ALL THE TREASURES OF WISDOM AND KNOWLEDGE

Christian Conviction
in a Controversial Culture:
Paul's Letter to the Colossians

ALAN D CATCHPOOLE

WESTBOW
PRESS®
A DIVISION OF THOMAS NELSON
& ZONDERVAN

WestBow Press books may be ordered through booksellers or by contacting:

WestBow Press
A Division of Thomas Nelson & Zondervan
1663 Liberty Drive
Bloomington, IN 47403
www.westbowpress.com
1 (866) 928-1240

Scripture taken from the English Revised Version of the Bible.

ISBN: 978-1-9736-1035-9 (sc)
ISBN: 978-1-9736-1036-6 (hc)
ISBN: 978-1-9736-1034-2 (e)

Library of Congress Control Number: 2017918745

Print information available on the last page.

WestBow Press rev. date: 02/20/2018

To my family: children, grandchildren, and great grandchildren.
They, above all others, have enriched the context of my life,
and have lovingly moderated all my living.

◆

'To the glory and honour of our dear Lord Jesus Christ, and
the establishment of our hearts in communion with Him, the
design of this digression is to evince that all wisdom is laid up
in Him, and that from Him alone it is to be obtained.'

Our Communion with God, John Owen, July, 1657.

◆

PAUL'S LETTER TO THE COLOSSIANS

AN APOLOGETIC PREAMBLE ...

It is not that I apologize for anything that I have written in this book, although I would ask the reader to be forgiving of my idiosyncrasies, foibles, prolixity, and blunders. Rather, I wish to explain that I have attempted in all that follows in these pages to present an introduction to an apologetic defence of the Christian faith and to do so in a manner that may be useful in the context of contemporary thought. Throughout most of my life, I have sought in my own fumbling way to explain the gospel of Christ and its implications for human life, and have done so in various circumstances, in a few different countries, in several diverse cultures, and to people of disparate ages and with various experience and education. Needless to say, I have not always – indeed, rarely – been successful, even by the standards of my own anorexic hopes and ambitions.

However, past events have left me with the conviction that I and my fellow Christians in this generation all need to be better equipped to "give answer to every man that asks" a "reason concerning the hope" that we have in Christ, as the apostle Peter required (I Peter 3:15). Or, as Paul writes in his letter to the Colossians, that we "may know how (we) ought to answer" (4:6) everyone who fails to understand what we believe and why we believe it. Therefore, I have written all that follows, being as definitive as I am able to be, to deliberately provoke the everyday, ordinary, thinking Christian to gain a greater appreciation of the pre-eminence of Christ and to pursue a philosophy that is dependent upon and compatible with all that He is, has said, has done, and will do. This, I trust, may help the reader to live a life that embodies His principles of personal ethics and of social morality that he might be better able to both manifest the truth and articulate the gospel effectively in this troubled world.

There is nothing original in all of this or in what I propose that we might overcome some of the difficulties we face in maintaining an effective Christian witness. In effect, I am only trying to emulate the apostle Paul, and to reflect as faithfully as I can the inspired defence he made of the original and essential gospel of Christ in his letter to the Colossians. From my perspective, this powerful little apostolic work, crafted under the inspiration of God's Spirit so many years ago, is the perfect expression of all that I am attempting to say. I do not think for one moment that I can improve upon what the apostle wrote, or that I can supplement it with my own ideas, any modern 'insights', or contemporary 'wisdom'. The epistle stands alone in its own integrity and strength, and it would be impertinent in the extreme if I thought I could add anything to it!

Rather, I write, as a man embedded in the world of my own generation, to my contemporaries who are struggling in the same philosophical and cultural environment – or in any other current intellectual climate – to encourage them to allow the teaching of the apostle – that is, the truth he penned about Jesus Christ – to penetrate into their own thinking and modify – indeed, to convert – their presuppositions, ideas, reasonings, and values. In other words, that they might learn from Paul what it means to "put on the new man, which is being renewed unto knowledge after the image of" God, who created them (3:10).

As far as I am concerned, the only thing of importance here is the truth about Jesus Christ, which Paul enunciates meticulously in his letter. In Him, we are told, "are all the treasures of wisdom and knowledge hidden" (2:3). The apostle is Christ's appointed authoritative representative, teacher, and preacher (1:24ff.), and as such he admirably explains to his readers the significance of the Lord Himself for all who believe in Him. At best, I am but a struggling provocateur, longing only to galvanize people into taking Christ, as Paul writes about Him, seriously. Giving the title that I have to this book is rather impetuous, and I hope no one mistakenly assumes that it implies that "wisdom and knowledge" can be found in my words. Be assured, if they are "hidden" in Christ, then they can only be found in Him – and to Him I would have you turn if you really desire to understand the realities of life.

Here and there, I write about the importance of contextualization. However, I am not particularly concerned about speculative theories concerning the contemporary context in which Paul was writing, and how this may or may not have modified his thoughts. There may be some value in such studies, but in my simplicity, I believe it sufficient – or, at least, that it is of primary importance – to read his letters in the context of the other divinely inspired works that are found in the Bible, wherein we have an infallible guide to the apostle's meaning. His words are thoroughly contextualized by all the revelation of truth God has given to the world through the preceding prophets, through the ministry of the other apostles, and, above all, through Jesus Christ Himself. So, it is to the whole canon of Christian scripture I would have you turn if you would understand Christ, and all the apostle writes about Him.

Neither am I particularly interested in current considerations about how the apostle's writing – or, for that matter, the whole biblical presentation of the gospel – can be moderated or restated that it might find acceptance among, or be understood by people in the context of our modern world with its malleable, multifaceted, and incongruous thoughts and cultural practices. There is a place for this reflection, but there is a dangerous tendency in such thinking to presuppose that today's men and women are fundamentally different from their ancient forebears, and in need of an innovative, new, state-of-the-art philosophy, suitable for 'our times'. But Paul makes it abundantly clear that he is writing to and about a very specific, ubiquitous, ageless kind of people – those who have been created in the image of God (3:10) but now suffer because they are alienated from and enemies of their Creator as a result of the misuse of their minds and the corrupted manner of their behaviour (1:21). It is impossible to 'contextualize' the gospel to accommodate those who think erroneously and act unethically! It is people who need conversion, not the gospel itself. The gospel is essentially timeless. So, it is to the intervention of the grace of God in Christ, "who delivered us out of the power of darkness" (1:13), that I would have you turn if you would be found "teaching every man in all wisdom" (1:28).

But what is of particular interest to me is to discover how the gospel, and the faithful teaching of it, delineates the context in which we, and all people in the world, actually live – indeed, the context in which all people of every generation have lived since creation and the Edenic rebellion. When Paul instructed us to "seek the things that are above, where Christ is seated on the right hand of God" (3:1), he was asking us to evaluate our present condition in reference to the eternal absolutes of the everlasting, sovereign God. He would have us bring "every thought into captivity to the obedience of Christ", as he mentions elsewhere (II Corinthians 10:5). Therefore, divine revelation – the biblical gospel that enables such basic and comprehensive evaluation – is, and must necessarily be, thoroughly contextualizing, affecting all our thinking, saying, and doing; but it is not itself amenable to being contextualized by anything we think, say, or do.

But perhaps I should apologise for some idiosyncrasies that may seem a little odd.

First, I would recommend that the last pages of this book – my summary comments on Colossians 4:7-18 – be read first. They are, in an indirect sense, Paul's own practical denouement of the mysteries he expounds throughout the letter. My own remarks there will also reveal a little of my own passionate concern in attempting to stimulate an interest in the apostle's words. Starting at the end, then, may give the reader a sense of direction and purpose as he attempts to make his way through the thoughts and argumentations that fill the preceding pages.

Then, throughout this book I have numbered sections, primarily to display what seems to me to be the logical order in the way Paul develops his exposition. However, this also enabled me to provide some internal cross referencing between various passages within the book itself where related information is to be found; and this I indicate by using the hash sign and section number (eg. #1.2.).

It is also an incurable, but unconventional, habit of mine to enclose quotations from the Bible in double quotation marks, and words from any other source in single quotes. I know this may be irregular, even confusing, but in doing this I attempt to privilege the divine text.

The English biblical text that I use throughout this book is substantially that of the old English Revised Version (c. 1880), and I do so mainly because I have been using it since my student days and it has become a familiar and much loved 'old and reliable friend'. However, to make clear nuances that I believe are there in the original language, and to avoid archaisms, I do not hesitate to translate where necessary as I think appropriate. With this in mind, I frequently include in parentheses quotations from the Greek text itself. But this, I must add, is rather pretentious, because I have very little expertise in that language. This whole work began years ago as a series of brief class notes. I, at that time, included the Greek text to encourage my students – and myself – to exegete as accurately as we were able in reference to the inspired original. So, I thought it might be helpful to some readers to retain this practice in the following pages. Hopefully, this will be no deterrent or hindrance to the English reader who has no knowledge of the Greek; such citations can be ignored.

This work will be, in all probability, my last attempt to write anything of such length. Therefore, I have made use of it to express some relevant but peripheral ideas that I think are particularly important. These sometimes appear as brief summaries, or essays, and are found within boxed borders. They are parenthetical to my main theme, but were written with some enthusiasm; indeed, with a touch of vehemence and affirmative aggression for the defence of the faith against what I believe to be serious dangers, not only for Christians, but for all people.

Numerous other contributory thoughts and comments that I think significant I have placed in footnotes. Keeping them on the relevant pages, rather than as endnotes at the back of the book, I rather optimistically hope that the reader might pause to consider them. All this amounts to a gallimaufry of my personal thoughts and concerns that I hope might be helpful.

Alan D. Catchpoole
Melbourne 2017

CONTENTS

◆

PAUL'S LETTER TO THE COLOSSIANS
INTRODUCTION AND SYNOPSIS

Paul is writing this letter, as an authoritative apostle of Jesus Christ, to a young church under siege. It was being assailed by some who were propagating what appears to have been a confusion of philosophical and religious notions that were contrary to the apostolic message. It was a congregation that had probably been established through the evangelistic ministry of Epaphras, one of the apostle's associates who may well have been a citizen of Colossae (1:7, 4:12). It is unknown whether the apostle himself had ever visited this city (2:1).

In reports he had received, Paul found sufficient evidence to convince him that there was an identifiable group of people in Colossae who had genuinely responded to the Christian gospel (1:3-4, 9). This gave the apostle cause for thanksgiving. However, it appears that some false teachers had entered the city and were troubling those young and inexperienced believers with their own peculiar and heretical doctrines. This was a serious danger that threatened the survival of this infant church as an orthodox community.

Just who these heretics were, we may never know. They were evidently erudite and eloquent (2:4). Their teaching seems to have been philosophically compelling (2:8), and to have contained elements of the Jewish religion (2:16-17). Whoever they were, they were apparently offering a deceptively appealing alternative to, or a potentially popular variation of Christian beliefs. However, to identify them precisely is not necessary for an understanding of this letter. What is significant is that God, in His providence, used that situation to motivate the apostle, as he reacted against these mischievous influences, to provide the Colossians with important, positive teaching and an explanation of principles vital for the Christian faith. These things they needed to know for their own spiritual well-being, and that they might defend their own beliefs. And from this instruction, we also can learn much.

In this introduction, I briefly analyze the letter to gain a summary understanding of Paul's concern, to quickly assess the purpose and content of his writing, and to focus attention on its most significant features. To do this, I give consideration to the following *three matters.*

A. PAUL'S CONCERN FOR THE TRUTH OF THE GOSPEL

This letter to the Colossians is, in the main, defensive. The message preached by the apostle and communicated to the Colossians by Epaphras was being impugned. The biblical doctrines of the faith and, consequently, the spiritual well-being of the Colossian Christians, were endangered. *Therefore, both the continuing preaching of the truth to those outside the believing community and the appropriate functioning of the believers within the community were at risk.* However, Paul's response to this problem was not negative, but a positive presentation of the theology and the values of the gospel. With this increased knowledge of the truth, the Colossian believers would undoubtedly be better able to discern the serious errors of the false teachers and maintain their orthodoxy and the moral health of the congregation.

We might suggest then, that throughout the whole letter Paul is concerned, *inter alia,* about *two things:*

- **First**, that the truth of the gospel be *adhered to* by the Colossians.

  This is a matter of contending "earnestly for the faith which was once for all delivered unto the saints" (Jude 3); and it is a continuing responsibility that devolves upon every succeeding generation of believers.

  The apostle begins by affirming the validity of the ministry of Epaphras, the man who appears to have been the first to preach the gospel in the city of Colossae. He was, Paul remarks, "a faithful minister of Christ on our behalf" (1:7). In saying this, he confirms that Epaphras had been preaching with the apostle's approval, perhaps even with his commission. The doctrine he taught was "the word of the truth of the gospel" (1:5). His ministry had been fruitful, and as a result, the people "knew the grace of God in truth" (1:6). His teaching, in contrast to that of the heretics, was, from the apostle's perspective, completely reliable. It is implied that there was, then, no reason to deviate from the message and the doctrines he had brought to them, and through which they became Christians in the first place.

  The apostle is concerned that the Colossians be men of such "spiritual wisdom and understanding" that they continue to "walk worthily of the

Lord", constantly "increasing in (or, by) the knowledge of God" (1:9-10). The apostle was ambitious for these believers, longing that they might be both intelligent Christians – people of wisdom, understanding, and knowledge – and also men and women of godly behaviour – walking in a manner worthy of the Lord Himself. And he seems to imply that they could not be one without the other.

However, there was the danger that they might be corrupted and turned aside from the way of truth. Therefore, it was important that they be aware of those who would make "spoil" of them "through (their) philosophy and vain deceit" and alert to the erroneous nature of their ideas (2:8). They needed to meticulously reject such teaching that would subvert the truth and lead them astray. This was no time for religious gullibility or naivety. To adhere to the truth of the gospel they needed to be both intelligently mature and consistently moral.

NOTE: Paul is suggesting that if his readers did not mature in true understanding and wisdom, and were unable to expose and resist the subtleties of human rationalism, moribund traditionalism, and pagan spirituality, they were in danger of being misled and of becoming ineffective in their ministry and mission. *In one way or another, this problem faces the church in every generation.*

- **Second**, that the truth of the gospel be *advanced by* the Colossians.

  This is a matter of making "disciples" and "teaching them to observe all things whatsoever (Christ) commanded" (Matthew 28:19-20); and this also is a responsibility that devolves upon every succeeding generation of believers.

  Paul's concern for the propagation of the truth and the advancement of the gospel is quite evident in this letter. Obviously, he approved the evangelistic ministry of Epaphras and was glad of his success in Colossae. This was an example of effective Christian witness "in all the world" (1:6). Evidently, the preaching of Christ was having a very significant and far-reaching influence. The apostle himself was willing to suffer, as much as the Lord required of him, to preach "the word of God" fully and "make known ... this mystery among the Gentiles" (1:24-29).

  Further, this evangelistic concern is clearly expressed in Colossians 4:2-6. He requests the prayers of his readers that his own preaching of the gospel might prosper, and is anxious that the Colossians also be able to "answer each one" when approached by "them that are without", that is, by the non-Christians. He would have them walk "in wisdom", speaking with gracious, seasoned words about their beliefs to their unconverted pagan neighbours.

B. PAUL'S COMPREHENSIVE BASIS FOR EVANGELISM

Where there is a genuine adherence to the truth and to the moral requirements of the gospel, together with an intelligent involvement in the advancement of Christianity throughout the world – the two matters mentioned above – there we will be able to find true and meaningful evangelism, which is simply but essentially a matter of both *godly behaviour* and *wise words*. It is with these two elements of effective Christian ministry in mind that Paul writes in Colossians 4:5-6 about the manner in which his readers should "walk", or behave, and the expected quality of their "speech". Therefore:

- **First**, their "walk" was to be "in wisdom" (4:5), and hence the need for being "filled with the knowledge of His will, in all spiritual wisdom and understanding" (1:9). Their personal growth as intelligent Christians was of vital importance, not only for their own well-being but also for the sake of a godly and convincing testimony through *the clear articulation of the faith*.

- **Second**, their "speech" was to be "with grace" when providing an adequate "answer to each one" (4:6). Paul seems to be suggesting that such an approach "towards them that are without" was to be cultivated in the congregational activities of the church. In that context, they needed to "let the word of Christ dwell in (them) richly in all wisdom" so that they might be found "teaching and admonishing one another … singing with grace in (their) hearts" (3:16). Their personal growth in Christian character was of vital importance, not only for their own well-being but also for the sake of a godly and convincing testimony through *the wholesome manifestation of the faith*.

And this should result in:

- **Third**, "whatever (they) do in word or in deed" – in speech and in practice – they should "do all in the name of the Lord Jesus" (3:17). The whole of a believing man's life should be subject to the lordship of Christ and directed towards the exaltation of His Name. Then, and only then, will he walk in the presence of, and talk to the unconverted as he should. This is, we suggest, Paul's *comprehensive basis for evangelism*.

We might summarize these things in the following diagram:

PAUL'S CONCERN FOR THE GOSPEL

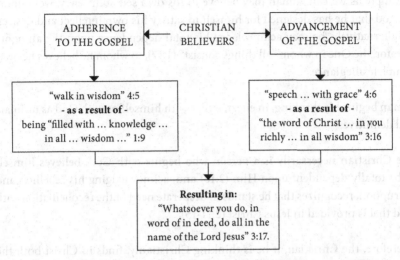

COPYRIGHT 1995. Alan D. Catchpoole, Olecko Pty. Ltd., Australia. coldia1.vsd

But we must now ask, what is involved in doing "all in the name of the Lord Jesus"? Paul presents an exhaustive answer to this question in Colossians. There is a comprehensive demand here that seems to embrace the whole of the Christian's life, with nothing excepted – "whatsoever you do". It would be no exaggeration to suggest that this whole letter is an exposition of this injunction in Colossians 3:17. It has implications for at least *five important and interrelated aspects of Christian living.*

1. RELIGION (2:8-19)

Basic to a man's attitude to his own existence, his sense of purpose, and his system of values is *his religious point of beginning*. It is the relationship he believes he has, or may have, with God – or with some god-substitute – that will determine every other aspect of his life. Every man, whether he will admit it or not, and even if he calls it by this or some other name, has a fundamental, religious commitment – be it theistic, polytheistic, or atheistic. This may not be developed or sophisticated, but it is his deepest and primary belief, his ultimate concern. It lies at the base of all his thinking about life, establishes his principles, and formulates his ambitions.

Despite the plethora of philosophical and religious theories, and when all is considered, there are in effect only two such points of beginning. As Paul suggests, a man establishes his philosophy either "after the traditions of men" or "after Christ" (2:8). He is either "vainly puffed up by his fleshly mind", or he is "holding fast the Head" (2:18-19). In other words, to summarize the apostle's suggestion as simply as we can, a man may believe in his own self-sufficiency, worshiping the god that he has designed for himself to satisfy his own intellect and desires; or, alternatively, he may acknowledge his total dependence upon the almighty Creator, the One in whom "all things consist" (1:17), to whom he believes he owes complete allegiance.

A man begins his thinking, in effect, either with himself or with God as ultimate and definitive.

The Christian necessarily is a person who begins with God, believes himself to be totally dependent upon Him (2:10) and, acknowledging his rebellion and corruption, recognizes that he stands in desperate need of the reconciliation with God that is provided in Jesus Christ (2:11-15).

Therefore, the Christian, if he is thinking Christianly, finds in Christ both the meaning of life and all moral principles, and the sustaining power of life and the restoration of all values (1:17, 21-22).

For the believer, the *doxastic* and the *axiological* cohere in our Lord.

Moreover, the believer is consciously and comfortably dependent upon God's self-revelation for his understanding of these things (1:24-28).

- *Christian religion is of first importance.*

II. PHILOSOPHY (2:20-3:4)

The Christian's faith and religion, being based upon Christ and holy scripture, provide for him not only personal reconciliation with God, hope, and eternal life, but also a comprehensive perspective for the interpretation of the whole of life that he might find value and significance in all his experiences. Biblical revelation certainly does not speak directly about every topic discussed by men, nor does it answer all the questions we might ask, but it does provide an adequate configuration within which all things might be discussed truly and meaningfully.

The problem with most human argumentation is that it is conducted in a vacuum, as it were, being without absolute points of reference. Being cut adrift from any sure anchorage, it drifts in an ocean without shores, being carried about by varying indiscriminate currents. Hence, human philosophies, each having its own presuppositions, are diverse, incongruous, and mutually destructive.

The biblical perspective will not allow the Christian to be dominated by the "rudiments of the world" (2:20, cf. 2:8). This implies, as I will suggest, that he is not locked into a purely materialistic system or restricted to such reasoning that is constrained by his own immediate experiences. He does not accept that life begins and ends with the limits of human ability, rationality, and science; or that it is guided by those earth-bound principles that the supposedly self-sufficient man has devised to direct his thinking and formulate his ambitions. He is no longer limited by the "wisdom ... of this world", having discovered "God's wisdom" in Christ (I Corinthians 2:6-7). *The principles moderating his thinking are distinctly different.*

In contrast to naturalistic and pagan thinking, the Christian, while being very conscious of the world in which he lives, seeks "the things that are above where Christ is seated on the right hand of God" (3:1). In other words, he works with an appreciation of a two-fold reality – the created and the uncreated, dependence and aseity. *The context within which he thinks is distinctly different.*

For the believer, the *ontological* is determined by Christ, in whom "all things consist" (1:17).

The Christian philosopher presupposes the existence of the biblical God, and believes that "all the treasures of wisdom and knowledge" are hidden in Christ (2:3). He could not think this way were it not for his religious convictions, which set the parameters for all his thinking. And, we might add, he also recognizes that the anthropocentric thinker reasons within an entirely different set of parameters.

It is, then, not man himself, but the risen, divine, self-revealing, and authoritative Christ that is at the centre of his understanding. He does think differently!

- *Christian religion is prerequisite for Christian philosophy.*

III. MORALITY (3:5-17)

Beginning with God, and recognizing that this material world is not the ultimate reality with which he has to do, the Christian looks for an immutable and eternal basis for his moral system. That he is a creature places him under the authority of the Creator. He believes himself to be, therefore, constrained to modify his attitudes and actions to conform to the divine will. Moreover, this divine will is not for him some theoretical abstraction, open to speculation, but is revealed in God-given, irrevocable laws found in scripture.

The Christian is also aware that, this being a fallen world, he is in constant moral conflict. In a sense, nothing is normal, but all is abnormal. The environment in which man must live is corrupted; paradise has been lost. This demands moral discernment and involves the deliberate rejection of negative actions and attitudes as well as the careful cultivation and practice of positive actions and attitudes, if we are to live as we ought. The believer, to use Paul's words, accepts the responsibility of both *putting away* immoral living, and *putting on* a moral disposition and moral behaviour (3:8, 12).

This striving after moral purity is no insignificant matter. Paul advises his Christian reader to have done with "anger, wrath, malice" and such things because he, the reader, is "being renewed unto knowledge after the image of Him that created" him (3:8-10). To recapture this "image" is to discover again the whole significance of being human as God designed it to be, and to anticipate the restoration of pristine purity. This renewal, then, is fundamentally important for all meaning and purpose in life, and to reject it is to opt for ultimate intellectual inanity and fatuous morality.

In association with this, Paul indicates, as I will suggest, that Christian philosophy contextualizes and moderates Christian morality, providing it with content and direction.

We should also note here the importance of the association that Paul makes between the restoration of morality and the renewal unto knowledge (3:10). Knowledge and morality can never be divorced from each other, and the one cannot be gained without the other. The man who would be wise and understanding must begin, continue, and conclude his pursuit of these things with profound and penetrating ethical considerations and responses. There must be purity and honesty in his attitudes, ambitions, and actions, or the knowledge of the truth will elude him. But on the other hand, and without contradiction, the man who persists in ignorance, which is a willful state, will never know moral purity or understand the principles of good ethics.

For the believer, the *epistemological* and the *ethical* cohere in Jesus Christ.

Such a morality as this can only be structured and sustained within an adequate Christian philosophy of life, built upon the basis of Christian religious beliefs.

The knowledge unto which the Christian is constantly being renewed is mediated to him through the "word of Christ". This ought, then, to "dwell in (him) richly in all wisdom". Further, this word is ministered through the congregation of believing men and women when they are found "teaching and admonishing one another" (3:16). The church, in other words, is the context in which believing men and women are – or should be! – "knit together in love and unto all the riches of the full assurance of understanding" (2:2). The efficiency of the church, then, is rooted in an affective and cognitive communion. The genuine Christian believes not only in 'God the Father Almighty' but also in 'the holy catholic church' (The Apostles Creed).

- *Christian religion and philosophy are prerequisite for Christian morality.*

IV. SOCIOLOGY (3:18-4:1)

Because of his faith in and love for God, the Christian will subject every aspect of his interpersonal life to the demands of His laws. When asked, Jesus explained that the great and first divine commandment is to love God, and the second is to love one's neighbour (Matthew 22:37-40). His laws, then, should moderate both religious and communal relationships. Moreover, our Lord also advised His disciples that their communal relationships *as Christians* ought to reflect their religious relationship with their God (John 13:35). We might say, then, that the practice of good Christian sociology is a manifestation, however imperfect, of divine truth; the practice that contextualizes the gospel. This is concomitant with being renewed after the image of God.

The Christian is impelled, therefore, to bring his moral principles to bear upon every social consideration. His sociology is necessarily more comprehensive, and far more beneficial, than that of the pragmatist.

The Christian is concerned that the whole of human society be moderated by God's moral standards. Love demands it! Further, he recognizes that the various relationships within human society which every human culture in every era has had to consider, are designed by God, purposeful, and governed by the divine order. To violate this order not only incurs the wrath of a holy God, but it also vitiates and impoverishes human life, robbing it of genuine significance, meaning, and satisfaction. The pandemic failure of interpersonal human relationships causes much sorrow in the heart of the compassionate Christian.

Such thinking will condition every interpersonal relationship in which the Christian is engaged – whether it be in marriage (3:18-19), family (3:20-21), or industry (3:22-4:1). He recognizes that these institutions, as such, are not man-made, but established by God for human society at the time of creation. Adam was to marry, reproduce, and work the Garden! We acknowledge that all three of these relationships are deleteriously affected by the fall and are now fraught with difficulties. Therefore, we will seek to understand them in reference to God's purpose in creation and to find redemption for them in Christ's sure purpose in His death and resurrection.

For the believer, the *sociological* is redeemed – or, is redeemable – in the sovereignty of Jesus Christ.

The Christian is not concerned primarily with some sociological technique whereby the greatest *individual satisfaction*, enjoyment, or 'good feeling' might be extracted from interpersonal relationships and social institutions. Rather, his first concern is for the enrichment of *interpersonal satisfaction* in all relationships and social institutions. But he is, above all, anxious that God be glorified through the re-establishing of His moral principles and meaningful order in human affairs. That is to be done which "is well-pleasing in the Lord" (3:20, cf. 1:10). And this, he believes, can only be beneficial and enriching for all people individually and in their associations with one another.

This prioritizing of interpersonal relationships is not only demanded by the Christian concept of love, but it is required by our creation in the image of God, the God who eternally exists in the interpersonal relationships of the Trinity. And both our understanding of love and of the God who is love (I John 4:8) are unique among all the schools of religion and philosophy in this world.

As a man becomes a Christian only when he repents of his rebellion and humbly acknowledges the sovereign authority of God, he is the first – or ought to be the first – to recognize and appreciate the hierarchical order in creation. He stands under the lordship of Christ. So, in discussing marriage, family, and industry Paul describes these institutions within this contextualizing, hierarchical framework. In each of them, there is to be an appropriate submission to and an appropriate exercise of authority. But this order is also to be moderated by love (3:19), sympathy (3:21), honesty of heart (3:22), justice and equality (4:1) – in fact, this order is the structure within which social benefits are truly defined, obtained, and preserved.

- *Christian religion, philosophy, and morality are prerequisite for Christian sociology.*

v. EVANGELISM (4:2-6)

Finally, Paul returns to the question of evangelism. He has mentioned the effect the preaching of the gospel was having in other places (1:5-7), and has made reference to his own commitment to the ministry he had been given to fulfil, or to fully proclaim, "the word of God" (1:24-29). But he only comes back to this matter after he has discussed his religious point of beginning, his philosophy of life and reality, and Christian principles of morality and social structures. It is only in this context that we can find an adequate foundation for true evangelism, because it must be made clear through the preaching of the gospel that those who respond are required to do all that they do "in word and in deed … in the name of the Lord Jesus" (3:17). Conversion, it must be explained, requires the re-contextualizing and the re-moderating of the whole of life.

Therefore, those who would evangelize are to exemplify the gospel in "word and in deed", or, as Paul now states, it requires of us not only the correct "speech" but also that we "walk in wisdom" and "with grace" (4:5-6). The gospel offers men salvation in this present, evil world, but provides no immediate escape from it. Therefore, we must learn to live in contrast to the unconverted, maintaining a distinct philosophy and a gracious, cultural attitude.

In this sense, we should shine as lights in the darkness – darkness of any form: intellectual, moral, or social. Nevertheless, for the believer, the only adequate *epitomization* of the gospel is in Jesus Christ.

If we are to propagate the gospel of salvation with understanding, we must appreciate the dangers from which men are to be saved. As every aspect of human life has been vitiated by the fall – man being 'totally depraved' – an adequate salvation must be comprehensive, affecting him at every point of his existence. The 'sin' from which we are redeemed is not abstractly 'religious', but intellectual, moral, personal, and social. It is rooted in the specific problem of man's anthropocentric philosophy. Because he "refused to have God in (his) knowledge", he was given up to "a reprobate/worthless mind", and so descended into all manner of immorality and social misconduct (Romans 1:28ff).

True evangelism, then, must begin with a religious declaration and then challenge human philosophy, morality, and sociology. In fact, evangelism, rightly understood, is *the total re-interpretation of the whole of human life* in the light of God's revelation in the Bible. But it must offer not only *reinterpretation* but also the *restructuring* of life through the grace of God, and the latter should be at least approximated in the church.

Our opening religious declaration might be the simplest of proclamations, but this must be extrapolated into all its ramifications and applications.

We should note that Paul encouraged his readers to engage in this ministry through prayer and by walking in wisdom towards the unconverted – "them that are without" – and by using their time appropriately (4:5).

- *Christian religion, philosophy, morality, and sociology are prerequisite for Christian evangelism.*

We can bring these things together in the following diagram:

COMPREHENSIVE BASIS FOR EVANGELISM

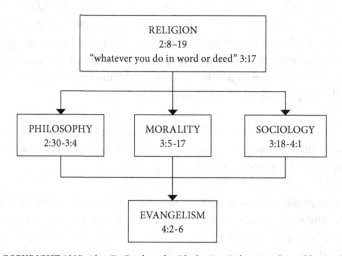

◆

C. PAUL'S BASIC DEFENCE OF THE TRUTH

It would seem that the false teachers who had disturbed the church in Colossae were denying the "fullness" of Jesus Christ (1:19, 2:9) and the sufficiency of His redemptive work (1:14). They may have accepted aspects of the Christian message, but they evidently wanted to supplement or modify it with notions and practices drawn from non-Christian sources. This is a far too common and exceedingly dangerous practice within Christendom! They were compromising the gospel, thereby distorting its meaning and denying its essential truths. So, Paul presents in this letter a defence of the apostolic message.

We might briefly summarize the way he does this under *three headings*:

- **First**, he presents Christ in His incomparable supremacy.

Christ, he insists, is "the image of the invisible God" (1:15), in whom "dwells all the fullness of the Godhead bodily" (2:9). He is, then, the ultimate revelation of God because He is God. Nevertheless, as a Man and "through the blood of His cross", He reconciles "all things unto Himself" (1:20). Therefore, as we shall consider, He "in all things" has "the pre-eminence" (1:18), being God and Man. His prominence is evident in *two particular ways*:

    i.   As Creator – "the firstborn of all creation" (1:15).

    ii.   As Redeemer – "the firstborn from the dead" (1:18).

Then, because He is both Creator and Redeemer, all wisdom and knowledge are found in Him (2:3). There is, then, no other ultimate source of definitive understanding. To appreciate the truth about God, we must find Him revealed in Christ. To appreciate the truth about man, and about man as we now find him in this world, we must see him in reference to this pre-eminent Christ. Man stands not only as a creature before his Creator but also as a condemned sinner before his Judge.

- **Second**, he presents man in his fatal alienation.

As a result of his condemnation, man has brought upon himself two intractable problems for which he has no solution – he is now both alienated from and also an enemy of this all-sufficient God (1:21). This enmity is located in *two things*:

    i.   Man's "mind" – he is alienated from God by the way he thinks. *His intellectual alienation.*

    ii.   Man's "works" – he is alienated from God by the way he behaves. *His moral alienation.*

Man has estranged himself from God by living, or attempting to live, in a philosophical and ethical world of his own making (2:8). If the problems he has thus created for himself are to be resolved, man needs and must turn to the pre-eminent Christ who alone has the intellectual and moral resources to rectify the human situation, and grace sufficient to intervene.

- **Third**, he presents the way this alienation is overcome.

All is not lost, "because of the hope which is laid up for (God's people) in the heavens" (1:5). The gospel offers those who believe a guaranteed and blessed future. However, believers only have this hope because they are "reconciled in the body of His flesh through death" that they might be presented "holy and without blemish before Him" (1:21-22). A man is reconciled to God by *two things*:

i.   The death of Christ. The *basis* of reconciliation.
   –   "in the body of his flesh through death". (1:22).
ii. The preaching of the apostolic gospel. The *means* of reconciliation.
   –   "the hope of the gospel ... whereof I was made a minister" (1:23, 25).

A man deceives himself if he thinks that he can find acceptance with God in anything other than the justifying death of Christ. He further deceives himself if he thinks that he has the intellectual ability to devise his own beliefs and refuses to submit to the authority of the gospel proclamation.

The preaching of the gospel, then, presents us with the supremacy of Christ to elicit *our trust* in Him; and it presents us with the alienation of man to elicit *our repentance* before Him. The heretics in Colossae, we might assume, were denying the first, Christ's supremacy, because they were not prepared to accept the second, man's comprehensive alienation. Therefore:

–   They may have reached out to Christ for help, but they did not do so out of a sense of total helplessness.
–   They may have been thankful for things Christ had done, but as we will see, they were not convinced that He had done enough.
–   They may have listened to "the word of the truth of the gospel" (1:5), but they subjected it to their own rationalizations.

Man, they would have suggested, must make his own contribution out of his own resources if he is to find reconciliation with God and have any hope of eternal life in heaven. This is a fatal misunderstanding, which is as widespread in today's world as it has ever been.

It was necessary for Paul to provide his readers with a comprehensive explanation of the Christian faith because the teaching of the heretics in Colossae evidently repudiated important, basic truths of the gospel. We suggest that they were mistaken in at least the following *three ways:*

•   **First,** they denied man's moral fallenness (2:16).
   For them, trusting in Christ was perhaps good, but not good enough. The benefits gained by such trust had to be supplemented by religious ritual and good works. This assumes that man's moral abilities are unimpaired, or at least still sufficient, even if perhaps somewhat weakened. He is yet able, through his natural capacities, to do things

that will be judged favourably and added to his credit. It is also, in effect, a denial of the divinely provided *basis* of salvation in Christ, rejecting His sufficiency and pre-eminence in *all things*, and attributing necessary merit to cultic obedience.

Here is *Pelagianism/humanism*.

- **Second**, they denied man's intellectual alienation (2:8).

  For them, to accept Christ's teaching was perhaps good, but not good enough. His teaching had to be supplemented with the knowledge that can be gained by independent human reason. This assumes that man's mind is adequate in itself, and that he reasons more or less as he should.

  Here is *liberalism/rationalism*.

- **Third**, they denied the sufficiency of the apostolic message (2:18).

  For them, to believe the apostles' message was perhaps good, but not good enough. The knowledge gained by listening to the apostolic preaching needed to be supplemented by one's own experiences or visions – or by some other person's experience and visions! This is in effect a denial of the adequacy of the divine *means* of salvation. No longer is salvation mediated through the preaching of the gospel alone but also by subjective enlightenment or intuition (cf. I Corinthians 1:21, Romans 10:12-15).

  Here is *subjectivism/existentialism*.

Again, in summary of what we have been saying, consider the following diagram:

QUESTIONS OF TRUTH AND ERROR
ABOUT MAN AND SALVATION

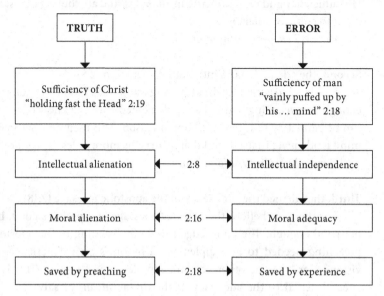

TRUTH	ERROR
Sufficiency of Christ "holding fast the Head" 2:19	Sufficiency of man "vainly puffed up by his ... mind" 2:18
Intellectual alienation	Intellectual independence
Moral alienation	Moral adequacy
Saved by preaching	Saved by experience

(2:8, 2:16, 2:18)

◆

A SYNOPSIS.

THE EPISTLE TO THE COLOSSIANS

1. THE DIMENSIONS OF SALVATION   1:1-23.

     Paul gives thanks and prays for the Christians in Colossae. In
     doing so he expresses his understanding of the benefits that
     their salvation had brought to them. There are three dimensions
     of this salvation:

1.1.   THE PROSPECTIVE: HOPE IN HEAVEN   1:1-8.

     Through the preaching of the gospel.

1.2.   THE PRESENT: MORAL STRENGTH AND FORTITUDE ON 1:9-14.
       EARTH

     Through knowledge and understanding.

1.3.   THE PERSONAL: RECONCILIATION WITH GOD   1:15-23.

     Through the person and work of Christ.

2.   PAUL'S MINISTRY OF THE GOSPEL   1:24-2:5.

     Paul may not have been to Colossae and was probably unknown
     personally to the believers there (2:1). If so, then why did he
     have an evidently strong, personal concern for them, and why
     the writing of this letter? Here the apostle explains that his
     interest in them is genuine, arising out of his responsibilities
     before God.

2.1.   HIS GOD-GIVEN STEWARDSHIP   1:24-29.

<table>
<tr><td>2.2.</td><td>HIS PERSONAL CONCERN FOR THE COLOSSIANS</td><td>2:1-5.</td></tr>
</table>

3. PRACTICAL IMPLICATIONS OF THE GOSPEL 2:6-4:6.

Paul has expressed his joy in and gives thanks to God for the conversion of the saints in Colossae. But, as with all Christians everywhere, they were evidently facing some difficulties in developing and working out the implications of being Christians in their own particular milieu. The apostle is evidently well aware of the opposition they were facing and writes to advise them accordingly.

3.1. THE EXHORTATION 2:6-7.

That behaviour be consistent with the confession that Jesus Christ is Lord.

3.2. RELIGIOUS PRESUPPOSITIONS 2:8-19.

The natural man's philosophy begins by assuming human moral ability. The Christian begins by acknowledging man's need of both regeneration (2:11-12) and justification (2:13-14). A man is only "complete" in Christ (2:10).

3.3. THE PHILOSOPHICAL IMPLICATIONS 2:20-3:4.

Every religion and philosophy is based upon some consideration of the nature of the reality of which man is a part. So it is also with Christianity. The Christian recognizes the place and importance of the space/time world, and of all that is in it. But these things never become matters of ultimate importance for him (2:20-23). More important to the believer are the "things that are above" (3:1-4). This metaphysical view provides a point of reference for our understanding and a source of values for our morality.

3.4. THE MORAL IMPLICATIONS 3:5-17.

Paul draws behavioural conclusions from his Christian philosophy. "Mortify therefore ...". (3:5). He allows this perspective to determine his morality. By doing so, he avoids vacuous 'moralizing' and ethical superficiality. He is able to give a reason for his value system. His whole life is thoroughly integrated.

But in human life in its postlapsarian condition, morality has both a prohibitive and an affirmative aspect for all people. There must be both a "putting off" and a "putting on".

| 3.5. | THE SOCIAL IMPLICATIONS | 3:18-4:1. |

As philosophy determines moral values, so moral values determine the structures of society. Ultimately, to alter a society and its structures requires a change in philosophy. (A fact that Marxism, for example, seems to understand far better than today's Christendom!)

| 3.6. | THE EVANGELISTIC IMPLICATIONS | 4:2-6. |

As the Christian is responsible for personal and social change – to be effected through his evangelism (understood in its most comprehensive sense) – he is, or he ought to be, very concerned about and sensitive to "them that are without" (4:4). He should be wise and understanding enough that he might "know how (he) ought to answer each one" (4:6). The believer must be able to communicate reasonably with the unbeliever, even when the unbeliever is blind to or resists all that he has to say.

| 4. | PERSONAL REFERENCES | 4:7-18. |

Paul never abstracts the gospel from the realities of human life and society, or from the space/time continuum. It was never for him merely a philosophy. He worked in this fallen world, together with a very diverse company of men and women. Hence, he could not conclude his letter without references to the actual situation in which he found himself, and to his companions in ministry.

◆

COLOSSIANS 1:1-23.

1. THE DIMENSIONS OF SALVATION

Paul, as he does in most of his letters, deliberately introduces himself as an "apostle" of Christ (1:1). Being an apostle, he is an authentic representative of Christ, and by presenting himself as such he infers that his readers ought to accept his words as authoritative. This is reinforced by his explanation that he holds this office not as a result of some human or ecclesiastical appointment, but because of the express "will of God". It is clearly not without good reason that he begins this letter in this manner. He wanted his readers at that time to know that he "was made a minister, according to the stewardship of God which was given" to him to make "the word of God" fully known for their sake (1:25). They needed to appreciate the jurisdiction of his ministry and the origin of his teaching, lest any of the misguided philosophers who were influencing the congregation "delude" them "with persuasiveness of speech" (2:4). It was important that they hear a definitive voice.

Then, from the beginning, the apostle also wanted his readers to know how he viewed them in the divine scheme of things. He carefully designated them as "the saints and faithful brethren in Christ at Colossae" (1:2). They are, he declared, "saints" *in reference to God*, which implies being set apart by their redemption for God's exclusive use and a life of holiness. They are "brethren" *in reference to each other*, being united together "in Christ", and thus incorporated into the Christian community. And they are "faithful" *in respect to their own individual character*, being genuinely dependent upon and obedient to their Lord. Paul is, then, writing to and instructing these people having in mind a comprehensive understanding of their relationships and personal standing as true believers. He was writing to a specific readership.

It is in praying for others that a man expresses his most profound concern for them, and in doing so he recognizes that ultimately their well-being is dependent

1

upon the grace of God. And it is the nature and content of his prayer for the Christians in Colossae that first occupy Paul in this letter. He explains the manner in which he makes intercession for them, specifying things he considered would be particularly beneficial in their lives (1:3, 9-11). In doing so, he is also instructing them concerning what they might anticipate from the Lord Himself, and, no doubt, indicating how they might prepare themselves to receive His grace.

Evidently, Paul is writing out of considerable personal concern for his reader's continuing welfare and spiritual development. In his prayer, we find both *thanksgiving* (1:3) and *request* (1:9): the former being grateful recognition in retrospect for that which God had done for them, and the latter expressing confident anticipation in prospect for all that He will yet do for them. The apostle, then, would have them remember the significance of their conversion to Christ, "the day (they) heard and knew the grace of God in truth" (1:6); and that they not forget that this was but a beginning upon which they, by the continuing grace of God, should build (cf. 2:6).

We should note that Paul's profound understanding of the theology of Christian salvation gives shape to his comments about and to the substance of his prayer. Indeed, prayer that is not based upon true theological comprehension is impertinent! Moreover, in writing about his intercession for fellow believers in Colossae, the apostle also reveals his understanding of *essential dimensions of the salvation they enjoyed*. Christian salvation is multifaceted, and we will be impoverished if we fail to investigate its intricacies.

So, we will briefly consider *three of the most important dimensions of our salvation* that the apostle incorporates into his prayers for the Colossians:

1.1. THE PROSPECTIVE: HOPE IN HEAVEN (1:1-8)

Paul was convinced of, and thankful for the fact that the first intended recipients of this letter were truly Christians. The evidence of their genuine conversion was their "faith in Christ" and "love ... toward all the saints" (1:4). The verification of an individual's true regeneration, that initial work of God's grace in the human soul that results in eternal salvation, is always bi-directional, being seen in his attitude of trust in God and in his attitude of concern for his fellow believers. It must always be so (I John 4:20-5:2).

Orthodox beliefs, catechetical correctness, and church association – as immensely valuable as they are – fail to be convincing confirmation of an individual's conversion to Christ if they are not supported by clear indications of sincere and consistent faith and love.

1.1.1. THE REASON FOR PAUL'S THANKSGIVING

Paul is thankful (1:3) not simply because the evidence of their faith and love convinced him that these Colossians were genuinely converted, but also "because of the hope which is laid up for (them) in the heavens, whereof (they) heard before in the word of the truth of the gospel" (1:5). Paul brings together these three great benefits of redemption – *faith, hope, and love* – elsewhere (Romans 5:2ff., I Corinthians 13:13, I Thessalonians 1:3 and 5:8). They are inseparable, they complement each other, and together they constitute genuine Christian character; to be deficient in one of them is to be impaired in the other two.

But here the apostle gives emphasis to hope when he mentions "the hope which is laid up for you in the heavens" (1:5). And it is important that we consider the link he makes between the faith and love that the Colossian believers already had, and the futurity of the hope that they anticipated. This demands some understanding of the true nature of Christian hope, and this requires that we distinguish between:

The hope of a *desired* positive result – or hypothetical hope.
The hope of an *assured* positive result – or categorical hope.

The *former*, it seems, is innate in the disposition of every human soul, even if it appears as little more than an indefinite desire or wishful thinking. It may be based on man's judgement of the possibilities, but is always provisional and hypothetical. The *latter* arises from the same innate disposition, but only when this has been redeemed and transformed by the grace of God. It is based upon divine revelation, assertions, and promises, reinforced by the Spirit of God in the human heart, and is always confirmed and categorical. And, obviously, I am concerned here only with the categorical hope.

Paul uses this word "hope" sometimes as a *verb* and in reference to the subjective, inward hoping of the Christian heart (eg. Romans 4:18, I Corinthians 13:7); and sometimes as a *noun* in reference to the objective thing hoped for (eg. Galatians 5:5, Titus 2:13); and then, quite naturally, he also blends both together (Romans 8:24-25). The understanding Christian has not only a sense of confident anticipation about the future – which alone might be little more than an inexplicable and perhaps unwarranted euphoria, an optimistic sentiment – but also an assured knowledge, a clear understanding of what the future holds for all those who believe in Christ, which gives substance to his anticipation and direction for his life. Here in Colossians 1:5 the apostle clearly has the objective sense in mind, as he writes of "the hope which is laid up ... in the heavens", not the hoping that lies in the soul of the individual. This objective sense is also seen in 1:23 ("the hope of the gospel") and in 1:27 ("the hope of glory").

Alan D Catchpoole

We must think more about this hoping and this hope, but first, there is an interesting grammatical problem in verses 3-5 that give rise to *two possible interpretations*. This demands some consideration.

1.1.1.1. FIRST POSSIBILITY: HOPE AS THE SOURCE OF FAITH AND LOVE

Some suggest that the words translated "because of the hope which is laid up for you in the heavens" at the beginning of 1:5, should be linked with the immediately preceding words, "your faith ... and the love which you have towards all the saints". This would suggest that hope is the grounds for or the origin of the believers' faith and love.[1] In other words, Paul is indicating that the Colossians had such faith and love because of their hope. If so, then hope is in some sense prior to faith and love.

But if hope has priority, we must enquire concerning the manner in which hope generates faith and love. It is reasonable to think that if, because of our redemption in Christ, we are assured of the future, and of our participation in the future, such confident anticipation may strengthen our confidence or faith in our God.

But it is not so easy to see how hope contributes to our "love ... toward all the saints".

We might hesitantly suggest that if love of the saints is understood as a person's correct attitude as an individual in community – as an intelligent willingness to do what is best for the other person – then the structure of the society in which Christians are to love one another is of vital importance. Because of the hope "laid up in heaven" for him, the Christian has – he must have! – a different sense of society, its values, and its ultimate purpose than the non-Christian might have. Material gain and earthly values are no longer of ultimate worth to him (cf. 3:1-2). He might then find himself entertaining a more altruistic attitude. Perhaps in this sense hope produces love, or at least provides the context in which it is facilitated, disposing an individual to be more generous towards others. For example, the man who confidently invests in eternity, laying up treasure in heaven (Matthew 6:19-21), will not be disposed to take advantage of his neighbour for his own immediate gain.

---

[1] The NIV, for example, translates Colossians 1:4-5: "... because we have heard of your faith in Christ Jesus and of the love you have for all the saints – the faith and love that spring from the hope that is stored up for you in heaven and that you have already heard about in the word of truth, the gospel ..." It adds the phrase "the faith and love that spring from" at the beginning of verse 5 (they are not in the original text) to interpret the simple word "because" (διὰ τὴν ἐλπίδα).

1.1.1.2. Second possibility: hope as the reason for Paul's thanksgiving

However, it is easy to understand the difficulty that many have had with this idea that hope is the reason or the motivation for faith and love. That we should love our fellow Christians because we ourselves have an inheritance in heaven seems dangerously close to violating the very principle of love. Indeed, in remarkable contrast to this, Paul was willing to forego his inheritance in heaven if only Israel could be saved (Romans 9:3). As he would sacrifice his inheritance for others, his love cannot be in any way dependent upon his having such an inheritance or any entitlement to it; or, if he would forego his hope for the sake of another, then his love for the other cannot be dependent upon or rise out of his hope. The true spirit of love is that a man lay down his life for his friends (John 15:13).

To avoid this difficulty, some would read verse 5 in association with verse 3, making hope the reason for Paul's thanksgiving. The connection of ideas would then be, "We give thanks ... because of the hope which is laid up for you in the heavens". If this is indeed in Paul's mind, he is exemplifying his own principle that when "one member is honoured, all the members rejoice with it" (I Corinthians 12:26). In giving thanks, he was rejoicing with them in their eternal gain. That he was thankful for their advantage is surely an expression of prior love.

There is an interesting parallel in Ephesians 1:15-18, where similar expressions are used. Here Paul, having heard of the Ephesians' "faith in the Lord ... and love unto all the saints", prays that, among other things, they might "know what is the hope of his calling" and "what the riches of the glory of His inheritance in the saints". Far from making hope the origin of, or the motivation for faith and love, the apostle is here indicating that faith and love, in the case of the Ephesians at least, preceded an adequate knowledge of the "hope of his calling". This implies, perhaps, that their faith and love are the source from which hope will come or develop.

Then, in Romans 5:1-2, having "access by faith into this (justifying) grace" precedes "rejoicing in hope". It is when grace is accessed by faith that we are able to rejoice in hope. The apostle is suggesting that only the man who has by faith entered into the redeeming grace of God, thereby being assured that he has "peace with God", will be in any position to rejoice in the hope (objective, the thing hoped for) of entering into God's glory. *Faith has priority over hope.* Moreover, in Romans 5:3-5, he also indicates that this "hope (subjective, the hoping) puts not to shame because the love of God has been shed abroad in our hearts". This, no doubt, refers to God's love for man, but it is His love for us that results in our love for Him (I

John 4:10-12). This further suggests that *love has priority over hope*, and that hope would be unable to support our rejoicing without it. This is perhaps one reason why Paul explains to the Corinthians that of the three abiding values – faith, hope, and love – love is the greatest (I Corinthians 13:13).

We might suggest, then, that in 1:4 we have *the occasion* for Paul's thanksgiving – "having heard of your faith ... and ... love" – and in 1:5, we find *the reason* for his thanksgiving – "because of the hope which is laid up for you". However, this problem is not easy to resolve, as the apostle would also have found good reason for giving thanks in the faith and the love of the Colossian Christians.

1.1.2. The Basis for the Colossians' Hope

We must ask if the Christian's hope is well founded, or just a sentimental aspiration born of desperation in a seemingly meaningless world. How can anyone possibly know about something "laid up ... in heaven" (1:5), it necessarily being outside our present experience and beyond examination and proof? And, moreover, how can he have any confidence that he might participate in it? In other words, how can a man have any hope (objective, something hoped for) and then hope (subjective, live in confident anticipation) that he will receive it?

Paul wrote in I Corinthians 2:9 about the "things God prepared for them that love Him", a concept not unlike that expressed in the words "the hope which is laid up for you in the heavens" (1:5). Both suggest things promised by God to His people that they will enjoy in the future. But these, he explained in I Corinthians 2:9, are "things which eye saw not, and ear heard not", so, presumably, they cannot be discerned by unaided, human sensory perception. Neither does knowledge of them arise in "the heart of man", so, presumably, they cannot be discerned through unaided human contemplation or philosophical consideration. However, although knowledge of such things is completely beyond scientific investigation and academic speculation, the apostle insists that it can be obtained through *revelation* (I Corinthians 2:9-10), but *only* through revelation. The situation is simple – if God has spoken to us about them, then there are things we might know that would otherwise be beyond our discovery; but if He has not spoken then we have access to nothing beyond the range of the human mind and the future is effectively closed to us.

However, Christianity is founded upon and has continued and grown through the belief that God has revealed Himself, having "spoken unto the fathers in the prophets" and "in His Son" (Hebrews 1:1-2). It is through this revelation that we discover that God has indeed "good works ... prepared" for His people to do in this world (Ephesians 2:10), so *their life now* is of true worth and meaning. But from this revelation we also know that He has "an inheritance incorruptible, and undefiled, and that fades not away, reserved in heaven" for them, so *their eternal life* is also of true worth and meaning (I Peter 1:4). God's word opens up to us both time and eternity.

And this revelation, the apostle explains, was brought to the Colossians when they "heard ... the word of the truth of the gospel" (1:5). This genuine preaching of the gospel is nothing more, and certainly nothing less than the verbal communication of truth that God Himself has revealed. Our task is simple. We are to "preach the word" – and to do so even when men "will not endure wholesome teaching" and "will turn away their ears from the truth" (II Timothy 4:1-4). But our confidence is that men and women "whose heart the Lord" opens will truly "give heed unto the things that (are) spoken" (Acts 16:14).

This establishes at least two things:

- **First**, the absolute necessity of divine revelation and the faithful preaching of the gospel if people are to be redeemed and a true perspective is to be obtained for this life and hope for the next. But if the gospel is not truly proclaimed, or if it is distorted or obfuscated by human rationalism or speculation, then we are left with no sure basis for any positive expectation for time or eternity.

- **Second**, that the gospel is only preached, as it ought to be, within an eschatological framework. If the gospel is preached only to achieve for others or ourselves a measure of wealth, health, and happiness in this present world it has not been truly declared. Such immediate physical well-being is incidental and is in no way guaranteed by the Christian faith (cf. Hebrews 11:32-40). However, an eternal hope is essential for man's salvation (Romans 8:24).

It is only through the preaching of the gospel that men might "know the grace of God in truth" (1:6). Much may indeed be known of God without the preaching of the gospel (Psalm 19:1, Romans 1:19-20). But He has chosen to make known His redeeming grace only through proclamation (I Corinthians 1:21-24) and in no other way (Romans 10:13-15).

For this evangelism, there is the constant need of "faithful minister(s) of Christ" (1:7).

◆

CONCERNING CHRISTIAN HOPE

It may be helpful at this point to survey the references Paul makes to Christian hope that we might see more clearly just what it is that he has in mind, understand the context in which hope is generated in the believer's heart and soul, and appreciate the benefits it conveys. My comments will necessarily be brief.

As we have seen above, faith, love, and hope are significant concomitants in Paul's thinking, and he evidently recognized nothing and no one as Christian that lacks them. Love and hope authenticate the true man of faith. They are not to be separated, but in I Corinthians 13:13 the apostle concedes that love, in some sense, has priority. But here in Colossians 1:3-5, no doubt because of the context in which he is writing, he gives prominence to hope. It is his immediate concern that we should notice that it is knowledge of "the hope which is laid up for (us) in heaven" that is conveyed to us by the preaching of the gospel.

With this emphasis upon the Christian hope in view, it might be helpful if we digress and think more specifically about it and its significance in God's scheme of things. In the following summary of Paul's teaching about this topic, we consider *three things*:

A. THAT WHICH PRODUCES HOPE

It is important first of all to understand how it is that Christian men and women obtained such hope as they do have, a hope such as no other religion or philosophy can provide, a true and sure sense of confidence in and longing for the future. There are several factors that combine to give and to strengthen this hope:

I. THE FUTILITY OF THE WORLD (ROMANS 8:20-21)

The "vanity" or "futility" of the creation in its present condition is, in a sense, productive of hope, or, at least, it forces man to long for something better. It shatters all human confidence and complacency in this evil world, engendering a longing to be "delivered from the bondage of corruption". As a result of the fall, the human stage is set to drive a man to look with expectancy beyond himself and his immediate circumstances. Therefore, the man of faith, believing in Christ and trusting His work of redemption, hopes "for that which we see not", and he "with patience waits for it" (Romans 8:24-25).

However, modern man in his rebellion, attempting to deny the existence of any god, desperately seeks to fabricate a better world through the exercise of his own abilities and drawing upon such temporal resources as he may find. Concealing or suppressing his inexorable despair, he attempts to convince himself that he is comfortably reconciled to the 'fact' that there is nothing to expect beyond this present, physical existence. Therefore, his great hope is that when he dies he will not exist in any way at all! He is driven to this hope, the desire for ultimate annihilation, by the futility of this world that he attempts to escape.

We only impoverish ourselves *"if in this life only we have hoped in Christ" (I Corinthians 15:19).*

ii. EXPERIENCE (ROMANS 5:4)

Paul wrote that those who are "justified by faith", the true Christians, "rejoice in … tribulations". They understand that tribulation works patience; and patience, character; and character, hope (Romans 5:3-4). Hope is cultivated through the experiences of life, even when they are distressing – at least it may be so for those who are the beneficiaries of Christian salvation and enjoy "peace with God" (Romans 5:1). If we appreciate what it means to have "peace with God", and have faith in His sovereign providence, we are able to understand that "all things work together for good", for them that love God and are "called according to His purpose" (Romans 8:28).

The word here translated "character" (δοκιμή) comes from a verb that was formerly used of assaying metals to discern their purity, and then meaning 'to test' or 'to prove'. But as a noun, in which form it appears here, it may refer either to *the process of being tested* (eg. II Corinthians 8:2, 9:13), or to *the acceptable result of the testing* (eg. II Corinthians 2:9, 13:3); that is, either being approved or being found of good character.

The implication seems to be that when tribulation is endured in faith the result is, by the grace of God, strengthened character or proven reliability. But this is not the end of the matter. Each character-building experience of the sustaining grace of God strengthens our hope, increasing the expectation that He is able and is willing to preserve those who are justified by faith. It is the man of refined character, the man of true godliness, who is well prepared to stand in the presence of God. This refining process as Paul writes of it is true only in the lives of men and women of faith and love – otherwise, experience can be embittering and corrupting.

We only impoverish ourselves if we resent tribulation or despise the patient endurance of it, because thereby we may become the more confident in our hope.

III. LOVE (ROMANS 5:5)

The hope of the justified man, the man who by faith now stands in the grace of God, the man who rejoices in tribulation (Romans 5:1-3), is not some unsubstantiated longing, or merely an exuberant anticipation, and far less the expectation born of wishful thinking. The unfounded hopes of men are frequently frustrated. But Christian "hope puts not to shame", and it never disappoints. It cannot do so because it is well founded through the ministry of the Holy Spirit who assures true believers in their hearts that God genuinely loves them (Romans 5:5). Christian hope is not self-enthused, so it cannot be imitated, but Spirit-born, so it cannot be denied.

But the assurance of God's love for His people that undergirds their hope is no mere sentiment, but a Spirit-given assurance, because "God commends His own love towards us, in that, while we were yet sinners, Christ died for us" (Romans 5:8). In other words, this love is truly known for what it is through the Cross of Christ. Therefore, the more we are able to embrace the significance of our Lord's redemptive death, the deeper will be our appreciation of the love of God, and so the stronger our confidence will be in our justification by faith alone, and then the more mature will our hope become. Ultimately, Christian hope, although a powerful motivation, rests not upon some sentiment or experience but upon assured knowledge of Christ and Him crucified.

Although it is a humble confession of his personal and moral inadequacy, the believing man is not ashamed of, or embarrassed by acknowledging his total dependence upon God and His grace. He freely and gladly admits that his anticipation of a blessed future rests upon God alone, not upon any worth or merit of his own, because he is aware in his heart of God's love for him.

We will only impoverish ourselves if we limit our understanding of the death of Christ as the measure of God's love for His people.

IV. PATIENCE AND THE SCRIPTURES (ROMANS 15:4)

Something of the process whereby patience or endurance produces hope, as we have seen, is found in Romans 5:3-5. We have also noted that Christian hope is no mere wishful thinking or vague longing for something better than we now know and experience. It is an informed, confident, and meaningful expectation, and is grounded in the love of God for His people, the love that is objectified in the Cross of Christ.

Here, in Romans 15:4, Paul again associates "endurance" or "patience" with hope. Indeed, it is because we have much to endure in this fallen world that our hope becomes critically important. The informed Christian, although he no longer stands among those who have "no hope" and are "without God in the world" (Ephesians 2:12), does not expect this life to be without its challenging difficulties – its pain, suffering, disappointments, sorrow, bereavement, and death. But not only does endurance engender hope, it is also our hope that provides us with the strength to endure (Romans 8:25).

However, hope is always prospective, looking forward to that which is yet to be. Although we might extrapolate from facts already known, even as we forecast the coming weather, this is always bothered by uncertainty because of our own limited ability either to know the 'facts' adequately or to rightly interpret them. Human prophecy is notoriously unreliable or vaguely oracular.

Therefore, as Paul indicates in Romans 15:4, Christian hope is always instructed by the "written ... scriptures". It is not the product of human extrapolation, but of divine revelation – revelation from the God who declares "the end from the beginning" (Isaiah 46:10). This provides it with thoroughly reliable information that gives our hoping meaningful content. We are not only given confidence that the future is governed by the God who loves us, but we are also provided with adequate information about the future so that our present life might have significance and direction. The Christian knows, for example, that the time is coming when "we shall see Him", and "everyone that has this hope in Him purifies himself, even as He is pure" (I John 3:3). Hope, then, is an important element in our sanctification, making a practical contribution to our present life.

Similarly, the apostle explains that we only know of "the hope which is laid up for (us) in the heavens" because we "heard" about it "in the word of the truth in the gospel" (1:5, cf. 1:23). Therefore, he encouraged the Colossians "to seek the things that are above" so that "when Christ ... shall be manifested, then shall (we) also appear with Him in glory" (3:1-4).

We only impoverish ourselves if we neglect the teachings of the scriptures.

v. Righteousness (Galatians 5:5)

This verse is perhaps a little ambiguous. The expression "the hope of righteousness" (Galatians 5:5) could refer to either 'the hope that we will become intrinsically righteous in a righteous world' – that which we hope for – or 'the hope that we have because we are already reckoned to be righteous through the merits of Christ' – the reason for our so hoping. I find it difficult to decide what the apostle may have had in mind when he wrote this verse. But then, I do not know that I have to decide between the two possibilities, as the one does not exclude the other.

There can be no doubt that when "we shall see Him" and we are "like Him" (I John 3:2), we will be intrinsically righteous, and fit to take our place in the "new earth, wherein dwells righteousness" (II Peter 3:13). This is our ultimate hope. But it is equally true that we can only anticipate entering into this perfect state because we have already obtained justifying righteousness in Christ. It is through the obedience unto death of that one Man, Jesus Christ, that "many (are) made righteous" (Romans 5:19). Herein is our "hope of eternal life" (Titus 1:2, 3:7).

We will only impoverish ourselves if we remain confused about the biblical doctrine of justification by faith alone.

vi. God Himself (II Thessalonians 2:13-16)

It is, Paul tells us, "our Lord Jesus Christ Himself and God our Father" who give "eternal comfort and good hope" to His people (II Thessalonians 2:16). As we have seen in all the items listed above in i. to v., there are various means that God uses to produce genuine hope in the hearts and minds of His people. But all these things only become effective "because God chose (His people) from the beginning unto salvation in sanctification of the Spirit and belief of the truth, whereunto He called you ... to obtain the glory of our Lord Jesus Christ" (II Thessalonians 2:13-14). Our God is "the God of hope" who gives "joy and peace ... that (we) may abound in hope" (Romans 13:15).

Hence Paul speaks of the "hope of his calling" (Ephesians 1:18, cf. 4:4). It is because God chose us to be His that we have such hope. This reflects the assurance Jesus gave to His disciples, "All that which the Father gives me shall come unto me; and him that comes to me I will in no wise cast out" (John 6:37).

We will only impoverish ourselves if we fail to see that our salvation and our hope are the gifts of God's sovereign grace.

B. THAT WHICH HOPE PRODUCES

Hope itself is productive – it gives birth to other benefits. This we will also consider briefly.

I. SALVATION (ROMANS 8:24)

Paul explains here that "by hope were we saved". This is no contradiction of his assertion that by grace we have been saved "through faith" (Ephesians 2:8). Hope, being an expectancy that is driven by circumstances to look beyond man and his abilities, and rising out of frustration and futility, fixes a man's attention upon God. In this sense, hope is the atmosphere of, or a necessary directive for faith, and hence productive of salvation.

The apostle further explains, our hope is necessarily a continuing aspect of Christian living, because that which we hope for – "the hope which is laid up for (us) in the heavens" (1:5) – is not yet realized, or not now "seen", but we "wait for it" (Romans 8:24). Therefore, we always "walk by faith, not by sight" (II Corinthians 5:7). It is necessary, then, to have "endurance" or "patience" in this world (see below, iv.).

It is Christian hope that enables us to reckon with the temporality and the brevity of our present life. Because of our constant anticipation of that "which is laid up in heaven" for us, we can accept that we "are a vapour, that appears for a little time, and then vanishes away", and we can comfortably say, "if the Lord will, we shall both live, and do this or that" (James 4:14-15).

Perhaps one of the main reasons why some Christians find little satisfaction in their salvation and complain that it does not bring them the immediate blessing they anticipated, is their lack of genuine, impelling hope.

II. REJOICING (ROMANS 5:2, 12:12)

In these two verses Paul uses two different words in association with "hope", and both are variously translated (καυχάομαι in Romans 5:2, and χαίρω in Romans 12:12). I shall attempt to distinguish them.

The first word implies a 'boasting' or 'exulting', suggesting an *outward expression* of delight or even pride in the hope that we have in Christ. Those who are justified and have peace with God will manifest exuberance in life, displaying their pride as Christians – not pride in self-accomplishments, but pride in all that Christ has done for them (Romans 5:2). Their hope, having substance in "the glory of God", restores *true worth* to human life.

The second word is perhaps best translated 'rejoicing', suggesting an *inner satisfaction* of delight, or sense of fulfilment. When Paul encourages his readers to "rejoice in hope" he, at the same time and in the same passage, would have them be "diligent ... fervent in spirit, serving the Lord ... patient in tribulation" and more (Romans 12:13ff). It is this joy in our hope that imparts delight and satisfaction to a Christian life of diligence, service, and suffering because it provides the context in which such a life has *true meaning*.

Therefore, hope in Christ is essential, at least contextually, for all that the Christian believes to be of genuine worth and meaning in a redeemed life. It adds a transcendent dimension to all that he does.

Perhaps one of the main causes of a lost sense of worth and meaning among some Christians in their lives, is the lack of genuine, intelligent, impelling hope.

iii. Boldness in Speech (II Corinthians 3:12)

If, as we have just considered, hope results in exulting and rejoicing, and if it contributes to the recovery of worth and meaning in human life, it is not surprising that it is compulsively expressive. Those who are possessed by this "hope of the glory of God" (Romans 5:2) cannot be silent about it! Therefore, Paul explains that those who have "such a hope" will "use great boldness of speech" (II Corinthians 3:12).

There is a connection between hope and evangelistic confidence.

Perhaps one of the main causes of reticence – even cowardice – among some Christians in their proclamation of the gospel is the lack of genuine, intelligent, impelling hope.

iv. Endurance (I Thessalonians 1:3)

Here Paul suggests that as faith produces work and love produces labour, so hope produces patience or endurance (ὑπομονή). The difficulty of any situation can be endured by believers because of the confidence and informed expectation of divine grace and the assurance of a meaningful, blessed, and eternal outcome.

But we have already seen that "tribulation works patience", which is a prerequisite for "hope" (Romans 5:3-4), and that it is only through learning the truths of the scriptures that "through patience … we might have hope" (Romans 15:4).

I would suggest then, that there is a reciprocal relationship between patience and hope, each producing and reinforcing the other.

Perhaps one of the main causes of impatience and the lack of endurance among some Christians in their tribulations is the lack of genuine, intelligent, impelling hope.

C. THAT WHICH IS HOPED FOR

I have, obviously, already mentioned things we hope for, but this needs further clarification, involving what we might call the dimensions or aspects of hope. Because, as we have seen, a distinction needs to be made between hope in the sense of 'hoping for', and hope in the sense of 'that which is hoped for.' Hope, then, has an immediate effect in Christian living, giving a *characteristic attitude* in this present life, and it has promise for future living, giving a *characteristic anticipation* of the life to come.

To clarify this somewhat, I suggest that there are *two immediate* and *two ultimate* aspects of the apostle's hope:

i. First Immediate Aspect: Grace sufficient for an effective ministry (I Thessalonians 2:19)

Hope gave Paul reason to believe that his ministry among men would not be futile. There would be those who would stand with him in glory "before our Lord Jesus" as a result of his service for Christ. His hope sustained him throughout his work on earth.

ii. Second Immediate Aspect: Grace sufficient for the day of his death (Philippians 1:20)

Paul anticipates that no matter what the outcome of his imminent trial, whether to live or to die, God's grace would be sufficient for him. His hope sustained him to the day of his death.

III. First Ultimate Aspect: The Lord's return (Titus 2:12-13)

Paul would have all his readers "live soberly ... in this present world, looking for the blessed hope and the appearing of the glory of our great God and Saviour Jesus Christ". This hope, in other words, is the anticipation of the final realization of the divine purpose in human history and the full discovery of God's greatness.

IV. Second Ultimate Aspect: Eternal inheritance (Colossians 1:5)

We also need to keep in mind that the hoping depends upon the thing hoped for – that is, the subjective hopefulness is the result of knowing what is the "hope laid up ... in heaven", or at least knowing that there is such a hope in the future. As Christians, we have been "begotten ... again ... unto an inheritance incorruptible, and undefiled, and that fades not away, reserved in heaven for" us (I Peter 1:3-4).

Such, in summary, is the Christian's hope.

◆

1.2. THE PRESENT: MORAL STRENGTH AND FORTITUDE ON EARTH (1:9-14)

By the grace of God and through salvation in Christ, the Christian's eternal future is secure; his hope "is laid up for (him) in heaven" (1:5). As we shall see, he and all true believers have been "made fit to be partakers of the inheritance of the saints" (1:12). However, as enthralled and encouraged as we might be by this hope, we have yet to live our present lives in many radically different and frequently difficult circumstances.

Whatever the future and eternal dimension of salvation may be, and no matter how important this aspect of the gospel is, or how confident the Christian may be about his imperishable inheritance, he must also be concerned about his present behaviour. Indeed, we might say that although our future is not made secure by the life we now live – for we are saved only by the grace of God – this future dimension of our faith must to some extent direct our immediate conduct in this present, evil world. Confident that we can invest "treasures in heaven" (Matthew 6:20), we allow this hope to determine our values on earth. We are to live consciously in the light of eternity and in reference to Christ who "is seated on the right hand of God" (3:1-2). Having been "translated into the kingdom" of Christ (1:13), we are bound by His purposes and principles.

Or, in brief, we are to "walk worthily of the Lord" (1:10). And this requires considerable moral fortitude!

Paul, having mentioned that he was always praying for his readers (1:3), now explains more specifically the manner and content of his prayer in which he intercedes for divine help that they might be able to "walk worthily", or behave in a manner acceptable to God. In doing so he indicates that *two things* must be considered:

- **First**, it is important that the Christian's behaviour be morally commendable in God's sight. It should, in other words, be "all pleasing" to Him (1:10). There is an *ethical dimension* to faithful Christian living.

- **Second**, the necessary prerequisite for such behaviour is "knowledge", which is to be applied with "spiritual wisdom and understanding" (1:9). There is a *noetic dimension* to faithful Christian living.

Here, then, as everywhere in scripture, morality and knowledge are seen to be mutually interdependent; one cannot be obtained or expressed without the other. A life of true godliness requires both a redeemed ethic and a redeemed understanding. Moral strength is born of knowledge, but degenerates through ignorance; even as knowledge is born of moral strength, but degenerates through immorality.

So profound was the apostle's concern for his Colossian readers that they walk in a manner worthy of their Lord, that he would "not cease to pray" for them (1:9). As we have seen, they had come under the influence of some sophisticated teachers who, it seems, would persuade them to think in a manner that would not produce such godly behaviour. Therefore, Paul interceded for divine intervention in their lives that they might be "filled with the knowledge of His will" (1:9). This implies that the understanding that leads to a morally acceptable life cannot be attained without divine assistance: that is, it not accessible solely by academic exercise (cf. #1.2.1.2.).

1.2.1. The Single Request (1:9)

Paul makes *only one request* in this prayer: "that you may be filled with the knowledge of His will in all spiritual wisdom and understanding". Everything that follows in 1:10-14 explains what he anticipates will ensue in the lives of the Colossian Christians if God is pleased to respond positively to his petition on their behalf.

Presumably, we might anticipate the same results if we make the same request for others or ourselves. The ramifications of such a positive response are potentially explosive – in a good sense. They include, for example, being fruitful "in every good work" and being "strengthened with all power" (1:10-11). These are no trifling considerations!

Indeed, the request is remarkable for its comprehensiveness. Paul would have his readers "*filled* with ... knowledge" which is to be effective "in *all* wisdom..." The two words "filled" and "all" suggest dominant and exhaustive influences that embrace every aspect of the believer's life. Nothing is to be left unaffected; the change must be radical and extensive.

This radical change is to be expected only when God intervenes in human life. When describing the catastrophic consequences of man's rebellion against God, Paul explained that "professing themselves to be wise" men became "fools", and refusing "to have God in their knowledge, God gave them up unto a worthless mind" (Romans 1:22, 28). Hence, adequate *knowledge* and effective *wisdom* were lost to mankind. Such a calamitous loss necessitates a comprehensive, profound transformation if true knowledge and wisdom are once again to effectively guide and establish our behaviour in a life worthy "of the Lord" (1:10). For the sake of His glory, we should seek to escape from ignorance and folly. There must be a reversal of the damages done by the fall. Paul, in effect, is praying for the restoration of lost intellectual abilities, anticipating that this will result in moral recovery.

We must enquire into the remarkable significance of the request itself, and then consider its ramifications.

1.2.1.1. Being "filled with the knowledge of His will"

It should immediately be obvious that without knowledge of God's will, no one is in a position to please Him or to live in a manner "worthy" of our Lord. How can a servant satisfy his master if he knows nothing of his master's intentions for both his household and for his servant? Even if well-meaning, he can make only blundering attempts to discharge what he thinks might be his responsibilities, assuming that his own standards will be acceptable. So it is with a Christian and his Lord; ignorance is inevitably detrimental to active Christian obedience.

However, knowing God's will must be seen in its biblical context.

1.2.1.1.1. Significant Christian knowledge

Here we might note three aspects – or *three stages* – of the knowledge Paul evidently believed was essential for his readers if they were to be effective as the servants of God:

- **First**, the knowledge of "the grace of God in truth" (1:6), which generates faith.
  This, as it were, is the exclusive commencement.
  The first thing as far as the gospel is concerned that a man needs to know – and to know appreciatively of its wonderful truth – is the grace of God. This involves knowing that, despite all he is and all that he has done in his sinfulness, there is a way in the kindness and the underserved love of God that people such as he might be redeemed and find an inheritance in heaven, as is declared in "the truth of the gospel" (1:5). Until something of the truth about this grace has penetrated into his understanding, he, together with all who do not believe, will remain "alienated and enemies in (their) minds" (1:21). But when this grace is received and a man grasps the truth of it, he is "translated … into the kingdom of the Son" (1:13). By grace the alien becomes a citizen of heaven!

Hence, being the recipient of this grace, such a man becomes a servant in the kingdom of God, and this is nothing less than the position for which he was originally created and in which he will receive all the blessings of his Lord and find fulfilment in his life.

- **Second**, the knowledge of "His will" (1:9), which generates obedience.

    This is, as it were, the necessary continuation.

    Once someone has received the grace of God and has become the servant of the Great King, the knowledge of God's will becomes crucial. We must at all costs avoid the contemporary superficiality that imagines that, once we become Christians, then God is at hand to serve us and see to our pleasures. As much as we may confidently believe that God, in His mercy, will always have our well-being in mind and that His love for us is unwavering, the dominant self-awareness of the truly converted man is that he has been drawn into the service of the Lord Jesus Christ. It is burning in his consciousness that, because God loved him, he loves God; and then, because he loves God, he will "keep His commandments" (I John 4:19, 5:3). *Therefore, obedience becomes a priority.*

    Hence, knowing the grace of God, the next thing the thoughtful Christian would know – indeed, needs to know – is the will of God. Only then will the maturation of his obedience result in his living being more and more "worthy of the Lord" whom he now serves.

- **Third**, the knowledge of "God" Himself (1:10), which generates love.

    This is, as it were, the anticipated consummation.

    Now Paul would take his readers yet further into the fascination of Christian knowledge. It involves more than an appreciation of the saving work of God's grace, and more than a comprehension of God's will for the world and for His people. As profound as these aspects of knowledge may be, they, in a sense, are but preliminary to the knowledge of God Himself. Indeed, this is the pinnacle, the ultimate purpose of Christian salvation. As Jesus mentioned in His prayer to His Father, "This is life eternal, that they should know you the only true God" (John 17:3). This makes the whole notion of knowledge infinitely personal, embracing more than facts, figures, and theories, and incorporating compatibility and fellowship with the Creator of all things.

    The servant in his master's house will do well if he knows the master's will, but he will do much better if he knows his master. Then his service will not be perfunctory in response to his master's demands but done with sensitivity in response to his master's character. Therefore, Paul would see his readers' service in the kingdom of Christ "increasing in/by the knowledge of God" (1:10). The better we know Him and His holiness, the more acceptable and more consistent will our good works become.

1.2.1.1.2. THE SIGNIFICANCE OF FULLNESS

Now we must ask what the apostle had in mind when he prayed that his readers be "filled" with the knowledge of God's will. Knowing the limitations of the human mind, the immensity of God's creation, and the eternity of His intentions, Paul obviously does not mean that any Christian can have plenary knowledge of God's will. All too often we have to acknowledge that we simply do not know what His intentions are. We exclaim with the apostle, "O the depth of the riches both of the wisdom and the knowledge of God! How unsearchable are His judgments, and His ways past tracing out!" (Romans 11:33) Frequently, in our confusion, we long to know what His will might be, in particular matters if not in general, that we might know how best to decide what we ought to do – but we so often do not!

To appreciate what Paul does mean, we need to consider the following.

The theme of 'filling' or 'fullness' is common in Paul's writings. Perhaps the reason for this is that the apostle had no doubt that there is a *completeness* or *total sufficiency* in the Christian gospel. In needs no modification, supplementation, addendum, or correction. We might note *two fundamental biblical implications* of this:

- **First**, it is God's intention in the "dispensation of the fullness of the times to sum up all things in Christ, the things in the heavens and the things upon the earth". This is "the purpose of Him who works all things after the counsel of His will" (Ephesians 1:10-11). Here it is implied that His intentions for His creation are complete, need no augmentation, and will be effected.

  We can trust implicitly in *all that He is doing and will do.*

  In the final analysis, nothing is ignored by, lies outside of, or evades the will of God.

- **Second**, we are told that "all the treasures of wisdom and knowledge" are hidden in Christ, in whom "dwells all the fullness of the Godhead bodily" (2:3, 9). This signifies that our Lord's divine being and His comprehension are complete and need no addition.

  We can trust implicitly in *all that He is and says.*

  In the final analysis, nothing is explicable or has any significance, meaning, or purpose apart from the being of God that is comprehensively revealed in Jesus Christ.

And because we through faith are "reconciled in the body of His flesh through death" that we might be presented before Him "holy and without blemish and unreproveable" (1:21-22), we have been "made full (or, complete)" in Him (2:10). He alone is sufficient if we are to recover the fullness of life for which man was created, and the fullness of knowledge we need to live as we ought. As we shall see, Paul's intention in this letter is to establish the pre-eminence of Jesus Christ "in all things" (1:18).

We might assume that Paul has written about these things so that we might always understand that we need look nowhere else than to Christ and the Christian gospel if we would be found living in the truth. And this was perhaps particularly significant in his writing to the church in Colossae, because evidently the false teachers there were insisting that neither Christ nor the gospel were sufficient but needed the additions and corrections that they could provide from their own philosophical system.

1.2.1.1.3. THE SIGNIFICANCE OF BEING "FILLED" WITH KNOWLEDGE OF GOD'S WILL

This word 'to fill' – or 'fulfil' – and its cognates may, in various contexts, have different nuances. For example, in 1:25 the phrase "to fulfil the word of God" probably means 'to fully preach the word of God', possibly reflecting the apostle's assertion in Acts 20:27, "I shrank not from declaring unto you the whole counsel of God". Then, in Ephesians 3:19, to "be filled unto all the fullness of God" – as breathtaking as this expression is! – cannot mean that we will in some way reach an equality in being or in knowledge with God Himself, or possess within ourselves all that He is. Probably Paul means that we are to achieve the fullness of the life God intends for His people, or, in other words, that we attain "the measure of the stature of the fullness of Christ" (Ephesians 4:13), or become truly Christ-like – and what more could we want?

However, here in 1:9, when the apostle writes about being "filled with the knowledge of His will" he seems to have another emphasis in mind. As we have suggested, plenary knowledge of the will of God cannot be implied. Then, elsewhere in the New Testament, we read in different expressions, for example, about being filled with anger (Luke 4:28), fear (Luke 5:26), and foolishness (Luke 6:11); or more positively, with wisdom (Luke 2:40), joy (Acts 13:52), faith (Acts 6:8), and goodness (Romans 15:14). Each of these things appears as a dominant attitude or a determining factor in a man's life. In this sense, that which fills him impetuously at any given moment, or persistently as a matter of character, motivates a man to act as he does. It becomes occasionally or consistently a driving force in his life. (We might note in passing that this perhaps gives us an understanding the expression, "filled with the Holy Spirit". When the Christian is so filled, his whole life is directed by the Spirit of God.)

With this in mind, we suggest that when Paul prays that his readers be "filled with the knowledge of (God's) will", his concern is that the knowledge they have of His will – the knowledge that was conveyed to them initially by Epaphras though "the word of the truth of the gospel" (1:5) – might be the driving and directing influence in their lives. Being filled with the knowledge of the will of God is the precursor, or, indeed, the substance of true obedience. And only such obedience will result is a walk worthy of the Lord (1:10).

There is, then, little value in knowing the will of God if this makes no dynamic difference to the manner in which we behave. A man, through careful and scholarly study of the Bible, might know well what the will of God is and this understanding remain for him nothing more than an academic exercise, having no impact in his life. So, we do well to pray, that by the grace of God, the knowledge we do have of His will might progress from being an intellectual consideration and develop into a compelling ambition. Then the purpose of it will indeed be fulfilled, at least to some extent, in our lives.

We should note that, in this single request, Paul brings together what we have called above the noetic dimension of Christian living – in reference to "knowledge" – and the ethical dimension of Christian living – in reference to "His will". And this requires that we obediently respond to God's will by effectively implementing the knowledge we have of it in the manner in which we behave. This knowledge, as we have suggested, comes from hearing "the word of the truth of the gospel" (1:5). But, as the apostle indicates, the implementation of it requires "all spiritual wisdom and understanding" (1:9) – and it is this intelligent use of knowledge that we must now consider briefly.

NOTE: It is impossible to read 1:9-10 with understanding and suppose that Christian living can be reduced to sentiment, emotion, and enthusiasm. It does require a great deal of 'heart' if we are to engage meaningfully in this world with all its pathos and yet rejoice in the hope of eternal life. We remember that our Lord wept at the tomb of His friend (John 11:35), and then we repent – or we should do! – of our own lack of compassion and sorrow. Nevertheless, we cannot live as we ought, no matter how passionate we might be, without an adequate measure of knowledge, wisdom, and understanding. And, we might suggest, it is only this knowledge, wisdom, and understanding that provide the context in which sentiment, emotion, and enthusiasm can be expressed without degenerating into self-indulgence, lust, and obsession.

1.2.1.2. Living "in all spiritual wisdom and understanding"

Knowledge, as we all know, can be and often is misused, for not all people are sufficiently wise and understanding in its application. And this is true for "the knowledge of His will", even as it is for any other knowledge. The Pharisees, for example, being dedicated students of the Law of Moses, used the knowledge of God's will they gained in their studies to structure a monstrous and soul-destroying legalism that burdened their followers and angered our Lord (Matthew 23:1ff). Wholesome principles that were designed to strengthen, guide, and bring freedom to the people – as prescribed in "the royal law ... the law of liberty" (James 2:8, 12), that is, in the "word of God" – were made "void" by their "traditions" (Mark 7:12). They appear to have used their knowledge of scripture for their own self-aggrandizement and at the expense of the denigration of others (Matthew 23:4-7). But such seems to be the way of any and every Christ-less religion, and of every form of rationalized, humanized, secularized, and unsanctified Christianity.

The only safeguard against the misuse of the knowledge of God's will – including the misuse of the "word of the truth of the gospel" (1:5) from which we gain such knowledge – is that His people learn to live "in all spiritual wisdom and understanding".

We should not confuse knowledge with wisdom, as each has distinct noetic significance. Paul would evidently have us distinguish between the two, as he places "the word of wisdom" in juxtaposition with "the word of knowledge", while acknowledging that both are gifts of the Spirit (I Corinthians 12:8). To appreciate this, we need only realize that a wise man may indeed have little knowledge; and a most knowledgeable man might be a crass fool! We would resort to the former if we needed guidance and advice, but to the latter, perhaps, if we needed information and facts. The man notably both wise and knowledgeable is exceptional; but to some extent every man requires a measure of wisdom and knowledge.

Wisdom, we might suggest, is *the ability to use knowledge well*; but well in *the dual sense* of both efficiently and ethically. The evil man who uses knowledge for wicked ends may do so with remarkable efficiency, but from a biblical perspective, we would not consider him to be wise. Alternatively, a good man might use knowledge for a good purpose, but do so inefficiently, and we would not consider him to be wise either. Therefore, Paul prays specifically that we might be "filled with the knowledge of (God's) will in all ... wisdom and understanding" (1:9). A thorough Christian education – whether at home, in Sunday school, or in seminary – demands something more profound than an academic impartation of knowledge.

To better understand this biblical wisdom, a comparison of two Pauline expressions might be helpful. Here, as we have seen, he writes of "wisdom and understanding" (1:9, ἵνα πληρωθῆτε … ἐν πάσῃ σοφίᾳ καὶ συνέσει); but in Ephesians 1:7-8, the apostle writes of the grace which abounds towards us in "wisdom and prudence" (sometimes translated "wisdom and understanding/insight", ἐν πάσῃ σοφίᾳ καὶ φρονήσει). The words for "understanding" and "prudence" are different, and at the risk of over-refinement, I suggest that the former implies a *critical thinking* that results in the *analysis* of whatever complex is being considered. But the latter implies a *practical thinking* that results is the *synthesis* of whatever disparate things are being considered.

In these two verses, Paul associates both "understanding" and "prudence" with "wisdom". This combination suggests that the apostle was aware that knowledge can only be used well when a man is wise enough to think both critically and practically, analyzing and synthesizing the information he receives and the situation in which it is relevant.

We might associate these things as in the following diagram:

THE COMPOSITION OF WISDOM

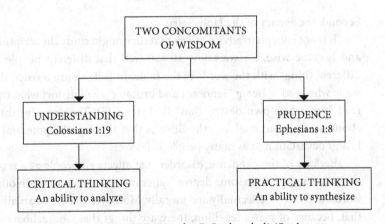

COPYRIGHT 2006 Alan D Catchpoole dia17.vsd

The use of knowledge through critical and practical thinking is something that man created in the image of God is designed to do, and is constantly doing. But our particular concern is to ask how this might be done well, both efficiently and ethically. In other words, we want to know how it might be done Christianly, that is, in a manner that is "worthy of the Lord" (1:10).

We have already seen that because Paul prays that his readers might be "filled with the knowledge of (God's) will" he is well aware that divine intervention is essential and that without it no man will be Christianly wise. There has to be, in other words, a salvation or redemption of man's mind. And this, we suggest, is done by God through *two things*:

- **First**, the instrumentality of the Bible.

  In Ephesians 1:17 Paul prays that his readers might be given the "spirit of wisdom and revelation", indicating that true wisdom must be associated with God's revelation. Elsewhere the apostle explains that the wisdom we need is not "the wisdom of this world", but "God's wisdom in a mystery", which enables an appreciation of things "God revealed ... through the Spirit" (I Corinthians 2:6-10).

  In other words, central and fundamental to Christian knowledge and wisdom is a revelation from God, or, in the language of Colossians 1:5, "the word of the truth of the gospel". Therefore, if we would be wise and truly think and reason as God would have us do, we must be familiar with and captivated by the teaching of the Bible.

  This requires a positive response in *humble obedience* (cf. Joshua 1:8, Psalm 119:9-11, II Timothy 3:14-17).

- **Second**, the agency of the Holy Spirit.

  It is not enough to advise others that they might study the scriptures and become wise, for we know all too well that different people do different things with the words of the Bible. In fact, we are warned that some who read it, being "ignorant and unstable", will distort what they read "unto their own destruction" (II Peter 3:16). The dreadful thing about reading and studying the Bible is that this has the potential to brings devastation to as many people as it saves!

  Because of the pandemic disorder that affects all people as a result of the fall, we are all to some degree "ignorant and unstable", or, in other words, depleted intellectually and morally. Moreover, our Lord explained that, because of man's rebellion, there are things that God deliberately hides "from the wise and understanding" (ἔκρυψας ταῦτα ἀπὸ σοφῶν καὶ συνετῶν, the two words here being cognate with those in Colossians 1:9) of this world (Matthew 11:25). Human noetic ability alone is not sufficient, no matter how sophisticated! Therefore, we all need reconciliation with God and the divine assistance for which Paul prayed on behalf of his Colossian readers. And this assistance is given through the ministry of the Holy Spirit (cf. John 15:13, I Corinthians 2:12-15).

  This requires a positive response in *simple faith* (cf. Proverbs 3:5-6).

These two requirements are found together in II Timothy 2:7 where the apostle writes, "Consider what I say" – that is, 'think about the apostolic word', or, as it was to become, the 'scriptures' – "for the Lord shall give you understanding in all things" (δώσει γάρ σοι ὁ κύριος σύνεσιν ἐν πᾶσιν) – that is, divine assistance will be given that you might understand. But Paul extrapolates! Those who understand the apostolic teaching – which is "the word of the truth of the gospel" (1:5) – will then have an adequate basis upon which to appreciate "all things". Obviously, Paul does not expect his readers to become omniscient! Nevertheless, those who develop a biblical perspective are well placed to gain an effective working knowledge of all necessary aspects of life that they might truly walk in the ways of their Lord. Life then can be approached with confidence and becomes meaningful and satisfying. Or, as Jesus said, they shall not "walk in darkness, but shall have the light of life" (John 8:12).

But we should note carefully that in writing about "spiritual" wisdom, Paul is not speaking of some mystical or merely intuitive understanding, or about comprehending things that are neither physical nor secular, or having insight into some realm that is beyond normal human experience or comprehension. He uses this adjective as the opposite of "carnal", and being "carnal" is the equivalent of being "sold under sin" (eg. Romans 7:14). Therefore, to think or act carnally, or "after the flesh", is the antithesis of thinking and acting "after the Spirit" (Romans 8:5-6). Either we think and act, in other words, under the dominion of our own sinfulness, or we think and act by the grace of God, under the dominion of God's Spirit. The most critical issue, then, is a matter of reconciliation and moral regeneration, not of greater natural intelligence or academic learning.

Therefore, we must understand "spiritual wisdom and understanding" as the perceptive use of knowledge that is in accord with the will of God and under the guidance of His Spirit. That is, redeemed thinking!

1.2.2. THE ULTIMATE PURPOSE (1:10A)[2]

There can be little doubt that Paul would have his readers "filled with the knowledge of (God's) will", that they might stand their ground theologically and not be distracted or confused by the heretical teachings of those who would make them captive to a false philosophy (2:8).

---

[2] There is an interesting grammatical structure here. What I have called 'the ultimate purpose' is introduced with an infinitive, and the following 'explanatory comments' by dependent participles.

But this, for the apostle, is far more than an academic exercise. The ultimate purpose of being filled with the knowledge of God's will is that men and women might "walk worthily of the Lord", or that they behave in a manner that pleases God. As man's rejection of God resulted in a worthless mind, which precipitated unbecoming behaviour and moral corruption, so any escape from corruption and unbecoming behaviour requires the redemption of the mind (cf. Romans 1:28ff.). It is important, then, that we be "renewed in the spirit of (our) mind" and that we be "not foolish, but understand what the will of the Lord is" (Ephesians 4:23, 5:17).

Paul's concern here is not so much that the Colossians *attain* the knowledge of God's will, as important as this is, but that they be *filled* with it. That is, as we have suggested above, he would have such knowledge be the driving and directing influence in their lives. *And the evidence that this is so is found not in academic excellence, as valuable as this might be, but in the moral quality of the way they live.*

Then, we should note, only that which pleases Him makes our "walk worthy of the Lord". God Himself, especially as we see Him incarnate in Christ Jesus, is the standard of godly living. It is God's intention – and so it should be our ambition – that we be "conformed to the image of His Son" (Romans 8:29). Therefore, as we shall see, it is important that we increase "in the knowledge of" Him (1:10).

Paul leaves us in no doubt about what characterizes those who do walk worthily of the Lord, writing elsewhere of this matter, for example, in the following three verses:

- **First**, the believers who walk worthily of the Lord are characterized by "all lowliness and meekness, with longsuffering, forbearing one another in love", giving "diligence to keep the unity of the Spirit in the bond of peace" (Ephesians 4:1-3). Such qualities of character, as difficult as they are for us to sustain, are evidence of Christ-likeness, and are essential for the maintenance of Christian unity.

  This verse explicates the meaning of the words "standing fast in one spirit" in Philippians 1:27, which is mentioned below. It explains that the unity we need to maintain the "faith of the gospel" requires much humility and love that are only available to us through the ministry of God's Spirit.

  We cannot walk worthily of the Lord when intolerant or hardhearted! *This is a matter of personal attitude.*

- **Second**, the Christians who walk as they ought, are also characterized by behaving "as citizens" in a manner of "life ... worthy of the gospel of Christ" while standing "fast in one spirit … striving for the faith of the gospel" (Philippians 1:27). Paul uses a word for behaviour ("let your manner of life") here that, more literally, means 'to conduct oneself as a good citizen' (πολιτεύεσθε). And the word translated "striving" or "striving together" (συναθλοῦντες, which is behind our word 'athlete') suggest being in a contest together, much like a team of sportsmen representing their country, or a company of soldiers fighting for their nation.

We cannot walk worthily of the Lord in disarray or in disunion.

But the contest in which we are engaged is not for personal or for communal glory, but for the defence and the propagation of the gospel of Christ. This involves not only faithfully and intelligently preserving "the word of the truth of the gospel" (1:5) – there is a *noetic* element involved – but also the presentation of it through wise and gracious behaviour in this world (4:5-6) – there is an *ethical* element involved. There is here a unity of belief *and* a unity of purpose; not the one without the other.

We cannot walk worthily of the Lord as eremites, nincompoops, or miscreants!

This is a matter of communal attitude.

• **Third**, Christians should also "walk worthily of God, who called (them) into His own kingdom and glory" (I Thessalonians 2:12). This reference to the divine "kingdom and glory" immediately confronts us with the responsibility of both obeying our sovereign Lord and of accepting His immaculate standards. Being called into His kingdom – which is an act of His pure grace, providing all the necessary elements of salvation (Romans 8:29-30) – is an immense privilege that, if profoundly understood, must generate both humility and thanksgiving in the beneficiary's heart. But it also imposes great obligation and responsibility. We strive "for the faith of the gospel" in the name of the Great King.

This verse expands the meaning of the expression 'behave as citizens' in Philippians 1:27, which is mentioned above. We are citizens of no insignificant city, but of the kingdom of almighty God, participating in His glory.

We cannot walk worthily of the Lord as aliens and enemies (1:2).

This is a matter of attitude towards God.

1.2.3. Four Explanatory Phrases (1:10b-14)

Paul now adds four explanatory phrases that amplify the meaning of his words "walk worthily of the Lord" – "bearing fruit", "increasing in knowledge", "strengthened with all power", and "giving thanks unto God". We might suggest that if the three verses we have just considered (Ephesians 4:1-2, Philippians 1:27, I Thessalonians 2:12) help us to understand the significance of the word "worthily", then these four additional expressions here help us to understand what the word "walk" entails. In other words, we have given some consideration to the *quality* of worthy behaviour, and now we must give some thought to the *structure* of worthy behaviour.

Evidently, the apostle wanted to impress upon his readers the responsibility they had to maintain a moral life such as is befitting anyone who, calling himself a Christian, has become the servant of the Great King. This is an awesome consideration, and the honest believer would sense that any real success in this endeavour is beyond his natural abilities.[3] Therefore, Paul would also have them know the resources that are at their disposal – indeed, the gracious interventions of God Himself – that enable them to proceed with some anticipation of actually doing that which is "pleasing" (1:10) to their Lord.

NOTE: It is important to note that these four expressions are in the present tense, and this indicates that we are not reading here about singular, momentary experiences that Christians have, or may have. Rather, they refer to the enduring and developing effect of God's unrelenting grace in the lives of all His people. *Fruitfulness, knowledge, strength, and thanksgiving are increasingly to characterize the true Christian.*

1.2.3.1. To walk worthily requires "bearing fruit in every good work"[4]

In 1:5-6 Paul wrote that "the word of the truth of the gospel" was "bearing fruit and increasing". There he is referring to the preaching of the gospel as it made a significant moral impact in human lives ("fruit", cf. Philippians 1:11), and was significantly influencing an "increasing" number of people. Its effect was both intensive in the lives of individuals, but extensive in world's communities.

Now, in 1:10, the apostle again uses these two words – "bearing fruit" and "increasing" – but here with a different application and in reference to personal Christian development, not specifically to the social influence of the preaching of the gospel. But the two cannot be dissociated from each other, and we might assume that Paul repeats these two words to suggest to the reader that there is a direct connection between Christian proclamation and the resultant Christian society. If the preaching is to change human individuals and communities, as it

---

[3] Consider Paul's own confession in this matter – Romans 7:14-18, 15:17-18.

[4] It seems preferable to me to take the words "bearing fruit in every good work" with the following words, and not with the preceding "unto all pleasing".

does, then it can only be seen to do so as men and women, being affected by "the word of the truth (1:5), are "bearing fruit in every good work, and increasing in the knowledge of God". Or, in other words, the *community* is transformed only as there is both *ethical* and *noetic* change in the lives of *individuals*. If God is pleased to bless our ministry, we should expect nothing less when we preach the gospel today.

Although we have separated "bearing fruit" and "increasing" here in these notes for particular comment, Paul does not do so. In fact, he clearly links them together in his writing (καρποφοροῦντες καὶ αὐξανόμενοι). Therefore, as they are so closely associated, we must not imagine that we can be fruitful in good works without increasing in the knowledge of God. Both are complementary, each depending upon the other as the Christian is being built up in Christ (2:7). This suggests an interactive development in Christian maturation. As we are guided in our obedience by "the knowledge of His will" that we have, the more fruitful we will become in "good work" that pleases our God. Then, the more fruitful we are in good work that pleases God, the more knowledge we will obtain of His will and the more perceptive we will become in His service.

Jesus explained in His parable of the sower that the "word of the kingdom", despite difficulties, would bear "fruit … some a hundredfold, some sixty, some thirty" in the lives of those who "hear … and understand" (Matthew 13:18-23). Similarly, Paul in this letter remarks that those who "received Christ Jesus as Lord" were "rooted … in Him" (2:6-7). We might extrapolate from the apostle's words that all true Christian growth, and hence all fruit, depends upon our relationship with Him, as we draw nourishment from Him as a plant does from the soil. And that fruit is "in every good work" (1:10). If we have genuine, even if limited understanding of the relationship Christians have with Christ, its rebirth, redemption, and reconciliation, it is impossible to imagine that it would have little or no effect in transforming people's lives for the better. *This relationship has its own irresistible dynamic.* Or, as our Lord said elsewhere, "As the branch cannot bear fruit of itself, except it abide in the vine; so neither can you, except you abide in me … apart from me you can do nothing" (John 15:4-5, cf. Romans 7:4-5).

Now, because the relationship the Christian has with Christ is most profound – an intimate, interpersonal relationship between a man and his God, in the sense that He is forever with His people and will never forsake them, and not necessarily, I might add, in any subjective sensation they might have of His presence – it necessarily has this irresistible dynamic. It has such an effect that Paul can write that "in Him (we) are made full" (2:10). Here he does not specifically tell us *by what* we are filled, but the context leaves us in no doubt about *by whom* we are filled – he implies that Christ did the filling. And in this Christ, as verse 2:9 states, "dwells all the fullness of the Godhead bodily". We might take this to mean that our lives, as Christians, are comprehensively, or fully, influenced by Him who is comprehensively and fully divine.

Therefore, we should not be surprised when we read here about bearing fruit "in every good work" (1:10). Struggling as we do with the temptations of this life and the moral deficiencies of our own souls, *any* truly good work seems to be beyond us (Romans 7:21). Nevertheless, although present perfection eludes us, by God's gracious enabling we can be involved even now in human activities that have genuine worth, and "as we have opportunity" we can "work that which is good toward all men" (Galatians 6:10).[5] Hence, if we are in every way influenced by Christ as a result of our communion with Him, we might indeed expect that this influence will affect everything that we do.

As we are "filled with the knowledge of His will" and so enabled to "walk worthily of the Lord", there ought to be an increasing goodness in everything we do. Sanctification has a pervasive influence in Christian life.

1.2.3.2. To walk worthily requires "increasing in the knowledge of God"

These verses, 1:9-10, establish beyond doubt that Christian behaviour should be characterized by knowledge and wisdom, as well as by moral worthiness. Therefore, all believers should approach life thoughtfully and intelligently, deliberately engaging their minds that they might be found "increasing in the knowledge of God".

As with all people, we must think, and the manner and content of our thinking do much to condition our conduct. And we must give the highest priority to the knowledge of our God Himself. For only as He is known will we rightly understand what He has done and is doing for His people, and then we will better appreciate *what* we should do and *how* we should do it to please Him. But we should not pursue this personal knowledge of God simply for its undoubted practical value, but also because it is necessary if we are to realize and enjoy all that a personal relationship with Him means. Moreover, our Lord said, "This is life eternal, that (we) should know ... the only true God" (John 17:3), implying,

---

[5] Perhaps we might say that even activities that are less than perfect – in motivation, intention, or execution – in God's sight, might nonetheless through His providence do good among men on earth, proving to be genuinely beneficial to others.

inter alia, that this is knowledge that makes life meaningful for both time and eternity.

However, bearing fruit in every good work requires both a morally perceptive mind that is able to distinguish between what is and what is not good, and also an adequate measure by which such distinctions may be made. For the Christian, the ultimate standard is God Himself. Therefore, it is imperative that we are constantly "increasing in the knowledge of God", never assuming that we know Him adequately, that we might be increasingly sensitive to His moral and other values. It is, then, imperative if we are to be "good servants of Christ Jesus" that we are "nourished" or "nurtured in the words of the faith and of the good doctrine" (I Timothy 4:6, ἐντρεφόμενος τοῖς λόγοις τῆς πίστεως καὶ τῆς καλῆς διδασκαλίας).[6] Thereby we will increase in the knowledge of God. But without such knowledge the conscience is weak (I Corinthians 8:4-7), and true moral judgement becomes difficult, if not impossible. The servant must appreciate his master's character if he is to discern the things that are pleasing to him.

NOTE: If we are to be filled with the knowledge of God's will (1:9, #1.2.1.1.2.), then we must have knowledge also of two other things – "the grace of God" (1:6) and "God" Himself (1:10). To know the grace of God is to be aware of His redemptive purpose in this world, into which purpose we are drawn by the Great Commission (Matthew 28:18-20), which also gives *direction* to our work in His service. And to know God Himself is to be aware of the purity of His character, and this delineates what it is to be "conformed to the image of His Son" (Romans 8:29), and this gives *quality* to our work in His service (cf. #1.2.1.1.1.).

1.2.3.3. To walk worthily requires being "strengthened with all power"

That Christians are "strengthened with all power, according to the might of His glory" is an astonishing concept! Paul evidently chose these forceful words and formulated this statement to impress upon his readers a sense of both their own inadequacy and the complete sufficiency of God's assistance.

However, it is important to understand the nature and intent of this empowering. We suggest the following factors need to be considered:

---

[6] Paul uses a word here that is variously translated 'nourish' or 'nurture' (ἐντρέφω). This compound verb is only found here in the New Testament, but elsewhere it has the meaning 'train' or 'bring up', but the basic word (τρέφω) is more frequently used in the New Testament with the meaning of 'feed' or 'nurture'.

- **First**, as the power is to be continually given (see #1.2.3. NOTE), the Christian is not at once strengthened so that he becomes self-contained and able to proceed on his own or to accomplish his own purposes. The power and the purpose for which it is given are always God's, and we continue to walk by faith (II Corinthians 5:7). We might say that we are not given power to use, but are used by the power of God for His purposes; or, we are not made powerful, but empowered.

- **Second**, the power given, although unlimited, is not unqualified – it is "according to the might of His glory". It is power that flows from the glory of God. It is, therefore, qualified not only by His omnipotence but also by His holiness. It is not brute force; it is not corruptible; it is not inexplicable; it is not meaningless – it is always expressive of the pure nature of, and intended to exalt the propriety of His own glory and to advance His own will and purpose. It is never given to glorify man.

- **Third**, the power is given by God, as the context clearly indicates, that His people might "walk worthily of the Lord unto all pleasing, bearing fruit in every good work". Therefore, we should note carefully, it is given that Christians might live a morally acceptable life, not that they might become miracle workers. This is, in other words, redemptive, moral power; not creative, physical power.

- **Fourth**, the moral significance of this power is also evident in the effect it has in the lives of Christian men and women. When "strengthened with all power" they will be people of "all endurance and long-suffering" (1:11, εἰς πᾶσαν ὑπομονὴν καὶ μακροθυμίαν). And it is most significant that the apostle considered his readers to be unable to live such patient and selfless lives without this magnanimous, divine assistance.

  The word "endurance" suggests a moral resilience that enables the Christian to accept the difficulties that come upon him and to stand his ground in serving his Lord. But the word "long-suffering" suggests a generous tolerance that enables the Christian to accept difficult people that come his way and to assist them as they may need. These are truly characteristics of a person of moral strength.

We should understand, then, that to be "strengthened with all power" – this power! – is not seen in miracle-working, powerful influence, forceful personality, or uniquely gifted individuals, but in the godliness of life manifested in holy living that is available to every Christian believer, even the lowliest and the most unexpected. And it is just this that makes divine empowerment most desirable.

1.2.3.4. To walk worthily requires "giving thanks unto the Father"

Undergirding a walk that is worthy of the Lord is thanksgiving (cf. Ephesians 5:20, I Thessalonians 5:18). The Christian is no querulous wimp! Being required to endure difficulties and to be long-suffering with difficult people, even when doing so comes with personal loss and pain, the strengthened Christian is not dispirited or dissatisfied. He is always "joyfully giving thanks unto the Father" (1:11-12).[7] This implies a sense of personal fulfilment in the service of God in the midst of pressures and problems. Paul knew that this disposition does not come easily to anyone, but needs divine assistance. Those who are "filled with the Spirit", he writes elsewhere, are found "giving thanks always for all things in the name of our Lord Jesus Christ" (Ephesians 5:18, 20).[8]

However, there is more than divine assistance behind the Christian's joyful thanksgiving; he also has exceedingly good personal reasons for it (1:12-14). We will briefly consider such reasons as are mentioned here:

- **First**, a change in *orientation*: the Father "made us meet/sufficient to be partakers of the inheritance of the saints in light" (1:12, τῷ ἱκανώσαντι ὑμᾶς εἰς τὴν μερίδα τοῦ κλήρου τῶν ἁγίων ἐν τῷ φωτί).
  The Christian is assured of a certain and enriching future, to which he aspires.

  If God had not come to our assistance, we would not have been able to make ourselves sufficient, or to qualify ourselves, to take our place among those who share in the eternal inheritance of God's redeemed people. It is only those who, by His grace, "turn from darkness to light, and from the power of Satan unto God" who "receive remission of sins and an inheritance among them that are sanctified" (Acts 26:18). These are they who, having turned "unto God", have become His servants and "shall receive the reward of the inheritance" (3:24, τὴν ἀνταπόδοσιν τῆς κληρονομίας).

  However, this inheritance is not ours simply because we are faithful servants of God. It is far more secure than we could ever merit, even by the most assiduous and acceptable service. Inheritance is associated with family descent, as the son inherits from his father (cf. Galatians 4:7). But all Christians become God's children through adoption and therefore, are "heirs of God, and joint-heirs with Christ" (Romans 8:15-17, κληρονόμοι

---

[7] Here "with joy" (μετὰ χαρᾶς) is best taken with "giving thanks" (εὐχαριστοῦντες).

[8] It is significant that these words from Ephesians are also found in the context of "understand what the will of the Lord is" (Ephesians 5:17, cf. Colossians 1:9).

μὲν θεοῦ,συγκληρονόμοι δὲ Χριστου). Our future – in effect, "the hope which is laid up for us in heaven" (1:5) – is intimately associated with the Father's purpose for His Son, with whom we are co-heirs.

We are then "made sufficient" or "qualified" to share in the inheritance with "the saint in light" by the remission of our sins and our adoption into God's family. And this is ours only by the pure grace of God and the love of the Father.

The "saints", a reference to all Christians, have this inheritance "in light". Paul no doubt adds this comment to make the clearest possible distinction between believers and non-believers. Having turned "from darkness unto light" (Acts 26:18), the believers, as it were, live in a different realm. They have been "delivered ... out of the power of darkness" (1:13), as we shall now consider.

- **Second**, a change of *dominion*: the Father "delivered us out of the power of darkness, and translated us into the kingdom of the Son of his love" (1:13, ἐρρύσατο ἡμᾶς ἐκ τῆς ἐξουσίας τοῦ σκότους καὶ μετέστησεν εἰς τὴν βασιλείαν τοῦ υἱοῦ τῆς ἀγάπης αὐτοῦ).

  The Christian is 'relocated' under a different and benevolent lordship.

  Not only are Christians now qualified through their adoption into God's family to participate in the inheritance of the saints, but also, they have been removed out of the dominion or tyranny of darkness and transferred into the "kingdom of the Son" of God. They are now subject to the gracious, sovereign rule of Jesus Christ.

  Although we have still to wrestle "against the principalities, against the powers, against the world-rulers of this darkness" (Ephesians 6:12, πρὸς τὰς ἀρχάς,πρὸς τὰς ἐξουσίας,πρὸς τοὺς κοσμοκράτορας τοῦ σκότους τούτου), "the principalities and the powers" (τὰς ἀρχὰς καὶ τὰς ἐξουσίας) have been overcome by Christ in His death and resurrection (2:15). To escape from darkness is to escape from "the power of Satan" (Acts 26:18), to find immunity from all his evil works, and to rise above the influences of ignorance and immorality. Therefore, we are encouraged to "show forth the excellencies of Him who called (us) out of darkness into his marvellous light" (I Peter 2:9). The privilege carries a responsibility.

  Without further comment, I might mention that in the Bible "light", in this sense, is indicative of the very character of God – Jesus said, "I am the light of the world" (John 8:12), and John wrote, "God is light, and in Him is no darkness at all" (I John 1:5). Hence, the "darkness" is all that is ungodly, all that is deficient in the truth, the purity, and the love of the Almighty.

Having escaped "the power of darkness" and being now numbered among "the saints in light" suggests a momentous change. This, we are told here, is the case with all who have been converted to Christ. Nevertheless, in so many obvious ways, life for the Christians is much like the life of all other people – they struggle, they suffer, they grow old, and they die. Paul was obviously aware of this, entertaining no naive misunderstanding of the difficulties with which believers must contend (Romans 8:22-23).

But the apostle would have us understand that the greater context in which we live as Christians, even while in this troubled world, is different. It is different because our Lord guarantees that "all things work together for good" for those who love Him (Romans 8:28), and that nothing "shall be able to separate us from" His love (Romans 8:39). This reciprocity of love is secured by the relationship we have with God "in Christ Jesus our Lord", as we shall now see.

- **Third**, a change in *relationship*: in the Son "we have our redemption, the forgiveness of our sins" (1:14, ἐν ᾧ ἔχομεν τὴν ἀπολύτρωσιν, τὴν ἄφεσιν τῶν ἁμαρτιῶν).

The Christian has been "reconciled" (1:21), and now enjoys a positive relationship with God.

Paul is stating quite clearly here that Christians now have "redemption" and "forgiveness of sins". But these are only found in Christ. Therefore, we might say that, on one hand, we only have redemption and forgiveness because of the relationship we have with Him; and on the other hand, that we only have a positive relationship with Him because of our redemption and forgiveness.

The apostle does write about *waiting* for our redemption (Romans 8:23, Ephesians 1:14, 4:30). Nevertheless, he assures us that we *already have* redemption (1:14, Ephesians 1:7). As this word implies a deliverance from bondage, and here the bondage to sin, we can understand both the immediate and the yet to be redemption. In Christ, we are already delivered from the penalty and the estrangement of sin, even as in Him also we are guaranteed deliverance from all the effects and the physical death of sin when our salvation is consummated.

But it is this immediate redemption from the penalty and the estrangement of sin that secures our reconciliation (1:21-22). Therefore, the Christian, being a beneficiary of our Lord's death and resurrection, already has a secure and irrevocable, positive relationship with God.

It is these things – our new *orientation* before Him, our life under His *dominion*, and our personal *relationship* with Him – that give Christians good and intelligent reason to remain thankful in the fallen world with all its pain and sorrow. We ought to be most grateful to God, even for the least of His mercies, but we should be overwhelmingly comforted by these everlasting blessings we have received from Him.

NOTE: Thanksgiving is an essential element in Christian living, being frequently mentioned and encouraged in the New Testament. Paul is emphatic that it should be unrelenting, writing, "Giving thanks always for all things ... unto God" (Ephesians 5:20, εὐχαριστοῦντες πάντοτε ὑπὲρ πάντων), and "in everything give thanks, for this is the will of God" (I Thessalonians 5:18, ἐν παντὶ εὐχαριστεῖτε). Evidently, then, this thanksgiving is not the product of or dependent upon our individual circumstances or occurrences; neither is it unduly influenced by the minutiae of daily life. It is, rather, the product of genuine faith in Christ.

The conditions in which such thanksgiving in faith is generated are the three things we have just considered: that we have been qualified by God to participate in His inheritance, that we have been delivered out of the power of darkness, having been transferred into God's kingdom, and that we have been reconciled with God through Christ. The greater our appreciation and recollection of these Christian benefits, and the contribution they make to our lives, the more consistent and the more exultant our thanksgiving will be.

And these three things correspond to what we have called the 'dimensions of salvation', the prospective, the present, and the personal aspects of the redemption we have in Christ (#1.)

Having considered what is involved in walking worthily of our Lord, we should no longer think it to be a trivial or secondary matter. Therefore, we should understand that to walk in a manner pleasing to God is far better and far more important than walking successfully in this world. It is perhaps a serious deficiency of the contemporary church that in it we are far more likely to be taught techniques for success in life than the ways of godliness.

◆

1.3. THE PERSONAL: RECONCILIATION WITH GOD (1:15-23)

This third dimension of our salvation, reconciliation with God, is fundamental to all the other benefits of being Christian. As Paul is about to explain, those who are unconverted and in their natural state are "alienated and enemies" (1:21), having no positive or beneficial association with God. But with those who are reconciled, it is very different. They have hope in heaven and moral strength to live on earth.

However, this third dimension, being less captivating than the contemplation of our coming hope and less pressing than the demands of moral behaviour in this world, is perhaps the most easily forgotten in the disciplines of Christian living. Or, possibly, we tend to be more preoccupied with the benefits we gain through our redemption than with the One from whom they come, and in whose fellowship, they are to be enjoyed. Not only should we "walk worthily of the Lord" (1:10), but we should also "walk in Him" (2:6). This suggests that there is a personal intimacy with the Lord that is essential for all who would be "rooted and built up in Him" (2:7).

Moreover, if we are to consider the significance of this intimacy the Christian has with his Lord as a result of his reconciliation, we must appreciate that it is not an association of equals.[9] The apostle evidently would have us remember that "in all things" He has the pre-eminence (1:18), being both "firstborn of all creation" and "firstborn from the dead" (1:15, 18). This surely implies that our sense of intimacy should be replete with awe and worship, lest we be guilty of impudence. Hence Paul presents the person of Jesus Christ here in a manner that reflects something of the magnificence of His being and the majesty of His office.

Now, we might suggest that the apostle, in writing as he does, is evidently concerned with more than that his readers cultivate a truly godly intimacy with their Lord. This was essential for their personal growth in grace. But the context of this letter suggests that a sense of awe and wonder was a necessary prerequisite if they were to resist the enticements of the heretical teachers who were seeking to captivate them with their own philosophies (2:8). If we are not entranced by the magnificence of such a pre-eminent God and inspired by the remarkable salvation He provides for His people, we might easily be deceived by the "persuasiveness of speech" (2:4) of those who would deceive us.

---

[9] There is a biblical basis for equality among all people created in God's image. However, today we seem to have lost the idea that there can be rich, satisfying, and true relationships where there is no equality in other matters (eg. between the adult and the child, between the strong and the weak or retarded). Problems arise when we are not subject to divine authority, nor contented in His service.

Only those who are driven by a godly heart and a devout spirit, those who tremble before the Almighty – that is, only those who are awed by His pre-eminence – will make good theologians. "The fear of the Lord is the beginning of wisdom: and the knowledge of the Holy One is understanding" (Proverb 9:10).

As Christians, we have been "translated into the kingdom of the Son" of God (1:13). Therefore, we ought to be impelled by a desire to know and understand the King whom we now serve (#1.2.1.1.1.). Here Paul gives us serious instruction. In what is a magisterial declaration, he presents his readers with a description of the unquestionable supremacy of Christ in the creation of all things and in the redemption of the church and His own people. No adequate assessment of human life can be formulated without acknowledging His sovereignty in matters both cosmic and religious. No doubt the false teachers in Colossae were ignorant or seriously deficient in their understanding of His might and dominion, being given over to their anthropocentric assumptions.

As a necessary corrective for any flawed theology or misguided faith, Christ is presented here in reference to His pre-eminent position both in the creation and in the church.

1.3.1. CHRIST AND THE CREATION (1:15-17)

Paul makes *three remarkable and complex statements* about Jesus Christ, God's beloved Son, and His involvement in the creation of the universe. These apostolic words need to be carefully considered, for if we capture their significance – and if we are captured by them – they will not only enlarge our appreciation of Him but will also greatly strengthen our faith in Him. Moreover, they will also provide us with a framework within which we can develop a true philosophy of life, and not be deceived by "the traditions of men" and "the rudiments of the world" – a philosophy that is indeed "after Christ" (2:8).

These are not, then, irrelevant, merely abstract, or conjectural statements designed only for the academic interest of erudite minds, but are concepts of profound importance for every Christian who would live meaningfully and intelligently.

1.3.1.1. HE IS THE "IMAGE OF THE INVISIBLE GOD, THE FIRSTBORN OF ALL CREATION" (1:15)

Here Paul is writing about Jesus Christ, the person known intimately by His apostles, as He relates on the one hand to God, of whom He is the visible image, and on the other hand to the creation, of which He is the firstborn. The reference to the "image" not only suggest that through Christ God is made known to man, but it also points to His divinity; and the reference to the "firstborn", having no reference to time, is descriptive of His sovereign authority and right of possession over all things. We will look briefly at these two concepts separately.

1.3.1.1.1. THE IMAGE OF THE INVISIBLE GOD

Elsewhere, when distinguishing between "the wisdom ... of this world" and "God's wisdom", Paul explains that there are "things which eye saw not, and ear heard not" that God has "revealed ... through the Spirit" (I Corinthians 2:6-10). And on another occasion, he declared that "we faint not ... though our outward man is decaying", because we "look not at the things which are seen, but the things which are not seen" (II Corinthians 4:16-18). There is, then, truth that is invisible but, by the grace of God, not inaccessible. It is this access to otherwise unknown wisdom and understanding that gives us assurance ("we faint not") of "the hope which is laid up for (us) in heaven" (1:5), and enables us to increase "in the knowledge of God" (1:10, cf. #1.2.1.1.1.). Nothing else can give us confidence in the future and acquaintance with the Almighty but cognitive, propositional, and unmistakable revelation from God Himself.

But how do we gain access to this wisdom and understanding, and obtain knowledge of things not seen?

God has indeed revealed Himself to us as worthy of our worship and trust through things we see in His creation, to which we should have responded appropriately, but did not (Romans 1:18-21). Then, in addition to this self-disclosure, further knowledge of "things not seen" is also "revealed ... through the Spirit" (I Corinthians 2:10), and we should recognize that there is no other way mankind could have obtained it. Such knowledge is inaccessible to human science and philosophy. There is, we read, a deposit of divine truth, given in history, which was delivered "to the fathers in the prophets" (Hebrews 1:1) and subsequently to the apostles (John 16:13, Galatians 1:11-12, Ephesians 3:2-5, cf. Matthew 11:25-27, II Peter 1:15-18). God has deliberately made Himself known to men at various times and in different ways (Hebrews 1:1), according to His own will and mankind's requirements.

But above all, God has "at the end of these days spoken unto us in His Son" (Hebrews 1:2). Jesus said to His Father, "The words which you have given me, I have given to them" (John 17:8) – that is, to His disciples. However, by his own declaration, He did far more than give words to the apostles to deliver to us. He also "glorified (God) on earth", "accomplished the work (God) gave (Him) to do", and "manifested (God's) name unto men" (John 17:4-6). His whole life and demeanour during the days of His incarnation on earth were the climax of God's self-revelation to men. Although "no man has seen God at any time, the only begotten Son, who is in the bosom of the Father, has declared Him" (John 1:18). Therefore, our Lord could say, "He that has seen me, has seen the Father" (John 14:9).

And as this most comprehensive of all revelations from the invisible God is in the incarnate God, the man Jesus, it is also, in a sense, the most comprehensible. Here, in the human Christ, God is revealed in a manner we can see and appreciate; in our form, He acted and spoke as man in the presence of men.

From this, it is evident that if we would know the invisible God and gain some true insight into the all-important "things which eye saw not", we are invited to look to Jesus Christ. He is the "image of the invisible God" (ἐστιν εἰκὼν τοῦ θεοῦ τοῦ ἀοράτου, 1:15, cf. II Corinthians 4:4).

The "god of this world has blinded the minds of the unbelieving", but through the preaching of the gospel "the glory of Christ, who is the image of God" has been made known to those who believe (II Corinthians 4:4). Here Paul associates, or even identifies the "image" with divine "glory", and this "glory" is the wonder and majesty of God's very being and character. Only in Jesus Christ could there be such a revelation, because, as Paul writes in Colossians, "in Him dwells all the fullness of the Godhead bodily" (2:9), and only in Him are "all the treasures of wisdom and knowledge hidden" (2:3). So, He is the "image of God" *because He is essentially God and necessarily omniscient. He has no equal in representing the likeness of God.*

◆

In the Bible, man is also referred to as being in the image of God (Genesis 1:27). This image was seriously defaced in the fall and further corrupted by men throughout history. Nevertheless, it is God's intention that His people, by His redeeming grace, be "conformed to the image of His Son" (Romans 8:29, cf. II Corinthians 3:18, I John 3:2). However, there is not only similarity but also dissimilarity between Christ as "the image of the invisible God" and the image to which we are being conformed.

Paul writes in Colossians that the Christian "is being renewed unto knowledge after the image of Him who created him" (3:10). This obviously does not mean that we will at any time participate in the essential being, or in the omniscience of our Creator. Every devout and understanding Christian seeks to emulate the Jesus we read about in the New Testament, but he also knows that He was unique in many ways that we cannot replicate in our own lives. And this is so not only because we are yet imperfect and sinful, but also because we are *created man* whereas He was *incarnated God*. Therefore, He is both God and God's image.

We might ask, then, in what dimensions ought we seek to be like Him? I would suggest we be concerned first of all with the importance of true righteousness, holiness, and knowledge (Ephesians 4:24, Colossians 3:10), which are the essential moral prerequisites for Christ-like behaviour. Then, the anticipation that one day we will indeed be like Him, should be powerful motivation for us to "purify" ourselves (I John 3:2-3).

But such a pursuit of Christ-likeness is not to be abstracted from physical life and sought in monastic living or mystical preoccupation. When man was created in the image of God (Genesis 1:27) he was made a physical creature to live in this material world. Therefore, we should also seek so to live that "the life also of Jesus may be manifested in our body", even in our "mortal flesh" (II Corinthians 4:10-11). Nothing is gained, as Paul writes, by "severity to the body" (2:23). Moreover, the apostle assures us that one day our "body … will be conformed to the body of His glory" (σύμμορφον τῷ σώματι τῆς δόξης αὐτοῦ, Philippians 3:21). This ultimate physical likeness with Christ – no doubt in a manner we cannot yet comprehend – is integral to being "conformed to the image of His Son" (συμμόρφους τῆς εἰκόνος τοῦ υἱοῦ αὐτοῦ, Romans 8:29).

I would conclude from all this that if we are truly concerned to live as those who are being restored to the image of God – according to the dimensions relevant to being created for this end – we will pursue righteousness, holiness, and knowledge for the sake of moral behaviour. But we will also seek to glorify God through our physical presentation in appearance, practical work, the artistry of our hands, the possession and use of property, our stewardship in this world, and every other matter in which our bodies and things tangible are involved. Nothing is exempted! (See further, #3.4.1.2.2.)

◆

1.3.1.1.2. THE FIRSTBORN OF ALL CREATION

This expression has no chronological significance. Being "firstborn of all creation" (πρωτότοκος πάσης κτίσεως) does not imply, as ancient and modern heretics suggest, that 'there was a time when the Son was not'.[10] That would indicate that

---

[10] 'If the Father begat the Son, he that was begotten had a beginning of existence: and from this it is evident, that there was a time when the Son was not.' (Arius, c. 330 AD. The Church condemned his views as heretical.) This, as I understand, continues to be the opinion of today's Jehovah's Witnesses.

He is Himself part of the creation and not eternally one with the Father. But quite evidently, He is not part of creation, "for by Him were all things created" (1:16); and, obviously, He who creates, or He through whom creation is effected, cannot be part of creation itself.

The significance of this appellation is found in the Old Testament. There is a remarkable regulation in the Mosaic Law stipulating that if a man has two wives, one loved and the other hated, and the hated wife gives birth to a son before her rival, the man is not to "make the son of the beloved the firstborn" when his inheritance is divided. The son who is *chronologically* the second born, in other words, is not to be considered *legally* the firstborn (Deuteronomy 21:15-17). The rights of the firstborn were not to be transferred to another.

Then, there was the infamous case where Jacob deceived his brother Esau – who was technically born first –into selling his birthright (Genesis 25:27-34); and subsequently, he contrived also to steal their father's final blessing (Genesis 27:1ff.). The result was that Isaac, their father, said to Esau, "I have made him (Jacob) your lord, and all his brothers I have given him for servants" (Genesis 27:37). Under normal circumstances, the son who was chronologically born first would inherit the controlling interest in the father's estate, authority over the whole family, and the associated religious responsibilities and privileges. Jacob's contriving subverted this principle.

Therefore, we suggest, the *primary* significance of being the firstborn was not a matter of the timing of the birth but *the position of ownership and authority*. We might assume that if the son born first died before coming of age, then the second born son would be deemed the "firstborn" and inherit the estate.

In Psalm 89 reference is made to the covenant God made with King David in which the Lord assured him that even when he slept with his fathers, one of his sons would inherit his throne and his kingdom would be established forever (cf. II Samuel 7:12-13). In this Psalm, God exclaims, "He shall cry unto me, You are my Father ... (and) I will make Him my firstborn, the highest of the kings of the earth" (Psalm 89:26-27). Evidently, this is a reference to the Messiah King, the descendant of David, Jesus Christ. And for Him to hold the position of God's firstborn makes Him the King of all kings. He has, in other words, sovereign rights of possession and authority in the kingdom of God over the whole of the created order. He has been "appointed heir of all things", being seated "on the right hand of the majesty on high", being "begotten" of God and Son of the Father (Hebrews 1:2-7).

It is precisely this position of ultimate sovereignty over "all things", which "in Him ... were created", that is in view here in Colossians 1:15-16 in the reference to Christ as the Firstborn.

1.3.1.2. "In Him were all things created" (1:16)

This sixteenth verse explains why it is appropriate to refer to Jesus Christ as "the firstborn of all creation". He is so "because in Him were all things created" (ὅτι ἐν αὐτῷ ἐκτίσθη τὰ πάντα) and "all things have been created through Him and for Him" (τὰ πάντα δι' αὐτοῦ καὶ εἰς αὐτὸν ἔκτισται). It is implied here that God is the Creator, but that He created "in", "through", and "for" Christ, His beloved Son. This indicates that the Son of God is *the context* in which, *the agency* through which, and *the reason* for which all things are created. And this can be so only because the Son is equally God with the Father. He does indeed, then, have both the right of possession and authority over all things! We live in His world.

NOTE: In passing, and lest we lose sight of the fascination of these words, we should keep in mind that Paul is writing about the person he and the apostles first knew as the Babe of Bethlehem, the Man from Galilee, the Carpenter in Nazareth. This is He of whom John could write that he, and others, had "seen with our eyes, which we beheld, and our hands handled" (I John 1:1). As transcendent as He may be, He is immanent in the incarnation! So, when we look into the vastitude of the universe, we see the creative genius of the One we can truly know and love (I Peter 1:8).

I suggest we might draw some definitive conclusions from Paul's words here:

- **First**, that all things were created "through" Him necessarily implies that the Son of God was agential in the whole process; He was directly involved in the making of all things.
  Therefore, the Christian cannot consider the creation to have anything other than a personal origin, in which its *essential meaning* is to be found. With this as a fundamental principle of their ontology, Christians cannot be materialists.

- **Second**, that all things were created "for" Him necessarily implies that whatever is brought into existence is for His ultimate satisfaction; He is not only the alpha, but also the omega, both the beginning and the end (Revelation 21:6), determining the course of history.
  Therefore, the Christian cannot consider the creation to have anything other than a personal consummation, in which its *essential*

purpose is to be found. With this as a fundamental principle of their teleology, Christians cannot be naturalists.[11]

- **Third**, that all things were created "in" Him[12] necessarily implies that nothing exists beyond or without Him, that He upholds "all things by the word of His power" (Hebrews 1:3), and that in Him we "live and move and have our being" (Acts 17:28).

  Therefore, the Christian cannot consider the creation to be self-sufficient or self-sustaining, or 'mechanically' independent, or capable of becoming independent of its Creator, and in this the *essential power* of the universe is to be found. With this as a fundamental principle of their religion, Christians cannot be deists, or acknowledge only an 'absentee' god that made, but does not manage, the world. But because we "live and move and have our being" in Him, we reckon with and enjoy the intimacy of love for and faith in our gracious and personal God, made possible through reconciliation.

These things are fundamental to Paul's comprehension of human life – and hence, for all Christian understanding – and they serve to raise the whole of human existence out of the meaningless, materialistic, and mundane. And in the immediate context of the first chapter in Colossians, it is only against this background that we can anticipate the "hope which is laid up in heaven" (1:5) with any assurance, or set our minds "on things that are above" (3:2) with any confidence.

But more broadly, what the apostle is saying in 1:16 lays a foundation which, if understood and trusted, will arm the Christian to resist the subtly persuasive "philosophy and vain deceit, after the traditions of men, after the rudiments of the world" which the non-Christian uses in an attempt to demolish our faith. In contrast to their theorizing, we are advised by Paul to develop a true philosophy "after Christ" (2:8) which demands that we begin with an appreciation of the Son of God as He is depicted here, and find in Him the source of all meaning, purpose, and faith. Then we will not be beguiled or misled by this world's materialism, naturalism, or deism, or by any of their various derivatives.

◆

---

[11] "Naturalist", not in the sense of botanist or zoologist, but one committed to the philosophy of naturalism, that nature is self-determining.

[12] In this verse (1:16) "in Him" is sometimes translated "by Him". This is not without some good reasons, but we prefer the former. If ἐν αὐτῷ is translated "by Him" it adds little or nothing to the following δι' αὐτοῦ, "through Him", and loses the connection with "in Him" in verse 1:17.

We must also note *the extent of Paul's claim* here. The Son of God is not one creator among others, but "all things" are created by Him, things "in the heaven, and upon the earth, things visible and things invisible" (1:16). Obviously, the apostle would have his readers understand that there is nothing in the whole of existence that has not been made by God. The heretics who were troubling the young church in Colossae were possibly promoting the pagan idea that there are two competing and contrasting systems, two primordial originating sources, one benevolent the other malevolent, that make reality such as it is. In this, perhaps, they were trying to provide a rational explanation for good and evil. But the Christian, following these words of Paul and the general teaching of the Bible, rejects all kinds of dualism. There are not and cannot be two such competing systems, two contending 'creators', because all things are created by God – the God we know in Jesus Christ.

The word "heaven" appears hundreds of times throughout the Bible, from Genesis 1:1 (where heaven is declared to be created by God) to Revelation 21:10 (where heaven is seen as the source of the New Jerusalem and the renewed creation). But it is used in various ways. It may refer, for example, to the sky above the earth from which the stars will "fall" (Revelation 6:13, 9:1); it is seen as a place of warfare between the angels (Revelation 12:7), and possibly the sphere of the conflict in which Christians are engaged (Ephesians 6:12). Yet heaven is the location of God's throne (Revelation 4:2ff) and where Christ entered "to appear before the face of God for us" (Hebrews 9:24). Moreover, it is where we invest our everlasting treasures (Matthew 6:20), and where we are to find the "hope" which God Himself has "laid up" for us (1:5) and enter into our imperishable inheritance (I Peter 1:4). Therefore, it does refer, *inter alia*, to the situation in which we will finally find ourselves, having been redeemed by the grace of God.

This very brief consideration is perhaps sufficient to indicate that we must consider the significance of the word "heaven" within the context in which it is used.

Here in Colossians 1:16 Paul seems to be referring to "heaven" in the most general sense, as an equivalent of all "things invisible". His purpose is not to refer to any particular aspect of "heaven", but only to indicate the inclusiveness of God's creation.

Even elements of the unseen world that appear to be evil and hostile – the thrones, dominions, principalities, and powers (cf. Ephesians 6:12) – are not uncreated, independent of the Creator, self-sufficient, or beyond the sovereignty of God (cf. Ephesians 1:21). There are no eternal malevolent forces. However self-corrupted and corrupting these things may be, they cannot escape the control and the judgement of the Almighty. Moreover, the apostle assures his readers that these wicked entities have been overcome by Christ through His crucifixion (2:14-15) and that He will ultimately abolish them (I Corinthians 15:24). Paul's immediate concern here in 1:16 is not to expound upon the various aspects of "heaven", but to embrace every conceivable thing within God's creation, and to draw attention to His supremacy.

We must realize that there are these two categories of created reality: the visible and the invisible. Not everything is within the reach of human observation. And among the invisible things, there are, *inter alia*, evil constituents. But whatever these thrones, dominions, principalities, and powers may be – and the Bible does speak of a devil, fallen angels, and demons – and despite any conflict we may have with them, the Christian always has the assurance that they are but creatures and "in subjection under (Christ's) feet" (Ephesians 1:22). This has extensive implications for our faith and life.

1.3.1.3. "He is before all things, and in Him all things consist" (1:17)

It is implicit in the statement in 1:16 concerning all things being created "in Him ... through Him, and for Him" that Christ is "before all things" (αὐτός ἐστιν πρὸ πάντων, 1:17). And our Lord says as much about Himself when praying to His Father: "Glorify me with your own self with the glory which I had with you before the world was" (John 17:5). He also said of Himself, "I am ... the truth" (John 14:6). This requires us to believe that the ultimate reality at the back of all things is neither a philosophical postulate or hypothesis, nor a mathematical equation, nor a chemical formula, but a person – indeed a Person both pre-existent to this world and pre-eminent in it. And this, we might add, makes personal life and interpersonal relationships matters of the highest priority in His estimation and in our existence.[13]

Then Paul adds another important consideration. Christ is not only the *pre-existent cause* but also the *providential sustainer* of all created things. That is, "in Him all things consist" or "cohere" (τὰ πάντα ἐν αὐτῷ συνέστηκεν, 1:17). This implies that the whole of creation is a dependent reality. It does not have "life in itself" (unlike Christ Himself, cf. John 5:26); it does not and cannot substantiate or interpret itself. It cannot exist without God, for it was never so designed. Or, as we read elsewhere, it is "by faith we understand that the worlds have been framed by the word of God", and that He is "upholding all things by the word of His power" (Hebrews 11:3, 1:3).

Then, as we shall see, Paul anticipates that through the death and resurrection of Christ God has purposed to "reconcile all things unto Himself ... whether things upon the earth, or things in the heavens" (1:20).

---

[13] God did not create a machine to make people, but He created man and woman to procreate people. Our very existence is, by his design, rooted in interpersonal relationships.

◆

Christ is seen in these apostolic words, first of all, in *an essential relationship* with God. He is the "image of the invisible God". The implication of this is that He is, Himself, very God of very God. But He is also presented here in *a covenanted relationship* with the whole of Creation. As the "firstborn of all creation" He possesses and rightfully exercises sovereign authority over all that is in the created order. He has such authority because by Him "all things were created". He exercises this authority through His providential control of "all things" that necessarily "consist" in Him.

We might summarize all this as follows:

CHRIST AND CREATION

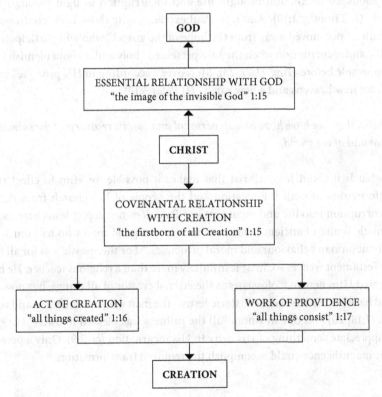

Alan D Catchpoole

1.3.2. CHRIST AND THE CHURCH (1:18-23)

Not only in creation, but also in the body of the church, Jesus Christ has the pre-eminence. He, then, has considerable interest in both the creation *and* the Christian community.

Being the servant of Jesus Christ, the Christian also has considerable interest in these two entities – the creation *and* the church – as together they constitute the comprehensive context in which he is to live. He, unlike the non-Christian who has no part in the church at all, is irrevocably involved in and concerned for the well-being of the world *and* the believing community. The serious problem with creation in its present, fallen condition is that it and all those who dwell on this earth are subject to death and decay (Romans 8:20-22). But in the midst of all the vanity and corruption of this world stands "our Saviour Christ Jesus, who abolished death, and brought life and incorruption to light through the gospel" (II Timothy 1:10). And it is, Paul explains, only those who "continue in the faith ... not moved away from the hope of the gospel" who will participate in this life and incorruption when they are presented "holy and without blemish and unreprovable before Him" (1:22-23). Moreover, "according to His promise" they "look for new heavens and a new earth" (II Peter 3:13).

In Christ, then, we have hope of both personal and cosmic recovery: of the salvation of man and of the world.

But what is it about Jesus Christ that makes it possible for Him to effect this transformation of both the creation and the people of His church from death and corruption into life and incorruption? Paul does not depict Jesus here as an enigmatic figure of ancient history, or merely as a good man who had much to say about human behaviour and moral principles.[14] For the apostle – as for all the New Testament writers – Christ is infinitely more than a religious teacher. He has presented Him here in Colossians as the eternal creator of all things, but now he would have his readers see the historic Jesus – the man who was crucified and rose again (1:18, 20) – as one in whom "all the fullness was pleased to dwell" (1:19)[15], and appreciate something of His deity in His incarnation (cf. 2:9). Only a person of His magnificence could accomplish the required transformation.

---

[14] Jesus is a figure of ancient history, and a good man who had much to say about human behaviour and moral principles. But this is not the whole story, and we should seek to know and worship Him as God incarnate.

[15] So this phrase from 1:19 might be translated (ὅτι ἐν αὐτῷ εὐδόκησεν πᾶν τὸ πλήρωμα κατοικῆσαι).

NOTE: We cannot but be moved by the astonishing presentation we have of Jesus Christ in these verses in Colossians. They should forever prevent us from trivializing Him in our thoughts and words and preserve us in constant adoration. Well might the church in time and in eternity say, "Unto him that sits on the throne, and unto the Lamb, be the blessing, and the honour, and the glory, and the dominion, for ever and ever" and fall down and worship Him (Revelation 5:13-14).

To the end that we might worship Him, as we ought, and trust Him, as He deserves, we will briefly consider the implications of some of Paul's specific statements here.

1.3.2.1. CHRIST, "THE HEAD OF THE BODY" (1:18)

The apostle is now introducing his readers to the incarnate Christ – He who was raised "from the dead" (1:18) – by whom it has been made possible for His people to participate in life and incorruption.

The person Paul has been describing as "the image of the invisible God, the firstborn of all creation" (1:15) is now presented as "the head of the body, the church; who is the beginning, the firstborn from the dead" (1:18). Elsewhere, the apostle has spoken metaphorically of the church as Christ's body. He does this *first* in I Corinthians 12:12-13, 27 to explain the interrelatedness and interdependence of all individual believers in the Christian community. *Then*, he later develops this metaphor by stating that the church is not only dependent upon its members, but also upon the Lord of the Church. We should, he writes, "grow up in all things into Him, who is the head, Christ", not only as a result of the contribution made by each believer to the community (Ephesians 4:15-16), but also through the nourishment provided by Christ Himself to all those who are "members of His body" (Ephesians 5:29-30).

These emphases upon the interdependence of Christians on one another and their ultimate dependence on Christ Himself, as members of His body, reappear in Colossians 2:19. But here in 1:18 Paul uses the same metaphor to draw attention to the authority that "the head" has over "the body" as a result of His pre-eminence. Then, as the apostle goes on to explain, this authority He has over the church is grounded upon our Lord being both "the beginning", and "the firstborn from the dead".

It is important, then, if we are to appreciate the extent of His authority over the church, that we have some understanding of the significance of these two expressions:

- **First**, Christ is "the beginning".[16]

   That Christ is "the beginning" (ἀρχή) no doubt refers to the fact that He was the first, chronologically, to rise from the dead.[17] "Christ ... raised from the dead" has become "the firstfruits of them that are asleep" (I Corinthians 15:20). For Paul, it was a biblical principle rooted in the Old Testament that "the Christ must suffer ... that He first by the resurrection of the dead, should proclaim light" to His people (Acts 26:23). The great light of the gospel, as we have seen above, is the conquest of the darkness of death.

   But more is implied, because the word "beginning" that we find here also is also used of 'rulers' – whether, on earth, of synagogue authorities (Luke 12:11) and Roman governors (Luke 20:20, cf. Titus 3:1); or of evil dominion among the "spiritual hosts of wickedness" (Ephesians 1:21, 3:10, 6:12). But as far as Paul was concerned, all such were of little consequence, because Christ "is the head of all principalities" having triumphed "over them" (2:10, 15). Then, at the end when Christ returns, "He shall have abolished all rule (ἀρχή) and authority and power" having "put all His enemies under His feet" (I Corinthians 15:23-25).

   And for our comfort, we should note the apostle's confidence that Christ in His authority is already seated at God's right hand "in heavenly places, far above all rule (ἀρχή), and authority, and power, and dominion, and every name that is named" and that we, His people, are seated "with Him in the heavenly places in Christ" (Ephesians 1:20-21, 2:6).

   There must be a sense, then, in which we are invulnerable to all the forces of evil because Christ our Saviour is "the beginning" and has the "pre-eminence". So, although we anticipate a final assertion of Christ's authority and the ultimate abolition of all evil rule (I Corinthians 15:23-25), it is already true that when God "raised him from the dead" He at the same time "put all things in subjection under His feet" making Him the "head over all things for the church" (Ephesians 1:20, 22).

- **Second**, Christ is "the firstborn from the dead".

   This assertion that Christ is "the firstborn from the dead" – or, as it might be translated, "the firstborn from among those who are

---

[16] This word, "the beginning" (ἀρχή), may indicate 'first in time' (eg. John 15:27, Hebrews 1:10), or 'first in authority' (eg. Luke 20:20, Ephesians 1:21, 'rule').

[17] There were those who recovered from death, coming back to life, before our Lord's resurrection. See, for example, I Kings 17:17-24, Luke 7:11-17, John 11:34-44. However, all these remained subject to death – and indeed, died again! But Christ not only came back from death, but also triumphed over death. Or, as Paul wrote, "Christ being raised from the dead dies no more; death no more has dominion over Him" (Romans 6:9). In this He is unique, the progenitor!

dead" (πρωτότοκος ἐκ τῶν νεκρῶν) – adds little to, but explicates the preceding comment about Him being "the beginning". We have already seen that being "the firstborn of all creation" defines His ownership of and authority over all things God has made (#1.3.1.1.2.). But now we are looking at His sovereign position in another and distinct – although related – realm, the community of God's redeemed people. He owns and has authority over the church.

It is assumed here that the readers were aware that Jesus Christ was God incarnate, although He was "found in fashion as a man" and was "obedient even unto death" (Philippians 2:8).[18] Then, being firstborn "from among those who are dead" implies that He was the first of many who would escape the penalty of sin (Romans 6:23) and return to life.[19] So Paul can affirm that "since by man (Adam) came death, by man (Christ) came also the resurrection of the dead" (I Corinthians 15:22). Therefore, all those who are in Christ "shall all be made alive", and so "death is swallowed up in victory" (I Corinthians 15:21, 54).

And this establishes Christ pre-eminently as the head of a vast number of redeemed men and women (cf. Revelation 5:9-11, 7:9, 14), who, through grace, have received eternal life (cf. John 5:24).

1.3.2.2. CHRIST AND "ALL THE FULLNESS" OF DEITY (1:19)

Paul writes, "Because in Him all the fullness is pleased to dwell" (ὅτι ἐν αὐτῷ εὐδόκησεν πᾶν τὸ πλήρωμα κατοικῆσαι, 1:19). This is intended to be explanatory (ὅτι), making clear to the reader how it was possible for Christ to hold such a position of pre-eminence and power. Since He possesses "all the fullness" we are not at liberty to diminish or denigrate His character in any part or to any degree. If we attempt to qualify His "fullness" – suggesting that He is less than He really is – we will only depreciate the gospel and impoverish ourselves. Indeed, we would do well to remember that the most exalted conception of Him we might entertain in our minds is, because of our own limitations, always inadequate. In Him, there is a prodigious incomprehensibility!

Finding this clause a little awkward, some translators add '*of the Father*' to this verse. Thus, they suggest it was the Father's "good pleasure" that determined that the fullness would dwell in Christ. This is not unacceptable and reflects satisfactory

---

[18] If there had been no incarnation, the notion of the one who is "the image of the invisible God" and in whom "all things were created" rising from the dead would be inconceivable.

[19] I do not think it inappropriate to say that Jesus escaped 'the penalty of sin', although having lived a sinless life. He would not have died at all were it not that He "bore our sins in His body upon the tree" (I Peter 2:24).

theology. However, if we take the words "all the fullness" as an abbreviation of "all the fullness of the deity" in 2:9 (πᾶν τὸ πλήρωμα τῆς θεότητος), then Paul is making a strong statement about the incomprehensible and complete divinity of our Lord. He is comprehensively everything indicated by the biblical concept of God. This reading serves to secure the sense of His pre-eminence and denies any lesser interpretation of the "fullness" mentioned in this verse. Jesus is no less a God than God![20]

1.3.2.3. Christ reconciled "all things unto Himself" (1:20-23)

Now we must ask how this pre-eminent Christ, being "the firstborn from among those who are dead" (1:18), achieves this transformation of both the creation and the people of His church from death and corruption into life and incorruption, as we are considering. This He did, Paul explains succinctly, by reconciling "all things unto Himself, having made peace through the blood of His cross" (1:20). It is important that this be understood.

We should no more diminish or denigrate the astonishing accomplishment of Christ's death than we should belittle or degrade the magnificence of His personal character. But we should always speak of both – His person and His work – with awe and reverence, and worship Him in humility and thanksgiving.

1.3.2.3.1. Christ and the cataclysm

There is an intimation here of something cataclysmic, the suggestion of an historic disaster of disconcerting proportions. Somehow, He who created "all things" (1:16) is now seen taking necessary action to "reconcile all things to Himself" (1:20). How could it be that God and His creation were estranged from each other? The disaster and the restoration seem to be as extensive as the work of creation. As He made "all things ... in the heavens and upon the earth" (1:16), so He reconciles "all things ... whether things upon the earth, or things in the heavens" (1:20). All that was intrinsically His as Creator, He must now recover as Redeemer.

---

[20] Paul may well have been motivated to write of our Lord's pre-eminence and "fullness" in this fashion because, perhaps, the false teachers in Colossae were disparaging Him. The worth of a man's theology is determined by and revealed in his evaluation of the person and work of Christ. The word 'fullness' (πλήρωμα) had currency as a technical term among the pagan religions of Paul's day. However, by using this word the apostle was not dependent upon or importing anything of its pagan significance. It assumes its meaning here entirely from the apostle's biblical theology and Christian understanding.

How, we might ask, and under what circumstances did "all things" created become alienated from the Creator? What event or process could have been so devastating that it resulted in cosmic disorder, affecting everything God had made?

Paul does not refer specifically to this cataclysmic event in Colossians, nor does he attempt to answer these questions directly. However, there can be no doubt that the historic fall recorded in Genesis 3 is in view here. It is evident that this would have been in his mind, it being fundamental to his theology (See Romans 1:18ff, 5:12ff). He wrote of this problem in Romans 8:19-24, declaring that "the whole creation groans and travails in pain together until now". The whole creation![21] But we might suggest that what he does say here in 1:20-23 reflects the enormity of the catastrophe and serves to emphasize – against the bleakest of all possible backgrounds – the necessity of a redeemer with the fullness and the pre-eminence that we find only in Christ. Only someone with the power of the Creator is able to restore the "whole creation" to normality.

If the whole creation groans because it has been "subjected to futility" (Romans 8:20), then it cannot have the ability to restore itself. Every human effort to effect such a change is indeed futile. We must look beyond creation and all that it has to offer if we are to find any hope at all of recovery (1:5, and cf. Romans 8:24-25, "by hope we were saved"). The creation could not redeem itself. Humanism inevitably fails. God Himself has to intervene.

1.3.2.3.2. CHRIST'S CONTROL OF ALL THINGS

The scriptures leave us in no doubt that the God we worship in Christ Jesus, being sovereign in all things (see eg. Ephesians 1:11), will most certainly accomplish all that He has planned to do. And this is true despite any fall or catastrophe that may have devastated His creation. "The heaven and the earth" of His original design (Genesis 1:1), despite all damage done, will at its appointed time emerge in all its intended glory.

There is also evidence enough in the Bible that even the catastrophe that has had universal effect does not lie outside the sovereign rule of God. As a consequence of the fall, man needed to understand that all things would be difficult and frustrating for him in a broken world – "toil ... thorns ... thistles ... sweat ... return to the dust" – because the ground had been "cursed" by God Himself (Genesis 3:17-21).

---

[21] The suggestion that the whole of creation is corrupt and in need of reconciliation to the Creator would have been an outright rejection of any form of pagan dualism that may have been circulating among the Colossians. Or, for that matter, of much contemporary, evolutionary philosophy!

Or, as we have noticed above, "The creation was subjected to futility ... by reason of Him who subjected it" (Romans 8:20). When man rebelled against God, the pristine perfection of the Garden of Eden was denied him (Genesis 1:31, 3:22-23).

Subsequently, natural disasters – whether flood (Genesis 6:17, cf. II Peter 2:5), famine (II Kings 8:1, Ezekiel 5:17), plague (Deuteronomy 28:61, II Chronicles 21:14), pestilence (Leviticus 26:25, Jeremiah 14:12), or earthquake (Isaiah 29:6) – were seen by believing men as expressions of God's judgment. Even our Lord Himself considered these things to be "great signs from heaven" (Luke 21:11). *But being subject to His sovereignty, they are also subject to His redemption. If they are solely matters of chance, there is no redemption.*

Many fail to appreciate the significance of this, but the Bible is consistent in associating the imperfections of and the disasters we endure in this world with man's rebellion against God and his violation of the covenant God established with him. If we are to ask why life is so difficult, why we must deal with so many tragedies, why we suffer so much frustration and disappointment, why our joy is so often turned to grief, and why life ends in the total loss of dignity in death, we, as Christians, must reply that it is because we – the whole human race – have all corrupted our proper relationship with our Creator. There has been an insurrection against heaven that began with Adam in the Garden of Eden and has been perpetuated relentlessly by all his descendants.

Therefore, as Paul writes, we have all become "alienated and enemies in (our) mind in (our) evil works" (1:21). The cause of our estrangement from God is, then, not only in our tragic history and the lamentable heritage we have received from the past but also in our own individual thoughts and actions.

Now if the creation is subjected to futility because of our alienation from and enmity towards God – as it is – then we might expect that there will be no recovery of the pristine perfection of the Garden of Eden, nor will God's plan for His creation be fully realized, until man is reconciled to God and living in peace with Him. And as God, from the beginning, has been introducing men and women to the hope of reconciliation, there is in scripture a confident anticipation that His redeemed people will eventually find their place in a new or renewed heaven and earth (Isaiah 11:5-9, 65:17, 24-25, 66:22, II Peter 3:13, Revelation 21:1).

It is true, as some have commented, that the word "reconcile" refers primarily to the restoration of good relations between persons – between man and man, between God and man – but not to things. If this is so, it has been suggested, we should limit this reconciliation of "all things" (1:20) to personal creatures only, perhaps both human and angelic, but not to include anything non-personal. But the difficulty with this, it seems to me, is that it requires us to understand that "all things ... in the heavens and upon the earth" in 1:16, refers to a different category than "all things ... upon the earth, or things in the heavens" in 1:20. Is the apostle saying that God created "all things" without exception, but that He only reconciles "all things" with the exception of the non-human, physical world? This seems very unlikely.

If the primary reason for the catastrophe is the willful rebellion of His creatures (angels, seemingly, and then men), which resulted in alienation and expulsion from the Garden, then surely any reconciliation between God and man must be accompanied by some resettlement in an Eden-like situation. Evidently the apostle John thought that this is so (Revelation 22:1-5). Therefore, it does not seem erroneous or incongruous to me – or a hopeless catachresis – that Paul should include the notion of a renewed creation, with all that is in it (cf. Romans 8:21-22, "creation itself", "the whole creation"), when writing of God's reconciliation with His people. That of which they were deprived because of their alienation is, or will be, suitably restored through reconciliation. After all, we rightly assume that reconciliation between estranged parties on earth may involve some form of 'property settlement', and not merely the pacification of personal sentiments. If the "ground" was "cursed" for man's sake (Genesis 3:17), so it will be blessed for the sake of redeemed man when there is "no more curse" (Revelation 22:3).

In other words, we cannot think of God being truly reconciled with His people and then leaving them outside the Garden of Eden, as it were! Or, there would hardly be any reconciliation at all if we were left without the required environment in which to be all that we – as people risen eventually from the dead (1:18) – were created to be and therein to glorify Him. Therefore, Christ does not save His people *from* the physical creation, but together *with* this creation.

1.3.2.3.3. CHRIST AND THE CRUCIFIXION

Although not speaking directly about the cosmic catastrophe that lies in the background here in Colossians, Paul does point immediately to the most unexpected of all events, "the blood of His cross" (1:20).[22] The ignominious crucifixion of a country carpenter seems to be entirely disproportionate to the

---

[22] For those who had a sufficient understanding of the Old Testament, the cross of Christ was to be expected. John the Baptist, for example, recognized Jesus as the Lamb of God (John 1:29). Nevertheless, for those not so perceptive as the Baptist, our Lord's crucifixion was a violation of all this world's wisdom (I Corinthians 1:18ff.). So the Cross is perceived to be irrelevant by most modern thinkers.

problem! And indeed, it would have been, had that country carpenter been anyone other than the pre-eminent, firstborn Son of God. The potency of the crucifixion is to be found in the person of the Crucified. Paul does not elaborate here upon the magnitude of the catastrophe – nor, in a sense, need he do so for all people everywhere are caught up in and painfully aware of it, needing little or no reminder of their dire condition and the tragic state of the world. But the apostle has sagaciously declared the magnificence and supremacy of the one Person who alone is competent and willing to rectify the damage done, and whose sacrifice is sufficient to "reconcile all things unto Himself".[23]

Two comments might be added here:

- **First**, concerning cosmic reconciliation.

     We must never trivialize the cross of Christ, or limit the efficacy of our Lord's death. There is much more here than an example of loving dedication, which we might emulate. Neither is this historic event merely a demonstration of God's intention to guide men into a life of self-sacrifice for others, or simply an act of divine solicitude in identifying with the suffering and oppressed. It may indeed contain elements of all these, *but it is above all a sublime act of cosmic reconciliation.* This ignominious crucifixion has, by virtue of the deity and perfect humanity of the Crucified, the potency to save the world, to redeem all of God's people, and to guarantee a new heaven and a new earth.

     Paul speaks similarly elsewhere. In the beloved Son of God, he wrote, "we have our redemption through His blood, the forgiveness of our trespasses, according to the riches of His grace ... according to His good pleasure". However, the blessings of this redemption and forgiveness, the personal benefits of the cross of Christ, which His people enjoy, are antecedent and prerequisite to cosmic restructuring. God in the "dispensation of the fullness of the times", the apostle continued, will "sum up all things in Christ, the things in the heavens, and the things upon the earth" (Ephesians 1:7-10). Again we see that the ultimate reintegration of a troubled and fractured universe is achieved by the crucifixion.

     Borrowing terminology from John, we might say that the creative power of "the Word" by whom "all things were made" is isometric with the redemptive power of "the Word" made flesh, who dwelt among us and was crucified (John 1:1-2, 14).

---

[23] Hence, perhaps, the opening lines of John Bowring's hymn: 'In the cross of Christ I glory, Towering o're the wrecks of time.'

- **Second**, concerning personal reconciliation.

Now if, as we have suggested above, the whole creation is subjected to futility and in need of recovery because of man's alienation from and enmity towards God (1:21), then the "restoration of all things" (Acts 3:21) must logically commence with man's reconciliation with God, or at least with provision being made for this reconciliation. It might be suggested that there is little point in the creation of a new heaven and a new earth if there is not a renewed man to occupy and have dominion over it, as God originally intended (Hebrews 2:8-10). Therefore, Paul explains, God is working to "reconcile all things unto Himself" because He has "made peace through the blood of His cross" (1:20). It is this "peace" that overcomes the alienation and enmity (1:21).

Man's estrangement from God must not be underestimated. As a direct consequence of Adam's rebellion in the Garden of Eden, all people are left "alienated" in that they have no place in the kingdom of God; and they are "enemies" in that they remain hostile to God's sovereign rule. This is tantamount to saying that they are *homeless* and *disoriented* in the divine order of things, and grappling in mortal conflict with their Creator. A perilous condition in which to be!

Neither should we underestimate the reason for this minacious condition. It is not the result of misadventure or inopportunity. Rather, it is a culpable state arising not only from our own "evil works" but also from the wicked machinations of our "mind" (τῇ διανοίᾳ ἐν τοῖς ἔργοις τοῖς πονηροῖς, 1:21, cf. Ephesians 2:3, 3:17-18). It is inevitable that if our minds are depraved, then our behaviour will be corrupted (cf. Romans 1:28ff.). Hence the modification of our conduct through the reconditioning of our thinking is required.

Therefore, in this letter, Paul is concerned with the "works", or the behaviour, of his readers, as he explains in 3:5-17. He concludes that section of the letter with the exhortation, "Whatsoever you do, in word or deed, do all in the name of the Lord Jesus" (ἐν λόγῳ ἢ ἐν ἔργῳ, 3:17). Because Christ is our Lord, all that we say and do should be modified in respect for His name (#3.4.2.2.3.).

But the apostle is obviously well aware that there could be no improvement in his readers' works without a profound noetic change in their disposition. Therefore, he points to Christ as the source of all "wisdom and knowledge" (2:3), and to the importance of a Christocentric philosophy (2:8), a mind set on things that are above (3:2), and the necessity of "the word of Christ" and the encouragement of a believing, "teaching" community (3:16, cf. 2:2). Our "mind" and our thinking are to be modified by God's grace, as we are "renewed unto knowledge after the image of Him" (3:10).

However, despite the outrageousness of our alienation and enmity, God has "now ... reconciled" His people "in the body of (Christ's) flesh through death" (1:21-22, cf. "we were reconciled to God through the death of His Son", Romans 5:10). And so effective has this reconciliation been, that He is now able "to present you holy and without blemish, and unreprovable before Him" (1:22). That Paul writes of his believing readers that God has "now ... reconciled" them (νυνὶ δὲ ἀποκατήλλαξεν) implies that all that was needed for this reconciliation has been done and applied in their case.

Moreover, in Christ, all of God's people, being reconciled to Him, have escaped the alienation and the enmity that threatened their eternal well-being. There was no doubt a time when the truly believing individual consciously recognized and accepted this reconciliation, through faith, and began to enter meaningfully into its benefits, having become a Christian.

But this, as Paul writes elsewhere, involves both reorientation and responsibility. Those who are reconciled are given "the ministry of reconciliation", and entrusted with "the word of reconciliation". This necessarily involves a reorientation, a new purpose. Life cannot remain the same once such a "ministry" in the service of God has been received. Moreover, now being custodians of the "word of reconciliation" Christians have a new responsibility. Consequently, they are now under the obligation to entreat others to "be reconciled to God" (II Corinthians 5:18-20).[24] We should, in other words, appeal to others to find peace with God through faith in Christ, thus escaping their own alienation and enmity.

But in making this appeal, we should leave no doubt in the minds of those to whom we speak that *all that needs to be done for their reconciliation has been done*. There is nothing left for them to do in this matter, but to thankfully accept and trust in all that Christ accomplished "in the body of His flesh through death" (1:22).

In making this entreaty and explaining the adequacy of the reconciliation, our focus should be on the crucifixion of Christ. This event is no mere story to be told for its sentimental value or its demonstrative force; neither is it only an enigmatic, historical conundrum. It is the real death of a real Man – and as we have indicated above, of the Man who is nothing less than God incarnate.

---

[24] We should always remember that the free grace of God that provides us with this reconciliation does not relieve us of the moral obligation to serve Him – rather, it heightens this responsibility, and increases the motivation and the ability to do so!

Paul leaves us in no doubt about this, explaining that we are reconciled "in the body of His flesh through death" (1:22). In this there was no apparition, no mystical being, but a person with a physical body; and no misdiagnosed syncope, but actual death! The apostle's words are simple and emphatic. He could not have written of "the blood of His cross" or "the body of His flesh" if he had not been convinced of the historicity and the physicality of the crucifixion, and he could not have attributed to it the power to "reconcile all things" if he had not believed in the immensity of that moment.[25]

However, the apostle does not only look back to the historic event that secured reconciliation, but he also looks forward to the ultimate benefits that each individual Christian will enjoy as a result of Christ's death. Reconciliation is but the prelude!

Because of our standing as Christians before our Lord, there is a sense in which we as Christians can now "enter into the holy place by the blood of Jesus" and "draw near" to our God (Hebrews 10:19-22), and being reconciled "we ... have access in one Spirit unto the Father" (Ephesians 2:16-18). Were it otherwise, we would have no immediate communion with Him. But as it is now, through Christ and the Spirit, we already enjoy proximity and intimacy with our Lord.

However, we have yet to be presented "before Him" (1:22), and when we are we shall stand "before the presence of His glory without blemish in exceeding joy" (Jude 24). This evidently refers to that coming moment when we will "see Him even as He is" (I John 3:2). There will be a day when we will "with Him be manifested in glory" (3:4). Then we will be "holy and without blemish and unreprovable" (ἁγίους καὶ ἀμώμους καὶ ἀνεγκλήτους, 1:22). We know little of what our life will be like when we join our Lord in His resurrection – it being beyond our present ability to comprehend – but *these three words* indicate what are perhaps the most significant aspects of our final redemption:

1. Being "holy" suggests that our whole disposition will be fully aligned with the will and purposes of God. This is a matter of orientation and direction. Perhaps we might say that it is the perfection of having our minds set "on the things above, and

---

[25] It is possible, as some have suggested, that Paul wrote in these terms to correct the false teaching of the heretics in Colossae, who may have been diminishing the significance and effectiveness of our Lord's death. But his words make perfect sense without this assumption.

not on the things that are upon the earth" (3:2), a principle of Christian living that now we only vaguely approximate at best.

Here is redeemed man in reference to *the intended purposes of God*.

2. Being "without blemish" implies that we will no longer suffer from the moral contamination of character that is now so troubling and often painfully distressing for sensitive believers. This is a matter of personal purity. We continue to have difficulties in "putting on ... as God's elect ... a heart of compassion" and the "love, which is the bond of perfection" (3:12-14), and all the associated graces. But in that coming day such perfections will be fully realized.

    Here is redeemed man in reference to *the intended image of God*.

3. Being "unreprovable", or 'free from accusation', explains that nothing from our past failures and misbehaviour will be held against or continue to encumber us. This is a matter of answerability to external moral standards. This will be the final benefit of the blotting out of "the bond written in ordinances that was against us" and "contrary to us" (2:14). We will enjoy the complete freedom of having the record of our violations of divine law expunged.

    Here is redeemed man in reference to *the moral law of God*.

We conclude, then, that when we are "with Him manifested in glory" we will have been completely restored to the pristine flawlessness from which we fell as the consequence of sin (Romans 3:23), and, moreover, raised to the exalted position in God's economy for which we were created.

1.3.2.3.4. THE CHRISTIAN AND PERSEVERANCE

Here is the link between what we now enjoy in Christ and all that we anticipate. Had Paul written, 'You *He will reconcile* in the body of His flesh through death' (cf. 1:21-22), we might conclude that 1:23 suggests that the crucifixion of our Lord only made a future reconciliation *possible* and dependent upon our continuing in the faith. Then our eternal salvation would remain an uncertainty, and, knowing the moral instability of our own lives, we would be left insecure and fearful. But what he said emphatically is that "now He has reconciled" His people "in the body of His flesh through death". Now! Reconciliation has been secured! This implies that our eternal salvation is certain because it only depends upon the work of Christ, historically accomplished.

So, we should note that when Paul writes of the Colossian believers, "You ... he has now reconciled ... if you continue in the faith" (ὑμᾶς ... νυνὶ δὲ ἀποκατήλλαξεν ... εἴ γε ἐπιμένετε τῇ πίστει, 1:21-23), he is not making reconciliation dependent upon continuing faith. Just the opposite! He is saying in effect that continuing in the faith rather than being *the prerequisite* of our reconciliation, is *the evidence* of it. The rationale for this is perfectly simple. Because we have been reconciled with God through the death of Christ, He also graciously gives us the sanctifying influence of His Spirit – together with "all things" needful (Romans 8:32) – that also secures our unfailing faith in Him.

The genuine Christian, Paul explains, continues "in the faith" and does not move "away from the hope of the gospel" (1:23). Here is *the corroboration of genuine conversion* to Christ. There are two factors involved that we should consider:

- **First**, perseverance in faith: a persuasive foundation.
  The authentic Christian constantly believes the truths of the gospel.
  Writing here about continuing "in the faith" (ἐπιμένετε τῇ πίστει) the apostle evidently has in mind the Christian faith, that set of beliefs that constitutes "the word of the truth of the gospel" (1:5), or "the word of God" (1:25) that he had been commissioned to preach at whatever cost (1:24). This is "the faith which was once for all delivered unto the saints" (Jude 3).
  This implies that there is a Christian orthodoxy and that any divergence from it is indicative of religious deviation and dubious confession of faith. Although biblical doctrines are indeed extensive, sufficient to establish a meaningful and effective life; and although they are to be applied in numerous, changing, and various situations; and although much thought needs to be given constantly to their implications in differing circumstances, they are in themselves consistent and unalterable.
  If anyone is truly converted by the grace of God to believe wholeheartedly in the Christ in whom "dwells all the fullness of the Godhead bodily" (2:9), and if he has accepted Him as "the image of the invisible God, the firstborn of all creation" (1:15), and if he has an appreciation of His pre-eminence (1:18), then it is inconceivable that he would subsequently abandon his initial belief in the doctrines

appropriate to such a faith.[26] His understanding of these doctrines may need to develop and be refined, but as they were initially conveyed to him in "the word of the truth" (1:5), and if he truly perceived the substance of them in Christ Himself,[27] he will not abandon or distort them.

Then, we should note, it is implied here that there is an inextirpable conservatism in Christianity, it being the proclamation of Jesus Christ who "is the same yesterday, and today, and forever" (Hebrews 13:8). Although the Christian may be enthusiastic about modern developments, greater learning, scientific and engineering advancements, and aspects of social change – all of which in the grace of God may be to the advantage of humankind – he has no need of novel alterations or additions to his fundamental beliefs.

We need, then, to be wary of theological innovations, and cautious in accepting new expressions of Christianity that claim to be nothing more than a rewording of the old, conservative ideas in contemporary language – which they may or may not be, and frequently are not! We are perhaps the more easily deluded by "persuasiveness of speech" (2:4) when the words used are biblical but the content of the teaching is not, or when Christian phraseology is subtly distorted to convey non-Christian thoughts. This kind of deceptive persuasion is common, subtle, and often scholarly.

Our faith is rooted in the historicity of the life, death, and resurrection of Christ. And this is immutable.

Therefore, we would suggest, the genuine Christian can be identified, in part at least, by his concern for the preservation and propagation of "the sound doctrine" that the disingenuous "will not endure" (II Timothy 4:3). Then the more the genuine Christian "continues in the faith" the more he will himself be "grounded and steadfast" (1:23), and hence he becomes the more confident in the genuineness of his own Christian standing. The greater the appreciation of "the faith" – in the objective sense of Christian teachings – then the greater will be the assurance of one's own personal faith – in the subjective sense of his believing.

- **Second**, perseverance in hope: a motivating aspiration.

    The authentic Christian constantly relates the truths of the gospel to his present life.

---

[26] A man may indeed diverge from or repudiate his original confession of Christian belief, but this serves only to indicate that his confession was without genuine commitment or faith.

[27] This making his original commitment the response of a personal faith in Jesus as his Redeemer, and much more than a personal convenience in accepting an expedient religious or philosophical position.

Then, the second indication of genuine Christian conversion mentioned here is that the true believer will not be "moved away from the hope of the gospel" (1:23, μὴ μετακινούμενοι ἀπὸ τῆς ἐλπίδος τοῦ εὐαγγελίου). This is necessarily concomitant with continuing "in the faith". As we have seen above (#1.1.2.), we confidently anticipate the secure future "laid up for (us) in heaven" because in the "word of the truth of the gospel" (1:5) we were exposed to divine revelation. But this revelation also gives us everything that is formulated in the Christian faith.

Therefore, if we are "grounded and steadfast" in our faith (1:23) – it being established firmly upon revelation – it is inevitable that we will not abandon the Christian's hope. Looking back to the historic life, death, and resurrection of Christ with the understanding provided by the word of God is the logical prerequisite to any confident expectation we might have for our coming days.

The Christian cannot and does not desire to escape from his dependence upon the ancient past, the pristine beginnings of his religion, when God became man in Jesus Christ. There the foundation was laid upon which his life is now established; there eternal truth was exhibited; and there the explanation of human destiny and ultimate purpose was given. This compelling, retrospective appreciation of the most significant events in time provides him with confident, prospective anticipation for the future.

If we do not clearly understand, then, that we have been reconciled to our God "in the body of (Christ's) flesh through death" that we might be "presented ... holy and without blemish and unreprovable before Him" (1:21-22), we will all too easily abandon, or drift away from our hope (cf. Hebrews 2:1). To be ill informed or ignorant of this past accomplishment serves only to obfuscate the future and to devitalize our present life.

It is imperative that Christians be taught about the factual death and resurrection of Christ, and the salvific effect this has in the lives of all who are given genuine faith to believe in biblical reconciliation. Without this, Christian hope evanesces; dissolving into whimsical thinking, or into some misguided notion that man is able to make sufficient contribution to secure a place for himself "in heaven". Any denial that Christ has in His own incarnation and death successfully and finally secured reconciliation for all His people, thus suggesting that man has to augment His work with works of his own, immediately makes any assurance of salvation, any certainty of hope, inaccessible.

Inasmuch as we are able in this contemporary evil world to "lay up ... treasures in heaven" (Matthew 6:20), then our time on earth need not be in vain (I Corinthians 15:59). The understanding Christian recognizes the importance and the worth of our present life and is conscientious in all that it requires of him. His "work of faith and labour of love and patience of hope in … Christ" (I Thessalonians 1:3) will be evident. Indeed, his faith, love, and hope will permeate and condition everything he does in this world now.

This perseverance in the faith and in hope presupposes a genuineness of Christian conversion, not merely a profession of it. It is only to be found in those who are "grounded and steadfast" as Christian people (τεθεμελιωμένοι καὶ ἑδραῖοι, 1:23). The doctrines can be learned, and even convincingly expressed and theologically defended even by an unbeliever or nominal Christian. But it is hardly likely that any will faithfully adhere to them unless they are enabled to do so by the grace of God (cf. I John 2:18-24). In this matter, a man may even deceive himself! And this is a prevalent danger (cf. II Timothy 3:13).

But if there is the possibility of self-deception, how is the true believer to be so grounded and made steadfast? As the word "grounded" is passive (τεθεμελιωμένοι, as also in Ephesians 3:17), it implies that it is a work done by God in the believer's life. We cannot ground ourselves but must trust in Him to generate the necessary sure foundation within His people. And this, we suggest, He does when we are "begotten again, not of corruptible seed, but of incorruptible, through the word of God" (I Peter 1:23). Only then will we be "steadfast" in our Christian life (ἑδραῖοι, this implying, at least, control over our will, cf. I Corinthians 7:37, ἑδραῖος … ἐξουσίαν δὲ ἔχει περὶ τοῦ ἰδίου θελήματος). Neither will we be "tossed to and fro, and carried about by every wind of doctrine" (Ephesians 4:14).

Then it is important to notice that Peter explains that God's people are begotten again "through the word of God". Undoubtedly the Holy Spirit is God's agent in regeneration (John 3:5), but the Christian is 'brought to birth' through the instrumentality of the "word of God" – that is, the "word of the truth of the gospel … bearing fruit and increasing" (1:5-6). Therefore, it is most significant here in Colossians that having mentioned the importance of being "grounded and steadfast" Paul immediately refers to "the gospel, which you heard, which was preached in all creation under heaven" (1:23). Grounding and the word of the gospel are inseparable.

It is through the preaching of the gospel, and thereby hearing the word of God, that men and women become Christians – and there is no other way that they may do so (Romans 10:12-14, I Corinthians 1:18-21). His word alone can ground a man in eternal truth and stabilize his life. Any attempt to establish the faith upon some other basis – upon human philosophy, intuitive insights, visions, experiences, and the like – can only result in instability in both the individual and in the congregations of the church, because such alternatives are themselves unstable. But His word "endures for ever" (I Peter 1:25) and is able to make men "wise unto salvation (II Timothy 3:15).

Paul does not hesitate to write that the word of the gospel had come to "all the world" (1:6) and had been preached "in all creation" (1:23). He was well aware that it had not been proclaimed in every country on earth, or to all races and peoples. He was always looking for new fields into which to take his ministry, other people to evangelize (cf. Romans 15:22-25). But he is indicating in 1:6 that wherever the gospel was preached it produced positive results and did so in "all the world" irrespective of geographical location. Then in 1:23 he is probably referring to the fact that the gospel having been preached, first by the pre-eminent Christ and then by His apostles, was a universal proclamation to "all creation", and hence it was to be taken to "all the nations" (Matthew 28:19).

We might well say, then, that when Christ gave the words that the Father had given Him to the people His Father had given Him (John 17:6-8), then the gospel "was preached in all creation under heaven" (1:23). This was, in other words, the original, definitive proclamation. God had spoken! He has spoken to the whole world! Therefore, what He said is universally significant.

Perhaps the most important thing here is to see that this is tantamount to saying that *there is one, and only one gospel,* and that it is a gospel sufficient for everybody in the world and throughout all history. There is no other gospel, and it cannot be modified for changing circumstances and popular preferences. The gospel is not and never could have been a message requiring adaptation to diverse cultures, ethnic groups, nationalities, and changing times. Neither is it person-relative, being of different significance to different individuals. We are commissioned to go to "all the nations", to teach "them to observe all things whatsoever (Christ) commanded" us, and to do so "even unto the end of the world" (Matthew 28:20). The message, then, is invariable. If Christ is the same yesterday, today, and forever, then "all the treasures of wisdom and knowledge hidden" in Him (2:3) – including His commandments – are as consistent as He is Himself. In other words, and despite much modern belief, we live in a world of absolutes because it is the creation of an absolute God.[28]

---

[28] Needless to say, I do not believe in the god of process theology.

Alan D Catchpoole

NOTE: I have suggested above that divine revelation is *necessary* for Christian belief, because our faith embraces truths that can be known in no other way (#1.1.2.). Now here, observing that the gospel has been "preached in all creation" (1:23), I suggest that the teachings of Christ and the promulgation of His word by the apostles is the only salvific message, the only message of truth that is applicable to the whole, created world. This is because there are no 'local deities', 'ethnic gods', or 'tribal totems' providing other ways of redemption (cf. I Corinthians 8:5-6 and John 14:6, Acts 4:12). Therefore, the revelation given by God is *sufficient* for all people at all times, needing no supplementation.

Then, as this revelation is preserved for us in the scriptures of the Old and the New Testament, we must insist upon the *necessity* and the *sufficiency* of the Bible.[29] And only such a Bible can provide the grounding and steadfastness to which Paul refers.

◆

We associate the three dimensions of salvation we find in these verses (1:1-23) in the following diagram:

THE DIMENSIONS OF SALVATION

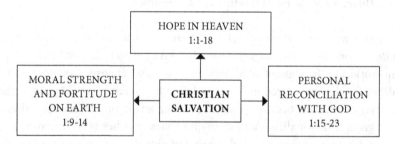

COPYRIGHT 1995 Alan D. Catchpoole, Olecko Pty. Ltd., Australia. Colossians coldia5.vsd

◆

---

[29] We must maintain our belief in the Bible's necessity, inspiration, authority, self-authentication, perspicuity, sufficiency, and finality. These seven attributes of the Christian scriptures make them of eternal worth and universal application.

THE NON-CHRISTIAN ALTERNATIVES.

We see clearly in these verses (1:1-23) three dimensions of Christian salvation – hope in heaven, moral strength and fortitude on earth, and personal reconciliation with God. But modern man – including, sadly, not a few church-going people – seems to have little interest in these things. He has rejected, or seriously modified, the revelation God has given in the Bible and has embraced a different concept of the nature of reality, which he believes offers a radically different kind of human salvation. Consequently, he is motivated to seek after a different set of values in a life that is set within *three entirely different parameters*.

We might briefly mention these alternatives.

A. HOPE ON EARTH

A desire to realize the fullness of human potential on earth now and in a purely materialistic context has replaced the Christian desire to find the fullness of human potential in heaven in an age yet to come. The Christian also anticipates discovering and enjoying the fullness of human potential on earth in his physical state, but only in the final "regeneration" when there will be "new heavens and a new earth". The difference is that the non-Christian assumes that the world is now in its normal condition and does not reckon with the fall and its cosmic effects. Further, the unbelieving modern man assumes that the universe is continuing in a steady, unchanging state and anticipates no climax – except in some terminal, cataclysmic disaster, or in a final state of universal exhaustion – or any divine intervention.

The means of realizing this modern hope is not through the preaching of the gospel, but through the means of science, material prosperity, human ingenuity, and self-government. It requires, then, the preaching of humanism in one or other of its many forms.

B. POWER TO ACCOMPLISH

No longer is the ability to live a moral life a thing much to be desired or sought after. Indeed, it is more likely to be considered that such a desire is 'puritanical', and the search for wholesome morality is thought to be the path to sterility and frustration. The man now to be admired is not he who has maintained a life that is pure in reference to the laws of God, but the man who has succeeded in his ambitions or attained the standards required of him by his peers. Success is applauded, and purity of life disparaged. Only the relative ethical principles of pragmatism and expediency are acknowledged.

The means whereby this success is attained is found in technique and methodology. Wisdom and understanding are now seriously discounted and men are trained not so much to think and to reason, but rather to be technicians in a particular field of endeavour that they might make a suitable contribution to the functioning of a materialistic society, or earn a wage for the sake of some hedonistic pleasure. Pragmatism has replaced morality and meaning.

C. Reconciliation with Oneself

Having imprisoned himself within the restrictive limitations of a purely materialistic perspective, modern man has no interest in any reconciliation with any kind of supernatural 'god'. All the 'gods' are to him nothing more than the projection of the true essence of humanity into a supposedly spiritual realm that does not actually exist. By doing this, the 'religious' man, it is suggested, has succeeded only in alienating man from himself. Therefore, the only reconciliation that he needs is reconciliation with himself. The internal strain and the discomfort that the individual feels are not the result of any fallen state or corrupted condition. Rather, he now believes, they result from the tension that is caused when a man sets himself over against another – whether it be man against 'god', ethnic group against ethnic group, class against class, gender against gender, or individual against individual. The distress is relieved only when man accepts himself as he is within himself.

This being so, there is no need for the person and the work of Jesus Christ. Rather a man is reconciled to himself through his own person and work – that is, through his own self-realization.

◆

COLOSSIANS 1:24-2:5.

2. PAUL'S MINISTRY OF THE GOSPEL

Having made mention of the preaching of the gospel (1:23), Paul now writes about his own participation in this ministry. In all probability, he had not been to Colossae and did not know personally the people to whom this letter is addressed (2:1). But, despite this, he obviously was deeply interested in and concerned for them and their well-being. We might wonder about this altruistic solicitude for unseen strangers!

Paul's personal concern for people unknown to him was evidently generated by his appreciation of the particular ministry that God had given to him, and the sense of obligation that this carried with it (cf. Romans 1:14). That is, his relationship with God determined his relationships with and ministry to others. His divine commission and sense of stewardship (1:25) evidently in some way engendered human compassion in his heart.[30] This caused him to "rejoice" even as he endured "sufferings" (χαίρω ἐν τοῖς παθήμασιν, 1:24, #2.1.1.2.) for the Colossians' sake, and to "labour" in "striving" (κοπιῶ ἀγωνιζόμενος, 1:29) for their well-being. His concern for others was evidently far more than a cursory personal or merely academic interest.

However, the apostle would claim no *personal credit* for this assiduous and sacrificial ministry on behalf of others because he believed he was doing no more than "fill up on (his) part that which is lacking in the afflictions of Christ" (ἀνταναπληρῶ τὰ ὑστερήματα τῶν θλίψεων τοῦ Χριστοῦ, 1:24). This was his duty in the service of his Lord. Neither would he claim to have been able to do this, executing his God-given responsibilities, though his own *personal abilities*, because he knew he would have accomplished nothing but for the fact that God

---

[30] This is the more remarkable in Paul's case, because he was once a bitter persecutor of the Church (Acts 9:1). But such is the power of the grace of God.

"work(ed) in (him) mightily" (κατὰ τὴν ἐνέργειαν αὐτοῦ τὴν ἐνεργουμένην ἐν ἐμοὶ ἐν δυνάμει, 1:29). He was, then, motivated by both his obedience to and his faith in Christ, and these are always associated with love (cf. John 14:15, Galatians 5:6-7). And the quality of his love explains his self-sacrificing altruism.

NOTE: The apostle's few, brief comments here about his own ministry are in themselves sufficient to transform any thoughts we might have about our own involvement in the service of our God. It is impossible to mistake Paul's burden. There is here no hint of self-aggrandizement. He is compelled by a sense of responsibility, being well aware of the mistreatment and the misunderstanding he would have to face. His ambition was for the glory of Christ, and not his own acclaim. The work demanded the exhaustion of the labour it required; and it required far more than the sum of his personal physical, intellectual, and technical abilities (1:29). He was the man he was and served his Lord in the manner that he did, not primarily by virtue of natural talent or developed skills, but through the profound disposition of a self-effacing, inner godliness and his dependence upon the intervention of God. This above all else is the precondition, or predisposition – rare as it may be – that should be apparent in all those who would preach the gospel of Christ.

2.1. HIS GOD-GIVEN STEWARDSHIP (1:24-29)

It was his awareness of his stewardship and his sense of responsibility before God that produced in Paul a concern and a compassion for other people. It seems critical to me that this order is never to be reversed. If a man is motivated in ministry *primarily* by his concern for suffering people, then such a concern might well be *merely* philanthropic – and essentially no different from the social concern of benevolent non-Christians. But if a man is primarily motivated by his concern for the glory and the service of God, then his concern for people will be of a different and much higher order – that of self-sacrificing love in devotion to the Lord.

The atheistic humanist, believing he lives in a world without any god, may indeed by kindly disposed towards other people and manifest communal responsibility, conforming to some kind of 'social contract'. However, it seems to me that in this he can have no higher motivation than a measure of narcissistic values – and this inevitably diminishes the worth of all he does. Ultimately, his social concern is riddled with subliminal egocentricity.

In contrast, in Christian service there should be a superior motivation that ideally is devoid of all self-serving – or, at least, whatever legitimate self-interest there might be is moderated by unalloyed benevolence. Jesus made this demand of His disciples: "A new commandment I give unto you, that you love one another; even as I have loved you, that you also love one another" (John 13:34). By asking His followers to love "even as" He loved, Christ made Himself the paradigm of true service and social concern. Our Lord also explained that "greater love has no man than this, that he lay down his life for his friend" (John 15:13). In this fallen world, this excellent love inevitably leads to suffering.

In the spirit of such love, Paul insists here that he actually rejoiced in suffering for the sake of others, because it is the Christ-like thing to do (1:24). Therefore, as the apostle draws attention to his own exemplary ministry, it seems to be important that we examine carefully all that he is saying in these verses:

2.1.1. PAUL'S UNDERSTANDING OF SUFFERING (1:24)

Paul, we might suggest, rejoiced in his sufferings for no other reason than that they were integral to the very nature of the ministry God had given to him. He was no masochist who would delight in pain for its own sake, or in some mistaken belief that suffering somehow increased his own spirituality.[31] But when his afflictions contributed to the advancement of the gospel and the enrichment of his fellow Christians, and thus brought glory to Christ, he endured them with joy.[32]

2.1.1.1. THE INEVITABLE STATE OF AFFAIRS

Ananias was commissioned by God to advise Paul, at the time of the apostle's conversion, of "how many things he must suffer for (His) name's sake" (ὅσα δεῖ αὐτὸν ὑπὲρ τοῦ ὀνόματός μου παθεῖν, Acts 9:16).[33] This has much significance, and perhaps not the least in that his conversion had interrupted and brought an end to his vicious program of inflicting suffering on Christians when he was "yet breathing threatening and slaughter against the disciples" (Acts 9:1). Now he was to suffer, and for the very cause that he had been seeking to destroy. This volte-face he would have attributed solely to the grace of God (I Corinthians 15:10).

---

[31] This latter idea, that suffering produced a greater spirituality, seems to be openly denied by Paul in Colossians 2:20-23.

[32] That Paul rejoiced in sufferings is significant for our understanding of joy itself. It is evidently an attitude or condition of soul that is not dependent upon circumstances, but has a more intrinsic and intimate origin. It is contra-circumstances and born of faith in Christ. We might suggest that in the biblical context it is confidence in and the satisfaction of meaningful accomplishment.

[33] One has to wonder how often this advice is given to other young men who are about to commence their ministry for Christ! Not to imply that all will suffer as Paul did.

Subsequently, no doubt, Paul would often have had occasion to remember this original counsel. Many years later and after considerable experience, he would catalogue the numerous and diverse sufferings of his long career in preaching the gospel (I Corinthians 4:9-13, II Corinthians 11:23-33). Few engaged in Christian ministry, if any, have suffered as much as he did. He mentioned, seemingly as a rebuke to the self-satisfaction of some, that in his estimate "God has set forth us the apostles least of all, as men doomed to death ... a spectacle to the world, and to angels and to men" (I Corinthians 4:9). And, we should note, our Lord Himself had advised those who "were apostles before" Paul (Galatians 1:17) that "in this world (they) have tribulation" (John 16:33). Suffering was the apostles' lot!

Clearly, the nature of Paul's ministry, which involved a God-given stewardship and the authority to "fully preach the word of God" (1:25), exposed him to unique sufferings. It was not without "tears and ... trials" that he courageously "shrank not from declaring ... and teaching" the gospel publicly and in private, even when he was aware that "bonds and afflictions" awaited him (Acts 20:19-22, cf. #2.1.2.2.1.).

Now, this opposition to apostolic preaching need hardly surprise us. As point men in the advance of Christian forces into the alien territory of this fallen world, the apostles had to bear the severe, initial brunt of opposition. It was their responsibility to take the challenge of the gospel to the apostate Jews and to the pagan world (Acts 1:8). They had to wrestle for the first time as believing, Christian men with the false religions and anthropocentric philosophies of non-Christian men, to rebuke all people for their moral decadence, and call the world to repentance. The very confrontational nature of their ministry would inevitably attract *resentment* (Acts 13:50, 14:19 et al).

Moreover, Paul knew, and his experience confirmed, that "the word of the cross" which he preached was "to them that are perishing foolishness" (I Corinthians 1:18). This, obviously, excluded him from intellectual acclaim among the learned of his day, and only attracted *ridicule* (Acts 17:32).

And this *resentment* and *ridicule* have not abated as and wherever the church has perpetuated, through faithful preaching, the original apostolic ministry. In this, if we remain as faithful, we stand in line with both the apostles and the prophets that preceded them (Matthew 5:10-12).

NOTE: In the initial advice given to Paul – that he must, for it was unavoidable, suffer many things (Acts 9:16) – there is an indication of a critically important element in the ministry of the gospel. As important as, or in some ways more important than the positive activity of the Christian in preaching Christ to the world, is his response to the negative activity of the hostility he faces in the world. His proclamation is constituted not only by what he does but also by his reaction to what is done to him. The former, we might suggest, is the more dependent upon the preacher's *skills*, but the latter is the more dependent upon the preacher's *character*. The former comes more cheaply, the latter only at considerable cost. But the former will always lack the ring of sincerity, the persuasive depth of conviction, without the reinforcement of genuineness in the latter. *The truly godly are more important for the ministry of the gospel than the merely erudite and eloquent.*

2.1.1.2. THE RATIONALE OF THE MAN OF FAITH

In all his sufferings Paul was aware of his own inadequacy. But in a sense, in this he found his strength, for it concentrated his attention on the presence and the providence of his Lord, upon which he was always dependent. (Note our Lord's remark in John 15:5, "Apart from me you can do nothing". Honest helplessness is a prerequisite for acceptable service.) Knowing that God's "grace is sufficient", he was able to "take pleasure in weaknesses, in injuries, in necessities, in persecutions" and "in distresses for Christ's sake", knowing that when he was "weak", then he was "strong". Therefore, he would rather "glory in (his) weaknesses, that the strength of Christ may rest upon" him (II Corinthians 12:9-10).

Ultimately, Paul realized, anything of true worth in his ministry was the product, not of his own efforts, for which he was *always responsible*, but of the intervention of God Himself, upon which he was *always dependent*. Therefore, he would "not dare to speak of any things except those which Christ had accomplished through" him (Romans 15:18).[34]

Suffering, then, when rightly understood and patiently accepted can become an accelerant for our faith. Hence, the apostle's developed sense of utter dependence upon the gracious working of God in his life is no doubt reflected in his words here in Colossians 1:29, "striving according to His working, which works in me mightily".

There is, then, significant blessing in suffering for the development of an individual Christian's own character and faith; and these are also significant factors for all

---

[34] We must wonder if this rationale is now a quaint and foreign concept in the minds of modern Christians who seem to be entranced by schemes that depend entirely upon human abilities and personalities for the desired results.

Christian ministry, which is best prosecuted by people of genuine godliness and strong belief.

But Paul provides a *much more important* and *completely unexpected rationale for his sufferings*.

Sufferings are important, he wrote, because they "fill up that which is lacking in the sufferings of Christ" (1:24). For anyone who is familiar with the biblical doctrine of reconciliation, any suggestion that there is something "lacking" in His sufferings is, to say the least, astonishing. Did not our Lord achieve enough for His people "in the body of His flesh through death", that they might be presented "holy and without blemish and unreproveable before Him" (1:22)?

Without hesitation, we would insist that the Bible is perfectly clear in all that it teaches about the death and resurrection of Christ. We are left in no doubt that He did *everything necessary* to secure the salvation of His people. By His death, and by His death alone, He is our "propitiation" that we might be "justified by faith" alone (Romans 3:25-28). To this, we can add nothing at all in any way whatsoever. Our sufferings make no contribution to our redemption.

Nevertheless, the apostle is obviously saying something here, as startling as it may be, that was important for the Colossians to hear, so it needs to be carefully considered. Several explanations of the significance of these words have been suggested. Some, for example, see here a reference to a kind of mystical 'suffering together' with Christ as members of His body; others suggest that Paul is only referring to suffering 'as our Lord did', or, simply, 'for His sake'. However, these interpretations fail to do justice to *two important phrases* – "that which is lacking", in reference to Christ, and "for His body's sake", in reference to Christians.

A consideration of these two phrases is helpful in determining Paul's meaning, or at least in setting some parameters for our understanding of the thoughts he was conveying to the Colossians. So, first, we should note that Paul saw in his own sufferings not only a beneficial stimulation of his own faith – as we have mentioned above – but also a positive advantage for his fellow Christians, "for your sake". And then we must consider what the apostle thought to be "lacking" in Christ's afflictions.

- **First**, Paul emphasizes by repetition that his sufferings were "for your sake" and "for His body's sake, which is the church".

    Whatever Paul suffered it was always for the well-being of Christians, both individually and in the community of the church, "for (their) sake". "If I am offered upon the sacrifice and service of your faith", he wrote elsewhere, "I joy, and rejoice with you all" (Philippians 2:17). In II Corinthians 11:23-28 he seems to be suggesting that his seemingly endless sufferings were evidence of the genuineness of his own ministry. The threatening dangers, the attempts on his life, and the persecution he endured recorded for us in the Acts of the Apostles were clearly *the result of his preaching* the Christian message, but he would not allow these harassments to deter him from doing so (cf. Acts 21:10-14). Had he not been prepared and willing to suffer in this context, many individuals would not have heard the gospel, churches would not have been established, and world evangelism would have been delayed.

We might say, then, that Paul suffered for *the propagation of the gospel.*

- **Second**, Paul unhesitatingly refers to something "lacking in the afflictions of Christ".

There is no doubt that Jesus Christ also suffered because He preached the gospel. His message, for example, so offended many that they branded Him as a blasphemer (John 5:16-18). And then His teaching so angered his fellow townsmen in Nazareth that they attempted to throw Him off a cliff (Luke 4:28-30). His own brothers did not – at first anyway – believe in Him (John 7:5). The authorities plotted against Him (John 11:48-50). And, as we well know, His ministry eventually led people to crucify Him.

This is indication enough that our Lord also suffered for the propagation of the gospel. Then, in passing on to His followers the responsibility for this ministry of proclamation, He inevitably drew them into His own sufferings in this regard, asking of them no more than He required of Himself. Paul, obviously, was well aware of this and accepted the responsibility of suffering for the same cause.

However, we might say that Jesus suffered *for the preaching* of the gospel *only in Israel*, and in this, it was restricted. But He commissioned His apostles to do so among "all the nations" (Matthew 28:19), a vast and multifarious arena of service. In this sense, in its geographical limitation, our Lord's afflictions were insufficient or "lacking". His followers were asked to suffer through the ensuing centuries for the sake of *the whole world*.

Nevertheless, Christ's afflictions that lead to and incorporated His death were also the unique, exclusive, and immense suffering for *the propitiation of the gospel*. This suffering was His alone.

It is important, then, that we distinguish between the *propitiation* of the gospel – solely the work of Christ – in which we rest, and the *propagation* of the gospel – jointly the work of Christ and the church – in which we wrestle.[35]

NOTE: Christ's sufferings were unique, in both their agony and their significance, and no doubt far greater than any other man has ever suffered, being profoundly intensified somehow by His estrangement from His Father (Matthew 27:46). And we might say that in some ways, and to a limited extent, even Paul's sufferings were unique and exemplary among believers. But all Christians are called upon to suffer for Christ and for the church (see, Matthew 5:10-12, Acts 14:27, II Corinthians 1:6-7, Philippians 1:29, I Peter 4:12-14, and cf. II Timothy 2:10). And, almost by definition, to suffer is to be more affected by one's circumstances than one is able to affect those circumstances, to be acted upon by others rather than to act upon others. *In a sense, then, our 'defeat' is almost more important than – or preparatory to, or concomitant with – our 'victory' (Romans 8:36)!*

2.1.2. PAUL'S UNDERSTANDING OF THE MINISTRY (1:25)

As an apostle, Paul was an authentic representative of Christ, authorized to speak in His Name. This was a position of considerable importance and influence. Nevertheless, here in Colossians 1:25 he explains that he was "made (or, became) a minister" (ἐγενόμην ἐγὼ διάκονος) of the church. The word the apostle uses here, "minister" or "servant" (*diakonos*, or 'deacon'), is humble enough in its origin, referring to someone who waits on tables, or one who is at his master's disposal.

However, *the status of a servant* is relative to the position of his master, and *the significance of his service* is determined by the task he is given to perform. Some serve kings (Matthew 22:13), and some at wedding feasts (John 2:5); some serve God (II Corinthians 6:4), and some Satan (II Corinthians 11:14-15). Evidently, each would have his particular status, and his service its distinctive significance. And Christ Himself, we should note, dignified the servant's position by His own serving, in obedience to His Father (Matthew 20:28, cf. John 17:4).

2.1.2.1. THE STATUS OF THE MINISTER

Although Paul was forced on occasions to assert his authority as an apostle (II Corinthians 11-12), he sought no greater status than being known as a servant

---

[35] There is no sense in which the sufferings of the apostles and all who followed them were meritorious, adding to their eventual justification. Even less is there any biblical suggestion that by works of supererogation in suffering and in good deeds some were able to gain more merit than they needed personally for their own justification that the church could later distribute in indulgences.

of Christ (Philippians 1:1) and of God (II Corinthians 6:4). But being well aware of his own inadequacies (Romans 7:18, I Timothy 1:15), he knew he would be ineffective in this service but for the fact that God made him and his fellow apostles "sufficient as ministers/servants of the new covenant" (II Corinthians 3:6). It was not a position they claimed for themselves, but one to which they were appointed; and being appointed, they were also enabled. As a result, in their service they had a responsibility similar to the Lord's "servant Moses" (Exodus 14:31, cf. II Corinthians 3:7-8).

Then, as Moses pioneered the ministry of the Old Covenant in obedience to the Lord, so Paul and his fellow apostles pioneered the ministry of the New Covenant in obedience to Christ. The apostle refers directly to this new ministry, it marking the beginning of the new, Christian age (1:25). That which had been hidden in previous ages, he explained, is now manifested in Christ – and he was responsible for making this new revelation known through his proclamation of the gospel (1:26-27). What His master had revealed, he was to teach. In this, the servant's task is to prosecute the work of the Master.[36]

It was this service of the Almighty that gave the apostles their *status* in the economy of God. They preached as the ambassadors of Christ (ὑπὲρ Χριστοῦ οὖν πρεσβεύομεν, II Corinthians 5:20).

2.1.2.2. THE SIGNIFICANCE OF THE MINISTRY

At the same time as indicating his status as a minister, Paul was also explaining something of the *significance* of his ministry as a servant of Christ. He states specifically in Colossians that he was also a minister/servant of *the gospel* (1:23) and of *the church* (1:24-25) – of a body of truth and a body of people. His remit was to *preach* the gospel and *build* the church, for he was serving the joint cause of both. To gain some appreciation of what this demanded of him, we need to consider two expressions he uses here:

---

[36] It is interesting that Joshua reminded the Reubenites and the Gadites that Moses had said, "The Lord your God … will give you this land" (Joshua 1:13). But then he spoke of "the land of your possession … that Moses the servant of God gave them" (Joshua 1:15). Moses only gave what God gave, for as a servant he was but an agent of the work of God. Similarly, Jesus said of Himself, "The Son can do nothing of Himself, but what He sees the Father doing: for what things soever He does, these the Son also does in like manner" (John 5:19). Paul, aware of the responsibilities of a servant, wrote, "I will not dare to speak of any things, except those which Christ wrought through me" (Romans 15:18).

Alan D Catchpoole

2.1.2.2.1. To fulfil the word of God

Paul states that he was "made a minister ... to fulfil the word of God" (πληρῶσαι τὸν λόγον τοῦ θεοῦ, 1:25). These words are variously translated or paraphrased as "to make the word of God fully known", "fully carry out the *preaching of* the word of God", or something similar. The difficulty is that the word "fulfil" has various nuances: to fill, to make full, to complete, to accomplish, to finish, to proclaim, to make fully known, etc. But we might suggest that the apostle's sense of his own ministry, "according to the stewardship of God" given to him (1:25), must help us to understand his meaning here.

Paul's ministry was to preach the gospel and to build the church, and in doing so "to fulfil the word of God". Therefore, 'fulfilling the word' was an essential aspect of, or the means of accomplishing, those two activities, and hence it was required for the completion of his service. In no sense of the expression would he have 'fulfilled the word' outside of this context. *Or, in other words, the word of God is fulfilled only when the gospel is preached and the church established.*

It may be, then, that Paul himself explained his meaning in this matter when he said to the Ephesian elders late in his life: "I shrank not from declaring unto you anything that was profitable, and teaching you publicly, and from house to house, testifying both to Jews and to Greeks repentance toward God, and faith toward our Lord Jesus Christ" (Acts 20:20-21). And he added, further describing his service, "But I hold not my life of any account as dear unto myself, so that I may accomplish my course, and the ministry which I received from the Lord Jesus, to testify the gospel of the grace of God" (Acts 20:24). This surely was to comprehensively "fulfil the word of God"! At least we know that it was the accomplishment or fulfilment of his ministry. Then, if the word 'fulfil' carries a sense of intensity, as it seems to do, this is also evident here: he declared "anything that was profitable" in public and in private, to Jew and Greek, speaking of repentance, faith, and the grace of God, and hazarding his own life in the process.

2.1.2.2.2. According to the stewardship of God

To further clarify the *significance* of his service, Paul remarks that he "became a minister, according to the dispensation/stewardship of God which was given" to him (ἐγενόμην ἐγὼ διάκονος κατὰ τὴν οἰκονομίαν τοῦ θεοῦ τὴν δοθεῖσάν μοι) for the sake of the Colossians (among others, no doubt). This implies that the "stewardship of God" was the primary determining factor – as is indicated by the preposition "according to" (κατά) – in his ministry, defining its content, setting its parameters, and specifying its objectives. We need, then, to discover just what this "stewardship" is.

The word "stewardship" (οἰκονομία) originally referred to the management, or the managing of a household – that is, to the task itself or to the implementation of the task. In this sense, but in a far greater context, the word appears in Ephesians 1:9-10. There Paul explains that "having made known unto us the mystery of His will" and "according to His good pleasure which He purposed in (Christ) unto a stewardship of the fullness of the times", God works "to sum up all things in Christ, the things in the heavens, and the things upon the earth". This, we suggest, implies that God through Christ is exercising His own stewardship, working out His managerial intentions throughout all "the times" and through redemption for the sake of the whole of creation. *In other words, God as His own steward effectively completes His own stewardship.* Under His management, His objectives will be accomplished, because He "works all things after the counsel of His will" (Ephesians 1:11).

Then, we read in Ephesians 3:2-3, Paul also writes of "the stewardship of God's grace which was given to" him. This occurred, he explains, when "by revelation was made known unto (him) the mystery".[37] Here he again brings together the knowledge of the mystery and the stewardship of God, as mentioned in Ephesians 1:9-10. Having been made aware of God's managerial intentions in and through the gospel, and knowing himself to be the servant of the Lord, it was inevitable that he was immediately burdened with the responsibility to serve God in His stewardship, and in this sense, the stewardship was "given" to him. Again, as we have suggested above, *the Master's work became the servant's endeavour; the Master's objective became the servant's ambition; the Master's intention to "sum up all things in Christ" (Ephesians 2:10) became the servant's vision.*

Therefore, in reference to his own ministry, Paul was aware of his obligation – "necessity is laid upon me" – to "preach the gospel", because, he said, "I have a stewardship entrusted to me" (I Corinthians 9:16-17). Being the Lord's servant and knowing his Master's managerial plans for the redemption of His creation, made it imperative for him to be involved with and obedient to his Master in the execution of those plans. He was the great Steward's steward!

All this helps us to understand the apostle's words – "the stewardship of God which is given to me for you" (1:25). Paul, it seems, is referring to God's own managerial plan, in which he had become involved for the sake of the Colossians and others to whom he ministered. Consequently, he was a servant of the gospel and the church.

---

[37] See Galatians 1:12.

This understanding of his stewardship no doubt contributed to the high motivation that enabled Paul to continue in his ministry despite the sufferings.

NOTE: Although we do not share in Paul's apostolic responsibilities, these being unique in the first generation of Christians, we are all ministers of the gospel for "the building up of the body of Christ" (Ephesians 4:11-12). So, the principles and the motivation for Christian ministry that we find here should instruct and encourage us in our own service for Christ. In this, the apostle would have us be "imitators" of him (cf. I Corinthians 11:1).

2.1.3. PAUL'S UNDERSTANDING OF THE MYSTERY (1:26-27)

Now Paul writes specifically about the "word of God", which he mentioned in the previous verse. This "word of God", which he and his fellow apostles were commissioned to proclaim to the world (a responsibility that devolves to some extent upon all Christians), he equates here with "the mystery which has been hidden from all ages and generations, but now is manifested to his saints" (1:26).

This immediately indicates that the new, Christian age was inaugurated with a new revelation – the manifestation of a "mystery" previously concealed. But as we consider this, we must understand that this new revelation does not expunge the old "word of God" found in the Old Testament scriptures, but it extrapolates the old into the new "word of God" of the New Testament. The prophets of the Old Testament were not entirely ignorant of Christian salvation They wrote of "the grace" that they anticipated would come, while they were "searching what time, or what manner of time the Spirit of God which was in them pointed" to concerning "the sufferings of Christ and the glories that should follow them" (I Peter 1:10-11). Therefore, being aware of the preliminary and basic nature of their own ministry, they anticipated further revelation. They knew that something was hidden from them.

Nevertheless, the Old Testament revelation was foundational for the Christian gospel. Paul himself wrote of his "preaching of Jesus Christ, according to the revelation of the mystery", a mystery "now ... manifested", and through "the scriptures of the prophets" is made known (Romans 16:25-26). His "preaching of Jesus", in other words, was rooted in and drawn from the writings of the prophets. As is evident in the record of his ministry in the Acts of the Apostles, and in his letters, Paul constantly quoted the old scriptures to establish the validity of his own presentation of the mystery. He even advised Timothy that these ancient "sacred writings" were able to make him "wise unto salvation through faith which is in Christ Jesus" (II Timothy 3:15).

Apostolic dependence upon the old scriptures was in keeping with the principles of our Lord's own ministry to His disciples, seen most clearly when He "beginning from Moses and from all the prophets ... interpreted to them in all the scriptures the things concerning Himself" (Luke 24:27). So, we might say that Christ is the hermeneutical principle for the final interpretation of the Old Testament; and that the Old Testament scriptures provide the initial revelational context for the true understanding of Christ.

Therefore, we might conclude that as the revelation of the mystery arises out of the Old Testament, we might anticipate that the meaning of the word "mystery" and the significance of it in the New Testament must be found first in the Old Testament.[38] There, in the ancient Greek version of the Old Testament, which was known to Paul, this Greek word is used to translate the original word that appears in our English Bible as "secret". In Daniel 2:22, 28, the prophet writes, "blessed be the name of God" who "reveals the deep and secret things", and he then announces to king Nebuchadnezzar that "there is a God in heaven that reveals secrets".

Paul, being an assiduous student of the Old Testament, evidently uses this word "mystery" to refer to matters of immense importance that are now known to the Christian community. But because they were divine secrets they could only be known as God was pleased to reveal them from heaven, and only at the time of His choosing and by no other means. He mentions various truths that could only be accessed in this way – for example, knowledge of the true wisdom of God (I Corinthians 2:7); that at the end of time we "shall all be changed" in the resurrection (I Corinthians 15:51); God's purpose to integrate all things in Christ (Ephesians 1:9-10); the "mystery of godliness" seen in the incarnation and triumph of Christ (I Timothy 3:16); the substance of the Christian gospel itself (Ephesians 6:19); and, we might add from Matthew, the reality of the kingdom of heaven (Matthew 13:11). *Anthropocentric philosophy and human science leave us in complete ignorance of these things.*[39]

Understanding Christians are openly and unashamedly dependent upon the revelation of mystery for all their fundamental beliefs, their philosophy, their system of morality, and their hope in life and in eternity.

---

[38] This is an important consideration, because the word "mystery" was frequently used in the pagan religions of Paul's time, giving some to suggest that the apostle not only borrowed the word from that source, but also imported its pagan meaning into his teaching. But this, for several reasons, I cannot accept.

[39] This is the point where the rationalism of the secular man departs from the reasoning of the Christian man.

However, there is evidently one aspect of the Christian mystery that is uppermost in Paul's thinking here in Colossians. He writes about "the riches of the glory of this mystery among the Gentiles, which is Christ in you, the hope of glory" (1:27). What is particularly rich and glorious about the mystery is not only the social impact it has upon believing Gentiles, but also the intimate, hope-giving association that they now have with Christ.

There can be no doubt that "the riches of the glory" of the gospel are just as wonderful among the Gentiles as they are among the Jews. Paul indicates what this imparted wealth is when he writes of "all riches of the full assurance of understanding" and "all treasures of wisdom and knowledge" in 2:2-3. The true believer, then, has access in Christ to "all ... understanding ... wisdom and knowledge", and greater treasures than these are inconceivable. They do not make man omniscient, but they allay the wretchedness of ignorance and remove the confusion of mind that leave men blind, disoriented, and aimless in this world, and in conflict with the purposes of God (cf. #1.2.1.2.). Christ came to bring light and truth into this world (John 8:12, 31-32).

From the beginning, the Old Testament acknowledges that the Gentiles will participate in the blessings of Abraham (Genesis 12:2-3) and in the kingdom of God (Isaiah 11:10, Romans 15:12). But what was made abundantly clear by the revelation of the mystery given to the apostle Paul was, in effect, that God's intention was that the incorporation of the Gentiles into the believing community be comprehensive – they were to be "fellow-heirs, and fellow-members of the body, and fellow-partakers of the promise in Christ Jesus through the gospel" (συγκληρονόμα καὶ σύσσωμα καὶ συμμέτοχα τῆς ἐπαγγελίας ἐν Χριστῷ Ἰησοῦ διὰ τοῦ εὐαγγελίου, Ephesians 3:6). In Christ "the middle wall of partition" has been removed (Ephesians 2:14); the Gentiles were no longer restricted to the outer court, as in the old temple regulations. Now, in the community of God's redeemed people, they, as Christians, were not in any way disadvantaged or inferior in position.

But if this was God's intention, then the substance of His plan is explained by the words, "Christ in you, the hope of glory" (1:27). They were constituted as "fellow-members of the body" – that is, the body of Christ (1:24) – because Christ was in them. Whether this implies that Christ was among them as a group, or indwelling each individually (which is probably more likely here, but both are true), the indissoluble, intimate, personal association of our Lord Jesus Christ with all the Gentile believers is indicated. This is the participation in Christ that is common to all believers, and in effect the answer to our Lord's request, "I pray ... for them ... that believe on me ... that they may all be one; even as you, Father, are in me, and I in you, that they may be one in us" (John 17:21).

It is only this intimate and irrevocable union the true believers, whether Jews or Gentiles, have with Christ that guarantees they, when Christ is fully manifested in the days to come, will also "be manifested with Him in glory" (3:4). This is "the hope of glory" (1:27), "the hope which is laid up for (us) in the heavens" (1:5) of which Paul writes. And it is this that lies behind the apostle's exhortation to the Colossians to "set your minds on the things that are above ... for ... your life is hid with Christ in God" (3:1-2).

2.1.4. PAUL'S UNDERSTANDING OF THE METHOD AND THE OBJECTIVE OF MINISTRY (1:28-29)

We have already noted that Paul had a developed sense of his utter dependence upon the gracious working of God in his life (#2.1.1.2.). He knew that he had accomplished nothing of worth in his ministry apart from, he said, "His working, which works in me mightily." Nevertheless, this exacted its toll on the apostle himself, demanding of him much "labour" and "striving" (1:29, κοπιῶ ἀγωνιζόμενος). We might suggest that the first of these two words implies 'working to the exhaustion of one's own strength'; and the second, 'working against the strength of opposition'.[40] We should not be mistaken! The ministry of the gospel, the preaching of Christ in this godless world, is an intimidating enterprise, not to be undertaken impetuously or frivolously.

Moreover, acknowledging the demanding implications and the seriousness of preaching the gospel, and being mindful of our responsibility to participate in this ministry, we should be aware of the manner in which it should be conducted. In 1:28, using a few carefully chosen words, Paul gives us a remarkable summary of the essential aspects of his own sense of responsibility in his ministry, as he saw it.

We will note these words briefly:

- **First**, the ministry is *declarative*, the proclamation of Christ – "whom we proclaim".

  Primarily, the ministry of the gospel is a proclamation, an open, public declaration (ὃν ἡμεῖς καταγγέλλομεν). It is not the expression of a personal opinion, the recounting of an individual experience, or a philosophical disquisition. It is not in itself an explanation, but an announcement. But in particular, it is an announcement about Jesus Christ – "whom we

---

[40] The first comes from a word for 'a beating', and hence took on the derived meaning of 'growing weary'; the second comes from a word for 'a gathering', was used of an athletic contest, and hence took on the derived meaning of 'contending against opposition' (this latter word being behind our word 'agony').

proclaim". It is not, then, the presentation of some theory, but, as it were, the formal introduction of a person. This is paramount!

Paul made this introduction when he "proclaimed the word of the Lord" (Acts 15:36), or "the word of God" (Acts 17:13). It is then only *the biblical Christ*, the Christ revealed through the word of God, who is to be presented to the world. Only the proclamation that is faithful to the scriptures will distinguish accurately between the true Christ and the many "false Christs" (Matthew 24:24).

The apostle's proclamation was true to the person of Christ.

Moreover, in Paul's proclamation, he not only carefully identified the true Christ but also accurately declared the significance of His presence on earth. "Be it known", he said, "... that through this Man is proclaimed unto you remission of sins" that leads to believing people being "justified from all things" (Acts 13:38-39). His purpose was to so introduce Christ to the people that they might appreciate His work and find eternal salvation in Him.

The apostle's proclamation was true to the purpose of Christ.

Then we should note that although the apostle's ministry was *declarative* – and authoritatively so – Paul did not for one moment doubt that it was also *defensible*. When he proclaimed Jesus to the Thessalonians he also "reasoned with them from the scriptures, explaining and pointing out that it behoved Christ to suffer and to rise again from the dead" (Acts 17:2-3, διελέξατο αὐτοῖς ἀπὸ τῶν γραφῶν, διανοίγων καὶ παρατιθέμενος ὅτι τὸν χριστὸν ἔδει παθεῖν καὶ ἀναστῆναι ἐκ νεκρῶν).

We should expect of those who would minister the gospel to us that they not only proclaim Christ faithfully but also that they are able to give "a reason concerning the hope" we have, "yet with meekness and fear" (I Peter 3:15).

• **Second**, the ministry is both *moral and didactic* – "admonishing ... and teaching ... in all wisdom".

Further to our consideration of Paul's ministry of the gospel, we should note here that his proclamation was supplemented with both "admonishing ... and teaching" (1:28, καταγγέλλομεν νουθετοῦντες ... καὶ διδάσκοντες). The ultimate results he desired could not be achieved by a solitary sermon, no matter how effective that might be. It required considerable, practical teaching to bring any interested neophytes to an adequate understanding of the Christian faith – and, perhaps, to bring an individual enquirer to genuine, informed personal faith in

Christ. As thankful as we might be for the enthusiasm and the courage of the evangelistic street preacher, we should be the more concerned for the wholesome ministry of the devout Christian community where understanding and belief can be nurtured. The church should provide the communal context in which wisdom, teaching, and admonishing will pervade the very atmosphere of the congregation, influencing all (3:16, cf. #3.4.2.2.2.).

It is important, I think, to see that Paul included admonishing with his teaching, suggesting that merely to impart truths and correct principles, as immensely valuable as this is, is not enough. The manner in which such knowledge is accepted and employed is also critical. The word "admonishing" (νουθετοῦντες, or, basically, 'to put in mind') involves warning and instruction, which we suggest includes moral guidance for the use of all that is learned. The gospel of Christ is no insipid or pallid philosophy that leaves men apathetic, but, as history has demonstrated, it is nothing less than "the power of God unto salvation" (Romans 1:16). But there is, and always has been, the imminent danger that some will attempt to use its dynamic for their own purposes and personal gain (cf. II Corinthians 2:17). That it might be preached in sincerity and humility, there must be admonishment in the church.

But admonishing, the apostle seems to suggest, is no facile task! It requires not only that we be "filled with all knowledge", but also that we be "full of goodness" if we are to "admonish one another" (Romans 15:14). It is, then, not only an academic, but also a demandingly moral activity, and not best done – if done at all – by either the simple or the unprincipled. Moreover, for Paul himself it was an emotional exercise, demanding both sedulity and tears (Acts 20:31). Therefore, as he writes here, it is to be done "in all wisdom" (1:28, ἐν πάσῃ σοφία), and with sufficient maturity.

We should expect much more of those who would minister the gospel to us than scholarly ability and communicative skills, for the minister of the gospel must also be a man of humble godliness and purity of character, able to admonish without hypocrisy.

- **Third**, the ministry is *unrestricted and unsophisticated* – "every man ... every man ... every man".

Paul, by this repetition, leaves us in no doubt that the preaching of the gospel, including both the admonition and the teaching, should be available to everybody to the end that all may be presented "perfect in Christ" (1:28).

This implies that the proclamation of the gospel, with the teaching of its principles and practices, was never intended only for an exclusively sophisticated, academic, or priestly class. There is nothing esoteric about the Christian message that is only to be shared with the privileged few.

Nor is there an inferior level of instruction for the 'average' believer, distinct from a superior level for the privileged or more capable 'academic' believer. Neither is there one 'gospel' for the young and another for the mature; nor is there one 'gospel' for men and another for women; nor is there one 'gospel' for one ethnic community and another for differing cultural conditions (see Ephesians 4:4-6).

There are no hidden doctrines so convoluted that they are beyond some believers, whether children or adults, whether neophytes or presbyters, or simple or sage. Everybody should be encouraged by all means to mature towards the ultimate perfection that is available for all in Christ.

We should expect of those who minister to us a sensitive concern for other people, without regard for their age, gender, ability, or social status; and the willingness to accommodate all manner of people within the Christian community, having regard for their age, gender, ability, or social status.

- **Fourth**, the ministry is *transcendent and extravagant* – "to present every man perfect in Christ".

  Here Paul returns to his statement in 1:22, that God's intention in reconciling His people "in the body of (Christ's) flesh through death" is that they be presented "holy and without blemish and unreproveable before Him" (#1.3.2.3.2.). This, we may assume, is the final condition of the man who is "perfect in Christ". The apostle obviously considers his ongoing admonishing and teaching to be instrumental in the process that matures Christian men and women, preparing them for the time when they will enter into the presence of their Lord.

  The primary motivation for the proclamation of the gospel is not to obtain immediate, temporal results – although these are undoubtedly important and should accrue from the admonishing and teaching, and become evident in the believers' behaviour. Rather, the final, magnificent objective of our ministry is to direct God's people towards the transcendent and extravagant glory of Christ, in which they will participate when they "shall be manifested with Him in glory" (3:4).

  It is important, I think, particularly in this pragmatic and restless age, to remember constantly that the aim of Christian ministry in all its forms – evangelistic, didactic, diaconal, societal, eleemosynary – is, or should be *the eternal well-being* of those to whom we minister. Our enthusiasm for instant results – especially for outcomes that can be quantitatively and even qualitatively evaluated – can soon become a distraction, attenuating our ideals and contaminating our motivation. We should never lose sight of our "hope that is laid up in heaven" (1:5).

However, with this ultimate goal in view and our anticipation that we will one day be holy and without blemish, it should be our immediate concern as Christians to "cleanse ourselves from all defilement of flesh and spirit, perfecting holiness in the fear of God" (II Corinthians 7:1).

We should expect of those who would minister the gospel to us a passionate interest in the eternal salvation of others and in the spiritual maturation of believers that will prepare them for eternity; being those ministers, in other words, for whom it is not the immediate, but the ultimate issues of life that are the primary concern.

With all this in mind, we turn our attention to Paul's own personal concern for the Colossian Christians.

◆

2.2. HIS PERSONAL CONCERN FOR THE
COLOSSIANS (2:1-5)

As suggested above, Paul's personal concern for the Colossians – and for others he had not met – is the product of his sense of the divine commission that he had received (1:25, cf. #2). We have also seen that his ministry and stewardship motivated him to "labour" and "striving" for the sake of "teaching every man in all wisdom" (1:28-29). Now he expresses specifically his solicitude in this regard for the people he is addressing in this letter, that they might know how he also strived for them (2:1) "that they might know the mystery, Christ" (2:2).

The education of Christian believers in the truths of the gospel of Christ was always an imperative for the apostle,[41] but evidently there was a specific urgency at that time for instructing the Colossians in particular. They needed a greater knowledge of Christ, "in whom are all the treasures of wisdom and knowledge hidden", that they might not only achieve some personal maturity, but also that they might resist the deluding philosophy and "persuasiveness of speech" (2:4) that were being introduced into their church by false teachers.

Perhaps because of the urgency of their situation, Paul wrote, "I would have you know how greatly I strive for you" (2:1, Θέλω γὰρ ὑμᾶς εἰδέναι ἡλίκον ἀγῶνα ἔχω ὑπὲρ ὑμῶν). Obviously, he wanted them to be assured of and comforted by his genuine interest in their well-being. Striving was a constant characteristic of his ministry, but now it is intensified "greatly". In saying this he may have been referring to his striving in prayer for the people, even as he commended Epaphras for doing (ἀγωνιζόμενος ὑπὲρ ὑμῶν ἐν ταῖς προσευχαῖς, 4:12). We do know that apart from his many physical sufferings, or the external "things that are without", he also wrestled inwardly and "daily" with his "anxiety for all the churches" (ἡ μέριμνα πασῶν τῶν ἐκκλησιῶν, II Corinthians 11:28).[42] He suffered a continuing apprehension for the welfare of Christian congregations everywhere.

We might wonder what aggravated this apprehension in the case of the Colossians. I suggested above that "striving" – as distinct from "labour" – suggests working against the strength of opposition (#2.1.4.). It is obvious from his letters that Paul was constantly combating not only *heretical teaching* which resulted in Christians misunderstanding the gospel, but also *unethical behaviour* in the churches. These two inevitably accompany each other. Christian congregations

---

[41] See II Timothy 4:1-3, Titus 2:1.

[42] Paul evidently distinguished between a commendable, even necessary, anxiety (ὅστις γνησίως τὰ περὶ ὑμῶν μεριμνήσει, Philippians 2:20), and unnecessary anxiety that should be avoided through prayer (μηδὲν μεριμνᾶτε, Philppians 4:6). The former is, *inter alia*, altruistic.

were and always have been susceptible to and threatened by both. Therefore, much of Paul's ministry involved him in an apologetic defence of the doctrines of the faith and in corrective ethical instruction. And these two concerns occupy him in this letter to the Colossians.

It seems likely, then, that apart from physical sufferings (1:24) and "wrestling ... against the spiritual hosts of wickedness" (Ephesians 6:13), Paul's striving also included his constant theological work to defend the truth of the gospel, the doctrines and moral standards of the faith, and the glory of Christ. He knew that this was essential for the very continuance of the true church, for the sustaining of its purity, and for the maintenance of its light in the darkness of this world.

But we should consider more carefully Paul's solicitude for the Colossian believers.

2.2.1. CONCERN FOR THE CHURCH'S INTERNAL INTEGRITY (2:2A)

First, the apostle was concerned for the believers that "their hearts may be comforted" (ἵνα παρακληθῶσιν αἱ καρδίαι αὐτῶν, 2:2). The word for 'comfort' may merely imply encouragement, but it seems in this context to suggest more than this. It appears here to be such encouragement as arises from adequate understanding. It demands more than words of assurance or sympathy, evidently being intended in the case of the Colossians to equip them to withstand the distraction and disturbance of the false teachers and their persuasive oratory. It was not, in other words, a palliative, but a corrective – *not only heartening but also intellectual empowering*. Paul continues by expressing his desire that his readers participate in "the full assurance of understanding" and in the knowledge of "the mystery", and this makes it clear that the comfort he is offering is far more than the sentiment of well-being, also involving *strength of mind*.[43]

This encouragement is immediately made dependent upon "being knit together in love" (συμβιβασθέντες ἐν ἀγάπῃ, 2:2). It is, then, encouragement within a specific context. It is more than individual satisfaction.

The word used here is somewhat ambiguous. It may mean 'to knit/hold together', but it is used also of 'teaching', being translated, for example, 'prove' in Acts 9:22, and 'instruct' in I Corinthians 2:16, or something similar. And having in mind that Paul is concerned that people be taught "in all wisdom" (1:28) and enjoy the

---

[43] We might note that Paul, in II Thessalonians 2:17, associates being comforted with being established "in every good work and word"; not only in action, then, but also in thought and expression.

riches of "understanding" (2:2), this second sense of the word may have been his intended meaning in this verse.

However, Paul then qualifies what he is saying here by adding the two highly significant words "in love" (2:2). In a sense, any instruction in the things of the gospel, any Christian teaching, fails in its purpose if it is not both given and received in love. Otherwise, the knowledge gained would possibly be seriously misrepresented and misused. There are the matters of godly motive and intention to be considered. But love is just as essential also for any Christian community to be truly integrated, or knit together. So, I suggest that the apostle may well have had in mind a complex of three parts, in which both Christian *education* and church *integration* are found combined, each being determined and moderated by *love*.

So, I would suggest, a church cannot be integrated without the contextualizing of a common doctrine or teaching, or without the moderation of a common love. Neither the one without the other!

In contrast, the disintegrated community, divided by schismatic teaching or internal discord, is utterly detrimental to learning the truth, being depleted in, or devoid of love.[44]

It is interesting that Paul in his letter to the Ephesians brings together the danger of being "carried away with every wind of doctrine" – for the want of teaching – and the importance of "speaking the truth in love" (ἀληθεύοντες ... ἐν ἀγάπῃ), when expressing his concern that "the body (the church) fitly framed and knit together" might build up "itself in love" (τὸ σῶμα συναρμολογούμενον καὶ συμβιβαζόμενον ... ποιεῖται εἰς οἰκοδομὴν ἑαυτοῦ ἐν ἀγάπῃ, Ephesians 4:14-16). In this, he undoubtedly has in mind both the integrity of the church and the importance that it be taught in good doctrine. And these things required both "speaking the truth in love" and building up "in love". A sentiment is expressed here that is very similar to that which we find in Colossians 2:2, and in similar circumstances. Here the same complex in three parts reappears.

Further, here in Colossians – as in Ephesians 4 – the apostle again uses the imagery of the church as the body of Christ in which all members are "knit together" (συμβιβαζόμενον, 2:19). Subsequently he urges them "above all" to put

---

[44] It is surely self-evident – even if so often disregarded – that study and instruction in theology without a devout concern for the glory of God, being driven by arrogance, self-interest, academic ambition, concern rather for a particular party or cause, or any other ulterior motive, can only result in confusion, debate, and divisiveness. It will certainly not produce "love out of a pure heart and a good conscience and genuine faith" (I Timothy 1:5).

on "love, which is the bond of perfectness", anticipating that this would contribute to their "teaching and admonishing one another" in the congregation, as they "let the word of Christ dwell" in them "richly in all wisdom" (3:14-16).

They were, then, to be "knit together" in love as they were "taught" together in love. Then, being integrated in the body of Christ and being instructed in the truth, both being effected through the moderation of genuine love, all these benefits merge in the establishment of an effective church.

Therefore, we might suggest that the "comfort" or "encouragement" of heart to which the apostle refers, arises from the knowledge that is gained from a loving congregation of believers who are well integrated in communion with Christ. *There is perhaps as much danger in a well-taught church with little love as there is in a loving church that is little taught.* Genuine and functional integration – true integrity – in the Christian community requires both the foundation of biblical knowledge and the structure of ethical love.

There must be love in ministering the truth and in integrating the body of Christ, and these two, it seems, the apostle would not have disconnected. And I suggest that to separate concern for the truth and concern for the integration from each other will result in the destruction of both; as will any attempt to promote either without genuine love. Therefore, this threefold complex is necessary not only to establish the context in which the church will flourish in integrity but also to provide the ambience required for wholesome theological learning.

2.2.2. Concern for the Church's External Viability (2:2b-4)

If *the internal integrity* of any church is the result primarily of its integration and instruction in love, then *the external viability* of the church is the result primarily of understanding, wisdom, and knowledge in the congregation. Facing the moral confusion and the complex philosophical theorizing of this world, and being required to distinguish between various ethical values and to differentiate between diverse rationalistic speculations, a church must not only be well integrated but also intelligently strong in its encounter with the unconverted. Otherwise, it will be defenceless – as churches often are – and probably compromise – as they often do. If they cannot defend their own beliefs, they probably have no well-defined beliefs to defend.

This infant church in Colossae was, it appears, suddenly and without warning exposed to external forces that threatened its existence, or at least its orthodoxy. Its viability was at risk. Was it able to respond appropriately to changing circumstances and unexpected theological and moral challenges? This depended first of all upon its internal integrity. Everything that a divided church might say to the world lacks credibility, and deserves little respect.[45]

However, Paul's immediate concern here, as we have suggested, is that the Colossian Christians might have the necessary strength of mind to be able to deal with the crisis they were facing. All that he had been saying about understanding and knowing the mystery was intended, as he wrote to them, "that no one may delude you with persuasiveness of speech" (ἵνα μηδεὶς ὑμᾶς παραλογίζηται ἐν πιθανολογίᾳ, 2:4). Evidently, the apostle was aware that they might be intellectually seduced by convincing argumentation, left confused, and fall prey to non-Christian philosophies. If, as seems probable, they were but recently converted and "without experience of the word of righteousness" (Hebrews 5:13), they were in significant danger, the survival of their church as a truly Christian congregation being at risk.

In this verse (2:4) we come to the very heart of Paul's concern for the Colossians and, no doubt, to the motive behind the writing of this letter. He evidently believed that the false teachers had nothing of real substance to offer, and for this reason, they resorted to "persuasiveness of speech" – mere oratory! But he was also aware of how devastatingly effective such speech can be (cf. Romans 16:17-18). And it is also evident that he believed that there was only one answer to this problem, only one way in which the young and the innocent could avoid such deception – they needed to access "all the treasures of wisdom and knowledge" that are hidden in Christ (2:3). And to this end, they must, *inter alia*, "let the word of Christ dwell in (them) richly in all wisdom" (3:16).

This has been Paul's concern from the beginning of this letter. He had reminded them of the importance in their lives of the first occasion when they heard "the word of the truth of the gospel" (1:5), and of the time when they first "knew the grace of God in truth" (1:6). And he assured them that he prayed that they "might be filled with the knowledge of His will in all spiritual wisdom and understanding" (1:9, see #1.2.). Now he urges them not to be deflected from these things – this truth, knowledge, wisdom, and understanding – by the "vain" or "empty deceit" (2:8) of skilful rhetoric or devious reasoning.

We would all do well, without becoming obdurate or self-satisfied, to keep in mind that we are all susceptible to this danger, and to be careful to maintain our faith

---

[45] It is of no surprise that Paul exhorted the Christians in Corinth to "all speak the same thing, and that there be no divisions among you" (I Corinthians 1:10).

in Christ. Whether it be by the skilful oratory, the charismatic personality, or the intellectual vigour of the preacher, or whoever would influence us, we may all be – and often are! – mislead. Many Christians are left to suffer from exposure to such disturbing influences for the want of adequate and true instruction. However, the apostle would empower his readers that they might avoid or be unaffected by deluding, damaging, and extraneous philosophical influences.

With this perennial danger in mind, it is worthwhile noting carefully something of the significance of Paul's comment that "all the treasures of wisdom and knowledge" are to be found in Christ (2:3). What he means by these words is, I suggest, best understood from the context of this letter to the Colossians. There are two things we might consider:

- **First**, knowledge in Christ is comprehensive.

  Paul makes a most remarkable assertion here, a bold affirmation. He insists that "all the treasures of wisdom and knowledge" are *hidden* in Christ, nothing being excepted. That they are "hidden" in Him is not intended to suggest that they are inaccessible – for there has been an open revelation of the mystery (1:25-26) – but only that those who are genuinely searching for such treasures must look to Him and nowhere else if they are to find them. *Nothing of wisdom and knowledge, the apostle is saying, is rightly comprehended if Jesus Christ is not first of all recognized for all that He is.*

  This assertion, I would suggest, is grounded in all that the apostle has written in Colossians 1:15-20, where he explains that Christ has the pre-eminence both in creation and in the church (#2.3.). It is common in our day for many to suggest that Christ might be of value in our search for religious truth, but that we must turn to science or anthropocentric reasoning if we would find the truth about other matters. So, faith and science are sharply distinguished, and more often than not considered to be contradictory or even mutually exclusive. However, if we would maintain a truly Christian understanding, we must begin with the belief that in Christ "were all things created" (1:16) and in Him "all things consist" (1:17). And this perspective will temper and enhance – and therefore, enrich, and not impede – our involvement in and consideration of scientific investigation.[46]

---

[46] And we might point out that if we as Christians bring our religious convictions to our study of the sciences, we are only doing what the atheist and the non-Christian do. Perhaps the only difference is that the atheist seems to have convinced himself that his religious position is one of honest neutrality, when in fact it is probably the most presumptuous and intolerant.

Then if we believe that Christ "is the beginning, the firstborn from the dead" (1:18), and if it is God's intention "through Him to reconcile all things unto Himself … whether things on earth, or things in the heavens" (1:20), we have in Him a unique and unsurpassed perspective on the critical matters of religion. In Him, we find the immense treasure of "wisdom and knowledge" concerning the meaning of life, questions about death, reconciliation with God, and eternal hope. This provides us with a confident religious orientation.

Therefore, we must conclude that all who are ignorant of or who refuse to consider the pre-eminence of Jesus Christ in the whole economy of God are tragically impoverished in every aspect of their lives, whether in matters concerning creation or religion. That Christ has this pre-eminence implies that He must be our primary and preliminary consideration in our search for wisdom and knowledge.

- **Second**, knowledge in Christ is personal.

It is also remarkable that Paul insists that all wisdom and knowledge are hidden *in Christ*. This not only traces all true knowledge back to God Himself, but it also implies that at the back of all things stands a person of great magnificence and holy character. Therefore, as the *methodology* of our search for the truth is to commence with our belief in Him as the source of knowledge, then the *mood* of our search for the truth should be one of awe and humility. Therefore, as "God resists the proud, but gives grace to the humble" (I Peter 5:5), the arrogant and self-satisfied know little of Him, and are, therefore, seriously impaired in their search for the truth.

It should not surprise us, then, that in this letter, in which Paul is anxious to establish the Colossian believers in wisdom and knowledge that they might escape the delusion of the false teachers, he emphasizes the importance of reconciliation. He reminds them of their former state when, before their conversion to Christ, they were "alienated and enemies" (1:21), and of their need of "peace through the blood of His cross" (1:19). Then "being dead through (their) trespasses", they had been quickened "together with Him" as they benefitted from "the cross" (2:13-14). Only those whose lives have been so radically transformed by the grace of God are in a position to find the treasures that are hidden in Christ. Their conversion to Christ has opened to them the possibility of wisdom and knowledge.

The implication of this is that repentance and faith, which result in communion with God, are prerequisite for all who would truly understand the "deep things of God" (I Corinthians 2:10) and become scientists indeed.[47] In a sense, as knowledge in Christ is personal, it is not open to impersonal enquiry.

In summary, we would suggest that Paul's comment in 2:3 has profound significance for the whole of our life, both in our appreciation of our creation and of our religion. It is imperative that we proclaim the centrality and comprehensiveness of Christ. In all our thinking as Christians in every sphere of our lives, we should commence with Christ, always keeping our knowledge of Him in mind. Being the revealed mystery (2:2), He is the beginning of Christian thought, not the conclusion reached through a supposedly logical reasoning process. Therefore, any "persuasiveness of speech" that distracts us from Christ Himself and His self-revelation, weakening our faith in and love for Him, can only have calamitous consequences for both our thinking and spiritual well-being.

2.2.3. Confidence *for* the People in the Colossian Church (2:2)

As we have had to consider the difficulty arising from the ambiguity of the word "knit together" (συμβιβασθέντες) in this verse (#2.2.1.), there is a similar problem with the expression "full assurance of understanding", which might also be translated "fullness of understanding" (τῆς πληροφορίας τῆς συνέσεως).

The use of this word for 'full' or 'fullness' in the New Testament seems to favour the first of these two possibilities.[48] If this were Paul's intended meaning, as seems to me to be more likely, then he would have the believers in Colossae reassured of their own faith and confident about the truth of the teaching they had received. This would result from their "understanding", this being their comprehension of the "mystery". This being so, then it is evident that personal assurance of their own faith was secured not in individual isolation, but in the loving integration and teaching of the Christian community – as explained above (#2.2.1.). Therefore, apart from the apostle's concern for the internal integrity of the church as such, he would also have the church provide the context in which the confidence of individual believers – assurance of their knowledge, faith, and salvation – might be found and nurtured.[49]

---

[47] Much more needs to be said – and has been said elsewhere by many writers – about the relationship between Christian conversion and the possibility of true knowledge, but here this brief comment will have to suffice.

[48] Elsewhere in the New Testament this word "fullness" or "full assurance" (πληροφορία) is found in I Thessalonians 1:5, Hebrews 6:11 & 10:22. In each of these three verses, the translation "full assurance" seems to be more appropriate.

[49] For us, this should be a serious pastoral concern, for we would not want anyone to be falsely assured of his salvation in Christ, or to encourage him to find such assurance in and through anything other than the word of God, rightly understood.

However, if the translation "fullness of understanding" is adopted, there is not much difference in the outcome. Paul's primary meaning then would be that the Colossians be so filled with understanding that they might be able to discern between truth and error, and to protect themselves from false teaching. And this, surely, is a critical element in any personal assurance Christians might have about the validity of their own beliefs. We can hardly gain any confidence in our faith if we are unable to intelligently distinguish it from the theories of other religions and philosophies.

Undoubtedly the apostle would minister the gospel not only that others might be saved, but also that they be exposed to the teaching that would provide confidence for each believer in his own salvation.

2.2.4. CONFIDENCE *IN* THE PEOPLE IN THE COLOSSIAN CHURCH (2:5)

Our Lord warned His disciples that there would "arise false Christs and false prophets, and (they) shall show signs and wonders, that they may lead astray, if possible, the elect", advising His followers to "take heed" (Mark 13:22-23). We should take this warning seriously, and not be surprised when such deceivers penetrate into and do much damage within Christian churches. So, we should also be prepared to defend the faith (cf. Jude 3-4). Nevertheless, we may be encouraged by our Lord's assurance that the most subtle and influential of deceivers are not able to lead astray the "elect" – those who are truly His – for this is not "possible".

Therefore, although Paul was writing to warn and equip the Colossians when others were attempting to delude them, he was convinced that their conversion to Christ was genuine. Presumably, he would hardly have given the advice he had in 2:2-4 unless he had some good reason to believe that he was addressing authentic Christians. And there was enough tangible evidence to convince him that this was so. Although not being with them in person, he was sufficiently informed about them to rejoice, "beholding (their) order and the steadfastness of (their) faith in Christ" (βλέπων ὑμῶν τὴν τάξιν καὶ τὸ στερέωμα τῆς εἰς Χριστὸν πίστεως ὑμῶν, 2:5).

Now we might suggest that the "order" that he observed is what we called above their 'internal integrity' (#2.2.1.), and the "steadfastness" of their faith is what we called their 'external viability' (#2.2.2.).

Despite the persuasiveness of the heretics, the Christians in Colossae in the main seem to have remained faithful to the truth of the gospel, and Paul was seemingly convinced that they would continue to be so. The apostle, then, is perhaps writing not so much to save the believers from confusion as to enable them to counter false teachers and to assist the unconverted, and to "answer each one" as they ought (4:6).

With these two admirable features of the Colossian congregation so evident – their order and steadfastness – Paul was eager to exhort them, knowing that they had indeed "received Christ Jesus as Lord", to continue to "walk in Him" (2:6). In our next section, we will consider the significance of this exhortation.

◆

COLOSSIANS 2:6-4:6.

3. PRACTICAL IMPLICATIONS OF THE GOSPEL

So far in this letter, Paul has penned a profound summary of "the word of the truth of the gospel" (1:5), has reminded his readers about what I have called the three dimensions of the salvation they had received in Christ (1:1-23, #1.), and has assured them of his concern for and confidence in their Christian well-being (1:24-2:5, #2.). Now the apostle writes to exhort them to continue living in a manner consistent with their faith (2:6-7). This gives him occasion to discuss the intensely practical matters of appropriate and effective Christian thinking, ethical behaviour, social involvement, and engagement with the non-Christian world (2:8-4:6, see Introduction, B.), all of these being basic and necessary aspects of Christian life.

3.1. THE EXHORTATION (2:6-7)

In these two verses, we find what we might consider to be the heart of Paul's concern in all that he is saying in this letter. In effect, he is summarizing his primary burden by exhorting his readers to continue in their faith.

The Christians' daily and ongoing behaviour, or "walk", should be consonant with the fact that they have "received Christ Jesus the Lord"[50] (2:6). This immediately suggests that the relationship the believing man has with Christ is no trivial or intermittent matter, but should direct the whole of his life. All the apostle's doctrine and high theology, his practical considerations, and his instructions in

---

[50] We seriously diminish the significance of these words whenever we speak lightly, or without explanation, about 'receiving Jesus'. Receiving Him requires faith in His work as the Christ and obedience to Him as Lord (#3.1.2.).

biblical morality that we find in this letter are designed to promote and sustain consistent and comprehensive Christian living.

Paul was well aware that the deepest motivation in any person's life is his religious commitment, that is, his faith. The nature of his religious convictions will ultimately be expressed in all that a man does. This is true whether he be a theist, a polytheist, or an atheist. Central to the Christian's conduct is his belief that sinful men can only be reconciled to a holy God through the death of Jesus Christ; and that his behaviour should be motivated by this belief and guided by his obedience to Him as his Lord. This is a fundamental, religious 'point of beginning' and it determines, or should determine directly or indirectly, all that the believer thinks and does.

Being concerned that his readers behave in a manner consistent with their faith, and in accord with their acceptance of Christ Jesus as Lord, the apostle, having written this exhortation (2:6-7), immediately reminds them of the nature and the remarkable qualities of their association with Him. He directs their attention in the following verses to the sufficiency they have in Christ – "in Him you are made full" (2:10) – having been "buried with Him in baptism" and "raised with Him through faith" (2:12), and having "all … trespasses" forgiven (2:13). We must consider what these things entail, but a cursory glance must give the believing reader the sense that Paul is writing about matters of great significance that ought to have a salutary effect upon the Christian. There is nothing said here that we can trivialize or neglect without serious impoverishment. There are fundamental truths in these verses that must be understood, believed, embraced, and consciously allowed to affect every aspect of our thinking if we are to act appropriately in all things.

Having raised the question of the Christian's "walk" or behaviour that is grounded in his beliefs, Paul then proceeds to introduce the readers to the further implications of their faith for *philosophy* (2:20-3:4), *morals* (3:5-17), *social life* (3:18-4:1) and *evangelism* (4:2-6) that Christian praxis must incorporate, even as our beliefs inform and influence all these facets of human experience. Our faith is not a mere addition to a life established upon other principles, or only a religious supplement to that which we are already accustomed to think and to do. Our conversion involves a re-evaluation and reorientation of every aspect of our existence. Genuinely receiving Christ Jesus as our Lord will leave nothing unchanged.

Inevitably, a man's religious commitment will subconsciously influence his life. But, as Christians, we ought also to consciously, intelligently, and deliberately incorporate our faith in all our thinking, saying, and doing. This should make our philosophy, morals, and social life unique in this world, as unique as the Christian religion itself, distinguishing us from other people. Moreover, because this operating principle demands religious consistency, we are not able to accept without question any of the theories and practices devised by non-Christian philosophy, morality, and sociology, these being necessarily inconsistent with our faith. As difficult as this may be to avoid, and although we often willingly or unwillingly are caught up in compromise, to incorporate non-Christian concepts into our own philosophy and way of life entails a deleterious, if not a fatal accommodation of error (cf. I Corinthians 3:18-19).

It is not surprising then, that Paul bases the exhortation in these verses (2:6-7) upon his previous statements concerning the conversion and salvation of the Colossians. In effect, he is doing little more here than to urge them to continue as they began, building on the foundation already laid in their lives, or, in other words, to live consistently with "the word of the truth of the gospel" (1:5) that they had heard and received. What we have considered as the 'three dimensions of salvation' (#1.) provides the background and substance of all that follows. Hence, we find in 2:6-7 that Paul picks up earlier themes and incorporates them into this exhortation:

1. The "Lord Jesus Christ" (1:3) as pre-eminent in creation and in the church (1:15-18) has been reintroduced here as the one "received" (2:6) – and He is to be received as nothing less!

2. The importance of "walking worthily of the Lord" (1:10) is re-emphasized and commanded in the imperative "walk in Him" (2:6) – and this imperative demands obedience.

3. It is implied that "bearing fruit in every good work" (1:10) must result from being "rooted ... in Him" (2:7) – and this requires divine intervention that cultivates moral values in life.

4. Seeing "the steadfastness of (their) faith" (2:5), the apostle was confident that they were "stablished in (the) faith" (2:7) – their trust in Christ, and their knowledge of and confidence in Christian truth were evident and essential.

5. Having reminded them of the things they had "learned of Epaphras" (1:7), he advised them to continue "as (they) were taught" (2:7) – their faith was informed and is to be continually informed by the apostolic gospel.

Moreover, Paul was not only aware that in Christ "are all the treasures of wisdom and knowledge hidden" (2:3), and that He is, therefore, the ultimate source of all understanding, but he was also convinced of the "steadfastness" of his readers' faith in Christ (2:5). Christ, then, is genuinely trustworthy; and the Colossians genuinely trusted in Him. It is just this relationship between Christ and the Christian man that will transform human behaviour. "Therefore", Paul continues confidently, "as you received Christ Jesus the Lord, so walk in Him".

In other words, all things necessary for their Christian advancement were in place. So, Paul could write of the Colossian Christians, "In Him you are made full" (2:10). In other words, they needed nothing in addition to Christ for effective Christian living in time and eternity. The apostle similarly assured the Ephesians that God has "blessed us with every spiritual blessing in the heavenly places in Christ" (Ephesians 1:3).

NOTE: We might suggest, then, that Paul's purpose here is not to explain to his readers how they might obtain more, but how they might appreciate, engage with, and live according to all that they already have in Christ, as genuine Christian men and women. For an effective life of faith, we should not be confused about this.

But if we are to take the exhortation of 2:6-7 seriously – as every earnest Christian will want to do – we must look at it carefully to discover precisely what it requires of us. What, for example, does it really mean to receive Christ, and how are we to "walk in Him"? I suggest that there are *four aspects of this exhortation* that we should consider.

3.1.1. The Moral Obligation

We would suggest that what we have here in the words "walk in Him" (ἐν αὐτῷ περιπατεῖτε, 2:6) is more than advisory; it is obligatory for all those who have received Jesus as "the Lord". Being an imperative, we should respond actively in obedience, and obedience requires knowledge of what our Lord requires of us. We should proceed, in other words, with *an informed sense of duty*.

Elsewhere the apostle John explains that there are privileges attached to having "receiving Christ" (2:6) that confer the right to become the "children of God" (ὅσοι δὲ ἔλαβον αὐτόν, ἔδωκεν αὐτοῖς ἐξουσίαν τέκνα θεοῦ γενέσθαι, John 1:12), or, that is, to be assimilated into God's family. And as the Bible makes abundantly clear, there are countless benefits both in time and in eternity for all those who become 'family members' with their Creator. Among these advantages, not the least is that becoming the "children" of God involves a regeneration ("which were born ... of God", ἐκ θεοῦ ἐγεννήθησαν, John 1:13) that must issue in an evident transformation in character and consequently in more acceptable behaviour. It is not, we might say, only adoption (Ephesians 1:5) that we receive – which alone is wonderful enough! – but rebirth as well (John 3:3).

Therefore, the benefits of becoming one of God's children – being adopted – are inseparable from the obligation of appropriate and compatible conduct – being born again.

If our salvation offered us only forgiveness for our failures, but gave us no divine assistance to change our ways, then we could hardly expect those who are forgiven to do anything other than continue to live unreformed in their corrupt, sinful, and guilty ways. But forgiveness is always given together with the grace of sanctification that subsequent to our conversion we might grow in godliness (II Peter 1:3), living for the glory of God.

The privilege of receiving Christ, then, is not without its attendant responsibility, and it is this responsibility that concerns the apostle here in Colossians. Those who have "received" Him, he implies, are not only able, but are also *morally obliged* to "walk in Him". Or as John explained, "He that says he abides in Him ought himself also to walk even as he walked" (I John 2:6). There is this inescapable "ought" – this obligation – in Christian living! It is certainly to our advantage to meet the requirements involved, but it should be our ambition to do so primarily because our Lord asks it of us. And Paul, in effect, is explaining how it is to be done in all that follows in this letter. Our obedience should be an informed and intelligent response to the will of God.

3.1.2. The Primary Response

Although we do well when we invite unbelievers to 'receive' Christ that they might share in the benefits of being Christian, we may be doing them little good if we fail to explain what this involves and how it is to be done. The modern mood seems to demand that we make Christian conversion as easy, as inoffensive, and as 'user friendly' as possible, so little use is made of biblical terms that might outrage our hearers. It is easier to suggest that others 'receive Jesus' or 'ask Him into their hearts' than that they should repent and believe. Paul knew that preaching "Christ crucified" would be deemed by some to be scandalous, and by others to be stupidity (I Corinthians 1:28). It always has been and always will be! Nevertheless, the first readers of this letter to the Colossians had only received Christ because they understood that they were reconciled to God because He has "made peace through the blood of the cross" (1:20). And these are confronting concepts that offends many.

So, although we will seek gently, lovingly, courteously, and winsomely to preach the gospel, we recognize that there is no way we can do so without giving some offence. But I would suggest that one thing we must do to avoid unnecessary resentment when we invite others to 'receive Christ', is to carefully and clearly explain to them what it really means to do so. Then we might hope that, by the grace of God, they will respond, not only in repentance and faith, but also with conviction and understanding – as well as with informed hope and anticipation.

Therefore, we need to notice – and to make clear to others, especially to those we wish to see converted to our faith – that there are at least *three things* involved in the genuine and effective act of 'receiving' Christ that gains the privilege of becoming a child of God – an accepting, an acknowledging, and an appreciating:

- **First**, accepting Christ's teaching.

  Jesus said that the person who rejects Him does not receive His "sayings" (John 12:48). If Christ is to be accepted, then His teachings must also be received *as authentic*.

  Any man who claims to have received Christ, or to be a Christian, and rejects His teaching or deliberately attempts to modify it for his own purposes – which amounts to the same thing – is deceiving himself, and endeavouring to deceive others. Moreover, if he truly receives Christ – and no other – as His Saviour and Lord, then he receives Him as the one "in whom all the treasures of wisdom and knowledge are hidden" (2:3). Therefore, it would be incongruous and an act of folly if he were then to ignore His instructions.

  This further involves accepting Christ's teaching *as being of truly divine origin*.

  Our Lord claimed, "I spake not from myself; but the Father which sent me, He has given me a commandment, what I should say, and what I should speak" (John 12:49). And He explained concerning the content of His words, "My teaching is not mine, but His that sent me" (John 7:16). His ministry was *authentic* because of its *divine origin*.

  Moreover, our Lord stated clearly that if any man is reluctant to accept His words as the words of God, the problem was essentially volitional, for He said, "If any man is willing to do (the Father's) will, he shall know the teaching, whether it be of God, or whether I speak from myself" (John 7:17).[51]

---

[51] There are few who reject Christ because they *do not* understand; most reject Him because they *will not* understand.

If anyone is reluctant to follow our Lord's teaching, either by open disobedience or by subtly impugning or distorting His words as they are recorded in the scriptures, he is not willing to obey God. And it is inconceivable that such a person has sincerely "received Christ Jesus" as his "Lord" (2:6).

Our Lord's teaching defines who He is; specifying the capacity in which He is to be received.

- **Second**, acknowledging Christ's authority.

Christ also insisted that the person who received Him also received the One who sent Him (John 13:20). He came in His "Father's name" and the people did not receive him (John 5:43). Ministering in the Father's name was to minister with the Father's authority, acting as His true representative. By rejecting Jesus Christ, therefore, the people withstood the divine authority with which He taught and acted, failing to understand the person He is and the supremacy of His position in the economy of God. Because of their intellectual and moral blindness, they were unable to see that He was "full of grace and truth" (John 1:14).

Implicit in receiving Christ is submission to His divine authority, and the authority of His Father. His teaching is not a matter of opinion, it is not one way of thinking among others, and it is not susceptible to changing circumstances; and His word is not merely advisory. We may find His teaching both pleasing and convincing, but we must not hold it to be authoritative for this reason, for that would be to make it only a secondary authority, and subject to our own evaluation. Rather, we should accept His teaching as authoritative because of the intrinsic worth of His person and because of the nature of the commission He received from His Father. And this, I suggest, is perfectly reasonable!

Christ is to be trusted and obeyed, and this is only possible when His teaching and His word are available and irrefragable.[52]

To suggest that receiving Christ is to accept both the truth of His teaching and the divine authority by which He taught is not to make the receiving an impersonal or merely academic matter. But it is to define the nature of the personal response we are to make when we receive Him. We must accept Him for all that He is. Paul made this matter clear enough here in Colossians. It is "Christ Jesus the Lord" (2:6) to whom

---

[52] This makes it imperative that we defend the inspiration, infallibility, and eternal authority of the Christian Bible. If we do not, then our Lord's teaching – and we ourselves! – will be lost in the seething fog of human opinions.

we must respond. This is the Jesus who is rightly titled "Christ" and truly designated "the Lord".

Here the term "Lord" without doubt would have carried in Paul's mind direct reference to Jehovah, the God of the Old Testament. Therefore, the Jesus we are to "receive" is the One who is Himself God and who rightly reigns as the Messiah King, the Christ. He, as God, speaks from omniscience and His word cannot be questioned; and as He acts in omnipotence, the efficacy of His work cannot be doubted. Therefore, receiving Him is a response of *obedience* to His word and *faith* in His work, and this is an intensely personal and profoundly meaningful acceptance of Him as supreme.

- **Third**, appreciating Christ's person.

This receiving, then, is not some inscrutable experience devoid of understanding, neither is it merely an emotional response. Far less is it some inexplicable blending of His being with ours in ontological fusion, and certainly not a realization of our own supposed participation in deity. On the contrary, it is an intelligent appreciation of all that Jesus Christ is, an acceptance of the truth of His teaching and a willing response in obedience to do all that He as sovereign God and King asks of us. It is to trust Him as the only trustworthy person to whom we can ultimately turn for true understanding and eternal salvation.

Nevertheless, we would be seriously mistaken if we were to think that acceptance of Christ's teaching and obedience to His word are merely an intellectual exercise that only requires a measure of learning. Indeed, learning is vital and the teaching of the gospel is imperative (1:28). But the teaching must never be 'disembodied', that is, never separated from the Teacher.[53] Just because the teaching is all about the Teacher – He being both the subject and the object of it – then the appropriate learning should result in an ever-increasing appreciation of and love for the Teacher Himself. We should, then, not think of receiving only the teachings and words of our Lord, but of receiving Him in person. The gospel teaches us, *inter alia*, of the love of God in Christ for His people, and we should thereby learn to love Him because He first loved us (I John 4:19). Both learning from His teaching and obedience to His word are in danger of being reduced respectively to the superciliously erudite and the nominally perfunctory in the absence of genuine love for Christ Himself.

---

[53] And this, I fear, happens so easily and so quickly when the Bible is studied as an obscure, ancient text, and subjected to faithless, critical analysis. Then all too often Jesus is reduced to an historical enigma, to be examined, not received!

NOTE: We would conclude from these three aspects of receiving Christ that it involves – indeed, demands – the comprehensive reciprocation of all that we are: our *cognitive* response in accepting His teaching, our *conative* response in obedience to His word, and our *affective* response to His love. This, perhaps, reflects the wholehearted response God has always required, "And you shall seek me, and find me, when you shall search for me with all your heart" (Jeremiah 29:13).

3.1.3. THE CONTINUING RELATIONSHIP

Earlier in this letter, Paul wrote of his prayerful concern for his readers that they be "filled with the knowledge of His will in all spiritual wisdom and understanding, to walk worthily of the Lord unto all pleasing" (1:9-10). And as we examined briefly, in his writings the apostle leaves us in no doubt concerning what he considered to be characteristic of such behaviour (#1.2.2.).

We also saw that he believed that "walking worthily" required four things of the believer: bearing fruit in every good work, increasing in knowledge of God, being strengthened with power unto all endurance and longsuffering, and giving thanks (1:10-12, #1.2.3.). Paul's emphasis there is on the *character or disposition* that must be found in the Christian if he is to walk before God as he ought. These being subjective matters, and knowing that no one is yet perfect in Christ, the apostle does not "cease to pray" (1:9) that his readers might always be appropriately "filled" unto this end.

But now, still concerned about the believer's "walk" or behaviour, Paul turns to another matter (2:6-7). It is one thing to consider the necessary changes in personal character that are required for worthy Christian conduct, but it is another to understand how and upon what basis such changes might be made. And as the apostle now makes clear, such changes in character are not self-induced, or ultimately dependent upon external disciplines, but are the result of God's gracious assistance.[54]

Therefore, the apostle urges the Christian to "walk in Him" (ἐν αὐτῷ περιπατεῖ τε, 2:6). This implies that his behaviour, or "walk", is to be determined by his relationship with Christ; and this relationship is the immediate result of the reconciliation that Christ secured for His people through His atoning death

---

[54] This is not to suggest that personal and external disciplines are of no value in Christian development – far from it! But it is to suggest that such disciplines are but instrumental, whereas the source of genuine change is the grace of God.

(1:20-21). *And it is most important that we understand that the dynamic for change in character is to be found in this relationship.*

Paul refers succinctly to the relationship we have with our Lord as being "in Him", and elsewhere as being "in Christ", or with some other equivalent phrase. The apostle does not use this expression much in this letter to the Colossians, although it is frequently found in his other writings.[55] But it does occur here in *three significant places*, and it should help us to understand its meaning in 2:6 if we consider them. I comment briefly, then, on these three occurrences – and only on these three, as they are immediately relevant – that we might gain some appreciation of the thoughts that may have been in Paul's mind when writing to these early believers:

- **First**, "in whom we have our redemption" (1:14).

  It is "in Christ" that we have our redemption (1:14). This simply implies that Christ in His own death paid a ransom for our deliverance from judgement and condemnation, thereby securing forgiveness for the sins of His people. And this involved being "delivered ... out of the kingdom of darkness, and translated ... into the kingdom of his dear Son" (1:13). To be "in Christ" is then, among other things, to be a redeemed member of the divine commonwealth (cf. Philippians 3:10), citizens in the eternal kingdom.

  This, surely, is highly significant for our behaviour! We are to live as men and women for whom Christ died, whose sins have been forgiven, and who now stand willingly under His authority as our King. This demands sensitivity to the repulsiveness of all godless evil and a sense of responsibility in His service. It is to recognize that we are no longer our own, having been "bought with a price", and therefore, under the moral obligation to "glorify God" in our body (I Corinthians 6:20). It is to avoid all disloyalty in God's kingdom and to conduct ourselves meaningfully as the subjects of the Almighty Lord. We were "servants of sin", but are now "servants of righteousness" (Romans 6:17-18).

- **Second**, "in Him you are made full" (2:10).

  Paul explains that "in Him" we are "made full" (2:10). This surely may be taken to mean that we are to be brought to our full human potential through our relationship with Him. The apostle writes

---

[55] See, in particular, Ephesians 1:3-14 where Paul uses this expression "in Christ" – or the equivalent "in Him", "in whom", "in the Beloved" – some eleven times in reference to the relationship and the benefits Christians have as a result of their association with Him.

elsewhere, for example, of God's people being filled with righteousness, joy, peace, goodness, and knowledge (Romans 8:4, 15:13-14), all as a result of His redeeming grace. And he makes the most remarkable assertion in Ephesians 3:19 that through knowing the love of Christ we "might be filled unto all the fullness of God" – and this, I suggest, seems to imply at least that he would have us enjoy all that embracing divine love imparts to our lives.

However, there is a particular relevance in the comment about being "made full" at this point in the Colossian letter. The apostle is discussing here the deceitfulness of human philosophy that is built upon the "traditions of men" (2:8). That way of thinking leaves man ignorant and confused. But the corrective for this nescience is to be found in Christ Himself. In Him "all the fullness was pleased to dwell" (1:19, cf. 2:9), and in Him "are all the treasures of wisdom and knowledge hidden" (2:3). He is the source – in His eternal being, in His incarnation, in His life, in His teaching – of true philosophy. He is "the truth" (John 14:6).

Here in 2:10 Paul appears to be referring back to his prayer for his readers that they might be "filled with the knowledge of His will in all spiritual wisdom and understanding" (1:9). How else could they avoid the deceptive reasoning of the false teachers? How else could they find and develop a true philosophy of life? Such sound thinking must be drawn from Christ Himself though divine revelation and the guidance of God's Spirit. True knowledge is essential for correct behaviour. We cannot live as our Lord desires if we continue in ignorance or confusion. The apostle says this directly in Colossians 1:9-10, where he explains that being so filled will result in walking "worthily".

The apostle explains elsewhere that Christ is "made unto us wisdom from God" (I Corinthians 1:30), in whom we might escape "the wisdom of this world" (I Corinthians 3:18-19). Therefore, he exhorted the Philippians, "Have this mind in you, which was also in Christ Jesus" (τοῦτο φρονεῖτε ἐν ὑμῖν ὃ καὶ ἐν Χριστῷ Ἰησοῦ, Philippians 2:5).

And what could be more significant for our behaviour than this access to the mind of God?

• **Third**, "in whom you were also circumcised with a circumcision not made with hands" (2:11).

Here Paul is clearly referring, I suggest, to Deuteronomy 10:16, 30:6 and Jeremiah 4:4, where Moses and the prophet write about the circumcision of the "heart". Jeremiah was concerned that "all the house of Israel (were) uncircumcised in heart" (Jeremiah 9:26), and in this, as Ezekiel observed, they had found companionship and common worship with the alien nations (Ezekiel 44:7). This indicates that these Old Testament prophets were well aware that formal association with the people of the covenant, marked by physical circumcision, was of no avail where there was no inner life of godliness, no concern for covenant obedience, no circumcision of heart. This change of heart was essential – and a change of heart for which man is responsible (Deuteronomy 10:16), but that only God is able to make (Deuteronomy 30:6).

Ezekiel writes of this God-given change of heart: "A new heart also will I give you, and a new spirit will I put within you: and I will take away the stony heart out of your flesh, and I will give you a heart of flesh" (Ezekiel 36:26). Only those who benefit from this are the true people of God.

Paul also understood this principle, writing, "He is not a Jew which is one outwardly; neither is that circumcision, which is outward in the flesh: but ... circumcision is that which is of the heart, in the spirit ..." (Romans 2:28-29). Therefore, he explained that it is necessary – and possible – for Christians to "walk in newness of life" (Romans 6:4).

It is sufficient for our purpose here to point out that in Colossians 2:11 the apostle takes up this Old Testament terminology, together with all it signifies, to explain that the Christian is "circumcised with a circumcision not made with hands" as a result of being "in Christ". The implication is that if we are "in Christ" we will enjoy the spiritual regeneration that disposes us to keep the covenant requirements, obey God's law, and manifest an improving morality in life. Again, the significance of this for our behaviour is obvious!

We will return to this notion of "circumcision not made with hands" below (#3.2.2.2.).

NOTE: To be "in Christ" implies, then, at least these three things:

1. That we have a place in the kingdom of God by virtue of our redemption, *this providing the eternal context for a worthy life.*
2. That we have access to true knowledge, wisdom, and understanding in Him, *this providing the intellectual capacity for a worthy life.*
3. That we have a regenerate heart, that is, a change of disposition, *this providing the moral composure for a worthy life.*

This "walking in Him", then, is not to be considered as some mystical rapport, or a blending of our being with the risen Christ, although those who do so walk are in the most intimate relationship with Him (cf. Matthew 28:20, John 14:16-17, 20, 17:20-21, Hebrews 13:5). Rather, it is intelligent behaviour that reckons with all that our redemption in Christ has secured for us. At least part of this is the sum of the benefits mentioned above – redemption, knowledge, and regeneration. These alone, in a perfectly reasonable manner, should result in the total transformation of the way we conduct our lives. Our deportment should reflect our position in God's kingdom, the knowledge of the truth that we have in our Saviour, and the gracious, moral change that He has wrought in our hearts. Having then a moral obligation to "walk in Him", we should give serious attention to such matters.

3.1.4. THE PROVISION FOR DEVELOPMENT AND CONFIDENCE

We have suggested that the subjective changes in the lives of Christians – the regeneration of the "heart" – which result in walking worthily of the Lord, arise from the benefits they receive through the reconciled relationship they have with God "in Christ". We know that being no longer "alienated and enemies" (1:21), we are free to enjoy these benefits of His grace. However, to give confidence to his readers Paul further assures them they are "rooted and are being built up in Him, and are being established in the faith as they were taught". Although, as we have seen, they were being unsettled by erroneous teaching, they were well positioned to continue in their faith, not in stuttering uncertainty, but "abounding in thanksgiving" (2:7).[56]

It is most meaningful that the true Christian has been "rooted" and "is being built up in Him" (ἐρριζωμένοι καὶ ἐποικοδομούμενοι ἐν αὐτῷ, 2:7). The tenses of these two verbs are significantly different, the first past perfect and the second present continuous. They imply that there is a completed and established planting whereby a man has been "rooted" in Christ, and subsequently there is an ongoing "being built up" in Him. This is the result – and is, at least in part, the purpose – of the "in Christ" relationship (#3.1.3.). The metaphors used here, taken from the gardening and the construction industries, seem to suggest that He is both the source of their nourishment and also the guarantor of their growth and development. Both our fruitfulness and our stability are dependent upon Him.

The use of these metaphors need not surprise us. In the Gospel records of our Lord's teaching, we find that He refers to His words as "seed" that has been "sown in (the) heart" (Matthew 13:18ff.) and that He looks for "much fruit" from His

---

[56] It is of interest that when Paul mentioned how he prayed for his readers that they might "walk worthily of the Lord" (1:10), he explained his concern by adding four following phrases (1:10-14, see #1.2.3.). Now, having instructed his readers to "walk in Christ" (2:6), he similarly adds four explanatory phrases – "having been rooted ... being built up ... being established ... abounding in thanksgiving" (2:7). In both places, he concludes with a reference to Christian thanksgiving. This thanksgiving is an essential concomitant of genuine faith (cf. Ephesians 5:20, I Thessalonians 5:18).

disciples (John 15:8). Then He also assures us that He will build His church, and none shall "prevail against it" (Matthew 16:18).[57]

But in what sense are the words "rooted" and "built up" to be understood, and how are such things accomplished in the lives of God's people? Paul explains, I suggest, in the following words – "and established in the faith, even as you were taught" (καὶ βεβαιούμενοι τῇ πίστει καθὼς ἐδιδάχθητε, 2:7). In effect, the apostle is saying that having been rooted in Christ and being built up in Him are the result of, or are concomitant with being established or confirmed in the Christian faith. The apostle, it seems, is re-emphasizing and further explaining his concern for his readers that they "continue in the faith, grounded and steadfast" (1:23, #1.3.2.3.4.).

This being "established in the faith" may refer, as some suggest, to the development of the inner, personal faith or the trusting of the believers – hence they translate τῇ πίστει here, "your faith". But it seems to me more likely that "the faith", Christian truth, is in view. Paul's immediate concern was that the Colossians be able to withstand the "persuasiveness of speech" and false "philosophy" (2:4, 8) of the heretics among them, who were assailing the teachings of the Christian faith. His readers were in danger of being taken captive by false ideologies. This problem could only be resolved through the consolidation of the true believers' knowledge and understanding of good doctrine. By adding the words "as you were taught" (2:7), the apostle appears to be referring to the teaching the Colossians had, at the beginning, "learned of Epaphras", which had received his own apostolic approval (1:7). It was in this instruction in "the word of the truth" (1:5), in the teachings of Christian beliefs, that they needed to be increasingly established, and through it to be nourished and built up.[58]

We might say, if anyone is not growing in confidence *in the teaching*, then he is not being built up *in the faith*.

It was imperative that these young believers in Colossae not be uprooted and removed from the very source of their nourishment and development, the biblical doctrines of the apostolic gospel. Just the opposite was required – that they be "established in the faith", that is, in Christian beliefs. It was essential in such circumstances, and as Paul in fact prayed for them, that they be found "increasing in the knowledge of God" (1:10). And their growing confidence in the teaching would have overflowed in "abounding ... thanksgiving" (2:7), for we ought indeed

---

[57] And Paul makes a similar reference to these notions in I Corinthians 3:9.
[58] No doubt, personal trust in God would be strengthened through a better understanding of the doctrines of the faith. But the point here is that the Colossians *themselves* were being confirmed, or reassured, in the truth of the gospel message and in their knowledge of Jesus Christ.

to be thankful for the all truths of the gospel that we learn, for they all contribute to our maturation.

The word Paul uses here for 'establish' (βεβαιόω) is of interest. It appears to have been used in ancient legalese of guaranteeing or validating a document, contract, or title. And it and its cognates seem at times to have something of this meaning in the New Testament. For example:

1. It is explained in Romans 15:8 that Christ was made a "minister ... that He might confirm/establish the promises made to the fathers". It is, in other words, our Lord Himself who guarantees that God's promises will be kept (cf. II Corinthians 1:20).
2. And in I Corinthians 1:6, Paul wrote that the "testimony of Christ was confirmed/established among you". He is probably referring here to the apostolic ministry that confirmed or guaranteed our Lord's teaching for the Christian community (cf. I John 1:1-4).
3. Then we read that the truth about Christian salvation "which having at the first had been spoken through the Lord, was confirmed/established unto us by them that heard Him, God also bearing witness with them by signs and wonders and powers" (Hebrews 2:3-4). And the implication of this is that our Lord's teaching was further validated for His church by the original apostolic testimony, which was itself authenticated by their miraculous signs and wonders.

We might infer from these references that both the Old and the New Testament are ultimately validated by our Lord Himself, and subsequently by the apostles, in and through their teaching and life. It is in this context that the truth and the authority of the Christian gospel, of the Christian faith, are guaranteed – through Christ's ministry and the apostles' witness.

However, Paul's concern in Colossians 2:7 is somewhat different. It is that the *Christians themselves*, in distinction from the *Christian faith*, be established or confirmed. We would immediately suggest here that the former is very much dependent upon the latter. The doctrines may be sure enough, but our own grasp of them most insecure! We, as Christians, cannot be confident about or confirmed in our beliefs if there is no guaranteed word from God that is itself authenticated by faithful witnesses, and to which word we have access. There can be no other adequate authority to which we can turn to guide us into the truth, so that we may be assured that we are truly rooted in and being built up in Christ. Christ's own word, through the Christian scriptures, alone supplies the required objective means for our nourishment and strengthening.

The author of the letter to the Hebrews expressed a similar concern for the Christians to whom he ministered. They also were in danger of being "carried away by diverse and strange teachings" and, as a consequence, of not having their "heart ... established/confirmed by grace" (Hebrews 13:9).[59] To avoid this disaster they were urged to "remember them ... which spake unto (them) the word of God" and to "imitate their faith" (Hebrews 13:7). Again, confidence in believing is directly linked to hearing and believing the word of God.

Paul, here in Colossians, seems to be suggesting that we are nourished and built up as we draw upon the truths of the gospel, "the treasures of wisdom and knowledge" (2:3), that are hidden in Christ and to which we have access as a result of our redemption, reconciliation, and the regeneration of our mind, and through the apostolic message.

It is of the utmost importance to maintain the teaching of the truth, "to contend earnestly for the faith which was once for all delivered unto the saints" (Jude 3), that Christians might mature and be strengthened. Without this, it would no longer be possible to "walk in Him" as we ought and behave in a manner well-pleasing in God's sight. The apostolic gospel is integrated, cohesive, and sufficient. There was, therefore, no reason for the Colossians to waver in their beliefs, or be distracted by misguided, philosophical speculators.

Nevertheless, Paul evidently believed it was necessary to warn his readers about the danger that they, or members of their congregation, be taken captive by false philosophy (2:8). There are deceptive concepts and specious nuances of which we should all beware.

◆

---

[59] These Christians were not faced with the same deceptive philosophical ideologies as the Colossians, but probably with the teaching of some who would convince them to turn back to the sacrificial ways of the Old Testament, failing to realize that our Lord sanctifies His "people through His own blood" (Hebrews 9:12).

3.2. RELIGIOUS PRESUPPOSITIONS (2:8-19)

As I mentioned in the Introduction, there is no certainty concerning the exact nature of the heresy that the false teachers were introducing to the young church in Colossae. Some of its features may be inferred from comments made by Paul in this letter, and some assumptions may be made about the possible influence of the surrounding, contemporary religious and philosophical beliefs, to the extent that these are known. It is commonly held that the apostle was writing to protect the church from a syncretistic blend of Jewish and Gnostic teachings, but opinions differ.

Our curiosity might impel us to find a more definitive description of the heresy, and much scholarly research has been done in this matter. However, I am more concerned to learn from the apostle's advice to the Colossians what he has to say to them that may assist us more generally to distinguish between the truth of the Gospel and *any* distorted theories that might disturb the Church and distress the believers at *any* time.[60] The so-called 'Colossian heresy' was, like all other humanly devised schemes, transient and unstable. Probably it did not last, or, at least, it did not endure in its original form. Therefore, we might assume that it cannot be directly relevant to those who are reading Paul's writings in our times. Nevertheless, the apostle's positive comments about Christ and the gospel are of timeless value for the church in its continuing defence of the truth.

It is also reasonable to assume, human nature being what it is, that something of the disposition and the methodology of those ancient heretics who repudiated the apostolic message and disputed the pre-eminence of Christ, lingers in the hearts of those who reject or modify the Christian faith today. At least, both ancient and modern heretics are of one mind in their opposition to our orthodox belief and seek some means to convince others to reject it. It is this commonality of thinking among anti-Christians everywhere that presents an alternative to Christian thinking that will concern us, as it surfaced in Colossae.

NOTE: In commenting on Colossians 2:8-19 I will be assuming that all the apostle has to say in these verses is primarily intended to advise the readers how to recognize and to avoid the influence of *any* "philosophy and vain deceit" which is "after the traditions of men and the rudiments of the world" (2:8). Or, in a positive sense, how they are to find and maintain a truly Christian mind and Christian understanding.

---

[60] And we might suggest that as he does not give us more information about the Colossian heresy, this more general advice might also have been the apostle's main concern.

3.2.1. The Alternative to Christian Thinking (2:8)

The history of the Church, from its inception until our times, could be considered from a negative perspective as the continuing record of the sufferings of Christian men and women and the chronicle of the constant battle they have had to maintain in conflict with the philosophical attacks that have been and are made upon our beliefs. Interestingly, the intellectual aggression of our opponents has motivated erudite and devout Christian thinkers not only to defend the faith of the founding apostles, but also to assiduously study the Bible to make its message clear, understandable, and significant to generation after generation of believers in constantly changing and diversified cultural and academic environments. The result of their endeavours is, to say the least, impressive, as is evident in the best of a constant profusion of Christian literature! But as long as time continues, this work will remain critical for the survival of the Christian faith.

The battle for the survival of the church in Colossae, about which we are reading, is a microcosm of the great conflict in which the Church universal has been involved subsequently. The parameters of the heresy then being taught to innocent young Christians have varied, changing from time to time and from place to place. Heterodoxy is a multi-headed beast, with chameleonic qualities, that speaks with diverse voices and modifies its colours as ambition and occasion require. But we suggest that the basic fundamentals of the dissension have remained the same from age to age. *The onslaught against us has always disputed the pre-eminence of Christ and the sufficiency of His word and work for the understanding of life and the salvation of mankind.*

There can be no doubt that the preaching of this biblical Christ has deeply offended the assumed intelligence of many who hear it – "for the word of the cross is to them that are perishing foolishness" (I Corinthians 1:18, cf. #2.1.1.1.). Moreover, as the Bible reveals the character of the God we worship, it also exposes, by comparison, the deficiencies of the *word* and the *work* of men and women in this world. Our Lord made this plain enough when He said, "If I had not come and spoken unto them, they had not sin … If I had not done among them the works that none other did, they had not sin" (John 15:22, 24). What He *said* and what He *did* both condemn our words and our works, revealing their sinfulness, and also deeply offend the presumed morality of many who hear about Him. Indeed, for this they crucified Him!

But the non-Christian man continues to protest! Surely, he will say, the thoughts expressed in man's words are not ineffective, and the accomplishments achieved by man's works are not without merit. Therefore, the non-Christian passionately desires such a religion or such a philosophy that enables him to construct his own truth, establish his own system of morality, and to achieve his own salvation – all structured upon his own theories, and endorsing his own endeavours. And in these assumptions, we find the heart of every rebellion against Christianity and every philosophical challenge to our faith. This should not surprise us because we see here nothing more than the spirit of Adam's revolt in the Garden of Eden, when he deliberately rejected the word of God and, in effect, disputed the significance of His work in creation.

Paul, in this letter to the Colossians, challenges these human assumptions. His first salvo is fired at the non-Christian's self-confident philosophy. We note his immediate concerns in this regard in the following:

- **First**, Paul was concerned that believers beware "any one that makes spoil of" others (2:8, βλέπετε μή τις ὑμᾶς ἔσται ὁ συλαγωγῶν). The word used here implies 'taking captive' – as prisoners of war – and suggests that there are those who would ensnare us by their oratory (2:4) and plausible philosophy (2:8), attempting to convince us to join their own cause, bringing us under their dominion. The apostle would not have his readers fall as such slaves of conquest, to be held in bondage not by sword and chain, but by the pseudo-logic and false creeds of men. And who would deny, in the light of the ideological fanaticism of people in all ages, that such bondage is real and typically abhorrent?

  In this, *the motive* of the false teacher is impugned. He is evidently more concerned for his own affairs than for the true well-being of others. He is driven by self-interest – be it fame, fortune, status, or influence. Few would openly admit that they are so driven, and some perhaps may be unaware that they are, as they habitually conceal their deepest desires, even from themselves. But it seems inevitable that eventually they betray themselves either by their disposition, their words, or their actions (Matthew 7:15-16). And it does not surprise us that this attitude is widespread because we find the spirit of it remaining in our own hearts. To repent of it is not only the first step to finding the grace of God to overcome it but the prerequisite to discerning it in others (Matthew 7:3-5). If we are aware of our own weaknesses, we know their evil potential and should beware the same weaknesses in those who would influence us. We passionately desire that both they and we might overcome them!

  In the light of and in contrast to this, it is appropriate that Paul has carefully written of the altruism of his own ministry in 1:24-2:3. He was always willing to acknowledge his own failings (Philippians 3:12-14, I Timothy 1:15), and to make plain his intentions to minister only for the sake of the church and the perfecting of every man in Christ (1:24, 28). *He had no cause but the cause of Christ.*

Avoiding *ad hominem* arguments and without falling into genetic fallacy, we must not be persuaded by philosophical arguments without considering their moral implications and intentions.

- **Second**, Paul was concerned that his readers recognize and avoid any "philosophy and vain deceit, after the traditions of men, after the rudiments[61] of the world" (2:8).

    It is not philosophy[62] as such that is the reason for Paul's concern here. In his epistles – including this letter to the Colossians – he wrote much about the importance of man's use of his mind, and his appreciation of true wisdom and understanding. Moreover, all that he penned is permeated with the most profound, comprehensive, and well-integrated view of the world and human life. He was, we might suggest, an enthusiast for the philosophy that is "according to Christ" (2:8).

    As the apostle sees it, the danger in anthropocentric philosophies generally – and in the teaching of the Colossian heresy in particular – is that they are nothing more than "vain deceit" (2:8) – gigantic human efforts, we suggest, in deception! As it is written (διὰ τῆς φιλοσοφίας καὶ κενῆς ἀπάτης), Paul is identifying such philosophy *as* vain deceit, or – as we might interpret – *as* 'vacuous fraud'. This seems to imply that the apostle saw in the oratory and logic of false teachers a deliberate attempt to deceive people, duping them into becoming their devotees rather than being the disciples of Christ. As other biblical references suggest, they did this, no doubt, by the promise of material wealth (Matthew 13:22), the satisfaction of human desires or lusts (Ephesians 4:22), freedom from the requirements of divine righteousness (II Thessalonians 2:10), and the accommodation of man's sin (Hebrews 3:13).[63]

    Although appearing to be the best of scholarly opinion, such philosophy presents a way of thinking that appeals primarily to the passions or lusts rather than to the intellect. The mind is persuaded so that the cravings might be legitimized. Thus, some of the most brilliant of men in framing their anthropocentric philosophies have conjured up

---

[61] I have more or less retained the older translation of this word, "rudiments", which is now frequently rendered 'elements' or 'elemental spirits'. Sometimes I use the combination "rudiments/elements" mainly for the sake of those reading different translations.

[62] This word 'philosophy' only occurs here in the New Testament. In Paul's day, it might be used to refer to any theory or lifestyle, popular, intellectual, or mystical. That is, it includes more than a reference to the academic discipline of philosophy.

[63] The same word for "deceit" (ἀπάτη) is found in all these verses.

the most fascinating of grand illusions! And we must all acknowledge that all too often a proposition appeals to us more for the license it gives to our desires than to such 'common sense' as we may have.

• **Third**, Paul was concerned that his readers distinguish two mutually exclusive schools of philosophy – those that are "after the traditions of men and the rudiments of the world" on the one hand, and that which is "after Christ" on the other (2:8). The latter stands in a class of its own.

If there is a philosophical genre that produces grand illusions through its deceit, then it is critically important for the Christian, according to his ability, to recognize it for what it is. He must understand, as Paul writes elsewhere, that there is "the wisdom of men" and, in sharp contrast, "the wisdom of God"; and he must appreciate that the former only and inevitably leads those who embrace it to the rejection, the crucifixion, of Christ (I Corinthians 2:5, 7-8).

There is a sense in which a philosophy can be recognized for what it is and its worth assessed by the results it produces. James acknowledges the importance of such an evaluation when he asks who might be a "wise and understanding" person among us, indicating that the wisdom that is "from above" can be distinguished from that which is not, by the moral quality of life it produces (James 3:13-18).

However, here in Colossians, Paul indicates that a different – although complementary – evaluation must be made, not by assessing the end results of someone's philosophy, but by a consideration of the fundamental principles upon which it is grounded. It is, then, proper and wise to ask *whither* some line of thinking might be leading us, but concurrently we should also ask *whence* it is coming.

Therefore, the apostle would have us begin our thinking with this latter distinction in mind – there are philosophies that are based on "the traditions of men and the rudiments of the world" which are to be differentiated from the philosophy that is based upon "Christ" (2:8).

The Christian approaches the problem of knowledge, and of understanding himself and the sphere in which he exists, from the opposite direction to the non-Christian thinker. People always want to postpone the religious question until they have resolved metaphysical, moral, and social issues. But the Bible will not allow us to do this. It demands that we ask and answer the religious question first.

In contrast to the non-Christian thinker, the Christian allows Jesus Christ – as He is revealed to us in the incarnation and through the scriptures – to determine the religious question for him and to provide the definitive answer. With this settled, he then seeks understanding in other areas of life.[64]

The initial religious question asks a man first of all if he is thinking in dependence upon and in obedience to God, or independently of and in disobedience to God. The non-Christian is not willing to face this question at the beginning of his enquiry. He would probably claim a neutral position, and to be reasoning with 'scientific objectivity'. But in doing so, he has deliberately postponed any decision about religious things, believing he has both the ability and the right to establish his philosophy first and then ask, grounding his thinking in his own deliberations, if there is a God at all, and if there is, whether He demands obedience. Only when he has confidence in the validity of his own philosophy, and having made this his criterion, will he give any consideration to the Christian faith.

Paul explains elsewhere that although men know God they neither respect nor depend upon Him, but trusting in their own "reasonings" they turned to idolatry, and consequently fell into all manner of moral corruption (Romans 1:21-13, 28ff.). Here he indicates *whence* human philosophy comes and *whither* it has taken us.

And from this erroneous methodology, together with its erroneous conclusions and disastrous consequences, Christ would redeem us.

We need to look at this a little more carefully.

- **Fourth,** Paul was concerned that his readers be aware of *two principles* that undergird anthropocentric philosophy, "the tradition of men and the rudiments of the world" (2:8).

  We mentioned above that Christian and non-Christian thinkers both strive for knowledge, which includes seeking an understanding of man himself and of the sphere in which he exists. And, I suggest, Paul indicates here that the non-Christian seeks to know himself in reference to "the traditions of men"; and to know the sphere of his existence in reference to the "rudiments of the world". Behind these expressions are two principles that need to be identified, understood, and avoided. They must never be allowed to dominate Christian thinking.

  Those who base their thinking upon these "traditions" and "rudiments" are, in effect, beginning with themselves and their

---

[64] Man, we believe, was created to exist in a living relationship with God. When this relationship was broken, man became a fool, and was plunged into ignorance (Romans 1:21, 28). Therefore, before man is wise enough, or rightly positioned to be able to construct a proper understanding of life once again and behave in an appropriate manner, there must be first a restoration of the relationship with God that has been lost. And this is at the heart of the religious question.

immediate environment. As the *traditions* that interest them are "of men" they demand an inquiry into the accumulation of human thought, the study of the manner in which both their predecessors and they reason within themselves, examining, in other words, the reflections of *self-conscious man*. And as the *rudiments* that interest them are "of the world" they demand an inquiry into their awareness of human surroundings, the study of the circumstances outside themselves, examining, in other words, the reflections of *world-conscious man.*[65]

In a sense, this is inevitable. We, being human, must commence with both our self-consciousness, which I associate here with the "traditions", and also some consciousness of our surroundings, which I associate with the "rudiments". Both press in upon us, demanding our attention, from the moment we begin to think. Both are ineradicable aspects of being human. They are, in effect, the context in which our minds must operate, and they provide the 'data' that we process into our thinking. This being so, it is unavoidable that Christians and non-Christians ponder the same questions, wrestle with the same intellectual conundrums, and have to deal with the same issues in life.

In this, we Christians have much in common with the non-Christian.

What is more, self-consciousness and world-consciousness, we believe, are essential for our knowledge of God Himself. He is not to be found in some intangible, paranormal realm, but in the world that He created for our habitation. The Christian ought not to seek some 'third way', some mystical consciousness, to find God.[66]

It is true to say that as we know God we are enabled rightly to know our world and ourselves. But it is also true that as we know our world and ourselves we are able to know God in whose image we were created and in whose created world we live. This reciprocity is the inevitable result of our being made in God's image and existing in God's world. If we were not self-conscious and world-conscious we would not have the categories of thought or the means whereby we might know our Creator.

---

[65] Secular philosophers have made much of this distinction between self-consciousness and world-consciousness – between the subjective and the objective, the inner world and the outer world, the immanent and the transcendent, the phenomenal and the noumenal. They dispute what may or may not be the relationship between the two. Their reasoning has been erudite and profound, and often recondite. But it frequently seems to have led to some kind of nihilism.

[66] This 'third way' was a feature of ancient Gnostic teaching, and there are those who suggest that some form of Gnosticism may have been influencing the Colossian heretics. This, as we will suggest, may be the problem Paul refers to in 2:18. It is perhaps worth noting that such 'third way' thinking has reentered the churches in our day and is having a devastating effect.

However, having "refused to have God in (his) knowledge" (Romans 1:28), the non-Christian philosopher is obliged to believe either that he is competent to explain all things by himself, or to assume that all things are comprehensively self-explanatory – or, perhaps, both. Alternatively, he might decide that we can know nothing but our self-consciousness, and everything else is lost in obscurity.

In contrast, the Christian, beginning with the same self-consciousness and the same world-consciousness, believes that God alone can truly interpret man and his environment, and acknowledges his dependence upon Him to do so. Therefore, the Christian and the non-Christian diverge in their thinking and in their understanding *from the beginning*, finding different answers to the same questions, to the same intellectual conundrums, and to the same issues in life.

In this, we Christians have nothing in common with the non-Christian.

To put it simply: The non-Christian, at least of *the most consistent kind*, in his self-consciousness and world-consciousness declares that he finds no evidence anywhere for a god of any kind, and then, because he can do no other, he depends only upon himself to make sense out of his existence. But in contrast, the Christian, at least of *the most consistent kind*, in his self-consciousness and world-consciousness declares that he finds nothing but evidence everywhere for a God of the omnipotent biblical kind, and then, because he can do no other, he depends upon this God to make sense of out of all existence for him. In doing so, the true believer acknowledges that "all the treasures of wisdom and knowledge" are to be found in Christ (2:3) – and nowhere else. Christ is his first and his final point of reference.

If we appreciate this distinction between non-Christian and Christian thinking, we will understand Paul's concern that his readers beware of those who would captivate them with their anthropocentric philosophies.

◆

TRADITIONS AND RUDIMENTS

In considering Colossians 2:8 I have thus far suggested some general implications of Paul's words as I have attempted to explain what I consider to be some of the basic principles that distinguish non-Christian from Christian thinking. I have, in effect, been immediately concerned with the two expressions "the traditions of men" and "the rudiments of the world", using them to introduce the concepts of self-consciousness and world-consciousness. Our self-consciousness, what we sense or interpret ourselves to be, is inevitably influenced by "traditions", and traditions incorporate the ideas, values, and practices passed on to us by our predecessors and are intimations of their self-consciousness. And our world-consciousness, what we sense or interpret our environment to be, is inevitably influenced by theories about the "rudiments" or "elements" that we assume to be the fundamental constituents of our 'world', whether these theories come to us from things we are taught or are formulated from our experiences.

Therefore, I would further suggest that our being self-conscious and being world-conscious are constant aspects of our being human in every generation; but our sense of, or the interpretation anyone might give to them, is determined at any given time by variations of tradition and fluctuating theories about the rudiments of life. That is, human awareness is constant, but the traditions and the theories about rudiments are constantly changing. Hence, all people are philosophers in common, but all do not have a common philosophy.

Philosophies – whether of the professional scholar or the common man – are always susceptible to the fickle moods of "traditions" and fluctuating theories of "rudiments". They, and their instability, affect us all in one way or another. It is important, then, for us to have some appreciation of these concepts that we might recognize them and be aware of their influence. So, I have added this extra section, giving some brief thought to the meaning of these technical words, at least as they are used in the Bible.

A. TRADITIONS

Concerning the meaning of this word 'tradition' (παράδοσις), we should note first that in the New Testament, mainly in Matthew and Mark, it is sometimes used with a negative connotation, referring to practices and customs passed down by former generations, and which had at that time assumed a religious authority above the words of scripture (eg. Matthew 15:2-3, Mark 7:8-9). And no doubt there has always been a tendency among us to elevate human traditions above any legitimate mandate they might have in the church. But here we need to remember that such troubling traditions are not to be rejected because of their antiquity, *but because of their heterodoxy*. From such degradation of true religion, we need to be redeemed (I Peter 1:18).

In contrast, Paul commends the Corinthians for holding fast "the traditions, even as (he) delivered them" to the church (I Corinthians 11:2). Similarly, he exhorts the Thessalonians to "hold the traditions" which he had taught them, and to "withdraw ... from every brother" who did not adhere to them (II Thessalonians 2:15, 3:6). There is a distinction here that we must take seriously – seriously enough to stand apart from any who despise or neglect the valid traditions of the Christian faith.

Obviously, then, we must distinguish between unacceptable and acceptable traditions, and it would be disastrous if we were to follow much modern sentiment that rejects all traditions upon the misconceived theory that progress renders everything received from the past otiose, passé, or inadequate, if not irremediably defective. And such, to our impoverishment, is the contemporary mood!

In particular, we should notice in the verses we have cited above, that Paul was insisting that we hold fast to the traditions that he "delivered" unto the churches and that he "taught" others through his words and writings. This implies that there is a continuing imperative in *the true apostolic traditions*, which we ignore at great cost.

However, the imperative in the apostolic tradition is not found in the authority the apostles had been given, as significant and important that this authority is for the church. Rather, it is found in the inherent, original authority, and in the provenance of the traditions that the apostles themselves had been given.

Human traditions – the "traditions of men" (2:8) – originate in human culture and are delivered by the people of one generation to the next, with and without modification. But Paul writes of his unique ministry, "I delivered unto you first of all that which I had received" that, he insisted, was never contrary to but "according to the scriptures" (I Corinthians 15:3ff.). Unless we misunderstand the importance of this, we should remember that he writes elsewhere that "the gospel which (he) preached" he did not "receive ... from man, nor was (he) taught it" – so it was not human tradition! – but it came to him "through revelation of Jesus Christ" (Galatians 1:11-12). And we should also note that the word "delivered" in

I Corinthians 15:3 (παρέδωκα, cf. I Corinthians 11:23) is the verb from which the noun 'tradition' (παράδοσις) is derived. *Therefore, that which was delivered to him by the revelation of Jesus Christ is authentic, authoritative tradition!*

These *apostolic traditions* must indeed be passed on from one generation of men to the next – for this is the preaching of the gospel – but they do not originate in human culture but in revelation from God Himself. *Therefore, they are not only imperative but also immutable.* And as such, they provide the essential prerequisite for a valid Christian philosophy and enable an adequate sense and interpretation of our self-consciousness. Human traditions, whether of some value or not, inevitably vary from time to time in changing circumstances; but the apostolic traditions, originating in the divine, never vary as they are the expression of the mind of God.

We ought, then, to be staunch and unashamed traditionalists – but only of a truly biblical kind!

B. RUDIMENTS OR ELEMENTS

This word "rudiments" or "elements" (στοιχεῖα) is more complicated and somewhat more technical. Coming from a word meaning a 'row' or 'line' – indicating, for example, the setting of posts in a fence, or in reference to a column of soldiers – it was used subsequently to refer to the basic constituent parts that compose the whole – for example, the phonemes of a word, or the elements of a physical substance. It is possibly used in this latter sense in II Peter 3:10, 12.

Like our word 'elements', this word may also be used for the elementary matters taught as an introduction to the principles of some studied discipline. This seems to be its meaning in Hebrews 5:12: "You need that someone teach you the elements of the first principles of the oracles of God". Here the problem was that some had forgotten – or had never really learned – the basics of the Old Testament revelation, and were as a result "without experience in the word of righteousness" (Hebrews 5:13).

However, in 2:8, 20, and in Galatians 4:3 Paul uses this word in the phrase "the rudiments/elements of the world" (τὰ στοιχεῖα τοῦ κόσμου). And here things become difficult! It has variously been suggested that the apostle is referring in these verses to theories about entities as diverse as the preliminary stages of a religious system as in the Mosaic Law (cf. Hebrews 5:13); the physical elements of which the universe is composed (cf. II Peter 3:10, 12); the heavenly bodies as the sun, moon, and stars; or the gods and goddesses the pagans supposed were associated with and thought to regulate these heavenly bodies. And to complicate matters, some suggest that one meaning is given to this phrase in Colossians and another in Galatians.

So extensive is the material and so complicated the discussions about this question that I withdraw from any debate about it here for the want of time and space in these notes. However, I cannot ignore the problem altogether, as it is an important expression in Paul's argument in Colossians, which we seek to understand.

In all the confusion about the various theories concerning the meaning of the words "the rudiments/elements of the world" there seems to be one common factor – the theorists all suggest that they refer to an attempt, whether by Jewish or pagan thinkers, to explain the phenomena of the universe in which we live. Or that they reflect man's struggling with what we have called human world-consciousness. Everyone wants to know how the world came into existence, of what it is made, and what controls it. If we cannot formulate some reasonable answer to these questions, we will be unable to find rhyme or reason for our lives.

Then, once a plausible – or even a specious – theory has been formulated and accepted, it becomes an essential plank in the philosophical platform of those who believe it – and this has far-reaching effects in all that they think and do subsequently. We surely do not have to prove, for example, that the theoretical explanation of the 'elements of the world' proposed by materialistic atheists produces a culture entirely different from any that result from the theory of 'elements' and of the 'world' accepted by Christian theists. Indeed, in our day, the former are openly and actively using their theory to undermine Christian culture! In stark contrast to both are the animistic theories of the causation of multiple spirits or demons, which still determine the morals and the values of millions.

It seems that Paul would have us understand that if we "died with Christ" we should abandon all such anthropocentric interpretations of our environment (2:20).

I suggest that for the Christian the only adequate theory of "the elements" must take into account all that Paul writes in Colossians 1:16-17. By Christ "all things were created in the heavens and upon the earth, things visible and things invisible" and "in Him all things consist." "All things have been created by Him and for Him", and therefore, it is in Him that we find the origin and the purpose of all things. Here is the biblical explanation of the "rudiments/elements". Here, *inter alia*, are the fundamentals of Christian cosmology. Only from this perspective will we have a true sense and adequate interpretation of our world-consciousness.

> **NOTE:** Therefore, we must first turn to Christ, in whom are "all the treasures of wisdom and knowledge" (2:3), to find immutable *traditions*. Then we must also turn to Christ, in whom "dwells all the fullness of the Godhead bodily" (2:9), to gain a true understanding of the *elements*. Then we will be adequately equipped to resist and overcome the persuasive oratory and the deceptive logic of non-Christian philosophy, which is based upon the very dubious "traditions of men" and the indeterminate "rudiments of the world".
>
> And only then will we be able to develop a philosophy that is truly "after Christj" (2:8).
>
> ◆

Obviously, in these brief comments I have avoided many of the technical difficulties involved in Paul's words in 2:8, and I have made no comments about more sophisticated explanations found in many commentaries. But, as mentioned above, I have deliberately done this to concentrate on what seem to me to be the most basic issues so that we can employ these in our own struggle with the anti-Christian philosophies of our day. We all need the necessary intellectual tools – no matter how scholarly we may or may not be – to be able to distinguish as best we can between the wisdom of man and the wisdom of God, and to understand why these are so divergent from each other.

But now we must turn to a consideration of the philosophy that is "after Christ" (2:8). And to do so, we begin by giving thought to *the religious presuppositions* upon which it is built.

3.2.2. The Access to Christian Thinking (2:9-15)

It seems to me to be particularly significant that having raised the spectre of deceitful philosophy Paul does not immediately turn to rational arguments for an apologetic defence of Christian beliefs. There may be a time and place for this, but it is obviously not the apostle's first concern here. Rather, he writes about the personal relationship his readers have with Christ and the "fullness" they have in

Him (2:9-10). And then, perhaps unexpectedly, he makes reference to the biblical ordinances of circumcision and baptism (2:11-12). We might well ask why this is so.

We have suggested that one of the fundamental differences between the philosophy that is "after the traditions of men, after the rudiments of the world" and the philosophy which is "after Christ", is that the former refuses to begin with the religious question and the latter demands that we do (#3.2.1. Third). Now Paul makes his own position in this regard abundantly clear. Having warned his readers to beware those who would take them captive through their persuasive oratory and convincing logic, he does not discuss the false propositions that may have been presented by the Colossian heretics. But he immediately draws attention to Christ, in whom "dwells all the fullness of the Godhead bodily", and to the fact that believers "are made full" in Him "who is the head of all principalities and powers" (2:9-10). In these comments, the apostle explains that both our *Lord as He is in Himself,* and *all that we are intended to be in Him,* are his foremost considerations.

NOTE: These two verses, 2:9-10, are freighted with greater meaning than we mere humans are yet able to comprehend. Nevertheless, they clearly provide the reader with two cardinal principles in Paul's defence of the Christian faith:

As "all the fullness of the Godhead" dwells in Christ, there can be *no other greater than He.*

As the Christian is "made full" in Him, there can be *no other needed than He.*

And with this comprehensive appreciation of Jesus Christ, the apostle Paul begins his philosophy and established his gospel. His thinking is clearly and emphatically Christo-centric.

This Christ-centered approach is not surprising, coming from a man who held that "the word of the cross is to them that are perishing foolishness", who believed that God has "made foolish the wisdom of the world", and who declined to debate with "Greeks" who "seek after wisdom" (I Corinthians 1:18-25). He was "determined" in his ministry "not to know anything … save Jesus Christ and Him crucified" (I Corinthians 2:2). He could hardly, then, begin by accepting the validity of the presuppositions and the methodology of his opponents!

Therefore, the apostle does not directly discuss the "traditions of men" or the "rudiments of the world", as there are far more important things to consider first. So regardless of any oblique references he might make to their ideas, he writes no forthright critique of the heretics' views about those things, or of their religious theories. He simply reminds his readers of the Christ in whom they believe and of the fullness they have in Him.

In other words, Paul begins with God and the religious question.

But how is the apostle able to set aside all the vexed and vexing philosophical questions – which, as we have seen, all men must ask (#3.2.1. Fourth) – that he might consciously and deliberately make his religion, the Christian faith, his starting point? Or, in other words, how does he find adequate presuppositions which provide a basis, or perspective, upon which the cogitative issues of life can be satisfactorily resolved? Or, again, how would he have us access true Christian thinking?

To find an answer to these questions, there are a number of things needing our consideration:

3.2.2.1. Access through Divine Revelation

It was one of Paul's fundamental beliefs that all men everywhere, although they might deny it, actually do know God, but they do not allow this to affect or moderate their thinking. Their problem is that "knowing God, they glorified Him not as God, neither were thankful". They "suppress the truth in unrighteousness" and refuse "to have God in their knowledge". They have no justification for this willful ignorance, because, as he explained, "the invisible things of Him since the creation of the world are clearly seen" (Romans 1:18, 20, 21, 28). Man, in other words, is in one sense capable of knowing God, and he has all the evidence he needs to know Him at least as sovereign Creator. Then, although he knows God, because of the awful implications and obligations this brings upon him, he chooses to expunge such knowledge from his consciousness as best he can. Thus, he leaves himself "without excuse", with a "worthless/unqualified mind" (Romans 1:20, 28), and in another sense incapable of knowing God.

However, as far as the Christian is concerned, there is much more to consider! He discovers truth about God not only in the world in which he lives, as all people should, but also in Christ "in whom are all the treasures of wisdom and knowledge hidden" (2:3). We recognize Him as "the way, and the truth, and the life" (John 14:6), who, as Paul adds, "was made unto us wisdom from God" (I Corinthians 1:30). This recognition is integral to genuine faith in Jesus as Christ the Lord. Not to accept Him as the source from which all truth emanates is to believe in some "gospel other than that which" the apostles preached, if in any 'gospel' at all (cf. Galatians 1:8).

131

But we also accept that our access to an adequate comprehension of the basic facts about God's self-revelation, both in the creation of the world and in the incarnation of Christ, is communicated through the inspired scriptures, the Bible, the Word of God. That is, we believe that God Himself has from the beginning explained the origin of our existence, the degradation of human life, and the possibility of our recovery by speaking "unto the fathers through the prophets" and finally "in His Son" (Hebrews 1:1-2).

Therefore, there can be no doubt that Paul believed his readers had access to the knowledge of Christ through "the word of the truth of the gospel" (1:5) which they had "learned from Epaphras" (1:7), and hence they knew that "all the fullness of the Godhead" dwells in Him "bodily" (2:9). Moreover, he knew that they had been "taught" and were now "rooted and being built up in Him" (2:7), and hence they had been "made full" (2:10) in Him.

Knowledge of and dependence upon Christ are the essential prerequisites for a true and adequate understanding of life, in comparison to which the anthropocentric "traditions of men" and the "rudiments of the world" appear feeble, inconsistent, and inconsequential. There is then, for all those who are of a heart and mind to find it, access to reliable information in the Bible, information that is otherwise inaccessible to human investigation or speculation (cf. #1.2.1.2.).

3.2.2.2. ACCESS THROUGH DIVINE RECONCILIATION

But the problem is far more complicated than finding a reliable source of desperately needed information. From the outset of our considerations, we must also reckon with the serious, subjective impediment of fallen man's blindness to and distaste for the truth.[67] There is serious concern expressed by Christ and the apostles concerning human intellectual impairment (John 12:40, II Corinthians 4:4, I John 2:11), and the inevitability that those who "received not the love of the truth" eventually "believe a lie" (II Thessalonians 2:10-11). Such blindness, Paul indicates, is only overcome when God shines "in our hearts, to give the light of the knowledge of the glory of God in the face of Jesus Christ" (II Corinthians 4:6).

---

[67] This impediment is perhaps a more acute problem in the modern world than it has ever been before. Once men would argue concerning the *nature* of truth, but today it is more likely that they will dispute the *existence* of truth. We seem to be developing a community in which nothing is more socially unacceptable than to claim knowledge of the truth – especially religious truth.

In these verses and elsewhere the Bible suggests that we all suffer this impairment that denies us insight into the truth about God until it is remedied by direct divine intervention.[68]

The significance of this divine intervention for our appreciation of Colossians 2:9-15 needs some explanation, and I suggest the following matters should be considered:

- **First**, the covenant community and the word of God.

  When Paul in his letter to the Colossians mentions "circumcision" and "baptism" (2:10-12) he brings to our attention the whole issue of God's covenant with His people. Circumcision among the Israelites and baptism among the Christians were both indicators of membership in this covenant, of belonging to God's people. Because he describes his readers as those who were "circumcised" in Christ and "buried with Him in baptism" (2:11-12) he, among other things, distinguishes them as a unique people, distinct from all others because of the relationship they have with God. The great and ultimately the only eternal division between the peoples of the whole earth is that between *the covenant keepers* – those who bow to the sovereignty of God, trust in Him, and live in obedience to His law – and *the covenant breakers* – those who defy the sovereignty of God, trust in themselves, and pursue their own purposes.[69]

  One of the primary advantages of being associated with God's people – indeed, of being formally accepted into the community and the congregation of believers – is that in this context we are exposed to and instructed in the Word of God.[70] Moses impressed upon the people of Israel that they were blessed above all other nations not only because the Lord was their God, but also because they had received His "statutes" and "judgements", for therein they would find their "wisdom and ... understanding" (Deuteronomy 4:5-8).

  Subsequently, the faithful in Israel recognized that God's "word (was) a lamp unto (their) feet, and light unto (their) path"; and being upheld by their knowledge of it, they were "not ashamed of (their) hope"

---

[68] When speaking of this, we must not be so arrogant as to imagine or to suggest that as Christians we have somehow been able by our own intelligence, diligence, or goodwill to overcome this blindness and distaste in our own heart and mind. We were as much blinded by "the god of this world" (II Corinthians 4:4) as others and were only delivered from this state by the grace of God.

[69] This is only a formal statement of the difference between these two categories. There is much more to be said, but my purpose here is only to identify them.

[70] And for this reason, it is of the utmost importance, when the people of God are gathered in congregation, that the Bible be read and faithfully and fully explained (I Timothy 4:13, II Timothy 4:1-2). We might say that the church has no greater responsibility!

(Psalm 119:105, 116). God's law gave them both *direction* in life and *confidence* to live.

And many years later Paul explained that the advantage the Jews had enjoyed, "the profit of circumcision", the benefit that others did not have, was "first of all, that they were entrusted with the oracles of God" (Romans 3:1-2). They were privileged and distinguished from others by having, learning from, and becoming wise through the Word of God.

Then, operating within the same covenantal relationship with God, Christians from the Day of Pentecost began and continued "in the apostles' teaching" which informed and directed their "fellowship ... breaking of bread ...and ... prayers" (Acts 2:42). And it needs only to be mentioned here that the apostles grounded all their teaching in the existing Old Testament scriptures (cf. II Timothy 3:14-15). Then by virtue of their unique, God-given apostolic authority and the guidance of the Spirit they received (cf. John 16:13), their teachings were also the word of God, subsequently inscripturated in the New Testament (cf. II Peter 3:16).

Paul's advice to Timothy, a younger man with responsibility in Christian service to the churches, is worth some brief consideration here. The apostle would have him be a "good minister of Christ Jesus, nourished in the words of the faith, and of the good doctrine" (I Timothy 4:6). This was an urgent matter. He knew that there were those in the congregations "desiring to be teachers of the law, though they understand neither what they say, nor the things about which they are so dogmatic" (I Timothy 1:7, μὴ νοοῦντες μήτε ἃ λέγουσιν μήτε περὶ τίνων διαβεβαιοῦ νται, my translation). There was the serious danger in this that people would be led astray from the truth (cf. II Timothy 3:13, 4:3-4).

The apostle also makes it clear how he thought young Timothy might become such a "good minister of Christ". He was to remember the things he had been taught from the "sacred writings which (were) able to make (him) wise unto salvation", having the confidence that "all scripture is inspired by God, and is profitable". Therein he might become "complete, equipped unto every good work" (II Timothy 3:14-17), and so present himself "approved unto God ... correctly handling the word of truth" (II Timothy 2:15).

And we might add, Paul expected that any man who would lead the church would hold "to the faithful word which is according to the teaching[71], that he may be able ... to exhort in wholesome doctrine"

---

[71] A reference, probably, to the apostolic teaching.

(Titus 1:9). In this way "the church of the living God" should be, and be respected as "the pillar and mainstay of the truth" (I Timothy 3:15).[72]

There is, I would suggest, a critically important link between the ministry of the church, the revelation of God in the scriptures, and access to Christian thinking. The "philosophy ... after Christ" (2:8) should be readily and constantly accessible in the churches, through the continuing proclamation, explanation, and application of "the word of the truth of the gospel" (1:5).

- **Second**, the covenant community and the salvation of God's people.

  Membership in the covenant community of God's people is in itself a privilege because it provides the context in which men and women can hear and respond to the Word of God and find the way of truth. But this membership does not in itself guarantee that anyone will believe the truth when it is heard, or obtain the eternal salvation that it offers. For example, the bona fide Israelites who were redeemed from slavery in Egypt in the days of Moses, all the males among them having received the covenant seal of circumcision (Joshua 5:4-5), provoked God, incurred His displeasure, and failed to enter into the Promised Land "because of unbelief" (Hebrews 3:19).

  The subsequent history of Israel contains a painful record of recurring rebellion and apostasy among God's covenant people – despite their access to the word of God.

  Similarly, in the Christian covenant community of the church there are accepted congregational members who are exposed to the truth of God's word but fail to benefit from it. For example, in Samaria, a man called Simon "believed" and was "baptized", and joined the congregation. Nevertheless, Peter declared that he remained "in the gall of bitterness and in the bond of iniquity" and called upon him to repent of his wickedness (Acts 8:13, 22-23).

  And the subsequent history of the Christian church contains a painful record of recurring rebellion and apostasy among God's covenant people – despite their access to the word of God.

  And this brings us back to a point made above (#3.1.3.). There we noted that the Christian's association with God "in Christ" involved being "circumcised with a circumcision not made with hands" (2:11). This, we suggested, referred to the Old Testament insistence upon the necessity of the inward circumcision of the heart of which Moses and the prophets wrote (Deuteronomy 30:6, Jeremiah 4:4, Ezekiel 44:7). We saw that participation in the outward religious ordinance of circumcision

---

[72] And, we might suggest provocatively, not as the 'theatre and the stage of light entertainment'!

and formal membership in the covenant community of Israel were of no enduring value without an inward change of heart wrought by the grace of God.

Circumcision was intended as a "sign" and "seal" for the people of Israel (Romans 4:11), both signifying and securing the promises of God. But all that was promised was only received "by faith working through love" (Galatians 5:6). In fact, Paul is at pains to make it perfectly clear that Abraham – "the father of all them that believe" – was justified by faith *before* he was circumcised, and centuries *before* any of the Mosaic and Levitical laws and rituals were instituted (cf. Galatians 3:16-17).

We would suggest from this that religious ordinances, whether they be of the Old Testament or of the New, may well have didactic value and be gracious indicators of God's promises, but they do not in themselves effect any change in the human heart or moral condition. They are "signs" and "seals" – being of great significance, because they are divine ordinances indicative of God's covenant and grace that invite men to believe – but they are not in themselves means, and have no direct instrumentality.

The matter of greater importance is the "circumcision made without hands" – the subjective ministry of God's grace within a man's soul, creating in him a "new heart" (#3.1.3. Third). Jeremiah – writing about the time when the temple in Jerusalem was destroyed and the Levitical system left in ruins – lamented the uncircumcised state of the hearts of the people of the covenant (Jeremiah 9:26). Therefore, the prophet understood that when God renewed the covenant relationship with His people He would do exactly what He said He would do in Deuteronomy 30:6 – "The Lord your God will circumcise your heart". Jeremiah understood this because God had said, "This is the covenant I will make ... I will put my law within them, and I will write it in their heart", and then "they shall all know me ... for I will forgive their iniquity" (Jeremiah 31:33-34, cf. Hebrews 8:8-12).

There is, as these verses indicate, a critically important link between the forgiveness of iniquity, the changing of the heart, and the knowledge of God. The inscription of God's law upon a man's heart evidently involves not merely a moral reorientation, but a moral reorientation that removes detrimental attitudes that preclude understanding; and that leads to a genuine knowledge of God – then "they shall all know me". In this, they escape their intellectual blindness and obtain access to Christian thinking.

Then the formality of covenant membership becomes genuine communion with God, and all that is signified and sealed by the ordinances of circumcision and baptism is realized in the fulfilment of God's promise.

3.2.2.3. ACCESS THROUGH THE DEATH OF CHRIST

So far, we have discovered that we have access to Christian thinking, and the means to defend ourselves from the deceptive and specious reasoning of anthropocentric philosophers:

- through divine revelation in the Bible,
- through the faithful ministry of the word of God in the church,
- and through the grace of reconciliation and regeneration in our hearts.

And these immense advantages are ours, Paul indicates, because we are "in Him ... made full" (2:10, #3.1.3.).

Now we need to think a little more about Paul's words in 2:11-12 to discover both how these things are activated, and also, in particular, how our hearts are affected, or "circumcised", that we might become positively responsive to the word of God.

We should note that Paul, in effect, is describing the life-changing consequences of Christian conversion in reference to circumcision and baptism. He associates the clause "in Him you are made full" with the following words, "in whom you were also circumcised ... in the circumcision of Christ, having been buried with Him in baptism" (2:10-11). He appears to be explaining that we can know nothing of the fullness that our Lord would have us enjoy without this circumcision and baptism. The language the apostle uses here is technical and difficult, and is variously explained. So, although we should proceed cautiously, the first thing we must take into account is the obvious emphasis upon *Christ's circumcision and Christ's baptism* – not our own personal, individual participation in such rituals. The benefits we have as Christians are, in some manner, the direct result of Jesus Christ's involvement in these very physical religious ceremonies.

This, incidentally, draws our attention to the important gospel fact that we are redeemed and receive the advantages of salvation not through our own work and experience, but through our Lord's unique work and His singular experience. Being "in Him", as Christians, involves us in *His* circumcision and *His* baptism, in both of which action was taken for our benefit. Jesus, obviously, was not circumcised or baptized for His own benefit.

Then, we should also keep in mind that Paul began his defence of the Christian faith with reference to the greatness of Christ's *person* – as "in Him dwells all the fullness of deity ... who is the head of all principality and power" (2:9-10). But now he continues his defence with reference to the greatness of Christ's redemptive *work* – to the "putting off of the body of the flesh, in the circumcision of Christ; having been buried ... in baptism" (2:11-12). The truth of genuine, biblical Christianity is embodied in His person and in His work, and any vindication of our faith must, therefore, always include reference to both. We cannot establish our beliefs and justify our faith – and hence do what we can to safeguard true Christianity itself against the philosophies of men – if we do not have some understanding of and ability to articulate a sound Christology.

Therefore, if we are to understand what the apostle is writing about here, we should be asking why Jesus was circumcised and why He was baptized. Evidently, His circumcision was immediately accepted without question, it being contemporary Jewish practice (Luke 2:21). In contrast, John the Baptist was quite nonplussed when our sinless Lord presented Himself to be baptized, for he was offering baptism "unto repentance" to those who confessed their sins; but Jesus insisted that it be done "to fulfil all righteousness" (Matthew 3:5, 11, 13-15). So, I suggest, in His baptism He declared His intention, to "bare the sin of many" (Isaiah 53:12, Hebrews 9:28).[73]

The principal issues are these:

- **First**, concerning Christ's circumcision.

     The significance of Christ's circumcision was that it identified the Lord as a member of, and incorporated Him into the people of God's covenant. This immediately brought Him "under the law" (Galatians 4:4), and made Him subject to both the blessings and the curses of the covenant (cf. Deuteronomy 27:15ff, 28:2ff).

     And this exposed Him to *the judgement of God*.

- **Second**, concerning Christ's baptism.

     The significance of Christ's baptism was that in it the Lord identified Himself with those people of God's covenant who, knowing they were condemned sinners, were genuinely repentant and looking in faith to God for redemption. He stood in the water of the River Jordan, as it were,

---

[73] Hence the testimony He received from heaven at His baptism identifies Him as the Christ and the Suffering Servant of Isaiah (Matthew 3:17, Psalm 2:7, Isaiah 42:1).

together with those contrite men and women for whom He would die on Calvary's Cross.

And this exposed Him to *the condemnation of God*.

NOTE: It is precisely these two things that make the life and the death of Christ effective in securing our salvation. He took upon Himself our humanity with all its *responsibilities*, and He took upon Himself our sin with all its *consequences*. Nothing else could be done, and nothing else needed to be done for our redemption – and no one else could do it. So, we also need to consider the following:

• **Third**, concerning our participation in Christ's circumcision.

Paul, as I have suggested, has in mind here *Christ's own circumcision*, which He suffered as a child.[74] Some would read "the circumcision of Christ" as a direct, if metonymical, reference to Christ's crucifixion. If so, one must wonder why Paul chose to use this word in this way. But it makes good sense that he is speaking of our Lord's childhood circumcision if we keep in mind that this made Him liable to the judgement of God – which, indeed, was necessarily prerequisite to and eventually led to His crucifixion (cf. Matthew 20:28). And, through its redemptive purpose, this secures for us the "circumcision not made with hands" (2:11).

But here we must consider an interpretative problem. The meaning of the words "in putting off of the body of the flesh" (ἐν τῇ ἀπεκδύσει τοῦ σώματος τῆς σαρκός, 2:11) is much disputed. There are two ways they might be understood:

1. Some, noting the *similar* expressions in 3:9 ("put off the old man"), in Romans 6:6 ("the body of sin might be done away"), and in Romans 7:24 ("the body of this death"), suggest that Paul is referring to the condition of man in his unconverted state, to those who are yet "in the flesh" (Romans 7:5). The words we are considering are then taken as an explanation of *the preceding clause*, "circumcised with the circumcision not made with hands". The implication of this is that the inner "circumcision" is equated with the "putting off of the body of the flesh", and seen as some *subjective transformation in the*

---

[74] The phrase "in the circumcision of Christ" (ἐν τῇ περιτομῇ τοῦ Χριστοῦ) is translated by the NIV as "the circumcision done by Christ". I certainly prefer the former, taking the genitive as objective.

believer. This gives rise to such interpretations as 'the putting off of the sinful nature'.[75]

2. Others suggest that when Paul writes about "putting off the body of the flesh" in 2:11 he may well be returning to his comment in 1:21-22, "yet now has He reconciled in the body of His flesh through death". If so, then the words we are considering are better taken with *the following phrase,* "in the circumcision of Christ". The reference would then be to the death of Christ – that is, His putting off His body through death – and to the reconciliation we have with God as a result. The benefit that the Christian receives is, then, not directly a subjective change in his 'nature', but an *objective change in his relation with his Lord.*[76]

    I am much more comfortable with this interpretation for several reasons, not the least being that it eliminates the vexed problem of defining 'sinful nature' (which, strictly speaking, is not a biblical expression) and clearly avoids the confusing and erroneous, although popular, dichotomy of a 'two natures' theory of the Christian life.

Following the second suggestion here, the significance of our having been "circumcised ... in the circumcision of Christ" (2:11) is that "in Him" (2:10) we benefit from His incorporation into the covenant people of God and from His subsequent death, so that having been reconciled through His death, we are no longer alienated from and enemies of God (1:21-2). That is, by entering into this world and being born under the law, our Lord became a member of the covenant people of God, so that through His crucifixion He might bring justification to those for whom He died and restore them to a renewed and secure covenant relationship with the Father. In this, He, a child of the covenant, became "the mediator of a better covenant", who "through His own blood ... obtained eternal redemption" for us (Hebrews 8:6, 9:12).

Therefore, by virtue of Christ's circumcision-unto-death, and our identification with Him, we have become members of the New Covenant, that the law of God be

---

[75] So the NIV. The "body of the flesh" – ἐν τῇ ἀπεκδύσει τοῦ σώματος τῆς σαρκός – is a literal translation, and quite sufficient. It at least leaves the interpretation to the reader and does not force upon him ideas that may or may not be in the text.

[76] I am of the opinion that there is much confusion in some Christian circles because greater importance is given to *intrapersonal* changes in the individual and their benefits, than to the *interpersonal* changes in our relationship with Christ and their benefits.

written on our hearts, that we might know the Lord, and have "boldness to enter into the holy place" of His presence (Hebrews 8:8-12, 10:19).

- **Fourth**, concerning our participation in Christ's baptism.

  The apostle immediately provides further explanation of the "circumcision" we have "in Him" by adding the words, "having been buried with Him in baptism, wherein you were also raised with Him" (συνταφέντες αὐτῷ ἐν τῷ βαπτισμῷ,ἐν ᾧ καὶ συνηγέρθητε, 2:12). The two compound verbs – "buried with" and "raised with" – preclude the idea that we were buried and raised in a baptism similar and subsequent to His baptism.[77] Rather, it is implied here that we gain whatever the saving benefit or advantage might be that Paul has in mind (see below) as a result of our participation in *Christ's own baptism*. And this we appropriate "through faith in the working of God, who raised Him from the dead" (2:12, cf. Galatians 5:6, "faith working through love").

  We might say that just as Christ's circumcision eventually led to His crucifixion, so His baptism necessarily led to His crucifixion being substitutionary and effective for the redemption of His people and their participation in newness of life.

  The tense of the two verbs – "having been buried" and "were ... raised" – implies that in some sense the Christian, simply because he is a Christian, has already died and has already received life of a new, specific kind. Paul has the historical death and resurrection of Christ in view, but is clearly not referring to our physical death or physical resurrection, for as yet we have experienced neither. He speaks similarly – and almost with a rapturous inference – in Ephesians 2:5-6 of Christians, who although once "dead in (their) trespasses", are now, as a result of their salvation, "made alive with Christ ... and made to sit with Him in heavenly places".[78] And in Romans 6:4, again using the terminology of baptism, he explains that his Christian readers "were buried ... with Him ... into death" that "like as Christ was raised ... we also might walk in newness of life".

  In these expressions, Paul is writing about what *has happened* in the process of becoming a Christian, not about what *will or might happen* subsequently. Nevertheless, what has happened determines what will happen.

---

[77] I would be tempted to translate this – συνταφέντες αὐτῷ ἐν τῷ βαπτισμω – "buried with Him in *His* baptism" (note the article).

[78] Surely Ephesians 2:5-6 implies that our present communion with Christ is both intimate and triumphant!

In what sense, then, are we to consider ourselves to be dead and buried with Christ and already raised into newness of life? What has happened to us, as Christians, in this revivification, and what will be the result of it?

This is an important question because we all discover that we have to face the same difficulties, feel the same pains, suffer the same misunderstandings, struggle with the same problems, and waste away with the same physical degeneration after our conversion to Christianity as all people must, converted or not. Once we have become Christians, we find ourselves recognizably much the same as we were before. Therefore, lest those who profess faith in Christ are left confused and disillusioned, having been told that Christian salvation makes 'all the difference', we must clarify as best we can what it means to be buried and raised with Him in baptism.

There can be no doubt that Paul is using exceptional expressions in the verses just cited to explain astonishing advantages that are provided for God's people through redemption – indeed, advantages that are in many ways ineffable – but we must think carefully if we are to grasp his meaning. And if we do not, then we are liable to expect what is not offered and fail to enjoy what is.

To comprehend Paul's meaning in Colossians 2:12 it is helpful to see what he has to say in discussing the same matter elsewhere. As we have seen, in a number of places in his letters he writes in a similar fashion.

Paul's theology in Romans 6 is complicated, but it is most helpful in understanding the verses we are considering in Colossians and is worth some reflection.[79] When he asks, "Shall we continue in sin, that grace may abound?" he is not raising the question of *the moral possibility of not sinning*, but the question of *the moral impropriety of sinning* once we have become Christians. In other words, it is not his immediate intention to discuss *how we might not sin* but to explain *why we should not sin*. So, he writes, in effect, that "we who died to sin" should not "any longer live therein" (Romans 6:1-2).

Now, obviously, we need to be able to make some sense out of the apostle's words, "were buried ... with Him ... into death" (Romans 6:4), lest we confuse his meaning altogether. To do so, it is important to note here that Paul not only said that Christians "died to sin" (Romans 6:2, ἀπεθάνομεν τῇ ἁμαρτίᾳ), but also that Christ Himself "died to sin" (Romans 6:10, τῇ ἁμαρτίᾳ ἀπέθανεν), and this must have the same

---

[79] It is wise to allow Paul, as it were, to explain his own terminology.

meaning in both places. This helps us to understand Paul's thinking. We cannot say, as many suppose, that the expression "died to sin" implies the death of some 'sinful nature' in man, because this cannot be true of Christ who had no such sinful nature; nor can we say that it suggests death to the evil influence of sin, because Christ was never so influenced. All Christians in their more thoughtful moments readily acknowledge that their conversion involved neither of these things, as they continually struggle with their own sinfulness, and often succumb to surrounding godless influences.

But there is one sense in which this expression is true of both Christ and all those who are in Christ – to "die to sin" is *to die to the penalty of sin*. Paul comments that "he that has died is justified from sin" (Romans 6:7, ὁ γὰρ ἀποθανὼν δεδικαίωται ἀπὸ τῆς ἁμαρτίας).[80] As the "wages of sin is death" (Romans 6:23), there can be no further condemnation when this death-liability has been discharged. As Jesus Christ paid the debt for the sins of His people (I Peter 2:24), then in Him their accountability for them was removed. Thus, those who receive the benefits of Christ's death are justified. "There is therefore now no condemnation to them that are in Christ Jesus" (Romans 8:1).

Or, in other words, Christ died to the penalty of sin, but to the penalty of the sins of His people and not of His own; but we who believe died to the penalty of sin, but through His death and not our own.

The indescribable magnitude of the divine grace and perdurable ramifications of this should leave us in wonder and humility!

It is most incongruous – and this is Paul's point – that anyone who is truly convicted of his sins and thankfully finds forgiveness and justification in Christ, should be content to continue living in sin – indeed, to continue living in the very sins that our Lord carried to the Cross. If a man is careless in this matter, we might well question his conversion (Matthew 7:20). Hence the apostle's answer to his own question, "Shall we continue in sin?" is an emphatic "God forbid!" or "By no means!" (Romans 6:1). Here there can be no dispute. A Christian *ought not* to go on sinning.[81]

---

[80] Most translations render this verse, "he that has died is freed from sin". This seems to be most unsatisfactory as the word is frequently and consistently translated as "justified" or "declared righteous" elsewhere in Romans. If "freed from sin" is intended to mean 'free from the penalty of sin' it might be acceptable, but unfortunately, it has given many readers the idea that they ought to be 'free from the power of sin' – and has left them confused or disillusioned.

[81] I am not for a moment suggesting some form of perfectionism here. Paul's concern is the motivation and intention of the heart, rather than any accomplishment.

However, although we might expect that a genuine Christian, because of his love for Christ, would desire to live in a manner pleasing to Him, we must ask what help is available to such a genuine penitent who sincerely longs to live in godliness and, like us all, finds it torturously difficult?

The answer to this is, I suggest, Paul's explanation that to have "died with Christ" has the immediate and ongoing result that we "also live with Him" (Romans 6:8) – and *living with Him is transforming*. Therefore, the apostle adds the imperative that we must "also reckon (ourselves) to be dead unto sin, but alive unto God in Christ Jesus" (Romans 6:11).

This reckoning is not some enthusiastic effort to convince ourselves that some subjective or mystical change has taken place within our souls, or that in some manner we must believe 'harder' or more fervently in our Lord to overcome any doubts that we may have. Neither is it dependent upon some confirming, religious experience we might have. Rather, it is simply to understand, through the scriptures, that because Christ died for His people, taking away their guilt and bringing them justification from heaven, everything that has alienated us from God has been removed and we are reconciled that we might, eventually, be presented holy and without blemish before Him (1:21-22).

Consequently, there is now nothing that can fatally destroy the living relationship we have with our Lord. We should live, then, in the clear realization of the benefits of our reconciliation, knowing that Christ will never fail or forsake us (Hebrews 13:5).

And this imperishable communion we have with Him is the newness of life Christians enjoy.

It is important, I think, if we are to understand Paul's theology in these matters, to realize that when he writes of being "raised with Him from the dead" and being "made alive together with Him" (2:12-13) – or walking "in newness of life" (Romans 6:4) – he is talking about *the restoration of a broken relationship.*

The benefit is the removal of our alienation and enmity, not our weakness and dependence.

The obvious example that the Bible uses such terminology in this way comes from our Lord Himself. In His parable, the father of the prodigal son declared when the wayward boy returned home, "This my son was dead, and is alive again; was lost, and is found" (Luke 15:24). Death was in the separation, but life was in the reunion. The broken relationship was restored.

Perhaps the most abhorrent of all the lamentable aspects of death is the separation it causes. Christians have good reason to believe that death is not annihilation, for the soul survives (cf. Matthew 10:28, II Corinthians 5:8, Revelation 6:9-10). The cause of our greatest grief is that, in death, we have lost the companionship of and communion with the deceased. The one we loved is no longer with us.

The Bible explains that the death most to be feared is alienation from God and banishment from His presence (Matthew 5:20, 7:23, Luke 16:26, Revelation 20:6). This is the state in which we once "were dead through (our) trespasses and sins" and "by nature children of wrath" (Ephesians 2:1-3).

The Bible also makes it clear that the life most to be desired is to live together with Christ, both in time and in eternity. This is the state in which "we were ... made alive ... together with Christ ... and raised up with Him, and made to sit with Him in the heavenly places in Christ" (Ephesians 2:5-6).

Hence Paul encourages the believers in Colossae to "walk in Him, rooted and being built up in Him ... abounding in thanksgiving" (2:6-7). That is, consciously and deliberately to keep His company and to constantly and faithfully depend upon His sufficiency and grace. But this we can only truly appreciate when we have some understanding of the benefits we have through and as a consequence of the circumcision and the baptism of Jesus Christ.

Therefore, by virtue of Christ's baptism, burial and resurrection, and our identification with Him, we have become members of the community of God's redeemed people, having therein died to the penalty of sin and entered into the newness of eternal life in fellowship with our Lord.

Having in mind that we are asking how we might gain a Christian mind (#3.2.2.), we suggest the following:

All this implies that the informed Christian in his search for truth and understanding is from the beginning well aware of the kind of person he is. He acknowledges his own moral impotence and is sensitive to the deleterious effect this has, prejudicing his reasoning. He also knows – and should always keep in mind – that his natural tendency is to relapse into his own egoism and return to his old ways of non-Christian thinking.

This makes any academic exercise – especially in the disciplines of philosophy and religion – a perilous activity, fraught with temptation. There is always the danger, we being the fallen, arrogant creatures that we are, that a man might "deceive himself". Therefore, "if any man thinks that he is wise … in this age, let him become a fool, that he may become wise" (I Corinthians 3:18).

The truly godly Christian student will discipline himself to proceed with humility in his repentance before God, and with thanksgiving through his faith in Christ. Repentance and faith will constantly moderate both his life and thoughts. He will take every step in his studies and ask every question in his research "clothed with humility" because he knows that "God resists the proud and gives grace to the humble" (I Peter 5:5). His constant concern will be for the glory of God, and not for the accolades of men. And to maintain this disposition he will always remember that he was buried with Christ and raised to newness of life.

Such a man will never forget "the day (he) heard and knew the grace of God in truth" (1:6) and will aspire after knowledge that he might "walk worthily of the Lord unto all pleasing" (1:9-10).

NOTE: We ought to be eternally thankful for God's prevenient grace that brought us sanctification and regeneration, set us apart from other people, opened our blind eyes to the truth, and disposed our hearts towards Him in love and faith. *But the overwhelming influence that now changes our lives is the vital, living, persistent, and inviolable fellowship we have with Him.*

This is no occasional or spasmodic relationship that may be influenced by circumstances or regulated by techniques, but it is the eternal state of everlasting life. It is the corollary of being "delivered … out of the power of darkness, and translated … into the kingdom of the Son of His love" (1:13). We now live with Him! "Being … justified … we have had our access by faith into this grace wherein we stand" (Romans 5:1). Now nothing "shall be able to separate us from the love of God which is in Christ Jesus our Lord" (Romans 8:39). And having delivered up Christ for us, "shall He not also with Him freely give us all things" (Romans 8:32)?

Every conceivable blessing that we have as Christians results from our reconciliation. Hence Paul can assure us that He has "blessed us with every spiritual blessing in heavenly places in Christ" (Ephesians 1:3).

Therefore, we should keep in mind that whatever benefits are suggested by being buried with Him and raised with Him, they are only obtained because we "are made full in Him" (2:10) – that is, we gain the blessings only through this relationship. This is the reality of Christian salvation with which we should reckon!

And this inviolable relationship provides us with the context in which we find "grace to help in time of need" (Hebrews 4:16). *And ultimately it is only this grace that enables us to resist the beguiling anthropocentric philosophies that would entrap us.*

3.2.2.4. ACCESS THROUGH THE TRIUMPH OF CHRIST

In 2:13-15 Paul develops the thoughts that he has expressed in the preceding two verses but is now looking at the benefits of Christian salvation from a somewhat different perspective. His focus has been on the *sufferings* of Jesus Christ in His incarnation, from the day of His circumcision, through His baptism, and concluding in His crucifixion. However, the apostle had mentioned, at the end of 2:12, His irrefutable resurrection – "God ... raised Him from the dead" – and now, taking up this idea, he directs the reader to the advantages true believers have because of the *triumph* of Christ.

We are still concerned here to discover how we might effectively access true Christian thinking (#3.2.2.), and follow the philosophy that is "after Christ" (2:8). So, I suggest, it might be helpful if we recall that all people, Christian and non-Christian, seek an understanding of both man himself and the sphere in which he exists. And they do so by exploring what I referred to above as *self-consciousness* and *world-consciousness* (#3.2.1., Fourth). However, the Christian and the non-Christian consider, explain, and evaluate these things differently.

Exploring himself, the Christian becomes acutely conscious, *inter alia*, of his *sin*; and exploring the world, he becomes acutely aware, *inter alia*, of its *evil*. He sees these as profoundly disturbing aberrations. Moreover, he acknowledges that his thinking is distorted by his sin and influenced by the evil forces that impinge upon him, both of which he seems impotent to overcome, struggle with them as he may. It is humbling to make such an acknowledgement, but it is a necessary aspect of genuine *repentance*.

The problem is twofold: subjectively, sin vitiates our relationship with God; and objectively, evil vitiates our relationship with God's world. And the Christian acknowledges that these two factors inhibit both moral behaviour and true thinking, recognizing that only divine intervention – Christian redemption – can resolve the problem. It is humbling to make such an acknowledgement, but this is a necessary aspect of genuine *faith*.

Now, both these aberrations – sin and evil – are at the back of the apostle's words in 2:13-15. It is the "bond written in ordinances" – or, as I suggest below, the law of God – that exposes and defines our sin; and it is the "principalities and powers" that corrupt our environment. Paul would have the Christian thinker remember, and take into account in all his thinking, that, having risen from the dead, our Lord has triumphed over both sin and evil to redeem His people from themselves and from this present, evil world. And this includes the redemption of both our mind and our morals.

Therefore, I suggest the triumphant victory of Christ might be considered under the following two headings:

- **First**, Christ's judicial triumph.

    Our Lord has secured for us forgiveness for "all our trespasses" and indemnification against legal condemnation (2:13-14).

    Paul reminds his Colossian readers of the state they were in before their Christian conversion. They were "dead", which implies, as we have seen, that they were condemned by and alienated from God. Two things, in particular, had contributed to this calamitous condition – their "trespasses" (or "transgressions") and the "uncircumcision of (their) flesh" (2:13).[82]

    The word 'trespass' (παράπτωμα)[83] connotes misconduct that has an element of deliberateness and rebellious intention about it. It is sinning with evil determination. A person might sin spontaneously simply because it is the nature of his imperfect character to do so; but he trespasses when he consciously violates a stated principle or requirement, defying a known prohibition or refusing a commandment.

    Hence Paul uses this word in reference to Adam's revolt against God in the Garden of Eden – "by the trespass of the one the many died", "by the trespass of the one, death reigned through the one", "and through one trespass *the judgement came* unto all men to condemnation" (Romans 5:15, 17, 18). The first man did not eat the fruit "of the tree of the knowledge of good and evil" (Genesis 2:17, 3:1ff) spontaneously, only because of an unsatisfied appetite, but with the determination to have what was categorically forbidden – and this was premeditated, subversive transgression. And because of it, Adam was banished from

---

[82] The NIV gives me some difficulty here. It chooses to translate the word for "trespasses" or "transgressions" (παράπτωμα) as 'sins' (ἁμαρτία) in this verse, although it does not do so with the same expression in Ephesians 2:5. This is an unnecessary obfuscation. Then it also, again, translates "flesh" as 'sinful nature', which I find unsatisfactory.

[83] This word is only found in this verse in Colossians, but is used by Paul on some sixteen occasions, nine of these in Romans. It is also found three times in the gospels, twice in Matthew and once in Mark. The cognate verb (παραπίπτω – 'to fall away') is found in Hebrews 6:6.

the presence of God and expelled from the Garden. He had deliberately and knowingly violated the covenant under which he was created.

This initial, human rebellion has had cataclysmic consequences for all of Adam's progeny. It was through this "one man" that "sin entered into the world, and death through sin … so death passed unto all men"; hence, the "one trespass" resulted in the condemnation of "all men" (Romans 5:12, 18). But Paul would have us understand that "all men" inherited not only Adam's condemnation but also his propensity for rebellion. All people, he explains, know God, but they "glorified Him not as God", "refused to have God in their knowledge", and all "practise the same things" (Romans 1:21, 28, 2:1).

Evidently Paul would consider all people – prior to Christian conversion – to be "dead through trespasses" (2:13), and suffering the same tragic consequences, being "alienated and enemies" (1:21).

It is particularly important to notice here that transgression, because of its willful nature, not only results in *condemnation*, but also in *the closure of the mind* as men refuse to know God, and if God is not known then nothing is known as it ought to be known. Moreover, if we accept the validity of Paul's comments in Romans 1:18-28, we must acknowledge that all people are *willfully ignorant* of God, not merely cognitively handicapped. These considerations, from the Christian perspective, again give us reason to emphasize the importance of raising the religious question first, before other matters are considered. Therefore, our primary concern – and responsibility – is not to debate the complexities of philosophical conundrums, as willing as we are to give the "reason for the hope" we have (I Peter 3:15), but to "preach the word" (II Timothy 4:2). First, then, we must place before the world the things God has revealed in Christ and in the scriptures, and explain to all who will listen that these are the fundamental principles, the substance, the building blocks upon which we establish our philosophy of life. Others will either accept or reject these principles, but all we ask is that they consider them openly and honestly. Then, if they do, they will at least know why Christians think and act as they do.

Because of our implication in Adam's rebellion and its consequences, there can be little or nothing of greater value than that, if we are His people, God has "forgiven us all our transgressions" (χαρισάμενος ἡμῖν πάντα τὰ παραπτώματα, 2:13). Both the comprehensiveness and the completion of such absolution are asserted in this clause – *all* our transgressions *are* forgiven! And we must recognize here the point of beginning in our positive dealings with God, the point where we can escape condemnation and receive "the light of the knowledge of the glory of God in the face of Jesus Christ" (II Corinthians 4:6). The point of reconciliation with God!

The word Paul uses here for "forgiveness", coming from the word for "grace" (*charis*, χάρις), implies acting kindly towards another, or giving generously. It is also used, for example, of cancelling another's monetary debt (Luke 7:42), and of forgiving iniquity/lawlessness (Romans 4:7) and sins (I John 2:12).[84] Those who are so forgiven are caught up in the infinite grace of the almighty God!

That the Colossian believers, before becoming Christians, had been in the "uncircumcision of (their) flesh" implies, I would suggest, that they were Gentiles. As it seems reasonable to assume there is a reference to our Lord's physical circumcision in 2:11 (#3.2.2.3.), so similarly this probably refers to their physical uncircumcision. In other words, they had not been converted from Judaism. And in this uncircumcision of their flesh, they would also, because of their pagan associations, have been uncircumcised in heart. Because, as Paul explains elsewhere in a similar situation, they "were at that time separate from Christ, alienated from the commonwealth of Israel, and strangers from the covenants of the promise, having no hope and without God in the world" (Ephesians 2:12).

However, all this had changed! Having been "forgiven all (their) trespasses", they had also been "made alive together with" Christ (2:13). Hence, they were now true citizens of heaven (1:13, cf. Philippians 3:20), members of the everlasting covenant (Hebrews 10:16), assured of "the hope which is laid up ... in heaven" (1:5), and reconciled unto God (1:19-23). In other words, they, in the providence of God, had been brought home and into renewed fellowship with the Father, somewhat like the prodigal son in our Lord's parable.

In 2:14, Paul, it seems, would assure his readers of the irrefragable and irrevocable character of their forgiveness. This, as we have mentioned above, suggests the cancellation of outstanding debt. Now he is saying in effect that there was documentary evidence of a legal nature – "the bond written in ordinances" (τὸ ... χειρόγραφον τοῖς δόγμασιν) – that was "against" and "contrary to us", evincing our indebtedness, and providing

---

[84] Another significant cognate of this verb is the noun 'charisma' (χάρισμα), the 'free gift'. There are two such free gifts that Christians enjoy that surpass all others – this gift of the free forgiveness of our trespasses, and the gift of "eternal life" (Romans 6:23). And both forgiveness and newness of life appear in Colossians 2:13.

damning evidence of our transgressions that could not be denied. That we needed forgiveness, then, is not in any doubt.

The word for "bond written", which only occurs here in the New Testament, was used at the time in commercial circles of a legal document in which the signatory committed himself to certain obligations, financial or otherwise. Paul seems to be suggesting that this particular written bond was given its binding force by "ordinances" (the δόγματα, official decrees).[85] This word is used of government decrees (Acts 17:7), Jewish laws (Ephesians 2:15), and apostolic instructions (Acts 16:4) – and on each occasion, authoritative sanction is implied. The bond, then, did not derive its power from a contractual agreement negotiated by different parties who together decided the terms of the settlement. Rather, it was empowered by sovereign jurisdiction.

But where are we to find such an authentic bond that is so "contrary to us" and to all people, that it exposes our transgressions and leaves us condemned?

We might well assume that if violation of its requirements requires forgiveness from God, then the bond must possess *divine authority*. And in Paul's mind, this could be nothing other than the law of God, written in the scriptures and resonating to some degree in the heart and conscience of all people, which is the standard by which He judges (Romans 2:12-16). It is exactly this law, he explains, that "speaks to them that are under the law, that every mouth may be stopped, and all the world may be brought under the judgement of God" (Romans 3:19).

If, then, our transgressions are defined, exposed, and condemned by divine law, how can they be forgiven?

Is it possible for a God of "consuming fire" (Hebrews 12:29), who is "of purer eyes than to behold evil" (Habakkuk 1:13), and who "hates all workers of iniquity" (Psalm 5:5), to forgive the transgressions of men who have deliberately rebelled against Him?

It is inconceivable that our God, who is "the same yesterday, and today, and for ever" (Hebrews 13:8) and with whom there "can be no variation" (James 1:17), who maintains every one of His "righteous judgements ... for ever" (Psalm 119:160), should, like some arbitrary or capricious autocrat, merely suspend or waive His moral principles to grant forgiveness. His law is the expression of His very character, and to violate or disregard His own law would be to prostitute Himself.

---

[85] The English 'dogma' is derived from this word.

We are often faithless, but "He remains faithful; for He cannot deny Himself" (II Timothy 2:13).

Therefore, if God is to forgive us our trespasses, there must be some righteous manner, some legitimate action He can take, by which He can do so without compromising His own moral principles or abrogating His own laws.

This He did, Paul explains, "freely by His grace through the redemption that is in Christ Jesus, whom God set forth to be a propitiation ... by His blood". Thereby the just wrath of God (Romans 1:18) was turned away from us. And this He did to demonstrate "His righteousness" – which was in no way subverted – "that He might be Himself just, and the justifier" of those who believe in Him (Romans 3:24-26). This implies that God found legitimate ground upon which He could forgive the transgressions of His people without violating His own immutable principles of righteousness (Romans 3:31).

Here we should notice that the apostle defends God's integrity, insisting that He always maintains the standards of His law. Nevertheless, He provides the redemption necessary for our forgiveness. But this redemption was secured *at immense cost to Himself* – the sacrifice and the shedding of the blood of His Son, Jesus Christ!

Here we are again confronted by the ineffable. Many find the whole notion of redemption through sacrifice and forgiveness impossible to accept. It seems to offend their sensibilities; they desire something less confronting. But the Bible insists that it is the outworking of God's infinite love for His people (John 3:16). As Christians, we acknowledge that we only appreciate the sacrifice involved because "the love of God has been shed abroad in our hearts through the Holy Spirit" (Romans 5:4, 8). Therefore, we "know the love of Christ" even while we confess that such love "passes knowledge" (Ephesians 3:19). And it seems that Jesus Christ knew that those who "have not the love of God in" themselves, inevitably fail to appreciate Him, His mission from the Father, and His teaching (John 5:42ff.).

We have been freely forgiven, but there was not and could not have been free forgiveness.

This consideration of Paul's theology in Romans 3:23ff. must help us to understand what he is saying in Colossians 2:14. The "bond written in ordinances" that was "against us" has been "wiped out", erased, cancelled, "blotted out". This cannot mean that the "ordinances", the authoritative law of God, has been removed or rescinded, for reasons we have already given. But it does assure us that whatever has been "written ... against us", whatever record there may be of our violations of the divine ordinances has been expunged. Using the same word, Peter urged his listeners to repent and turn back to God that their "sins may be blotted out" (Acts 3:19).

Then, in simple, graphic terms, the apostle reminds the Colossians how this was done: God took the damning record of our transgressions "out of the way, nailing it to the cross" (2:14). This is, in effect, a concise, vivid summary of all he had written explicitly in 1:19-23. But it also fixes our eyes upon Christ's crucifixion as the only place where we, or any other, can find justification before God.

However we might think about all this, I would suggest that it must be considered as a monumental judicial triumph. Jesus Christ, through His incarnation, death, burial, and resurrection, has overcome every legal impediment to secure our justification. "Who," then, "shall lay anything to the charge of God's elect? It is God who justifies; who is he that shall condemn?" (Romans 8:33-34).

In the light of all this, we must insist upon the following:

It is impossible that the erudite, anthropocentric philosophies of men, no matter how comprehensive or brilliant, could ever, in themselves, lead to Christian religious beliefs about the incarnation, life, death, and resurrection of Christ. Neither – even if their proponents believed in the historicity of His life on earth and His resurrection – could they establish on their own presuppositions any concept of divine righteousness and the forgiveness of trespasses. The unremitting tendency seems to be that those who begin with faith in their own philosophy will deny the Christian faith.

Alternatively, those who are truly Christian – being thankful for the love of, and motivated by a genuine love for God – will discover, if they continue to think biblically, the profound significance Christian beliefs have for establishing a true and powerful philosophy of life, which provides meaning and hope for human existence.

Therefore, the truly godly Christian student will proceed in all his academic endeavours, in whatever discipline, with a love for Jesus Christ as "the way, the truth, and the life" (John 14:6) that surpasses any love he may have for the discipline he is studying. The greater truth he desires to know is the eternal, living, personal truth of the God who "is love" (I John 4:8), which knowledge alone will give genuine warmth, relevance, meaning, significance, and purpose to the lesser truths he garners from his learning or scholarship.

- **Second**, Christ's executive triumph.

Our Lord has secured for us not only *deliverance* from the corruption and condemnation of sin, but also *protection* against the evil ravaging of those who oppose and would destroy us (2:15).

The Christ we proclaim, in whom dwells all the fullness of deity, and in whom we might find the fullness of our humanity, is, Paul explains, "the head of all principalities and powers" (2:10). We have already seen (#1.3.2.3.1.) that these "principalities and powers" were created by Christ (1:16), but they became destructive forces that have an evil influence in this world (Ephesians 6:12). Evidently, they are agents that effect "the wiles of the devil" (Ephesians 6:11). We see and feel their influence in moral corruption and physical disaster – even if we do not immediately recognize their involvement – but they are no doubt influential also in the propagation of "every wind of doctrine" (Ephesians 4:14) that troubles the churches. Hence, we might assume they played their part in promulgating the confusing false teaching that disturbed the Colossians. It is the devil's intention, as far as it is possible for him to do so, to blind "the minds of the unbelieving" (II Corinthians 4:4).

We cannot deny, then, that there is an element of spiritual wickedness even in the most scholarly of anthropocentric philosophies, and from this also we need to be redeemed. Not even in sophisticated academia are we beyond intellectual temptation and rationalistic seduction!

We are aware that it was the devil that, at the beginning, deceived man into trusting in his own anthropocentric philosophy and to deliberately transgress the commandment of God (Genesis 3:1-5). Our Lord Himself suffered, but resisted similar temptation (Matthew 4:1ff.). And the devil has not desisted from his evil intentions! We are warned to beware of his "designs" (II Corinthians 2:11, αὐτοῦ τὰ νοήματα, or his *thoughts*), his wiles (Ephesians 6:11, τὰς μεθοδείας τοῦ διαβόλου, or his *schemes*, or *methods*), and his snare (I Timothy 3:7, παγίδα τοῦ διαβόλου, or *trap*). The Bible, Christ, and the apostles take this personal, evil being and his malevolent enterprise very seriously, and we would be foolish indeed not to do the same.

We might conclude from this that if we are to maintain the true philosophy that is "after Christ" (2:8), we need not only a measure of intellectual integrity and wisdom, together with increasing moral courage, but we must also "submit ... to God" to obtain the spiritual strength we need to "resist the devil" (James 4:7).

Although the devil appeals to our appetites that he might tempt us into immorality, his ultimate aim is to so corrupt our morals that he diverts our mind and obfuscates the truth so we will adopt his philosophy. The last thing he wants us to do is to intelligently believe in God and in His Son, Jesus Christ. He rests content if we believe in Plato, Aristotle, Kant, Hegel, Hume, Nietzsche, or any other great thinker, ancient or modern. *However, there is more than enough evidence in this world to convince us that academic brilliance alone is not sufficient to save men from the thoughts, the schemes, the methods, and the trap of the archenemy of our souls.*

We are troubled and depleted not only by our own moral and intellectual weaknesses but also by evil in our environment. We must, then, constantly reckon with our Lord's victory over "the principalities and the powers" (2:15), and trust in our triumphant Saviour, for if we would do battle with anthropocentric philosophers – as we must! – we are putting ourselves in harm's way.

Therefore, it is not surprising that warning his readers about false philosophy and mentioning the need we have to be "rooted and built up" in Christ (2:6), the apostle not only mentions that Christ is the "head of all principalities and powers" (2:10) but also that He has triumphed over these evil forces through His death and resurrection (2:14-15). There is a spiritual dynamic here that we ignore at our peril – and not only the *moral* but also the even more malignant *intellectual* peril.

It is not without good reason that, as he was advising his readers to beware the philosophies of men, Paul reminded them that God "disarmed the principalities and the powers" and "made a show of them openly, triumphing over them in" Christ (2:15).[86] These threatening, evil agencies that are responsible for so much suffering and confusion have been rendered impotent in their assault against the kingdom of God and in their attempt to overthrow His people. And their defeat is open for all to see – clearly and triumphantly demonstrated – in the death and resurrection of our Lord.

Evidently, Paul would have us keep the knowledge we have of this triumph in mind when we engage with the thoughts and theories of the unconverted. There are at least two advantages in doing so:

1. The recollection of it, and understanding that it is the defeat of all evil powers by the incarnate Son of God, will provide an essential perspective for all our philosophical reckoning,

---

[86] So I understand ἀπεκδυσάμενος τὰς ἀρχὰς καὶ τὰς ἐξουσίας ἐδειγμάτισεν ἐν παρρησίᾳ,θριαμβεύσας αὐτοὺς ἐν αὐτῷ, reading ἀπεκδυσάμενος as middle voice with active meaning, hence 'disarm'.

distinguishing our beliefs from all others. The immensity of the implications of our belief in the person and the work of Jesus Christ, both Creator and Redeemer, and in His indisputable triumph over all evil has enormous ramifications for everything we believe. To the degree that this fades from our memory, so our philosophy ceases to be "after Christ".

2. The recollection will also provide us with a personal, defensive redoubt wherein we may find protection from "all the fiery darts of the evil one" (Ephesians 6:16). We will be reminded that we have very little spiritual or moral strength and that we are constantly dependent upon the presence with us of the victorious Christ. Those who would be faithful ministers of Christ would do well to confess with Paul, "Not that we are sufficient of ourselves, to account anything as from ourselves; but our sufficiency is from God" (II Corinthians 3:5).

A truly devout Christian student will fortify himself from the influence of the principalities and powers by taking Paul's excellent advice to put on the whole armour of God (Ephesians 6:13-18). He will reckon with the executive triumph of Christ who works all things according to His own will (Ephesians 1:11).

3.2.2.5. Access through faith in Christ

Paul, as we have seen, has been saying much in 2:9-15 about the access we have to Christ and to Christian thinking. His emphasis has clearly been upon all that God has done in Christ and through His death and resurrection to provide His people with an entrance into all the "treasures of wisdom and knowledge" that are to be found in Him (2:3). I have attempted a brief exploration of the implications and the ramification of His divine revelation to His people, His gracious reconciliation of His people, and their involvement in the circumcision and baptism of Christ, all of which open their minds to the truth and fortify them against the subtle errors of false philosophies.

However, in this complicated paragraph (2:9-15), with all its technical terminology, the apostle makes but *one relatively simple statement* to indicate how a man is to enter into the state of being "made full" in Christ (2:10). He explains that the true Christian has been "raised with Him through faith in the working of God, who raised Him from the dead" (2:12). *All that was required was faith! No sophisticated techniques, only faith.*

But the faith that was required was of a very specific kind. All people whom we would consider unconverted and outside the genuine Christian community, have faith of some kind, trusting either in a religious system dependent upon their imagined deity, or in a philosophical system dependent upon some "vain deceit", or in a combination of both. In contrast, Christian faith is trust in the God who was actively involved in raising Christ from the dead. It has, then, unambiguous historical content. It is not built solely upon logical syllogisms, or empirical, scientific discoveries. Its core principle is that God is "a God at hand", and "not a god afar off" (Jeremiah 23:23). That is, He is intimately involved in human affairs, and has acted decisively in time to accomplish His purposes.[87] We trust, then, not only in this God, but also "in the working of God" (διὰ τῆς πίστεως τῆς ἐνεργείας τοῦ θεοῦ, 2:12)[88].

Elsewhere Paul wrote, "If you shall confess with your mouth Jesus as Lord, and shall believe in your heart that God raised Him from the dead, you shall be saved" (Romans 10:9). Nothing less than faith with these components will do! The true believer openly acknowledges that he holds himself responsible to obey Christ as his Lord, and this involves – no doubt among other things – recognizing Him as "the head of all principalities and powers" (2:10), and gladly taking his place in "the kingdom" of God's Son (1:13).

But this confession of Christ as Lord, if genuine, is the inevitable result of "believing in your heart that God raised Him from the dead". Presumably, believing "in your heart" implies an attitude of far greater significance than making a formal, confessional declaration. The latter might be made for the mean reason of finding acceptance with others, being received into church membership, or conforming only to external requirements for the sake of appearances. But belief in the heart is faith that arises out of profound, inner conviction that necessarily drives a man's behaviour in accordance with the principles believed. And those who truly believe that God raised Jesus from the dead are compelled not only to acknowledge but

---

[87] We might add that we have no interest in arguing for the existence of some vague or ill-defined deity, a 'superior power', or a 'first cause'. We wish only to defend our belief in the biblical God, who is Father, Son, and Holy Spirit, eternal Creator and sovereign Redeemer.

[88] The word Paul is using is translated "working" or "power" (ἐνεργεία). I suggest the former is preferable here, as the apostle is referring to the effectiveness – the dynamic rather than the potential of divine ability (cf. use of the same word in Ephesians 1:19, 3:7). Then in Colossians 1:29, bringing two words together, he writes of God's "working ... in (him) in power (τὴν ἐνέργειαν αὐτοῦ ... ἐν ἐμοὶ ἐν δυνάμει). We should trust, then, in His "working" (ἐνεργεία), or dynamic activity, because of His infinite "power" (δύναμις), or potential ability: not simply in what He can do, but in what He has done and is doing.

also to trust the power of God that achieved such a triumph over evil, as they yield to the authority of the risen Christ.[89]

Moreover, the Christian trusts not only in that which the power of God *has effected* in Christ's resurrection but also in that which it *will effect* in our own resurrection. For we believe that "if the Spirit of Him that raised up Jesus from the dead dwells in (us), He that raised up Christ Jesus from the dead shall quicken also (our) mortal bodies through His Spirit that dwells in (us)" (Romans 8:11). And, as we saw in 1:29 (#2.1.1.2), we now continually trust in "His working ... in (us) in power" (τὴν ἐνέργειαν αὐτοῦ ... ἐν ἐμοὶ ἐν δυνάμει) for our present life in His service.

At no time, then, can we escape the importance of "faith in the working of God" (2:12).

And a man who has been given such a faith as this will never be able to think or to live as he did before. Being buried and raised with Christ, he now walks "in newness of life" (Romans 6:4).

One more thing of great importance needs to be added here. Paul explains that no one will ever "believe in Him, of whom they have not heard" and they cannot hear "without a preacher" (Romans 10:14-15). Therefore, the church has been commissioned to go into all the world and preach the gospel. He also made it perfectly clear that the gospel has not been preached at all unless it is announced that Christ died and was raised again, according to the scriptures (I Corinthians 15:1-4). In other words, the message we have to take to the nations involves a scriptural presentation of our Lord's death and resurrection, that, by the grace of God, others might call Him Lord because they believe from their hearts in the God who raises the dead.

If no other faith than this brings salvation to men, then no other preaching than this will bring faith to their hearts.

---

[89] Sadly, in much of modern Christendom – from the simple man in the pew, through the sophisticated theologian, to the church potentate – Jesus Christ is for many only a good, if enigmatic, man of history, His resurrection is denied, and faith is reduced to a religious sentiment with no specific objectivity. And much of this unbelief is concealed behind the subtle and devious use of the Bible and traditional Christian language. In this sphere also – and perhaps in this even more than in the secular world – we must "take heed lest ... any one makes spoil of us through his philosophy" (2:8)!

3.2.3. Deviation in Christian Thinking (2:16-19)

Despite the access the Christian has to all that the grace of God provides so he might develop a truly Christian mind according to the philosophy that is "after Christ", there is no immediate or sudden maturation in his thinking. We all need to grow in understanding (I Peter 2:2, II Peter 3:18). We should aspire to be mature in mind (I Corinthians 14:20) so that we may be "no longer children ... carried about with every wind of doctrine" (Ephesians 4:14). *Therefore, not being as sagacious as we need to be (James 1:5), there is always the danger that in our immaturity we may be exposed and succumb to some erroneous theological or philosophical influence.* And we might suggest that those most vulnerable to this peril are those who imagine they are already have sufficient intellectual competence (cf. I Corinthians 3:18, 8:1-2, 10:12, Galatians 6:3, Philippians 3:12-13).

This danger was, it seems, behind Paul's concern for a number of the young believers in Colossae, despite his confidence in the orthodoxy and reliability of the congregation in general (2:5, #2.2.4.). Otherwise, there would have been no need for his warning in 2:8.

When vulnerable members of the Christian community are influenced by the persuasive oratory and deceptive logic of non-Christian philosophy, the church may have to deal with one or all of the following hazards:

1. *Apostasy.* This occurs when some, having had only a nominal faith, are so influenced by anthropocentric philosophy that they abjure the former confession of Christianity they may have made, and openly reject Jesus Christ and the teachings of the church. They sever all meaningful contact with the believing congregation.
2. *Plagiarism.* This occurs when some, now having faith in anthropocentric philosophy, reject the biblical Jesus Christ and many of the doctrines of the church, but having found much in the Christian way of life and teaching that pleases them, they borrow some concepts from the Bible, incorporating them into their own theories. They dissociate themselves from the believing congregation, but surreptitiously take with them the benefits and values of much that it has taught them.
3. *Compromise.* This occurs when some, now having faith in anthropocentric philosophy but desiring to maintain their status as Christian believers, modify or reinterpret Christian beliefs to blend them into their new and extraneous ideas about human life. They continue to associate with the believing congregation, often determined to change its theological constitution through an attempted philosophical miscegenation.

The most dangerous of these is the last – those who compromise with anthropocentric philosophy and choose to remain within the Christian community, thus influencing others with their false or depleted theology. Paul warned the Ephesian elders of the disastrous effect such people can have in the church, saying, "From among your own selves shall men arise, speaking perverse things, to draw away the disciples after them" (Acts 20:30). They can be particularly insidious, because they may appear and sound orthodox, and often secure positions of authority. They are the false prophets, the wolves in sheep's clothing, of which our Lord warned us (Matthew 7:15).

NOTE: It is understandable that such false prophets continue to influence many innocent Christians in our congregations who are impressed by their personality or erudition. Believing that God has given man considerable intellectual ability, we recognize his potential for brilliant and creative – and often mischievous! – thinking. We are, then, not at all surprised by the genius of great philosophers and theologians. Moreover, we anticipate finding remarkable insights and, indeed, elements of useful wisdom in their writings. And this is true of the often-genial heretics who, intentionally or unintentionally, corrupt the faith. They can be most convincing and winsome.

However, there comes the moment when the professors of anthropocentric philosophies begin to impugn the supremacy of Christ, to question the fullness of His deity, and to dispute the sufficiency of His redemptive work for man's salvation, denying that "all the treasures of wisdom and knowledge" (2:3) are to be found in Him. Then we might well be fearful of the destructive influence they have in the world. They are in revolt against heaven.

Now, it would seem that such compromisers had appeared in Colossae and were causing problems in the church. If they were not actually within the congregation, they were at least close enough to the believers to seriously affect them with their heretical opinions. They seem to have been propagating *two erroneous and deleterious theories* that we will now consider.

3.2.3.1. THEY UNDERMINED THE FOUNDATIONS OF BIBLICAL AUTHORITY

There is abundant evidence that the first preachers of the Christian gospel and the authors of the New Testament found the authority for their teaching in the existing biblical scriptures (see Acts 2:17-21, 25-28, Romans 16:26, II Timothy 3:14-17, et al.). Hence, the Bible became the authority for all Christian faith and practice. But the heretics appear to have replaced this with either *ecclesiastic authoritarianism* or *mystical speculation*, or both.

• **First**, incipient, ecclesiastical authoritarianism. 2:16-17.

The word "therefore" in 2:16 indicates that the apostle is drawing an inference or conclusion from what he has just been writing. But what is the connection? Some would suggest that the link is only with the immediately preceding verse (2:15) and that Paul is saying that his readers should not allow others to judge them because the principalities and powers have been overthrown, have no authority, and are no longer able to make demands upon them. This I find rather inadequate, mainly because it assumes that the religious requirements of 2:16 were imposed in the first place by these evil principalities and powers. But this, as I explain below, I cannot accept.

I would suggest, then, that Paul is referring back to all that he has written in 2:8-15. It is *the warning* that his readers "take heed least there be anyone who would take (them) captive" by his anthropocentric philosophy, and lead them away from the philosophy that is "after Christ", that now provokes him to pen *this imperative*, "Let no man therefore judge you ..." So revolutionary is the Christian faith, and so transforming are the benefits of being in Christ, that the Christian is now answerable to a different authority and lives according to different principles than those the heretics would impose upon them. They should not be inveigled by clever and persuasive reasoning into abandoning the mind of and life in Christ.

Having asked, then, about what it is that precedes this verse and from which Paul draws this inference, we must now consider what it is that he is referring to when he writes of religious dietary and ceremonial requirements in 2:16. Why does he now mention these matters?

Some suggest that in 2:16 Paul has in view contemporary pagan practices of abstinence and asceticism, which, apparently, were common among the people at that time. If this is so, then he might have considered them to be associated with the heathen worship of principalities and powers.

But, it seems to me, one thing makes this suggestion completely unacceptable. It is that Paul himself defines what he has in mind when he adds, "which things are a shadow of things that were to come, but the substance is of Christ" (2:17). In this, he indicates that the religious practices he has mentioned were an adequate foreshadowing of a reality that is to be found only in our Lord. This function could not be attributed to evil principalities and powers or found in the practices of pagan worship. He is, I suggest in the light of this, referring to the Jewish practices of the Old Testament.[90]

We know that the first Christians had difficulty in separating themselves from the worship practices of the Jews and the orders of the Old Testament – they were Jews, they had grown up with the religion of Israel, and they evidently had some genuine affection for the old ways. But this, as was inevitable, became problematic when Gentiles, who had no such background, became Christians and joined the church. This complex, cross-cultural situation generated questions about Christian conventions and led to the Church council which met in Jerusalem (Acts 15), and at which some critical issues were settled.

Also, Paul had written forcefully in his letter to the Galatians to preserve the gospel, to assert the freedom provided by the new faith, to establish the sufficiency of the work of Christ, and to rebuke those who would bring the church back "into bondage" to the Jewish ways (Galatians 2:4). The lengthy letter to the Hebrews was also composed to demonstrate that the Christian religion was rooted in, but had grown out of the ancient religious practices of Abraham and Moses, and now offered a better way.

How the cultic and cultural practices of the Old Testament were to be transformed or translated into the life of the Christians of the New Testament was an important consideration – and continues to be so. Paul indicates here that the "shadow" (2:17) of the old had become fulfilment and reality in the new.

But I sense that there is something more sinister here in Colossians than confusion about the relationship between old Israel and the new church.

Paul would not have been motivated to write 2:16 unless there were dominant people influencing the Christian congregation in Colossae who presumed they were able and in a position to "judge" others. *They had arrogated to themselves, despite their misunderstanding of the apostolic gospel and confusion about Old Testament practices, an authoritative position in and over the congregation. To borrow Peter's words – and taking them out of context – they were "lording it over ... the flock", rather than being an example to them and teaching them in truth (I Peter 5:3).*

---

[90] Paul's earlier reference to circumcision (2:11) indicates that the Old Testament and its requirements were much in his mind.

Their superior attitude alone was in itself inimical to the best interests of the church, but their actions were probably far more disturbing. The fact that they were judging others in reference to Old Testament dietary and ceremonial laws suggests that they may have been using the old scriptures to maintain *the appearance of orthodoxy.*[91] The apostles, as we know, legitimately preached from the Old Testament. But they were aware that some having wandered away from "a good conscience and unfeigned faith", and listening to "vain talking" (ματαιολογία, or "meaningless discussions"), desired "to be teachers of the law" although they did not know what they were talking about (I Timothy 1:5-7). Paul does not say so here, but one wonders if he might have had in mind "false apostles, deceitful workers" who were making themselves out to be "apostles of Christ" (II Corinthians 11:13). There were such men who troubled the congregations of the early church (cf. Revelation 2:2).

If such pretenders as these were troubling the Colossians, this would have prompted Paul's warning. By preaching from the Old Testament they would have been *imitating the apostles,* and by judging and demanding obedience from the believers they were *usurping apostolic authority.* Christians should not give heed to such people, or accept their judgements.

These pretenders had seriously misunderstood the significance of the Old Testament dietary and ceremonial regulations, having judged them to be an end in themselves and not "a shadow of things that were to come" (2:17). In contrast, the apostles, following their Lord's teaching, interpreted "in all the scriptures the things concerning" Christ Himself (Luke 24:27). They had found, as Paul explains, that the Old Testament "law was (their) tutor to bring them unto Christ" (Galatians 3:24).

I would suggest that Paul has already explained why he and these heretics read and understood the scriptures in completely different ways. *The pretenders would have interpreted the Bible according to "the traditions of men and the rudiments of the world" (cf. Matthew 15:1-6) – the principles of anthropocentric philosophy – bringing their hearers into captivity; and the apostles interpreted the Bible "according to Christ" (2:8), bringing men and women into the liberty in the gospel.*

The high and comprehensive Christology of 1:9-23 had provided the apostles with a perspective not only from which to understand human

---

[91] Most innovative heretics who seek to change the established beliefs and structures of the church will make shrewd, disingenuous use of the Bible to maintain the appearance of orthodoxy and inveigle their way into the congregation.

life, but also from which to read and understand the Bible – a perspective vastly different from and superior to any that could be found in deceitful, human reasoning.[92]

I am aware that we only know Christ from the Bible, and that I am asking that we take this knowledge of Christ as necessary for our understanding of the Bible. But this is only to ask that we allow the Bible to interpret itself. It is all too often that Christians are so swept away by the persuasive oratory and the convincing arguments of influential men, that they deny the sufficiency of the Bible to interpret itself, and then use the principles of anthropocentric philosophies in an attempt to explain its meaning. This, tragically, has resulted in a cacophony of mutually exclusive theological opinions that has greatly troubled Christians and obfuscated the Christian message for others. Attempts have been made to avoid this confusion by imposing official or creedal beliefs by church or state legislation – but with little success, for the officials themselves are more often than not also affected by the same philosophies.[93]

So, I wonder if there may be here in Colossians 2:16-17 an indication of an incipient tendency, albeit limited and localized, to establish an ecclesiastical mandate to govern or teach the church based upon anthropocentric thinking, rather than upon the sole authority of the Christian scriptures.

I would not deny for one moment the commission and the authority the church has been given to maintain, to preach, and to teach the truth faithfully. But the church is not a law unto itself. It must always be subject to the authority of the Bible, and the responsibility for the promulgation of biblical truth within the church must only be committed into the hands of men "of a pure heart and a good conscience and unfeigned faith" (I Timothy 1:5). Therefore, if genuine ecclesiastic authority is to be established and maintained, the church must be truly submissive to the authority of the scriptures, and humbly follow the leadership of men of attested Christian godliness and orthodoxy.

What we should beware is the all too human tendency of learned men and women, being qualified biblical and theological scholars, insinuating

---

[92] It seems to me to have become a deeply engrained and pervasive practice in theological academia to read the Bible, consciously or subconsciously, from an anthropocentric rather than a Christocentric perspective.

[93] Nevertheless, in all the confusion I believe it is important that the church declares its beliefs in confessional statements. However, these at best can only be secondary authorities and must be subject to biblical truth.

themselves into positions of authority in the church on the basis of their erudition, rather than their character and orthodoxy.

- **Second**, incipient, mystical superiority. 2:18-19.

Often when there is theological confusion or open dispute, people are left in aching doubt about where the truth is to be found and what they are to believe. The pain this causes can be, and usually is, most distressing. This problem is more acute for the Christian when philosophical debate deliberately attempts to undermine the reliability of the Bible. Then the struggling believer – or the honest seeker – is left without any anchorage either in genuinely erudite human reasoning or in religious revelation, for both have been taken from him. He is abandoned to drift in the cross currents of a seemingly shoreless ocean. He knows not to which wind he should set his sails, for he knows of no destination that is to be reached. He is unable to return home, for he knows not from where he has come.

At such times, there is always the temptation to search for some existential or mystical moment that provides the individual with his own subjective point of reference and verification, which will give him a personal source of assurance – some confirming experience.[94] But this is contrary to Paul's desire for his readers that "their hearts may be comforted … in love, and unto the full assurance of understanding" (2:2). *In this, he writes of assurance that is found in Christian community, not in personal isolation, and that comes from understanding, not from mere experience (#2.2.3.).*

Perhaps something of such a desperate, experiential attempt – and desperate it is! – to resolve this dilemma is reflected in these verses (2:18-19).

Paul's meaning in 2:18 is difficult to discern, in part at least because two of the words he uses – "let no one disqualify" (καταβραβεύω) and "dwelling in", "intruding into", or "taking his stand on" (ἐμβατεύω) – are found only here in the New Testament, although they, especially the latter, are variously used in other Greek literature. Therefore, it is somewhat difficult to define them and to evaluate their significance in this verse, but I will attempt to do so below.[95] In pursuing my intention to

---

[94] I can only wonder if this search – this agonizing – for assurance has given rise to the remarkable increase of New Age mysticism in congregations which have been depleted by years of rationalistic, anthropocentric philosophies.

[95] In such situations, we must be careful not to select arbitrarily a secular use of the word and use it to import or insinuate some non-Christian concept into the text. The text should be interpreted and translated in a manner compatible with the overall teaching of the Bible.

discover the relevance this and other verses here may have for the church in our own day, I make the following comments hoping they will lead to some understanding of the apostle's concern:

1. First, we should note the obvious parallel in this passage between Paul's two imperatives: "Let no man therefore judge you" (2:16, μὴ οὖν τις ὑμᾶς κρινέτω), and "Let no man exclude you" (2:18, so it might be read, μηδεὶς ὑμᾶς καταβραβευέτω). Here *judging* is seen in contrast to *excluding*. Two entirely different verbs are used, and both suggest that the heretical teachers in Colossae were falsely appraising the quality of the lives of others. I suggest that the difference between these two words may be that the first involves judging the individual in reference to law (hence the following mention of Old Testament regulations); and the second involves judging the individual in comparison to other people considered to be more spiritual (hence, as we shall see, the following mention of the supposed superior experience of some). And does not this censorious and supercilious attitude always tend to discriminate against or denigrate others who do not conform to the arbitrarily required cultic/moral or social/personal behaviour? And is this not contrary to a truly Christian disposition (eg. Romans 15:7, II Corinthians 10:12)?

2. Such censoriousness seems inevitably to arise out of heretical teaching, which is necessarily divisive in its rejection of orthodoxy, and to become schismatic. It wants to form a distinctive or exclusive category of its own. To distinguish themselves and their faction, the false teachers in Colossae were evidently requiring of their followers "a voluntary humility" (θέλων ἐν ταπεινοφροσύνῃ) and their participation in the "worship of angels" (θρησκείᾳ τῶν ἀγγέλων). Were they forming their own, peculiar cultic structures?

    Here also are two difficult expressions, and they need consideration.

    This word for "humility" is usually used in the New Testament – where it is only found on five occasions – of a desirable Christian attitude, and is sometimes translated "lowliness" or "lowliness of mind" (Ephesians 4:2, Philippians 2:3). It is the very opposite of pride, arrogance, and willfulness. Paul uses this word in Colossians 3:12 to identify a quality that is concomitant with compassion, kindness, gentleness, and longsuffering. A good, if somewhat rare, characteristic indeed!

However, in 2:18 and 23, being associated with human volition and severity to the body, this word obviously takes on a negative sense, indicating something undesirable. Paul, I suggest, seems to be referring to *a self-imposed asceticism, a deliberate physical self-degradation – an extraneous, superficial, mock humility* – which was probably required by the false teachers. Perhaps a specific cultic, or ritual humiliation is in view.

When such religious asceticism is undertaken to improve one's spirituality or cultic status, it is not only evidence of theological misunderstanding (cf. I Timothy 4:1-5), but also, I suggest, the manifestation of profound egoism and self-assertion, a proud display of determination and willpower. Self-humiliation, especially when undertaken for ultimate personal gain, is far removed from genuine humility. How easy it is for fallen man to corrupt and distort all the true qualities of godliness, reducing them to emblems of superiority!

The expression "worship of angels" (θρησκείᾳ τῶν ἀγγέλων) presents us with an ambiguity. It could mean either *making angels the object of worship* or *participating in worship with the angels*. If the latter is intended, as I think it is,[96] Paul may well be writing about people who are not content with worship within the natural realm of human physicality, thought, emotion, and verbal expression – that is, not content with worship that I would consider thoroughly compatible with God's design that we should live and glorify Him within the created world. However, there are those who seek to move out of this context altogether through the appropriate mystical and meditative techniques, including self-imposed asceticism in various forms, and to worship in what they might consider a higher, ethereal level of existence. They desire a transcendental experience: they would, as it were, hold hands with the angels in their domain,

---

[96] Reading τῶν ἀγγέλων as a subjective genitive. It is also worth noting that the word for "worship" (θρησκεία) used here refers to the outward practices of religion, rather than to any devotional attitude of heart.

and share in their more immediate and intimate communion with God.[97]

We are reading here about voluntary "humility" and "worship", and the two words are grammatically coupled together suggesting that they are associated in the one religious exercise. And this might well refer to the practice of ascetic self-discipline as the means of obtaining a mystical experience or vision that enables a paranormal participation in worship that is above the common religious observances of average Christian men and women.[98] And this is certainly the path – the erroneous path – that many have followed and continue to follow that they might gain personal, religious assurance.

And if this is Paul's concern here, then he associates it with heretical teachings.

3.   Yet another obscure expression needs consideration, which is perhaps the most important element in the sentence. Paul adds words variously rendered as "intruding into those things which he has seen", "taking his stand on visions", "goes into great detail about what he has seen", "dwelling on visions", or some such translation (ἃ ἑόρακεν ἐμβατεύων).[99] Both the vocabulary and the syntax are technically difficult.

The Greek word responsible for such renderings as different as "intruding into" and "going into great detail" originally meant 'to step in/on', then 'to enter into', 'to frequent', and 'to possess'. It is used in the ancient Greek version of the Old Testament in Joshua 19:49 of entering into or possessing the Promised Land after the exodus from Egypt.[100] It was also used in the secular world, like English equivalents, of entering into an investigation of some kind.

But what are we to make of its use here in Colossians? We might suggest that it at least implies that the heretics would

---

[97] An interesting example of this is found, perhaps, in the claim made by some who have experienced the glossolalia and misunderstood I Corinthians 13:1, that the 'tongue' in which they speak is the language of angels. An experience they frequently recommend as evidence of their genuine Christianity, despite the fact that the same phenomenon is found in many religions.

[98] These practices of ascetic self-discipline to obtain mystical experiences are increasingly common in congregations today of various denominations and theological positions. To some extent, this is the result of the growing influence of New Age mystical spirituality.

[99] The "not" – "things … not seen" – found in the KJV is most unlikely.

[100] There is also evidence of this word being used by pagans for the entering of an initiate into heathen shrines.

seriously engage in some way with the matter in hand – and that matter is, the "things he has seen" (ἃ ἑόρακεν). And this may provide the key to unlock the continuing, practical significance of this verse, despite the little we know about the vocabulary and background.

Evidently, some heretical teacher was making much out of things he had seen. And this, being his own individual experience, evidently gave him a sense of his own unique qualifications. Hence he was "vainly puffed up by his fleshly mind" (εἰκῆ φυσιούμενος ὑπὸ τοῦ νοὸς τῆς σαρκὸς αὐτου, 2:18). He was conceited, suffering from an inflated ego! Paul was aware that knowledge, especially without love, could do this to people (I Corinthians 8:1). Such a person is doubly dangerous to himself and to others if he is puffed up by "knowledge falsely so called" (I Timothy 6:20). And this seems to be the case here because this man was "vainly" conceited – that is, as this word implies, holding a high opinion of himself without any good reason to do so! And this was sufficient to make all his talk about his own experiences of no consequence.

I suggest that whatever this heretic had experienced, he made the fatal mistake of interpreting it "by his fleshly mind" or "the mind of his flesh", in which, presumably, he was proudly confident. This we need to understand in reference to Paul's theology and technical terminology. First, he believed that the human mind, man's faculty for thinking, was defective as a result of the fall. He described it as depraved, or corrupt (I Timothy 6:5, II Timothy 3:8), and defiled (Titus 1:15). It was therefore futile or vacuous, and the driving influence behind non-Christian behaviour (Ephesus 4:17f.). It was a human faculty in urgent need of renewal (Ephesians 4:23, Romans 12:2).[101]

Then, using a different word for 'mind' but referring to much the same problem, Paul also wrote that "the mind of the flesh (τὸ φρόνημα τῆς σαρκός) is enmity against God, for it is not subject to the law of God, neither indeed can it be" (Romans 8:7). Although he uses the word 'flesh' in different ways, I suggest that here it is his term for 'man without God', or what we Christians were before our reconciliation with God

---

[101] This is a crucial matter that the genuinely repentant Christian will always keep in mind. As he thinks and reasons he remains keenly aware of the fallenness – and consequent limitations – of his cognitive and rational abilities. Even here – indeed, especially here – he remembers his dependence upon the grace of God.

(Romans 7:5), the 'unconverted man'. It does not refer only to our physicality or sensuality, but to the whole being – including noetic faculties – of those who are still among the "alienated and enemies" (1:21). This involves "being darkened in ... understanding, being alienated from the life of God because of the ignorance that is in them" (Ephesians 4:18).

This is a deadly serious matter, and even the most intellectually competent among the unconverted labour in their thinking with this impediment – and even we as Christians are not yet altogether free from its influence.[102]

Here, then, is the problem:

People are continuously engaged with their own consciousness, interacting with others around them, and constantly involved with the phenomena of this world. Life, then, is incessantly charged with experiences! The religious ascetic and mystic may attempt to supplement these common experiences with real or imaginary paranormal encounters. These experiences – whether common or paranormal, but particularly the latter – are rarely, if ever, self-interpreting, so those that suffer them must find an explanation for them, devise their own definition of the occurrences, or assume that they have occurred in a non-cognitive realm in which understanding is of no significance.

Whichever way they go, they must *seriously engage* with these happenings in their life, just as I suggested above the heretics were doing in Colossae. In one sense, they cannot help but "dwell in the things ... seen" (2:18). Everything then depends upon what they make of these experiences, or how they interpret them – and even consigning them to a non-cognitive realm is to make an interpretation of them.

And this brings us back to the question of anthropocentric "philosophy and vain deceit after the traditions of men, after the rudiments of the world" (2:8, #3.2.1.). All such philosophy is the direct product of those who are "vainly puffed up by (their) fleshly mind". And if this mind is "darkened in understanding ...

---

[102] We should not forget that Paul was advising Christians when he wrote, "be transformed by the renewing of your mind" (Romans 12:2). The imperative in this clause (μεταμορφοῦσθε) is in the present tense, implying an ongoing process of renewing. Similarly, the "being renewed unto knowledge" (τὸν ἀνακαινούμενον εἰς ἐπίγνωσιν) in Colossians 3:10 is a matter of progressing development, not instant transformation.

alienated from the life of God" (Ephesians 4:18), how can man ever rightly discern the truth?

A man will follow "the traditions of men and the rudiments of the world" because he is "vainly puffed up by his fleshly mind"; but if he would follow the philosophy that is "after Christ", he will hold fast "the Head" that he might "increase with the increase of God" (2:8, 18-19).

The disturbing complaint that threatens the health of the church is anthropocentric philosophy, and the aetiology of the disease is the pride of the unconverted mind.

4. Another important observation must be made here. The heretic Paul had in mind was, as we indicated, seriously engaged in the "things he has seen".[103] In the most obvious contrast, the apostle was urging his readers to remember and build upon *the things they had heard.* We should weigh the importance of his specific comments regarding this in the Colossian letter: "whereof you heard in the word of the truth of the gospel" (1:5), "since … you heard and knew" (1:6), "which you heard, which was preached" (1:23), "as you were taught" (2:6). And we should also note what he had to say in such passages as Romans 10:13-15, I Corinthians 1:21, 15:1ff, II Timothy 4:1-4 (cf. #2.1.3. and #3.2.2.2.).

To encapsulate the apostle's teaching in this regard, we need remember that he not only wrote that "we walk by faith, and not by sight" (II Corinthians 5:7), but also that "faith comes by hearing, and hearing by the word of Christ" (Romans 10:17).

Christian faith does not rest in experiences or visions, but in the word of God.

Paul's primary concern here in Colossians – which we find at the beginning of this letter – is that his readers be "filled

---

[103] One might wonder if this heretic in Colossae was attempting an imitation of the apostles who were appointed to be eye-witnesses of Christ's life and resurrection. They were specifically given this responsibility because they had been with Christ "from the beginning" of His ministry (John 15:27, cf. Acts 1:22, 10:39-42). It was required of them to speak of "the things which (they had) heard, which (they had) seen with their eyes" of the life manifested in Christ (I John 1:1f).

No one apart from the first-generation apostles has ever been given, or could have been given, this ministry – although there have always been those who would arrogate it to themselves.

with the knowledge of His will in all spiritual wisdom and understanding" and "increasing in the knowledge of God" (1:9-10). This, in other words, is knowledge of God Himself and His purposes that enables Christian men and women to live in wisdom and understanding, to live intelligently and thoughtfully in this present world. It also enables them to give a reason for their hope (I Peter 3:15), to articulate their faith, and to preach the gospel, as the apostle requires in 4:6.[104]

Moreover, knowing God and gaining wisdom and understanding through His revelation in Christ and the scriptures, enables His genuine people, as they relate intelligently to this present world, to appreciate something of the authentic significance of *every experience* they have. For them there is nothing other than religious experiences, because they know that they live in a world in which all things are created by God (1:15), who "works all things after the counsel of His own will" (Ephesians 1:11), and in whom "we live, and move, and have our being" (Acts 17:28). Those who truly respect and have faith in the magnitude of God's creation, providence, and redemption would probably find a paranormal or mystical experience something of an unnecessary distraction.

So, I wonder also if there may be here in Colossians 2:16-17 an indication of an incipient tendency, albeit limited and localized, to establish a mandate to govern or teach the church which is based upon experience and vision, rather than upon the authority of the apostolic scripture.

I would not deny for one moment the importance of the ministry of experienced men in the congregation. Indeed, this is implied by the apostolic use of the term "elder" (πρεσβύτερος) when discussing the appointment of leaders in the church (I Timothy 5:17, Titus 1:5).[105] And obviously, an elder is to be appointed because of his years of experience; he is "not a novice", a new convert, or neophyte (I Timothy 3:6, νεόφυτος).

---

[104] One of the disturbing features of ancient and modern Christian mysticism – and mysticism in general – is that its proponents speak much about religious techniques that are supposed to lead the devotee to his own transcendental experience. But they usually insist that nothing can be said about the experience itself, it being ineffable. Therefore, their message has no communicable substance, no intelligent context to be preached, no practical wisdom and understanding to impart, and no relevant moral principles. In this, at least, it is totally unrelated to the very expressive, content-full, ethically rich, perspicacious gospel of Christ. It provides no help for this life, only at best possible, brief moments of escape from it.

[105] Titus 1:7 uses the word "bishop" or "overseer" (ἐπίσκοπος, *episcopos*), as equivalents for the concept of "elder"; these are two terms for the one office.

He is a man, then, not of enhanced, unique experiences, but of prolonged, everyday, common experiences.

And for this maturity of the years, the occasional or mystical experience is no substitute at all. The biblical elder, out of his prolonged involvement in life, is positioned to lead the Christians under his care in and through the many and varied everyday adventures they must face in the world. But the 'charismatic' leader – using this word in its narrow, modern, popular sense among Christians – is more likely to lead them only into the experience of a mystical moment. And outside of that moment a believer is often left ignorant, morally naked, and unprotected against evil temptations and the anthropocentric philosophies of men.

3.2.3.2. THEY IMPUGNED THE SUFFICIENCY OF CHRIST (2:19)

To counter the misleading teaching of the heretics, the apostle stresses the total sufficiency of Jesus Christ. What was available to God's people in and through Christ did not need to be supplemented in any way by anything man could gain through the exercise of his own and unaided wisdom, moral ability, or experience. Such limited wisdom and moral abilities the Christian may have are to be redeemed and used to appreciate and to apply all that Jesus Christ has done and has to offer.

All Paul has written thus far in this letter exhibits his belief in the complete sufficiency of Christ and His ability to meet all the needs of His people – indeed, all that is needed for the redemption of the whole of His creation. We have already noted, for example, that he declares that "all the treasures of wisdom and knowledge" are to be found in Him (2:3), and that it is only "in Him" that we can discover the fullness of human life (2:10).

Now the apostle insists that it is futile to turn to asceticism or mystical experiences, because everything the Christian community needs for its "increase" (2:19) is supplied through Christ as the Head of the body, and not in individual isolation but in communion with other believers. However, the false teachers in Colossae were so engrossed in the things they "had seen" that they had, in effect, turned away from Christ altogether. They had in some way allowed egocentricity to displace Christocentricity in their religious thinking and practice. And as this displacement of Christ by anthropocentric concerns has been and remains a constant problem in the churches, it is worth giving it some thought.

There are *two matters* here we need to consider: the displacement of Christ and the misjudgement of purpose.

• **First**, the displacement of Christ.

The strongest condemnation of the Colossian heretics Paul made – and no greater could have been made – was that they were "not holding fast the Head, from whom all the body, being supplied and knit together through the joints and bands, increases with the increase of God" (2:19). Here the apostle picks up the image of Christ as the head of the body from 1:18, and we have suggested above that he used this metaphor to explain the interdependence of Christians upon one another, their mutual dependence upon Christ, and His supreme authority over the church (#1.3.2.1.).

Christ as the Head of His church, as 2:19 indicates, provides both the *sustenance* it requires for survival and growth, and exercises the *lordship* and authority it requires for its structure and purpose. Therefore, it is necessary – and indeed, obligatory – that the members of the church *trust* Him for the former and *obey* Him in the latter.

We might assume, then, that any who are not "holding fast the Head" are failing to trust Him or to obey him, or probably – as these are concomitants – both. And as such was the case with the false teachers, a serious and sinister danger becomes evident. It is tragically possible to write purportedly Christian theology and to conduct a plausible teaching ministry in the church, masquerading in both as an orthodox exponent of the gospel, without genuinely holding to Christ as the Head of the body and as the authority for all things Christian, that is, without faith and obedience. And this is a haunting possibility that persistently troubles even the devout (cf. I Corinthians 10:12).

The word for 'holding fast' (κρατέω) is variously used in the New Testament: often physically of laying hold of someone, to arrest or take into custody (Mark 6:17), of holding on to someone to give assistance or find support (Mark 5:41, Act 3:11); and sometimes metaphorically of keeping some matter in mind (Mark 9:10), and of maintaining traditions (II Thessalonians 2:15). Therefore, where there is no 'holding fast' either physical contact is relinquished, or intellectual association and social obligation are abandoned. Whatever Paul had in mind when using this word in 2:19, it seems evident that he censured the false teachers in Colossae for severing whatever attachment they may have had with Christ, and for renouncing their obedience to Him. The Lord, then, was of no central significance in their lives, having been reduced, at best, to a peripheral point of occasional reference.

This abandonment of Christ is a threatening possibility whenever anyone is unduly, or exclusively preoccupied with his own experiences – "the things ... seen". This can result in an introspection that excludes any serious consideration of our Lord, as it generates an obsession with one's self. Then the practice of religion becomes an expression of egocentricity.[106]

Interestingly, this attitude among the Colossian heretics involved not only a violation of the relationship they should have had with Christ Himself – He being the Head – but also a violation of the relationship they should have had with Christ's body, the church, and all its members. In this, heresy always contains the seeds of schism and exclusivity. Those who are rebellious against heaven are usually fractious among men.

By denying their dependence upon the Lord, through whom "all the body (is) supplied and knit together", they simultaneously deny their dependence upon other believers through whom He establishes and enriches His church. For them neither Christ nor the congregation are considered essential for their spiritual life, and neither have any authority for them, because these deceived intruders have found their fullness in their subjective mysticism. It was not without good reason that Paul strived for the Colossians "that their hearts may be comforted, they being knit together in love, and unto all riches of the full assurance of understanding, that they may know the mystery of God, Christ" (2:1-2); or that he reminds them here of the importance of their being "knit together" (2:19). It is only within the objective communion of the church, being united with other believers, that we understand God's mystery, and gain knowledge of Christ.

Any supercilious or arrogant claim to superior spirituality, or to some uniquely defining religious experience, is necessarily divisive and isolating. In comparison, we should think of Paul's mature statements about himself: "I know that in me, that is, in my flesh, dwells no good thing ... wretched man that I am" (Romans 7:18, 24); "I count not myself yet to have apprehended; but one thing I do ... (I stretch) forward to the things that are before, I press on ..." (Philippians 3:13-14); "Christ Jesus came into the world to save sinners, of whom I am chief" (I Timothy 1:15). He was thankful that he could stand together with others as repentant, redeemed sinners.

Those who seriously engage with their own individual or mystical experiences, making them the basis for their faith and their claim to authority, usually have little place for Christ other than to seek patronage in His name, and trade upon His reputation. Mention of Christ by them

---

[106] And I cannot but wonder sometimes if this has become the nemesis of contemporary church worship.

is usually cursory and often made to enhance the teachers' dubious claim to legitimacy. By making so much of their experiences in both their life and teaching, Christ is displaced. The historicity of Christ's life, death, and resurrection become inconsequential in comparison with their own supposed spiritual encounters. They make the most of every opportunity to draw attention to themselves and to talk about their own religious history. Their personal testimonies are more important than the testimony of Christ, or of His apostles. They would have people follow them into their mystical happenings, rather than follow Christ in the service of God.[107]

- **Second**, the misjudgement of purpose.

We might well ask those who pursue asceticism and mystical experience what they believe the purpose of such religious activities might be, or at least what their purpose might be in pursuing them. Paul evidently believed that if in the process they were no longer "holding fast the Head", then they would not increase "with the increase of God", or, as some might translate, grow "with a maturation which is from God" (2:19, αὔξει τὴν αὔξησιν τοῦ θεοῦ). If this were so, they would then be pursuing a misconceived goal, devoid of any godly advantage.

This presents us with the tragic possibility that some people, following the wrong teaching, might zealously and with much personal discipline (cf. 2:23), engage in futile spiritual exercises. And when this is done in anticipation of some ineffable experience of which they know nothing and can know nothing until it is experienced, their purpose can be little more than an experiment in blind faith. This carries the danger of ending in either disillusionment or despair – or in nothing but wasted effort and scepticism.

In contrast, those who hold to Christ in faith and obedience, drawing upon the wisdom, knowledge, and revelation found in Him, and who are nurtured and nourished within a congregation of genuine and humble Christian believers through the teaching of "the word of the truth of the gospel" (1:5), these will indeed "increase with the increase of God". And

---

[107] I know that there are many sincere Christians who speak much about their experiences – normal and paranormal – in their desire to bring glory to Christ. This practice may be laudable, but tends to become, I believe, dangerous. There comes a point where such devotees of experiential mysticism begin to introduce into the churches a religion that is simply not Christianity, despite the claims they make and the vocabulary they use. There are, for example, most erudite theologians who would have us believe that what happened two thousand years ago in the life of Christ is of no consequence, because, they insist, the only thing of importance is what happens in our hearts now.

in this, I suggest, they will not only discover the true purpose of religion, but also the God-given significance in being human.

But what exactly are we to understand by "the increase of God", or "the maturing that God gives"?

This is a question that at first glance might be thought inconsequential, and the answer obvious. But it seems to me to be an enquiry of immense importance that is too often sadly misconceived, ignored, simplistically answered, or taken for granted. *Ought we not to be seriously concerned to know what God requires of us, what goals we ought to pursue that are pleasing to Him, what are the parameters of Christian maturity to which we should aspire, and by what means we should progress in our faith?*[108]

Then, apart from confusion about personal maturation, Christians frequently seem to have drifted into the folly of attempting to prosecute the work and the ministry of the gospel when they do not really know what the increase is that God desires for His church. But they are constantly devising new techniques and programs that they consider to be suitable activities to succeed in their vague endeavours.

Whether, then, in individual, spiritual maturation or in church development, holy ambition desires – or should desire – nothing but the "increase" that God is pleased to give to His people.

In our modern, efficient, methodological age, in which human skill and programming have achieved the most remarkable things in contemporary society, I believe it has become difficult for Christians to keep in mind that the only "increase" – whether personal or congregational – that is of ultimate worth is "the increase of God", that is, the development that God gives. And if it is so given, it is of grace. Today churches seem more concerned to determine *what increase, of any kind, they are to achieve by their techniques.* If one scheme fails, then another, more sophisticated, must be found to replace it; if the first then becomes unfashionable or is considered otiose, another more marketable program is needed. If our self-chosen goals are achieved – or abandoned – then we choose another.

I am well aware that God is pleased with our obedience and rewards our good works, such as they are. Moreover, I would not deny that God is pleased to use our rather feeble efforts to serve Him and even our misconceived plans; otherwise, nothing at all would ever be achieved. But we must hold fast to Christ as our Head, being obedient to His word,

---

[108] And we should never confuse this with the egocentricity that asks how God and the gospel can be employed to prosper our own ambitions or to further our own cause.

always seeking to do that which is good in His sight, and not merely engaging in our own machinations. We should be diligent and thoughtful in all our service for Him and in the works of the congregation. We must continually keep in mind that whether we plant or we water, it is always "God that gives the increase" (I Corinthian 3:7).

But we need not be ignorant concerning "the increase of God" (2:19) of which Paul writes. He has already mentioned this matter twice in this letter, leaving us in no doubt.

He explained that "the word of the truth of the gospel" was "bearing fruit and increasing". There was a growing influence of the preaching of the gospel "in all the world" that was effectively bringing knowledge of "the grace of God in truth" to many people (1:5-6). This was a *geographically expansive growth of the church* that took the influence of the gospel throughout the local community and across national and ethnic boundaries, eliminating ignorance about God, and bringing Christian salvation – and, indeed, Christian civilization – to others.

Then the apostle mentioned his prayer for his readers that they might, by the grace of God, "be filled with the knowledge of His will … to walk worthily of the Lord … bearing fruit in every good work and increasing in the knowledge of God" (1:9-10). This was a *congregationally comprehensive growth within the church* that informed, sanctified, and strengthened individual believers that they might be godly in thought and deed.

Paul is evidently concerned, then, for both the increase of Christian influence in the world and for the increase of individual spiritual maturation in the lives of Christian people. And, I would suggest, these two must not be separated. It is impossible for immature believers – those who are not "filled with the knowledge of His will in all spiritual wisdom and understanding" (1:9) – to have any meaningful influence in the world; they are ill-equipped to proclaim and implement "the word of the truth of the gospel" (1:5) in the human community.

However, in Colossians 2:19, it is evident that Paul's primary concern is for the maturation of individuals within the congregation because he would have "the body" – the church, the congregation – "increase with the increase of God". He was anxious that this growth among his readers be not hindered by what appears to have been heretical teaching that advocated, among other things, asceticism and mystical experience.

◆

CHRISTIAN AUTHORITY

Assuming these comments more or less reflect Paul's concerns in 2:16-19, we might bring together some matters of fundamental importance in the hope of clarifying *the way to a truly Christian mind*. We need to ask how we might actually find such clarity when confronted by all the confusion and cacophony of many different theological and philosophical theories and opinions, fluctuating social conventions, multicultural practices, and gyrating moral relativism. And the problem is exacerbated by contemporary considerations which conclude, these things being so convoluted, that, truth be known, there is no such thing as 'truth' to be known, that there is nothing but opinion! Or, in effect, nothing but individual, subjective – or mystical – experience.

The thinking man is confronted by vast, labyrinthine, and intimidating philosophical notions that are sufficient to deter all but the most adventurous and audacious academics.

In contrast, to allay His disciples' fears and to facilitate their understanding, Jesus said, "I am the way, and the truth, and the life" (John 14:6). Setting aside for the moment all philosophical discussion, He simply drew attention to Himself. Here the simplest of His followers could find understanding and meaning embodied before them. He had already made one thing clear to them when He said, "Except you turn, and become as little children, you shall in no wise enter into the kingdom of heaven" (Matthew 18:3). The newborn child learns to know and to trust the most significant person in his life instinctively and immediately – and many years before he can master the knowledge of arithmetic, Euclidean geometry, or infinitesimal calculus! And we could argue that his first, infantile learning experiences ground him in two essential prerequisites for knowing truth – our inescapable human dependency and the necessity of trust. Only a subsequent and more sophisticated education undermines this early faith and understanding, making the cynic.

The Bible begins with an interesting and compelling parallel. "In the beginning God created ..." (Genesis 1:1). Here we might also set aside for the moment all philosophical debate about creation, and note that the author begins by simply drawing attention to a Person. He assumed that his readers would have had no problem with this, as he would, no doubt, have been of the opinion that as a human being Adam instinctively and immediately knew and trusted in a personal God. It was only the subsequent subtle, philosophical assertions of the serpent – his "persuasiveness of speech" (2:4) – that undermined man's primeval faith and understanding. Paul was in complete agreement with this assumption. He wrote many years later, "The invisible things of Him since the creation of the world are clearly seen ... His everlasting power and divinity" (Romans 1:20). And again, we would suggest, only a more sophisticated education undermined this fundamental trust and knowledge.

We sense, then, that there may be something treacherous about education.

The word 'education', I believe, comes from a word meaning to 'lead', and hence to 'rear', or 'bring up', as with a child. A perfectly good word for a worthwhile activity! Indeed, the wisdom of the Old Testament recommends it: "Train up a child in the way he should go" (Proverbs 22:6).

Here we must distinguish two words that are not altogether synonymous and represent ideas that are not necessarily concomitant – 'education' and 'learning'. Ideally, the teacher educates and the student learns, but the student may learn without a teacher, and the teacher may teach without the student learning. So, the two may be both related and unrelated. The autodidact only has himself to blame if his learning is inadequate, but the student in a classroom may blame either himself or his teacher if he fails to learn. Therefore, I suggest, any benefit that education may have is dependent upon the appropriate disposition and character of both teacher and student. If the teacher is at fault, then the education he offers is treacherous. He will lead his students astray. And if the student is at fault, he will be his own traitor. He will lead himself astray. There is, then, always the danger of "deceiving and being deceived" (II Timothy 3:13). Education is never far removed from deception.

We must not be so naïve as to imagine that education and learning can be separated from morality. Neither must we think that any educational system is neutral, without bias, or having no ulterior motive. We know well enough that a totalitarian regime will manipulate and politicize the educational system in its country to instill its own prejudices and values into the minds of its people to maintain its dominance and prosecute its agenda. And religions tend to do the same! But it is not the processes of education, the methodologies, that are the main problem, but the intentions of its manipulators. If the purpose of education is to lead, then it is important to ask about the direction in which it might be leading the people, and to remember that where it is leading is determined by whence it has come (see #3.2.1. Third).

And this raises the question of authority in education and learning, *especially in the church*. Can it be trusted?

It is of the greatest importance that all genuine Christian education and learning – devolving as they do from Christian thinking – begin with God as He is revealed in Jesus Christ, for He is the way, the truth, and the life (John 14:6). This involves no difficulties for the committed and wise Christian, because he acknowledges the authority of Christ, recognizing His pre-eminence in all things (1:14ff) and that in Him "are all the treasures of wisdom and knowledge hidden" (2:3). Moreover, Jesus said, "My teaching is not mine, but His that sent me. If any man is willing to do His will, he shall know of the teaching, whether it be of God, or whether I speak from myself" (John 7:16-17). In this, He asserted that His teaching, coming directly from the Father, had divine authority, but that those who are unwilling to believe and obey will gain no benefit from it. The volitional disposition of the listener, or the learner, is critical.

We have already seen that to receive Christ involves both accepting His teaching and acknowledging His authority (#3.1.2.). Only those who were willing to do so will learn from His tutelage. Therefore, the true Christian, by virtue of his rebirth and conversion, is obliged and enabled to hear the word of Christ and to obey it. If he does not, then he is immature, recalcitrant, or rebellious.

Moreover, learning from Christ is, at least in one aspect, different from all other learning. From other teachers, we may glean knowledge that we might effectively use once we have left the classroom, but we need have no further association with the teacher, and we are free to apply whatever we have learned as we please. But our Lord said, "If you abide in my word, then you are my disciples, and you shall know the truth, and the truth shall make you free" (John 8:31-32). In other words, we will only benefit from His teaching as we continue to be His disciples. We dare not learn from and then depart from Jesus Christ! Or, as He said elsewhere, "If you abide in me, and my words abide in you, you shall ask what you will, and it shall be done unto you" (John 15:7). This indicates that to live a life that is compatible with the will of God there must be an established and ongoing relationship between the believer and both Christ and His words. There is much more in this Christian learning than a merely academic exercise! We can neither learn nor apply Christian learning, as we ought, outside a redeemed and continuing association with Christ as our Lord. This learning is only effective in and through faith and obedience.

With this in mind perhaps, Paul admonishes the church: "If any man teaches a different doctrine, and consents not to sound words, the words of our Lord Jesus Christ, and to the doctrine which is according to godliness, he is puffed up, knowing nothing, but doting about questionings and disputes of words, from which come envy, strife, railings, evil surmisings, wranglings of men corrupted in mind and bereft of the truth" (I Timothy 6:3-5).

Here it is worth noting that the apostle is concerned that any teacher in the church be not only a man with adequate knowledge of the word of Christ but also that he knows and follows the ways of godliness – being both intellectually and morally sound! This translates into the knowledge of God and the willingness to obey Him. And in this, by the grace of God, we might regain that primeval knowledge of and trust in the Person.

There is no doubt, then, that Christian authority – the authority for both our teaching and our practice – is Jesus Christ Himself, and that we have access to His authority in – and only in – the Bible. We only *know Him* through the revelation of His word; we only *trust Him* in reference to the promises of His word; and we only *obey Him* by adhering to commandments of His word. *His word is of paramount importance in all things.*

It would be a rare occasion – although not as rare as we might expect – if we were to find someone in the Christian congregations who would deny that Jesus Christ is the Head of the Church and the Lord of all believers. After all, to confess that 'Jesus' is the 'Christ' is to acknowledge, *inter alia*, that He is 'King'. No one could honestly hold membership in a church, let alone seek a position of leadership in it, if he did not make such a confession. And it would be unusual – although not as unusual as we might expect – for a church to grant membership to or appoint to office anyone who denies the lordship of Christ. At least some semblance of genuine and orderly Christianity must be maintained.

However, it is not at all rare – indeed, it is far too common – to find those who do confess Jesus as Lord who do not know Him, trust Him, or obey Him. There are those, Jesus said, who "honour me with their lips, but their heart is far from me" (Matthew 15:8). Elsewhere He explained, "Not every one that says unto me, Lord, Lord, shall enter into the kingdom of heaven; but he that does the will of my Father who is in heaven" (Matthew 7:21).

Now, perhaps the most facile and probably the most popular way in which people confess Jesus Christ as Lord while at the same time caring neither to know, trust, or obey Him, is to suggest that He is too remote, a distant figure in history, and only the far removed 'founding father'. He may have left us an important heritage, but now we must build upon it, move forward, and 'progress with the times'. Then, if we suggest that Christ can truly be known and that He draws near to us in and through the pages of the Bible, we are told that the scriptures are ancient writings, obscure in meaning, culturally obsolete, and we must leave it to the academics to extract from them whatever little remains of practical value for our times, if any.

If we are going to confess Christ as Lord for the sake of gaining or maintaining status in the Christian community, but wish to continue doing and thinking as we please, all we have to do is to deny that there is any clear and unambiguous access to His word and commandments. If we convince ourselves that we really do not know exactly what He taught, or entertain the idea that what He taught is no longer relevant, then we might excuse ourselves from following His teaching.

To confess Jesus as Lord and yet continue in our own theories and practices, we need only to set ourselves in one way or another at a distance from the Bible: and this we can do either by sophisticated argument or by simple neglect. And sadly, both these are defections far too common in the churches.

◆

It appears that the heretics in Colossae did not believe in the sufficiency of Christ, or in the sufficiency of His redemptive work. Neither did they believe that salvation was obtained by faith alone. Rather, they believed in the supposed uncontaminated, natural ability in man, and that this must be exploited if the benefits of religion were to be enjoyed. Therefore, a man is to depend upon sources other than Christ to secure salvation and gain the advantages of 'faith'.

There was, it seems, a synergism of the worst kind being taught in Colossae. Failing to appreciate the pre-eminence of Christ (1:18), they confidently turned to "philosophy and vain deceit, after the traditions of men" (2:8) to supplement or to interpret whatever they might have considered of worth in the Christian message. In doing this, these false teachers were impugning the authority of Christ and the sufficiency of "the word of the truth of the gospel" (1:5).

However, Paul was clearly convinced that it was this "word of the truth of the gospel" – that is, the teachings of Christ – that established the Colossian church in the "grace of God" at its inception (1:5-7). Moreover, he was prepared to suffer for the church that he might fully preach "the word of God", knowing that "God was pleased to make known what is the riches of the glory of this mystery … which is Christ" (2:24ff). It was imperative that the new Christians in Colossae were "established in the faith, even as they were taught" (2:7) – as they were taught from the beginning in "the word of the truth of the gospel", in the "mystery … which is Christ". *Not to accept this word of the truth and the failure to learn from and obey it could lead only to disaster.*

And here is the one, fundamental heresy that has devastated the Christian church, the one deviation that gives rise to all other heresies: the impugning of the authority of "the word of the truth of the gospel" (1:5). To abandon the Bible, or to question its authenticity as the word of God, or to supplement it and its explicit teachings with additions from other sources – be they church dogmas, anthropocentric philosophies, or mystical experiences – is to diminish the value of Christ Himself and to contribute to the demise of genuine Christianity.

It is to be expected that the non-Christians will emphatically deny our Lord's authority, repudiate His teaching, and reject the Bible. This we anticipate, and it does not surprise or unduly trouble us. But we find it seriously distressing that historically His authority, as a person and in the scriptures, has been and is being compromised by many professing Christians *within the churches.* They have done this by deviating from the apostolic assertion that the Bible is the trustworthy, sufficient, and authoritative word of Christ (cf. II Timothy 3:14-17, II Peter 1:15-21). Wishing to find a place for man's independent skills and self-government, they have introduced numerous variations of human "philosophy and vain deceit", incorporating them into Christian theology.

NOTE: We might suggest that because the heretics in Colossae repudiated the sufficiency and authority of Christ and His teaching, they were unable to accept "the word of the truth of the gospel" (1:5) as it was originally "delivered unto the saints" (Jude 3). That they associated with the Christian congregation suggests that there was something about the gospel that they appreciated, but evidently, they did not consider it to be adequate. Therefore, it appears, they sought to modify the apostolic message with the following additions:

The supposed cognitive supplement of human rationalism. 2:8.
The supposed meritorious supplement of cultic practices. 2:16.
The supposed mediatorial supplement of mystical experience. 2:18.

And, we might say, those who would modify biblical Christianity today advocate, in one way or another, the very same additions. However, a careful consideration of these three supplements reveals that those who advocate them – or any one of them – no longer believe in the centrality and the sufficiency of Christ and His redemptive work. They call upon men to trust in themselves, in their own reasoning, in their own religious devotion, and in their own subjective experiences. Salvation then is not – as the apostles proclaimed – by faith alone, but by human thought and endeavour. And in this, "the truth of the gospel" is vitiated.

◆

3.3. THE PHILOSOPHICAL IMPLICATIONS (2:20-3:4)

At this point in our studies, it is worth keeping in mind *two particular aspects* of the apostle's teaching so far in this letter to the Colossians:

1. As we have seen, Paul has written a remarkable summary of the 'three dimensions' of Christian salvation, which is rooted in the reconciliation we have with God through the death of Christ. Benefitting from this, we are no longer "alienated and enemies" and we live in anticipation of being presented "holy and without blemish and unreproveable" in the presence of God (1:1-23, #1).

    In this we have a panoramic view of the Christian's *enduring association* with his Lord, historically established in time and reaching into eternity. He is now accepted by the Most Holy, the Almighty Creator, is granted knowledge and wisdom to live well and meaningfully in this present life, and is progressing towards a perfect future.

    Such is the "hope ... laid up" for His people (1:5).

2. We have also seen that considering the pressing intellectual and religious challenges they were facing in difficult and controversial times, the apostle considered it necessary that his Colossian readers also have an accurate view of the immediate, personal, and *intimate association* they have with Christ their Saviour that they might appreciate the fullness they have in Him (2:8-19).

    In this we have an insight into the benefits of the Christian's identification with his Lord in His circumcision and His baptism, so that he might grasp – and be grasped by – the fact that he died and was made alive together with Him. That is, Paul would have his readers understand and trust in that which God has done for them in Christ, rather than in the works, religious or ethical, that they might do for Him.

    Such it is to have "faith in the working of God" (2:12).

Now, any man who has *this hope* and *this faith*, together with some understanding of what they involve, is obliged to live – indeed, cannot but live – with a distinctive perspective on life that will set him apart from other people.[109] He will view and evaluate all things differently. He will have, and will hold to a philosophy, not after the traditions of men and the rudiments of the world, but after Christ (2:8). And it

---

[109] Everyone's religious presuppositions determine his philosophy, and his philosophy determines his manner of life. But as Christians, we should openly acknowledge this from the beginning, and cite the Bible as the source of our fundamental beliefs.

is just this new philosophical perspective and its demands that Paul now asks the reader to consider (2:20-3:4).[110] Genuine and informed hope and faith in Christ[111] have transforming potency, with, *inter alia, two significant ramifications.* For the believer, they determine both *the fundamental values* (2:20-23) and *the authentic purpose* (3:1-4) for human living. And these we must now consider.

3.3.1. Hope, Faith, and Human Values: and the Death of Christ (2:20-23)

Christian hope and faith establish for us the fundamental *values for human living* (cf. #3.3.2.).

In this respect, we should consider the following:

- **First**, the death of Christ and Christian living.[112]

    Paul draws our attention to *the true values for human living* when he writes, "If you died with Christ ... why ... do you subject yourselves to ordinances" (2:20). *He, perhaps in contrast to the advice of the false teachers, is referring to the kind of life we ought to pursue as Christians, and the manner in which it should to be lived.*

    Christian praxis is in view. We should live by faith.

    Evidently, the apostle is concerned lest we be adversely influenced by demands imposed upon us by others – both in life in general, and in a religious context – that are inconsistent with our redeemed association with Jesus Christ. Such extraneous impositions inevitably distort our system of values.

    He was aware that an unthinking or ill-informed Christian is susceptible to the inventions of the non-Christian mind that are contrary to the principles of the gospel. And one of these fundamental principles of our faith is that those who believe are justified through the death of Christ, and thereby fully reconciled with the Lord (1:21). Now, having escaped the condemnation of the law, they "live unto God" (Galatians 2:19). Subsequently, the dynamic of the living relationship we have with Him, rather than superimposed, alien regulations, should above all else determine the manner in which we live. There is far more to the Christian life than the rigours of religious discipline!

---

[110] We should always remember that Christ would have His disciples live in such a manner that they might be seen as lights in the world – distinctive and enlightening (Matthew 5:14, cf. John 8:12, 12:35-36). A solemn responsibility!

[111] See comments about faith, hope, and love in #1.1.1.

[112] cf. #3.3.2. First.

However, we should note immediately that these verses do not suggest that Christians should at all times, and in every circumstance avoid being subject to any rules or regulations whatsoever.[113] The word Paul uses here which is translated "subject yourself to ordinances" (*dogmatizesthe*, δογματίζεσθε) comes from the word 'dogma', and refers to established or officially proclaimed decrees. It is recorded elsewhere, for example, that Paul at one time carried official decrees or dogmas (τὰ δόγματα) from the Jerusalem Council to regional congregations for their observance (Acts 16:4). There are then, as this obviously indicates, ordinances to which we should willingly submit ourselves. We are not antinomians!

What is to be avoided is the dogma that is "after the precepts and doctrines of men" (2:22, κατὰ τὰ ἐντάλματα καὶ διδασκαλίας τῶν ἀνθρώπων) - that is, the religious demands and instructions that are according to and the product of anthropocentric philosophy (2:8). This is dogma that diminishes the joy and enfeebles the hope of men and women, imposing unwarranted burdens upon the human spirit and impoverishing human life (cf. Luke 11:46). They are always detrimental to Christian hope.

Following such misconceived dogma is an unrelenting, historic problem; an impediment that has its beginning in the Garden of Eden and, it seems, will persist until the day of our Lord's return (cf. Revelation 22:1-5).

In principle, Adam's rebellion, which has been perpetuated by all his descendants, was "after the precepts and doctrines of men". Although in Eden Adam responded to the suggestions proposed by Satan, they were nonetheless anthropocentric proposals in the sense that they placed man at the centre of the decision-making, recommending that he take charge of the situation, and leaving him responsible for his subsequent actions and their consequences. Things the devil insinuated, man chose to institutionalize.

Adam, then, accepted the specious principles of an anthropocentric philosophy that placed him at the centre of his own 'world'. He foolishly assumed that God's commandments or "precepts" were misconceived or malicious and could be rejected, so he ate the forbidden fruit. Then he apparently justified doing so by embracing false teachings or erroneous "doctrines", evidently being convinced that he could independently

---

[113] We must not be deceived into thinking that Christian freedom is anarchy.

decide the difference between good and evil (Genesis 3:1-5). And here is the origin of all "the precepts and doctrines of men".

The first man audaciously believed in his own self-sufficiency, and assumed that he could formulate his own beliefs, and then develop his own moral principles and way of life. He was convinced that he did not need God or divine law. He could devise his own commandments and construct the necessary religious and civil structures to impose them.

To this day mankind remains entranced by this delusion, and the lesson of Eden has not been learned! And sadly, man's "precepts and doctrines" do not, and never have, appreciably enhanced the moral quality of man's life on earth, and Eden has disappeared.

The phrase Paul uses here – "after the precepts and doctrines of men" – can be traced back to Isaiah 29:13. The prophet Isaiah was distressed by the superficial religious practices and vacuous profession of faith among the people in his day. These the Lord condemned because, He said, "This people draw near to me with their mouth, and with their lips they do honour me, but have removed their hearts far from me". They were spurious, religious conformists, social opportunists with no genuine belief in God. Their profession was the product of "a commandment of men" which they "had been taught", and was unrelated to divine revelation. The inevitable result of this travesty of true worship was that the "wisdom of their wise men shall perish, and the understanding of their prudent men shall be hid" (Isaiah 29:14). The intellectual consequences of their unbelief were alarming!

A vacuous religion – be it theistic or atheistic – is the prologue to a depleted mind (Romans 1:28).

Or positively, we might say, the genuine worship of God is an essential prerequisite for true wisdom. The Bible is replete with instructions in this matter.

Mark records that Jesus quoted this text from Isaiah (as found in the ancient Greek translation) to rebuke the people of His day who had, in effect, exchanged the word of God and its precepts for the anthropocentric "traditions of men" (Mark 7:6-9, τὴν παράδοσιν τῶν ἀνθρώπων). They, like the Israelites before them and the Colossians after them, had been exposed to a similar misleading philosophy (cf. 2:8).

And, interestingly, as a result of this aberration the Jews reduced religion to legalistic externals, much like the Colossian heretics who evidently required an ascetic life – "Handle not, nor taste, nor touch" (2:21). Therefore, Jesus had to explain to His followers after citing Isaiah 29:13, that, as Matthew noted, "Not that which enters into the mouth defiles the man, but that which proceeds out of the mouth, this defiles the man" (Matthew 15:11). The essential worship of God is not found in physical or ritual conformity – which may have an appropriate, secondary place, but it easily becomes vacuous – but in the heart of man.

False religion based upon anthropocentric philosophy inevitably leads to various forms of carnality as men worship the creation rather than the Creator (Romans 1:25). This, as we shall see, helps us to understand and define what is often referred to as materialism.[114]

Paul suggests that these anthropocentric theories, because of their severely limited perspectives, will inevitably result in the degradation of human life on earth, and in producing a manner of living that falls short of the fullness that we ought to enjoy in Christ. Paul was aware that the people in Colossae might be misled into a life of self-imposed, false humility, which actually results in dishonouring human physicality (2:23). Then, where this happens, created human life as God intended it to be is misunderstood, inadequately valued, and greatly impoverished (cf. I Timothy 4:1-4).

It is only our reconciliation with God through the death of Christ, and an appreciation of the intimate relationship that we have with Him as a result, that position us to live by faith in a significant and evident Christian manner.

• **Second**, the death of Christ and true philosophy.

Paul explains that we ought not to subject ourselves to futile ordinances or dogmas, because we "died with Christ from the rudiments of the world" (2:20). In this matter, then, the cross of Christ – and our being crucified with Him (Galatians 2:20) – makes a transforming difference.

How we understand this will depend upon what we take the "rudiments of the world" to be.[115] If this expression refers simply to the "principalities and powers" (2:10, 15), as some suggest, and these are understood to be demons or evil spirits of various kinds, then our crucifixion with Christ effectively sets us free from their domination. That we are set free from such personal, evil influences by the death of Christ is not in doubt[116]; but whether this is what, or all that Paul has in mind here is, I think, questionable.

---

[114] See below, Fourth, the death of Christ and things material.
[115] This we have discussed briefly above. See #3.2.1., especially TRADITIONS AND RUDIMENTS.
[116] See #3.2.2.4. especially, Second, Christ's executive triumph.

Throughout this letter to the Colossians, and central to it, is the apostle's primary concern that his readers be not deceived by the "persuasiveness of speech" (2:4) and the "philosophy and vain deceit" (2:8) of the false teachers. This is where the proximate threat to his readers' well-being is found. Therefore, he would have them remember "the word of the truth of the gospel" (1:5), and be established in the faith "as (they) were taught" (2:7). It was vital that they be thoughtful, and well instructed in the Word of God. The immediate danger was the influence of the heretics, their speculations, and their erroneous teaching.

First consideration, then, must be given to adequate Christian understanding.

But this, as we have seen, depends upon escaping the false anthropocentric theories about the "elements/rudiments"; the misconceived ideas people entertain about the nature of the world, man, human society, and all existence. These deceptions can only be avoided by knowing that Christ created all things, including the "principalities and powers" (1:14-17); that is, by thinking from a Christocentric perspective; or by "bringing every thought into captivity to the obedience of Christ" (II Corinthians 10:5). If we do not know that this world is created and governed by Almighty God who "works all things after the counsel of His own will" (Ephesians 1:11), then we will have to find some other explanation of life.

Only when we know that Christ has pre-eminence in all things "in the heavens and upon the earth", can we have the informed faith that will enable us to escape or overcome any evil forces that may emanate from the "principalities and powers" or from anywhere else. How can we expect deliverance from either the fear or the force of any form of wickedness or deception if we doubt the deity, the omnipotence, the sovereignty, or the grace of Christ? We dare not trust in any lesser redeemer! Who else is powerful enough to save us? Hence, no doubt, Paul would have us know that "in Him dwells all the fullness of the Godhead bodily" (2:9). He alone is sufficient. Our faith must be in Him who is seated at God's right hand in heaven, "far above all principality and power" (Ephesians 1:21); such a faith that is "rooted and built up" in Christ (2:7).

Moreover, if we have a restricted or diminished view of Christ, our Redeemer, then we will also be inhibited by a restricted or diminished understanding of our redemption in Christ. If we do not see Him as sovereign and omnipotent, or if we entertain the idea that He is obliged in some circumstances to limit the exercise of His own dominion, we will necessarily hold a reduced appreciation of the effectiveness of His redemptive work. We will underestimate the value of both His crucifixion, and the benefits we obtain from it.

And any diminution in our minds of the majesty and the ministry of Christ inevitably weakens our faith in Him. The less we think of Him, the less we will trust in Him.

Therefore, an undiminished faith in Christ must at first be based upon *a correct and adequate understanding of God and His creation*, an understanding of the personal and physical context in which we live – that is, with God in His world, not alone in 'our' world. In one sense, and in biblical order, this is where we must begin: because "in the beginning God created the heavens and the earth" (Genesis 1:1). This is the first thing God would have us know.

Subsequently, when we have gained some awareness of divine creation, a developed, redemptive faith must be based upon a true appreciation of, and confidence in God's gracious, saving intervention in this world in Christ. That is, a sense of divine creation is prerequisite for understanding salvation.

It is, therefore, a matter of primary importance that we heed Paul's warning and beware those who would take us captive by their "philosophy ... after the rudiments of the world" (2:8). This, we have suggested above, is the attempt of the non-Christians to explain the phenomena of the universe in which we live from their own perspective. But by following such anthropocentric theories, "the ... doctrines of men" (2:22), people fail to reckon with the fact that "all things were created" in Christ (1:16). And this misunderstanding of creation inevitably erodes faith, because it excludes God from the singular, sovereign position of Creator. Such people seem to be content to believe in a lesser god, or no god at all, and would have us join them in their folly.[117]

It is not, then, escaping the evil influence of the "principalities and powers" that is of first importance, but escaping the evil influence of any "philosophy" according to anthropocentric theories about "the rudiments/ elements of the world" that misrepresents God's creation and therefore undermines the very faith that saves us from the "principalities and powers". Only those who "know the truth" – the truth as it is in Christ and His word – will be made free (John 8:31-32).

---

[117] It is not surprising, then, that the enemies of the Christian faith are vehement in their opposition to our belief in creation and are enthusiastic proponents of evolutionary theories. If they can demolish the biblical cosmology of a divinely designed and constructed world, they can – and do – quickly excuse themselves from the obligation to believe in Jesus Christ.

Therefore, I suggest, it is important that we understand what Paul means when he writes that we "died with Christ from the rudiments of the world" (2:20).

We must keep in view here that the "rudiments of the world" that the apostle has in mind are such "rudiments" as are presented or assumed by those committed to a vain philosophy and "the traditions of men" (2:8). It is their non-Christian concepts and their ideological influence that must be overcome. And somehow, Paul declares, our identification with Christ in His death overcomes this for us.

Now we must keep in mind that those who reject the significance of biblical creation and the sovereignty of God as the Creator do so, not because of any intellectual incapacity to comprehend what is involved in these concepts, but because of their resistance to Christ's lordship (Romans 10:9) and their resentment at His teaching (John 7:7). Or, in other words, because of their "ungodliness and unrighteousness" (Romans 1:18, ἀσέβειαν καὶ ἀδικίαν ἀνθρώπων, man's refusal to respect the person and obey the law of God). The basic problem is not cognitive, but moral. They reason as men estranged from God, as those "alienated and enemies in (their) mind" (1:21).

Therefore, recovery can only begin when the problems of alienation and enmity are resolved. The mind-set of antipathy and antagonism towards God must be converted into one of love and obedience.

It is just this profound, comprehensive conversion of the heart and mind that we should expect and long for when we preach the gospel.

When Paul wrote in Ephesians 2:13-16 about the reconciliation of Jews and Gentiles to each other in the body of Christ, and the reconciliation of both to God in the blood of Christ, he wanted his readers to appreciate the extent of the personal transformation this requires. Before their conversion, people were not only "alienated from the commonwealth of Israel" and therefore did not share in "the covenants of promise", but they had also been walking "in the vanity of their mind", being "alienated from the life of God" (Ephesians 2:12, 4:17-18). But on their behalf God had graciously "through the cross ... slain the enmity" and renewed them "in the spirit of (their) mind" (Ephesians 2:16, 4:23). So complete was the change, the apostle declared that they had "put on the new man" (Ephesians 4:24).

Both the alienation and the enmity had been overcome together with the renewal of the mind!

Now we should note that overcoming the alienation and the resolution of the problem of the enmity, which involve the renewal of the mind, are inextricably linked with Christ's death: "You that once were far off are made nigh by the blood of Christ ... through the cross, having slain the enmity thereby" (Ephesians 2:13, 2:16).

Similarly, here in the letter to the Colossians, the apostle explains that although Christians were once in fact estranged from God because they were "alienated and enemies in their mind", they are "now ... reconciled in the body of His flesh through death" (1:21-22).

We might suggest, then, that we will not think Christianly until we are filled with an understanding of the death of Christ.

We really cannot anticipate that anyone will truly believe in Jesus Christ solely as the result of the Christians' convincing arguments. We must indeed be "ready always to give an answer to every man that asks (us) for a reason concerning the hope" that we have (I Peter 3:15). But we must remember that we will be giving our answers to men and women who may well be unresponsive because they are alienated from and the enemies of God. They will not be of a mind to give any credence to anything we say. They may be most polite and reasonable, even open and amiable, in their discussions with us – even as we should be with them. But we must keep in mind that there is something in their innermost disposition, no matter how carefully concealed, that is hostile to the lordship and teachings of Christ. Our convincing arguments may be useful, but the best of them are never adequate.

What is required if a man is to be truly converted is that he, as a genuinely repentant sinner, seriously and intelligently considers the crucifixion of Christ. He must first face the truth about his own moral condition, and then honestly ask if there is any solution to this problem in the Christian gospel. So, we must follow the apostle's example and speak to him of "Jesus Christ, and Him crucified" (I Corinthians 2:2), directing him to the one Person and the one event that give redemptive substance and ethical meaning to true religion. He must see and 'feel the power' of the death of our Lord. Then, if God is pleased to open his eyes, he may truly believe (II Corinthians 4:4-6).

It is only in reference to the cross of Christ, and through the realization of the immense significance of that event, that anyone will escape from himself, his propensities, and his "vanity of ... mind" (Ephesians 4:17), and begin to think Christianly. And when he does, he will also escape from those who would make a captive of him through their "philosophy and vain deceit after the traditions of men, after the rudiments of the world" (2:8).

And this, I suggest, is what it means to die "with Christ from the rudiments of the world" (2:20).

That we died with Christ "from (not 'to' as in some translations) the rudiments of the world" (ἀπεθάνετε σὺν Χριστῷ ἀπὸ τῶν στοιχείων τοῦ κόσμου, 2:20) suggests that our having been "buried with Him in (His) baptism" (2:12) removed us from the influence of such erroneous opinions. And this, we suggest, is effected in two concomitant ways:

1. *We are given a new disposition.*

    Having been reconciled "through the blood of His cross" (1:20) we are now exposed to all the assistance of God's grace. As He "spared not His own Son ... for us ... shall He not also with Him freely give us all things?" (Romans 8:32). Everything for our moral and intellectual recovery has been provided. And, *inter alia*, the reconciliation that delivers us from alienation and enmity – which are rooted "in (our) mind" (1:21) – also results in our being "renewed in the spirit of (our) mind" (Ephesians 4:23). This suggests at least that Christian conversion involves a change in our intellectual disposition, enabling us to think in a different manner and with a different attitude.

    Or, as Paul explained to the Colossians, from the moment we "put on the new man" – that is, when we became Christians – we are being "renewed unto knowledge" (3:10). Once our intellectual disposition has been changed, God continues to renew and develop our thinking.

    There is a new, inner, *subjective moderation* in our thinking.

2. *We are given new presuppositions.*

    Once our eyes are opened to appreciate the death of Christ for all that it is, we are not only constrained to trust implicitly in Him, but we are also enabled to develop a new perspective, a new framework, a new set of fundamental principles for our thinking. Before our Christian conversion we, like all people, "refused to have God in (our) knowledge" and therefore suffered from a "mind" devoid of true judgement (Romans 1:28). We were then reasoning with anthropocentric presuppositions and standards that inevitably led us into misunderstanding and confusion.

195

But now, as we seek to bring "every thought into captivity to the obedience of Christ" (II Corinthians 10:5), we have an entirely new set of presuppositions and standards. Our thinking, in other words, has been significantly restructured; we reason within the knowledge that we have of God in Christ. With a new point of beginning, we think towards a new objective.

Or, as Paul indicates here in Colossians, we, being raised with Christ, now "seek the things that are above, where Christ sits on the right hand of God" (3:1).

There is a new outward, *objective contextualization* of our thinking.[118]

People in general are unwilling – indeed, unable – to admit that they are aliens and the enemies of God; and, if some do acknowledge this to be a problem, they frequently fail to see the gravity of their condition, which appears to them to be the 'normal' state of affairs.[119] They may consider it to be an impediment, but not a terminal disorder that ends in death.

It is understandable that although we human beings are willing to acknowledge that we are all less than perfect, we resist the suggestion that we are 'totally' depraved. In one sense, we have to resist at this point! If we were to discover that we do not have the ability to improve ourselves and our situation, or to eventually reach some Utopia of our own making, we would be driven to despair. So, we cling to the vain hope that mankind 'has what it takes'!

At least, we cling to this tenuous hope and pursue the "philosophy and vain deceit" of men and "the rudiments of the world" until we discover, through the preaching of the gospel (1:5), the truth about Christ and the sufficiency of His grace for our salvation. Then, and only then, can we accept what we truly are in all our fallenness and impotence – that is, we can *genuinely repent* – knowing that there is hope of another kind – that is, we *genuinely believe*.

However, we can only discover the truth about and the sufficiency of His grace through an appreciation of the biblical significance of the death of Christ. If a man would but give a little serious thought to that remarkable, historic event, and search the scriptures to discover its meaning from a Christian perspective, he would find himself confronted with *some astounding concepts*:

---

[118] Concerning my use of 'moderate' and 'contextualize' see #3.4.1.1. and fn. 145.

[119] Hence the often-heard remark, 'Well, no one is perfect!' The universal excuse for all wrongdoing.

1. He would have to think about the Person who was crucified, and reckon with the idea that He was unique, being God incarnate. This immediately makes the event of His crucifixion one of the most important and most consequential moments in the whole of human history – the moment when the eternal entered into time, and the infinite into the finite. And this immediately invites him to reconsider all that he has previously thought about God, man, and the world.

   The ramifications of this for understanding the *world and mankind* are immense.

2. He would have to face the tragic state of humankind – not only in the appalling brutality of the execution of an innocent Man, but behind this in the extent to which God was prepared to go to deliver man from his own folly. To gain some, albeit limited, comprehension of what was happening on that Cross he will have to take very seriously matters that he had previously trivialized or ignored – divine law, God's righteousness, man's transgressions, and judgement.

   The ramifications of this for understanding *righteousness and morality* are immense.

3. He would have to reckon with the incomprehensibility of Christ's death – for it is ultimately inscrutable to the human mind, it being a divine transaction – if he is to see the Cross not only as an act of sovereign justice, but also as the greatest possible demonstration of God's love for His people (cf. John 15:13, Romans 5:8).

   The ramifications of this for understanding *interpersonal relationships and human salvation* are immense.

4. But he must then appreciate the crucifixion – the magnificent demonstration of the justice and the love of God that it is! – as the prelude to the unprecedented moment of divine triumph, the rising of Christ from the dead. All that Christ accomplished in His death comes to fruition through His resurrection, without which the Cross would effectively be nothing but yet another historic calamity. But as it is, the death of Christ is the death of death itself.

   The ramifications of this for understanding *Christian hope and anticipation of eternal life, and the ultimate significance of being human* are immense.

We might say, then, that it is in the crucifixion of Christ that we can penetrate most deeply into the character of God, see most clearly

His revealed justice and love, understand more comprehensively the possibility and the way of reconciliation with our Creator, make the greater sense of our present life on earth, and enjoy the hope of eternity.

None of these things can be gained from "the philosophy and vain deceit" of anthropocentric thought.

Therefore, I would suggest that when we "died with Christ from the rudiments of the world" (2:20) we were rescued by the grace of God from the foolish and devastating philosophies of fallen men, and also from the foolish beliefs of our own heart. Our understanding is relocated in a new realm of ideas.

Therefore, Christians inevitably think differently!

If, then, we are to be of help to those who are in bondage to demonic forces, disturbed by human evil, confused in thought, or distressed by the corrupting passions of their own souls, we should first preach the gospel to them. Then, knowing the truth about Jesus Christ and the salvific power of His death, they might turn in faith and flee to Him for forgiveness and deliverance, and the renewal of their minds. Paul insists on the priority of preaching the gospel – "the word of the cross" – because God has chosen "the foolishness of the preaching to save them that believe" (I Corinthians 1:18-21).

In becoming Christians, we were so drawn to Him, so impressed by the truth He proclaimed, so grateful for His extravagant sacrifice on our behalf, and so captivated by His ineffable love – so awed by the cross of Christ – that we could never view God, the world, and human life in the same way again. Having died with Christ we were raised into newness of life (Romans 6:4). We were born again!

- **Third**, the death of Christ and living in the "world".

    Now Paul raises a matter of incongruity. If his readers, as genuine Christians, have indeed "died with Christ" – as, by the grace of God, all true believers have – why, he asks, are they behaving "as though living in the world"? Remember, we have already considered that because of our identification with Christ in His death we should not "subject" ourselves to the dogmas of anthropocentric theories that are generated by "the precepts and doctrines of men" (#3.3.1. First). But this is not easy!

    We are now in a position, perhaps, to consider how Christians are so easily ensnared by such non-Christian dogmas, and how they might be resisted. We are all, to a greater or lesser degree, influenced by the popular – even the official, the 'politically correct' – intellectual theories and accepted moral values of our times, being exposed to them through our education, the media, and in the common concourse of social life. We take them in with the air we breathe and they permeate our thinking, even surreptitiously when we are unaware! It is far from easy for us to resist their impact upon us.

But if, as we have just suggested, a true appreciation of the crucifixion of Christ has immense ramifications for our understanding of the whole of life, and if as a result the Christian inevitably, in principle, thinks differently, we ought in our mind and in our practice to rise above the influences of any pagan or secular context in which we live. This is, perhaps, the supreme challenge that we face.

And this, I suggest, is the significance of what the apostle is saying here. If through the reconciliation of the Cross and the renewing of "the spirit of (our) mind" our thinking has been contextualized and moderated "after Christ" then, consequently, our daily living should also be contextualized and moderated accordingly.

Therefore, there is a sense in which we no longer live in the same 'world' as non-Christians.

We must think carefully about the significance of the word 'world' whenever it is used in the scriptures. Here, for example, it is clear that the apostle is not referring to the physical world. Obviously he has something else in mind, as he does not want his readers to act "as though living in the world" (ὡς ζῶντες ἐν κόσμῳ, 2:20), being well aware that they could not escape the material existence in which they found themselves. This implies that they were not, or ought not to be "living in the world" in one sense, when in another sense they were, and could not avoid living in the world, there being nowhere else for them to live. What, we might ask, is Paul talking about?

The problem is that this word for "world" (*cosmos*, κόσμος) is used with different connotations in diverse contexts in the New Testament. It may refer to:

1. The created universe, *the physical world* (eg. Acts 17:24, Hebrews 4:3, I Peter 1:20).

2. The human population of the earth, *the world of people* (eg. Mark 14:9, Romans 1:8, 3:6, Colossians 1:6).

3. The system and way of life man has established for himself in his rebellion against God, *the corrupted world-order of human society* (eg. John 17:14-16, Romans 3:19, I John 2:15-17, I John 4:54-5, 5:19).

Now, it ought to be obvious to the thoughtful Christian that he should be concerned for the well-being of the physical world, because of his understanding of its divine creation and God-given purpose. Therefore, he needs to have a keen sense of *environmental responsibility*.

Moreover, he should also be concerned for the well-being of the world of people, because of his understanding of their divine creation and God-given purpose. Therefore, he needs to have a keen sense of *sociological responsibility*.

Those well taught in Biblical truth know that through Adam man was given a covenanted responsibility to care for "the works of (God's) hand" (Psalm 8:6), and this commission has not been rescinded. They will also know that through Christ those who believe in Him have been given the covenanted responsibility to preach the gospel to "all the nations" of the world (Matthew 28:19), and this commission also has not been rescinded. Therefore, Christians should not question the importance of living in the physical world or in the world of the human community. They should not resile from their responsibility to both the earth and their neighbours. On the contrary! They should wholeheartedly be living in and involved with both, and to do so with greater enthusiasm and wisdom!

However, the Christian's concern for and involvement in the created world and with the human population of the world will be conditioned by his awareness of the corruption of both because of the fall and the distorted system of the human society that man has devised in his catastrophic rebellion against God and His law (cf. Isaiah 24:5). In other words, his environmental and his sociological concerns will be redemptive. *He will never think or act – as far as he is discerning and able – "as though living in" the corrupted world-order of those who reject God. He knows that he ought not to be "unequally yoked together with unbelievers", being aware that there comes a time when he must "come out from among them, and be separate"* (II Corinthians 6:14-16). This implies, *inter alia*, that both his environmental and sociological responsibilities will have their own distinctive, Christian characteristics.[120]

So, when Paul writes, "Why, as living in the world, do you subject yourselves to ordinances", he is asking in effect, 'Why are you allowing the evil environment of man's corrupted world-order with its mistaken theories to dictate the way you live?' For Christians, this is completely

---

[120] I might suggest in passing that contemporary, Western culture has little objection to the church's social welfare work in the community, but it deeply resents us doing this in a truly Christian manner, or in reference to our faith. And this drives many Christians to compromise.

incongruous, because, having been redeemed, they have been "delivered out of the powers of darkness, and translated into the kingdom of the Son" (1:13). They live in a different 'world'.

If we have died from the "rudiments of the world" then we should have nothing to do with the 'world' that is built upon such "rudiments".

To understand the distinction I am making here, to take this matter seriously, and to distinguish ourselves from those of the corrupted world system, are fundamentally important considerations for Christian living. The manner in which we respond exposes the depth – or lack of it – of our appreciation of God Himself. For John wrote, "Love not the world, neither the things that are in the world. If any man love the world, the love of the Father is not in him" (I John 2:15). If we are content to live in the fallen world of degenerate human society and to comply with its values, we have no genuine love for God. We have then, evidently, failed to understand what it really means to have "died with Christ" (2:20, cf. Romans 5:5, 8).

But if we love God with all our heart, all our soul, and all our mind (Matthew 22:37), then we will have a wholesome interest in the world of His creation, and a passionate concern for all the people whom He has made to inhabit it. We will, in other words, love our neighbour as ourselves (Matthew 23:39). Therefore, we should be the better citizens in our community, even when we are despised for our beliefs.

- **Fourth**, the death of Christ and things material.

Having suggested that the understanding Christian should live wholeheartedly in this material world that God has created, we must repudiate the common misconception that to do so is, or inevitably tends to *materialism*. There is no doubt that being both descendent from Adam and shaped to some degree by our culture, we always face the temptation to become materialistic. Avarice, covetousness, gluttony, opulence, prestige, and the like always appear to have a meretricious appeal. It is, then, perhaps because of the fear of becoming mercenary and acquisitive that some conscientious Christians mistakenly turn to lives of asceticism, but in doing so they expose themselves to other dangers.

It seems that the heretics in Colossae may have integrated into their teaching the theory of those ancient philosophies that reckoned physical things, including the human body and its longings, to be essentially inferior and antithetical to the non-material or 'spiritual' values of life. From this, perhaps, they deduced that physical appetites and desires were a hindrance to significant personal development and fulfilment, and that the latter were only to be experienced in an ethereal world. Then techniques were devised to suppress these inhibiting, sensual passions, such as self-denial – "touch not, taste not, handle not" – and rigorous physical discipline – "severity to the body" (2:21, 23).

But Paul, it seems, immediately and unhesitatingly dismisses such ascesis, these religious rigours, as having no place or purpose whatsoever in the Christian life (2:23).

The wording of 2:23 is grammatically complicated and how it should best be translated is debated. Following others, I would suggest it might, for the sake of clarity, be paraphrased:

> These things amount to – although they might be taken for wisdom in will-worship, humility, and severe treatment of the body, which have no value at all – the indulgence of the flesh.[121]

If this is the apostle's meaning, as I take it to be, then he is actually insisting that the ascetic life is, surprisingly, a form of "the indulgence of the flesh" (2:23), and not its repression. Moreover, self-denial and physical discipline, he suggests, have "no value at all", and add nothing to the benefits the Christian has as a result of being crucified and raised with Christ. No man can achieve through such abstemious and austere practices the advantages that are freely given by grace in Christian salvation; neither can this physical rigour add to or improve our relationship with God.[122]

It seems to me, then, astonishing that churches, claiming to be both apostolic and biblical, time and time again throughout history and until this day, have introduced such ascetic disciplines into their religious practices.[123] One would have thought – and hoped – that church leaders would have given better guidance to their congregations.

---

[121] I am aware that few, if any, English versions reflect this interpretation, but it is suggested by some commentators; and the word "will-worship" is variously translated (see fn.125).

[122] This is not to deny that there is a useful, physical discipline in life that contributes to our well-being in this world, improving our efficiency (eg. I Corinthians 9:26-27). But it is life lived in communion with God – reconciliation with Him and His purposes – that is in view here in Colossians. Having been justified through the death of Christ, "we have peace with God" (Romans 5:1), and this is complete and immutable. God, together with the gift of Christ Himself, will "also with Him freely give us all things" (Romans 8:32).

[123] Techniques devised to overcome physical desires and influences include not only bodily disciplines such as these, but also certain meditative practices – that often amount to physical discipline – that are intended to exclude both thought and desire from the mind to overcome the distractions of the physical world and to escape into the ethereal. Such meditative exercises are now rampant.

Nevertheless, it is understandable that conscientious, but ill-informed Christians might be enticed into an ascetic lifestyle. It has a certain, superficial appeal. As the apostle remarks, it was recommended by misguided teachers to the Colossians and continues to be presented to others, for its purported "wisdom in will-worship, and humility" (λόγον μὲν ἔχοντα σοφίας ἐν ἐθελοθρησκίᾳ, 2:23). We must remember that the heretics in Colossae were presenting themselves as the teachers of "philosophy" (2:8), which, presumably, made an appeal to man's mind, offering a form of wisdom.[124] And whatever it might have been, the "will-worship" they proposed evidently would have challenged and depended upon the volitional determination of the participants. Then, as we have considered above, they also required a "voluntary humility" (2:18) in their ascetic practices, a deliberate – albeit, spurious – self-abasement with its inevitable emotional content.

Failing to see the dissimulation, many are attracted by such presentations of wisdom, willingness, and humility, which, they assume, are desirable qualities – and obviously to be preferred to stupidity, stubbornness, and arrogance! And desirable qualities they would be, if only they were the wisdom, willingness, and humility found in Jesus Christ. But no ostensible, but merely human, substitutes – which are all that heretical teaching has to offer – are of any worth.

Through the advocacy of ascetic practices, the devotees of such pagan or sub-Christian belief systems are *being driven back into themselves* – into the assumed sufficiency of their own knowledge, emotions, and, above all, into their own will – to achieve whatever their religion, through its exponents, was offering them. Their system again appears in its unrelenting anthropocentric colours!

Nevertheless, the call to such egocentric wisdom, determination, and humility does attract the conscientiously pious. It offers a serious challenge to them to prove their own worth and ability. But sadly, the more they pursue such false 'spiritual' exercises which depend upon their own self-discipline and devotion, the more removed they are from Christ and from the simplicity of the grace, the faith, and the hope freely given in Him.

The techniques being recommended by such religious practitioners inevitably encourage self-trust and self-effort, because they are based

---

[124] It is important that we learn to distinguish between Christian wisdom and the wisdom of this world (cf. James 3:13-18).

upon "will-worship" (ἐθελοθρησκία)[125], and therefore any supposed personal progress or improvement becomes a source of self-satisfaction and pride. We have here what we might call a 'self-help religion', and this relies on 'willpower' or personal effort. People generally are more attracted to religions that appeal to their self-interest and the pride they have in their own abilities – systems that offer credit, merit, or success to the sedulous devotee – than they are to the biblical religion of repentance and faith.

The Christian faith offers far greater benefits, but in a manner "that no flesh should glory/boast before God" (I Corinthians 1:29).

If I am right in seeing religious asceticism as a source of self-satisfaction and pride, then perhaps we can understand why Paul – as we suggested above – is saying that such religious practices only amount to "the indulgence of the flesh" (2:23, πλησμονὴν τῆς σαρκός). It actually gratifies the flesh!

However, Paul does not always use the word "flesh" in reference to the body or physical appetites, but sometimes to identify the whole life of a man without God (eg. Romans 8:9). So here, I suggest, he is probably referring to egoistic self-satisfaction in general. Then enduring the self-denial and physical discipline is a triumph for a man's volitional commitment, a source of emotional indulgence, and a vindication of his wisdom in choosing this religious path. He has proved himself!

What genuine interest, then, does he have in the Cross of Christ?

The apostle's own reaction was remarkably different. Speaking of his religious involvement he said, "For that which I do I know not: for not what I would, that do I practise; but what I hate, that I do" (Romans 7:15). Here there is no sense of wisdom – "I know not" – no volitional triumph – "what I would not" – and no emotional gratification – "what I hate". Then, out of this sense of deep, personal dissatisfaction, he decided, "In me, that is, in my flesh, dwells no good thing" (Romans 7:18). He had failed himself – "O wretched man that I am!"

Therefore, he had a genuine and profound interest in the Cross of Christ (Romans 7:24-25, 8:1).

So, I suggest, the ascetic life with its neglect or abuse of things physical, including the human body, may have a "show of wisdom" (2:23),

---

[125] This word only occurs here in the New Testament, and not in earlier Greek. It combines two words – 'will' and 'worship' – and hence, obviously, is translated "will-worship". The latter refers to the outward practices of religion. The idea here probably implies something like 'religious lifestyle of their own choosing'. The volitional element and superficial display seem to be prominent.

but it only results in the satisfying of the "flesh" – an isolated, introverted, meaningless, humouring of one's own mind, emotion, and will.

And this gratification of the flesh amounts to nothing more than contentment in one's own achievements, as gratuitous as they are.

Instead of encouraging people to turn in faith and flee to Christ for forgiveness, deliverance, and "grace to help in time of need" (Hebrews 4:16), this religious system subtly requires its devotees to engage their own abilities and strength to find their own way to God and personal fulfilment.

But again, we need to return to Paul's earlier remark when he was writing about the 'three dimensions' of our salvation (#1). There he explained that by the crucifixion of Christ we, and "all things", have been reconciled to God (1:20-21). And we noted that the divine goal is to "sum up – or integrate – all things in Christ, the things in the heavens, and the things upon the earth" (Ephesians 1:10-11). Both man and the physical world, both so devastated by the fall, are to be restored for the sake of the glory of the Creator. Therefore, not only are man and God reconciled so that there be no conflict between them, but man and man, man and physical creation, and body and soul are also to exist together as complementary and without conflict. Therefore, we should seek the sanctification, not the suppression of our physical appetites. Our hope is in God, who "gives us richly all things to enjoy" – to enjoy, not to despise (I Timothy 6:17)!

The materialism that we should fear is not a love for material things, but the displacement of our love for God by our love for material things. It is to "worship and serve the creation rather than the Creator" (Romans 1:25). It is a love unredeemed. Paul assures the redeemed elsewhere that "all things are (theirs), whether ... the world, or life, or death, or things present, or things to come, all are (theirs) ..." (I Corinthians 3:22). You can love your teddy bear without becoming an idolater![126] But self-flagellation never made a saint!

Although we should wholeheartedly be involved in God's physical creation, we need to be so with understanding and an appreciation of its place in God's economy. Paul will soon be advising the reader to distinguish between "things that are above" and the "things that are upon the earth" (3:2) – and he clearly sees that the former have priority.

---

[126] But if you were to deify your teddy bear in your mind and worship it, you would be guilty of idolatry. Idolatry is both forbidden and dangerous, and must be eschewed in all its forms.

The intrinsic danger in materialism is that it reverses this order (see again, Romans 1:25). We ought not, then, to allow material things to become for us an end in themselves, but only be for us a means to an appropriate end. The earth was created to bring glory to God, and to sustain the man He created in His image, providing him with the context and the substance for his own derived creativity and expression, that man might also glorify God.

Moreover, physical things are temporary, and, as Paul comments, they "perish with the using" (2:22). Even the earth itself as it now is – because of its fallen condition – will ultimately "be dissolved with fervent heat ... and shall be burned up" (II Peter 3:10). Therefore, those whose sole ambition is to "lay up ... treasures upon the earth" (Matthew 6:19) will be sorely disappointed!

However, the apostle's point here seems to be to make clear to his readers that it is critically important not to confuse different categories – there are temporary, physical things, but there are also eternal, heavenly things. We must do justice to both, but the latter always have ultimate worth. It is obvious that we cannot avoid material things or escape physical existence – except through death. But even in death the Christian looks forward with confident anticipation not only to the "hope which is laid up in heaven" (1:5), but also to a return to the physical through the resurrection of the body, and to life in the "new heavens and new earth" (II Peter 3:13).

Surely, then, we fail in our God-given stewardship if we hesitate to be wisely and wholeheartedly involved in this physical world. On the one hand, we should avoid the materialism of engagement with the physical as if it were of ultimate – or the only – value; but on the other hand, we should avoid the asceticism of disengaging from or despising the physical as if it were of dubious value.

In 2:20-23, then, Paul has reminded his readers of the significance of having "died with Christ" (2.20). The reconciliation and reorientation this 'dying' provides redefine for us our associations with God, with His physical creation, and with the people who inhabit this created world. Our Christian salvation does not provide us with a way of escaping from these relationships but encourages a more energetic and ethical involvement in them. So, Christian hope and faith restore human values of every kind.

But the philosophical implications of our faith do not end here. Although they require of us a full participation in our present existence in this world, they will not allow us to think or act as if life on this earth is all that there is, or that it defines our purpose. The ultimate reason for our being in this world is not found in the world, nor does the world provide all the resources we need to attain the goal for which we were created.

Therefore, Paul continues, "If then you were raised together with Christ, seek the things that are above" (3:1). The inescapable reality is that we can only live wholeheartedly in this physical world – as suggested above – when our minds are "set ... on things that are above, not on the things that are upon the earth" (3:2). So, we now turn to a brief consideration of the implications of being raised together with Christ.

3.3.2. Hope, Faith, and Human Purpose: and the Resurrection of Christ (3:1-4)

Christian hope and faith establish for us the authentic *purpose for human living* (cf. #3.3.1.).

In this respect, we should consider the following:

- **First**, the resurrection of Christ and Christian living.
  Paul draws our attention to *the true purpose for human living* when he writes, "If you were raised together with Christ, seek the things that are above ..." (3:1). *He, perhaps in contrast to the advice of the false teachers, is referring to the objective for which we ought to live.*
  Christian aspiration is in view. We should live in hope.
  Evidently, the apostle is concerned lest the ultimate purpose of our creation and redemption be obfuscated by secondary, materialistic concerns and we become disoriented. There is an obvious relationship between *the manner* in which we live and *the purpose* for which we live. If we are confused about the purpose of our existence, then we will be in constant uncertainty about what we should be doing with ourselves – or merely pursuing temporal satisfaction in the immediacy of physical life.
  It is obvious enough, for example, that a consistent atheist, because of his severely limited perspective, faces insurmountable difficulties in finding any purpose for human existence – for such a purpose, according to his principles, is simply not there to be found! Purpose is precluded by his presuppositions. He might courageously admit this and then propose his own contrived purpose – perhaps of a pragmatic or hedonistic kind – as a temporary means of ordering his life. Then, to achieve his fabricated objectives, he determines for himself the means to obtain them and the moral principles that are compatible with his own scheme of things. He,

in effect, designs a life for himself – *and eventually and necessarily this becomes vacuous.*

However, all this will be somewhat different for a religious non-Christian. He, with his severely confused perspective, does not have the courage, or sufficient self-confidence to attempt a life of total independence. Understandably, he fears living all alone, finite, feeble, and dying in a vast and inexplicable universe, not daring to trust completely – as the audacious atheist does – in his own abilities. He looks, therefore, for a god that might support him in achieving his own purposes, whether they be pragmatic or hedonistic. Then everything depends upon the kind of god he is willing to accept, and sadly his fallen moral predilections obscure any vision of the holy and the almighty, so he worships an image like or less than himself (cf. Romans 1:22-23). He, in effect, designs his own god – *and eventually and necessarily this becomes self-imposed bondage.*

In contrast, the Christian, beginning with the God who has revealed Himself in creation, in Christ, and in the Bible (cf. #3.2.1.), is motivated neither by the audacity of the atheist, not by the timidity of the pagan. Because of his distinctively Christian perspective, and being motivated, as we have seen, by hope and faith, he accepts that he has been created with a God-given purpose and, therefore, he seeks "the things that are above, where Christ is seated on the right hand of God" (3:1). He believes that his purpose in life is prescribed for him, is abundantly clear, and by grace is achievable, despite his obvious imperfection. He reckons with the triumph of Christ's resurrection.

- **Second**, the exaltation of Christ and Christian living.

    Although it is impossible for any man to live as a Christian ought without being born again (2:13), the enabling that is most and immediately needed comes not from his own intrinsic, moral rehabilitation, which is a work in progress, but from the immutable reconciliation he has with God in Christ, which is a permanently established relationship.[127] (Nevertheless, both regeneration and reconciliation are necessary and concomitant.)

    As this relationship between a believer and Christ is so important, it must not be trivialized. It involves an ineffable and sacrosanct personal intimacy, which is implied, no doubt, in Paul's concern that "Christ may dwell in (our) hearts through faith" (Ephesians 3:17). And although we may – and often do – "grieve ... the Holy Spirit of God" (Ephesians 4:30),

---

[127] See #3.2.2.3., Fourth, concerning our participation in Christ's baptism.

He has promised that He "will never fail ... or forsake" us (Hebrews 13:5). This relationship, then, is both intimate and irrevocable.

But our comprehension of and delight in this intimacy must never be allowed to diminish our sense of awe and fear in God's presence, lest our relationship with Him be impaired (cf. #1.3.). Now that we are members of "the kingdom of the Son" (1:13), we should "offer service well-pleasing to God with reverence and awe, for our God is a consuming fire" (λατρεύωμεν εὐαρέστως τῷ θεῷ μετὰ εὐλαβείας καὶ δέους· καὶ γὰρ ὁ θεὸς ἡμῶν πῦρ καταναλίσκον, Hebrews 12:28-29). If our hearts become insensitive to the overwhelming greatness and burning holiness of our Lord, and we attempt to progress in our salvation without "fear and trembling" (Philippians 2:12), then we will inevitably trivialize our relationship with Christ. And this will leave us both impoverished and ineffective in the service of our King.[128]

It is a serious concern that much modern church activity and instruction has attempted to establish a delight in the intimacy without any concern for the awe and fear of a salutary, serious, and holy relationship with God. This has resulted in the misconception that we may legitimately have expectations of all that God might do for us, without a corresponding and sufficient concern for the expectations God might have of us. Then our relationship with Him is demeaned.

However, to effectively offset this tendency to trivialize our relationship with Christ, that is, our being "raised together with Him", Paul immediately adds that He, being raised, is now "seated on the right hand of God" (3:1). He would not have us forget the exalted position our Lord has in His sovereign dominion over all things, or disregard the magnificence of His person, His rightful place in the glorious transcendence of heaven, and the perpetual might of His power.

We are indeed thankful that through His crucifixion and death on our behalf Christ secured our salvation, and we should never lose sight of the fact that "He made peace through the blood of His cross" (1:20). But this vision of our Lord's passion and humiliation should not distract us from worshipping Him *as He now is*, seated "on the right hand of

---

[128] In Hebrews 12:28-29 and Philippians 2:12 there are four words which seem to have faded from our contemporary, Christian vocabulary – "reverence" (εὐλαβεία), "awe" (δέος), "fear" (φόβος), and "trembling" (τρόμος). And with their loss, or neglect, and, as a consequence, our ignorance of their meaning, we are diminished and our effective relationship with God is attenuated. We would do well to recover these words and restore them to their proper place in our thinking and practice. Also see #3.5.2., Third, 2. Subjective disposition.

the Majesty on high" (Hebrews 1:3), where "angels and authorities and powers (are) made subject to Him" (I Peter 3:22).

Our worship of our exalted Lord requires, *inter alia*, these *two indispensable constituents*:

1. First, we are now able to "draw near with boldness unto the throne of (His) grace, that we may receive mercy and find grace to help in time of need" (Hebrews 4:16). It is our immense privilege to turn to Him, assured that our God is sovereign over all things, to find comfort for our hearts, and to ask for assistance, as His children. *This is the response of faith, made in love.*

2. Second, having risen from the dead, Christ has all authority "in heaven and on earth" (Matthew 28:18); He "is the blessed and only Potentate, the King of kings, and Lord of lords" whose commandment is to be kept with meticulous care (I Timothy 6:14, 17). It is also our immense privilege to turn to Him to serve Him in His kingdom (1:13), as His humble servants. *This is the response of obedience, made in fear* (see #3.5.2., Third, 2.).

From this we might conclude that whenever faith or obedience is absent, there is no worship; and that *every* act done in faith and obedience is an act of worship.

Perhaps one other demanding aspect of this should be noted. Because we are "raised together with Christ" and "Christ is seated on the right hand of God" (3:1), Paul could confidently write elsewhere that God "raised us up with Him, and made us sit with Him in the heavenly places" (Ephesians 2:6). And we might boldly suggest that this being so, there is an exceptional and inextirpable nobility about the Christian – not in himself, but by virtue of all that he is as redeemed in Christ. He is clothed in divine righteousness and reassured in the divine presence. Those who are concerned to find some manner of dignity in being human – especially in this age of degradation in which people openly and even proudly display their depravity – should seek it here, in the sanctification of Christian salvation.

Moreover, our position with Christ in the heavenly places is the guarantee of Christian security, because Christ is seated in "heavenly places far above all rule, and authority, and power, and dominion, and every name that is named, not only in this world, but also in that which is to come" (Ephesians 1:20-21). We are seated with the all-conquering

King! Therefore, none of these forces can destroy us – or even touch us without divine permission (cf. Job 1, I Corinthians 10:13, cf. #3.3.2. Fourth).

We are commanded, then, to "seek the things that are above where Christ is seated on the right hand of God" (3:1, τὰ ἄνω ζητεῖτε,οὗ ὁ Χριστός ἐστιν ἐν δεξιᾷ τοῦ θεοῦ καθήμενος). This obviously implies an intelligent resolve to pursue what must be the highest possible objective, according to the highest possible standards, to which any human being can aspire. We should, then, "seek first the kingdom of God, and His righteousness" (Matthew 6:33), as we value above all else the "glory and honour and immortality" (Romans 2:7) that only God can give. In doing so, we must avoid the ways of this fallen world where "all seek their own, not the things of Jesus Christ" (Philippians 2:21).

And this, as we shall now consider, requires the reorientation of our mind.

- **Third**, the reorientation of mind and Christian living.

Paul, having commanded his readers to "seek the things which are above" (3:1), would now have them "set (their) mind on the things that are above, not on the things that are upon the earth" (3:2, τὰ ἄνω φρονεῖτε,μὴ τὰ ἐπὶ τῆς γῆς). The two imperatives in these verses – translated "seek" and "set" – are both continuous and concomitant; things that we should always be doing, and always doing in conjunction with each other.

It is not possible to attain the purpose for which God has created and redeemed us if we fail to use our minds as we ought.[129]

There is a responsibility laid upon all Christians to deliberately, persistently, and incrementally adjust their thinking that they might live increasingly in a manner pleasing to God. This is required of them, *inter alia*, that they "be of the same mind one with another according to Christ Jesus" (Romans 15:5), and that none "think of himself more highly than he ought to think" (Romans 12:3). In this, they should find a compatibility with the manner in which Christ Himself thought (Philippians 2:5).

We should all consider very carefully how we might attain, or at least approximate to this demanding standard. It requires maturity (I Corinthians 13:11).

---

[129] And this requirement – to "have this mind in you, which was also in Christ Jesus" (Philippians 2:5), with its radical change in one's way of thinking – is perhaps the greatest personal challenge presented to us in the Christian gospel.

This demands of us more than we are able to give! However, Paul explains in Romans 8:5-8 that the reorientation of our thinking is inherent in our Christian salvation. No matter what technique, self-discipline, or didactics might be employed, no Christianly significant change of mind is possible without the aid of "the Spirit of life in Christ Jesus" (Romans 8:2), because the "mind of the flesh is death, but the mind of the Spirit is life and peace". So "they that are in the flesh cannot please God".

Therefore, the apostle can say here in Colossians, in the light of the newness of life the Colossian believers had received (2:12-13), "If (since) you were raised with Christ ... set your mind on the things that are above" (3:1-2). Our association with our Lord enables the reorientation of mind, which should be as radical as our being reconciled to and raised with Christ. This renewed thinking is life changing.

Let no one imagine – or be misled into believing – that he can become a Christian and continue to accommodate his old manner of thinking. Nor let him imagine that he can change his thinking without divine, gracious assistance. A new mind emerges from our true worship – our faith and fear.

It is an essential aspect of this reorientation of our thinking that we embrace a new system of values. We should mind "the things of God" and not the "things of men" (Matthew 16:23). We must not, then, allow the contemporary thinking of our age, or the opinions of our peers, or the forces of mere expediency to dominate the way we think. So, to this end, we must deliberately set our "mind on the things that are above, not on the things that are upon the earth" (3:2). We are, in other words, to look beyond our immediate environment to find the principles and values that must be allowed to moderate our thoughts and actions and define our purpose in life. This involves making resolute decisions and astute choices, and investing in things heavenly – and this requires being "filled with the knowledge of His will in all spiritual wisdom and understanding" (1:9, #1.2.1.1.).[130]

Advocating that we set our "mind on things that are above, not on the things that are upon the earth", Paul has obviously not forgotten that we have no other option than to live, as God intended, "upon the earth".[131] Therefore, he would have been well aware that "things that are

---

[130] All the verses cited in the preceding four paragraphs contain the same original word for 'setting the mind' or 'thinking' (φρονέω).

[131] Here Paul uses the word "earth" (γῆ), as distinct from "world" (κόσμος) in 2:8, 20.

upon the earth" would necessarily and continually come into our minds. So, in one sense, we must think about them.

But it simply will not do to believe that we can find upon the earth all that is necessary for truly purposeful thinking or to allow our thoughts "upon the earth" to set the pattern or determine the parameters for our understanding. Not even in the pristine, prelapsarian Garden of Eden before man's mind was devastated by the fall, was this so. The earth was not fully self-explanatory; neither was human existence. Therefore, God immediately gave to Adam the principles or values by and the purpose for which man was to live.[132] From the beginning man was directed by the word of God to set his mind on "the things that are above" – to give heed to divine instruction – that he might accomplish that for which he was created and given a place on the earth. He was not left to deduce from empirical data what he was to do with his life or to pragmatically structure his own value system.

We have explained that we can only know God within His creation (see #1.3.1.1.1.). Therefore, God's revelation to Adam was given and received in, and in reference to the earth upon which man was to live. It was God's intention that man be a gardener and care for the earth (Genesis 1:28, 2:25). Indeed, so correlated are God and the earth that the very things God created were in themselves a revelation of His power and deity (Romans 1:20). But in the postlapsarian world, when men's eyes were blinded to these things by sin and the machinations of evil, God sent His Son to be light in the darkness (John 12:26, II Corinthians 4:3-6). Integral, then, to Christian understanding of the world and the gospel, is extraordinary, divine, authoritative revelation – revelation that explains both creation and redemption.

God has clearly expressed His intentions in the creative works of His hand, in the life and teachings of Christ, and in the inspired explanation He has given to us of these things in the scriptures. We have in them, then, access to knowledge of the "things that are above" – if only we can escape our blindness of mind (II Corinthians 4:4, Ephesians 4:18).

More fundamentally, if we are to think in the manner Paul is indicating, we must begin with the realization that there are "things that are above" distinct from "things upon the earth".

This immediately suggests that there is a reality that is beyond anything we might experience in this physical world where we live. And

---

[132] *Purpose* was given when man was "put ... into the garden of Eden ... to keep it"; and moral *principle* was established when God instructed Adam in what he should and should not do in the garden (Genesis 2:15-17).

as the "things that are above" are located "where Christ is, seated on the right hand of God" (3:1), the distinction in the apostle's mind is, I suggest, basically between the Creator and the created. *This is the foremost of all Christian beliefs* – "In the beginning God created the heavens and the earth" (Genesis 1:1) – *and it is the first point in the philosophy that is "after Christ"* (2:8), being essential for our ontology, our understanding of what reality actually is.

Then, that Paul can say so simply, "Set your mind on the things that are above", reveals something of his epistemology, his theory about how we might know the things most important for us to know. It is required that we deliberately adjust our thinking – because our natural tendency is to think with a mind that is "enmity against God" (Romans 8:7). But acquiring knowledge of the truth is, by the grace of God, assured – because, as the apostle is about to explain, we have "put on the new man which is being renewed unto knowledge" (3:10).[133]

If we wholeheartedly "set our minds on things that are above" – following a Christian ontology and epistemology – we will surely find that our thinking, with all its principles and values, will be at odds with the thinking of other people. There is no compatibility between the philosophy "after Christ" that we pursue, and the "philosophy and vain deceits … of men" (2:8). Therefore, the Christian who thinks Christianly may well find himself isolated, even despised, by his peers, and perhaps socially and professionally disadvantaged. A redeemed mind does not come cheaply!

Faced with such potential ostracism, the Christian has to ask himself whether it is worth the cost. And Paul, in effect, answers this question in Colossians 3:3-4, which we now consider.

- **Fourth**, eschatology and Christian living.

A changed perspective for living provides a new 'prospective'. If we convert to Christian thinking by setting our mind on "the things that are above" and disengaging our mind from "the things that are on the earth" then, although still living in this world, we will anticipate our eventual participation in "the hope which is laid up (for us) in the heavens" (1:5). Hence, we will be motivated, as Paul suggests elsewhere, to forget "the

---

[133] It is important – even unavoidable – that we work out our ontology and our epistemology together, as they are mutually implicit. That Christians work with a creational ontology and a redemptive epistemology usually makes their philosophy abhorrent to the non-Christian mind. "The word of the cross is to them that perish foolishness" and "the wisdom of this world is foolishness with God" (I Corinthians 1:18, 3:19). There is irreconcilability here.

things which are behind" and to "press on towards the goal unto the prize of the high calling of God" (Philippians 3:14-15).

This implies that the Christian needs 'moral strength and fortitude' (see #1.2.) to continue his life on earth with this goal in view, while at the same time drawing his values from and investing everything in the coming of the kingdom of God. This does not diminish the value of his present life but greatly increases it. Therefore, he must be intelligent about both the condition of his life on earth and also the ultimate life that he is yet to experience as the result of his salvation. And he must recognize the correlation between the two. Time and the end of time are determinative for purpose.

However, the Christian can only understand adequately his life now and his life then in reference to Jesus Christ (3:3-4). We must recognize that we are to discover in Him both *the most significant matters that determine our present condition* and *the most significant matters that determine our future condition.* Paul has something to say about both this present and future condition in these verses.

The most significant thing that determines our present condition as Christians is that our "life is hid with Christ in God" (3:3, ἡ ζωὴ ὑμῶν κέκρυπται σὺν τῷ Χριστῷ ἐν τῷ θεῷ). This is a puzzling expression, but it immediately indicates that at this present time we must reckon with hiddenness because there is much that we do not see and cannot understand. We only "know in part" and "now we see in a mirror, darkly" (I Corinthians 13:9, 12). And the apostle John, also being aware that our future is somewhat concealed from us, wrote, "Now we are the children of God, and it is not yet manifested what we shall be" but "we know that when He shall be manifested, we shall be like Him" (I John 3:2). There truly are things that we assuredly know – and such are fundamental for our faith – but our future is not fully revealed to us – but this is significant for our hope.

Although we may face uncertainty in this present darkness, we might take comfort in this – we are assured that our lives are hidden with Christ in God!

And in this hiddenness, I suggest, is to be found both our security and our destiny.[134]

We should note the following about perseverance in *our present condition*, our security.

---

[134] Is it not more often the things we see and know that leave us feeling insecure and hopeless?

The most significant thing that determines our security is reflected in Paul's words, "For you died, and your life is hid with Christ in God" (3:3). *We "died", but continue in "life"!*

One of the fundamental principles underlying the Christian gospel, and the salvation it offers, is that *death is not and cannot be triumphant; it is not and cannot be final for God's people*. To appreciate this conquest of human mortality, we need only trace the apostle's thinking in the following words. "I make known unto you the gospel ... Christ died for our sins ... He has been raised on the third day ... Christ is preached that He has been raised from the dead ... by man came death, by man also came the resurrection of the dead ... the last enemy that shall be abolished is death ... O death, where is your victory?" (I Corinthians 15:1, 3, 4, 12, 21, 26, 55).

So irrevocably is this principle embedded in the gospel that it fashions every aspect of our Christian salvation. Not only does it determine our hope in the resurrection of the body when Christ returns, but it also determines – as we have seen – the transformation of a man's life when he believes in Christ at the time of his conversion. Jesus explained, "He that hears my word and believes Him that sent me ... has passed out of death into life" (John 5:24). In some sense, then, the believer has already – by believing – passed beyond death! And then Paul wrote similarly, "And you being dead through your trespasses ... He made alive together with Him, having forgiven us all our trespasses" (2:13). *We will rise triumphantly in the resurrection of the body because we have already been raised graciously into the newness of life in Christ.*

We have seen that, *inter alia*, the Christian benefits as a result of Christ's death and resurrection in two ways (see #3.2.2.4.):

1. As a result of the judicial triumph of His death, we are justified, and the forgiveness of all our transgressions is guaranteed: we are reconciled with God. We might suggest, then, that *we are redeemed from the condemnation of God and from death, the wages of sin* (Romans 6:23), because our lives are hidden in Christ, covered in His righteousness.

    We are no longer exposed to divine wrath.

2. As a result of the executive triumph of His resurrection, Christ reigns at God's right hand "far above all rule, and authority, and power, and dominion" (Ephesians 1:21): we are protected by His supreme might from those who would do us harm. We might suggest, then, we are *redeemed from the powers of evil because*

our lives are hidden in Christ and we are saved from the ravages of wickedness by His sovereign power.

We are no longer exposed to demonic wiles.

There is, then, *comprehensive security* for those who are so united with the Lord. Their lives are unassailably and securely hidden with Christ.

And just because of this relationship we have with our Lord, Paul can confidently assert, "We are more than conquerors through Him that loved us" and that "nothing can separate us from the love of God, which is in Christ Jesus our Lord" (Romans 8:37, 39).

We might well compare the confidence of King David when confronted by the wickedness of evil men who threatened his life. He wrote, "In the day of trouble He shall keep me secretly in His pavilion; in the secret place of His tent shall He hide me" (Psalm 27:5). And of them that "put their trust" in God, he said to the Lord, "In the hiding place of your presence you will hide them from the conspiracies of men" (Psalm 31:19-20). This surely reflects the faith of a man who found his ultimate security only in his God.

But there is more in this puzzling expression. Because of our present condition, we look at ourselves and are usually disappointed because we see, if we are honest, little Christ-likeness. And if we are not what we ourselves desire to be, failing to live in true godliness, then how miserable do we appear in the eyes of a most holy God? And are we not often ashamed of ourselves and of our fellow Christians, and disappointed in how we must appear in the eyes of other people?

We all seem to be inveterate hypocrites! We proclaim the highest of moral standards, instruct ourselves in the ways of holiness, and declare the immaculate purity of our Lord. And then we consistently fail to live in a manner compatible with these principles. Even when we have done "all the things that are commanded" – which is surely a rare occurrence! – "we are worthless servants" (δοῦλοι ἀχρεῖοί ἐσμεν, Luke 17:10). We are always in pursuit of godliness.

However, in Colossians 2:3 Paul indicates another hiddenness. "All the treasures of wisdom and knowledge are hidden" in Christ (ἐν ᾧ εἰσιν πάντες οἱ θησαυροὶ τῆς σοφίας καὶ γνώσεως ἀπόκρυφοι). This implies that it is to Christ that we must look to discover the truth and find the ways of wisdom. Similarly, then, if our life is hidden in Christ, then it is to Christ that we must look to discover what it ultimately means to be a Christian in every sense. And as we have seen, John explains that the time is coming when "we shall be like Him" (I John 3:2).

This, then, is the *present position* of those who are united with the Lord. Their lives are hidden with Christ, wherein all the potential for our eventual Christ-likeness is also hidden.

And it is just because of this relationship we have with our Lord that we should be of all people the humblest. With Paul, we must say we are yet only "earthen vessels" – frangible and of little value – and whatever is of worth in our lives is the effect of "the exceeding greatness of the power" that belongs solely to God (II Corinthians 4:7). Therefore, we must indeed serve our Lord or live in frustration, but if by His grace we accomplish any "good works" the praise for them must be given to our "Father who is in heaven" (Matthew 5:16). *Thankful we might be, but never self-congratulatory.*

We are, I think, most foolish when we draw attention to ourselves as if we are in some manner exemplary of the 'good Christian' or the 'mature believer', for at best we remain sinners saved by the grace of God. All that we might judiciously ask others to see in us and emulate is the repentance and the faith our Lord has been pleased to give us. Our only proclamation to the world, the sole topic of our witness, the only person we would recommend without reservation is "Jesus Christ and Him crucified" (I Corinthians 2:2). If any would know what a truly mature Christian is and how he ought to behave, let them consider Christ, for there is no other adequate exemplar.

We turn now to Paul's remarks about the anticipation of *our future condition*, our destiny.

The most significant thing that determines our future condition is that "Christ ... is our life" (3:4, ὁ Χριστὸς ... ἡ ζωὴ ὑμῶν).

The Bible assures us that all things necessary which are now hidden from us will be fully manifested. The darkness will be dispersed and we will see clearly. "Now we see in a mirror, darkly ... now I know in part; but then I will fully know ... even as also I have been known" (I Corinthians 13:12). Our communion with God will be fully consummated. Then there will be no hiddenness, but a complete realization of the profound relationship we have with Christ.

We have suggested above that if we set our minds on "the things that are above" (3:2) we will think – and, hence, act – in a manner that distinguishes us from other people, and this may possibly result in social disadvantage and ostracism. Therefore, we need to appreciate that the present is a prelude to the future, and that we are the people redeemed and reborn for the future. To invest everything in "the hope that is laid up for (us) in the heavens" (1:5) demands not only courage but also the prescience of revelation. Or to overcome the seduction of materialism and the apolaustic enticements of immediate gratification, we need some insight into that which "the heavens" have to offer us.

And here Paul makes two important statements that help to prepare us to live for the future in the manner that Christians ought, and that give us a preview of the benefits we are yet to receive from our salvation in Christ. He writes that Christ "is our life", and that when He is manifested we "will with Him be manifested in glory" (3:4).

As we have suggested, there is a subtle complexity in the expression "your life is hid with Christ in God" (3:3). But there is a greater intensity in Paul's assertion that "Christ is our life" (3:4). The former statement encapsulates our absolution through, and consequent association with our Lord, as we have explained; but the latter refers to the more intimate and comprehensive communality of this association with Him. But they are both aspects of the Christian's present relationship with Christ, a relationship in which we are already securely established by God's grace, but are yet to enjoy in its fullness.

But can we understand more exactly what the apostle has in mind when he writes that Christ "is our life"? Here I prefer not to use the old expression 'mystical union'[135] that conjures up nebulous and enigmatic ideas in the minds of many, leading to some confusion and false anticipations. Perhaps Paul's meaning here is best understood in comparison with parallel expressions in his other writings.

The apostle writes in Galatians 2:20, for example, "I have been crucified with Christ; yet I live; and yet no longer I but Christ lives in me". Here we note again that whatever the relationship is that he claims to have with Christ, it is subsequent to and, therefore, dependent upon his identification with his Lord's crucifixion. That Christ lives in him is the direct result of Christ's death for him. He employs a subtle use of words that is somewhat cryptic – crucified, yet he lives; he lives, but it is no longer he that lives – but, I suggest, the point being made is clear enough. Paul wants us to know that prior to his Christian conversion he sought to determine the course of his own life; it was to be the product of his own understanding, volition, and self-confidence. But subsequently, he no longer considered his life to be his own, or himself to be sufficient, but as

---

[135] This term was originally used to explain that our association or union with Christ is only known through revelation – ie. in the Bible. But it is taken by many to suggest that the union is only known though an esoteric experience. Hence the expression can be confusing.

his Lord's servant the course of his life was to be determined by Christ's gracious intervention, so now he lives "by faith ... in the Son of God".

To summarize, *Christ had become the primary motivation for his life.*

In contrast, Paul wrote in Philippians 2:21, "For me to live is Christ, and to die is gain". The perspective has changed. In Galatians 2:20 he looks back to his *dying with Christ*, but now he is looking forward in anticipation of *dying for Christ*. He is in prison awaiting an unknown future and possible execution. He is willing to die if it be his Lord's will, but he also desires to continue his ministry on earth for the advantage of others (Philippians 2:23-24). But whatever the outcome was to be, only one thing was of paramount importance – that "Christ shall be magnified in my body, whether by life or by death" (Philippians 2:22).

To summarize, *Christ had become the ultimate intention for his life.*

From its beginning, Paul's Christian life was driven by and directed to Jesus Christ. He trusted always in Him and desired nothing but Him. Hence, he writes to the Colossians, "Whatsoever you do in word or in deed, do all in the name of the Lord Jesus" (3:17), and "Whatsoever you do, work from your soul, as unto the Lord, and not unto men" (3:23).

Christ is undoubtedly our "life" in *the ontological concept* that "in Him we live and move and have our being" (Acts 17:28), and inevitably so because "in Him all things consist" (1:17). Moreover, He upholds "all things by the word of His power" (Hebrews 1:3). As human beings, we are all utterly dependent upon Him, whether we realize it or not. Human existence is only possible because of His creative and providential genius. The apostle recognizes this.

But when Paul writes that He "is our life" in Colossians 3:4 he has in mind *the redemptive concept* that only Christians have an intimate reconciliation with Him. The unconverted necessarily are dependent upon Christ for life and survival, but for them in their alienation and enmity (2:21) He is neither the motivation nor the intention in the life they live. They are bereft of the qualities and the purpose that obtain in the lives of God's redeemed people.

Considering these things, and being thankful for our reconciliation, we must ask about *the prospect that now lies before us.* Where does it all end? How are we to conceive in our minds "the hope which is laid up for (us) in the heavens" (1:5)? How do we conceptualize the final state to which we aspire?

We might imagine for ourselves – and this would not be by any means a foolish thing to do – what life might be like in the new heaven and earth, and in the New Jerusalem, by considering the description given of this coming state in Revelation 21-22. Acknowledging the symbolic nature of the language used, we are assured here that when the time comes human life will be restored to the blessed condition for which it was originally created (Revelation 21:4), and all that corrupts will be excluded (Revelation 21:27). Then the most remarkable description of the Heavenly City, wherein we have our God-given citizenship, conveys a picture of sufficiency, serenity, security, and beauty (Revelation 21:10-21). All that had been lost in the Garden of Eden will be restored and enhanced, and there will be "no curse any more" (Revelation 22:1-4). We may anticipate life in perfect circumstances.

However, we must emphasize that existence in a paradisiacal milieu is not in itself the important factor. It was not in the Garden of Eden and it will not be in the new heaven and earth. What will be of supreme significance is that "the Lord God, the Almighty, and the Lamb" will be "the temple" there, and the "glory of God" and the lamp of "the Lamb" will be its light (Revelation 21:22-23). There we will be "His servants" and we shall "see His face" (Revelation 22:3-4).

In other words, that which we should desire above all else is that which Adam tragically rejected in Eden – the comprehensive, overt presence of God and fulfilment in His service. *The benefit beyond comparison that we anticipate is being "manifested" or appearing with Christ in glory (3:4).*

It is, we might conclude, the Christian's anticipation of the "hope which is laid up for (him) in heaven" (1:5) and his "faith in the working of God" (2:12) that provide him with values for and purpose in life. It is within this context that he is not only motivated but also enabled to "seek the things that are above where Christ is seated on the right hand of God" (3:1) and to "set (his) mind on things that are above and not on the things that are upon the earth" (3:2). He has a perspective and sense of being that lift him above the materialism and the corruption of "this present evil world" from which he will ultimately be delivered (Galatians 1:4).

However, we should remember that in anticipating the time when we will be "manifested with Him in glory" (3:4) we are obliged to live for the time being in this world with all its mayhem and sorrow. Nevertheless, despite the afflictions, perplexities, and defeats we suffer, "the life of Jesus" should be "manifested in our mortal body" (II Corinthians 4:7-11). *Our hope and faith should in measure be visible in the way we live now. And Paul, significantly, proceeds in this letter to describe this visibility in moral and sociological terms.*

NOTE: In this general context, it is worth considering Paul's words in I Timothy 6:17-19:

> Charge them that are rich in this present world, that they be not highminded, nor have their hope set on the uncertainty of riches, but on God, who gives us richly all things to enjoy; that they do good, that they be rich in good works, that they be ready to distribute, willing to communicate; laying up in store for themselves a good foundation against the time to come, that they may lay hold on the life which is life indeed.

◆

3.4. THE MORAL IMPLICATIONS (3:5-17)

We considered above the significance of our being both self-conscious and world-conscious in forming our philosophy of life and in understanding God and ourselves (#3.2.1.). It might be helpful at this point in our attempt to enter into Paul's thinking in Colossians to elaborate these ideas a little.

When any man seeks an interpretation of human life he must in one sense begin with his own self-consciousness.[136] There are *three important aspects* of this self-consciousness:

- **First**, man is self-consciously dependent.

  No matter how much he asserts his self-sufficiency in attempting to live independently, man is constantly aware that he is completely dependent upon his environment – the earth beneath his feet, the air he breathes, the food he eats, the people of his community. This leads him to make enquiry about a reality beyond himself, or, as we have suggested, to investigate the "rudiments of the world" (2:8).

  This implies that he does not have "life in himself". Such absolute self-sufficiency, this aseity, is a unique feature of God and God-incarnate (John 5:26).

  Man, therefore, is inevitably a *scientist*!

- **Second**, man is intellectually self-conscious.

  No matter how limited his experience and education, every man has a mind and a measure of rational ability. There is an irrepressible need within him for knowledge and understanding. His appreciation of life must be intellectually received.

  Even when men professed "themselves to be wise" and so "became fools", it required the processes of the mind for them to do so (Romans 1:22).

  Man, therefore, is inevitably a *philosopher*!

- **Third**, man is morally self-conscious.

  No matter how seared his conscience may be (I Timothy 4:2), no man can avoid asking himself what is right and what is wrong, what is good and what is bad. And no matter how primitive his axiology may be, he will employ it to calibrate his conscience as a basis for his moral

---

[136] I do not mean by this that his self-consciousness is to be considered either as sufficient or as authoritative, but only that it is the unavoidable point of beginning.

judgements. As with every other aspect of his being, his conscience has been corrupted by the fall, but it remains his conscience nevertheless.

This inexorable moral awareness is compounded – and complicated – by man's social instincts, his cultural milieu, and his need to adapt to various circumstances. But it persists, and demands attention.

Man, therefore, is inevitably a *moralist*!

These things being so, any interpretation of human life must provide:

A theory about reality to sustain man in his dependence.
A method of reasoning to satisfy his mind.
A system of moral principles to regulate his behaviour.

However, an anthropocentric interpretation of human life will not structure or evaluate these matters in the same way as a Christocentric interpretation. There is a Christian as well as a non-Christian approach to science, philosophy, and morals. This is commonly accepted with respect to morality and philosophy, *but it is often assumed that science is 'objective' and must exclude considerations of morality and philosophy, and be undertaken in exactly the same manner and upon the same principles by believer and unbeliever alike.*

One problem with this assumption is that genuine science – the sincere, open, and honest searching for the truth – does not exclude *anything, not even input from philosophy and morality,* from its investigation. Then there is a secondary problem, as some would accept this inclusiveness in principle, acknowledging that science must *include every consideration,* but then, through such disciplines as psychology and sociology, they subsume philosophy, religion, and morality as subsections of naturalistic science, denying them any intrinsic standing of their own. Everything is reduced to 'science', and 'science' is considered to be potentially omniscient.

Thus, the autonomy and self-sufficiency of the 'scientific' human mind are asserted in all matters, and, as a result, Christians are given no voice in science *as Christians.* The atheistic 'scientists', in other words, would have us play their game, on their home ground, and according to their rules! Then there are some among them who insist that if we are even to be considered as rational beings, we must accept their assumed presuppositions, and abandon what they consider to be our belief in 'religious superstitions'. If we do not, then we are considered to be unreasonable, are excluded, and cannot engage with them. They would silence Christians in obscurity!

Paul seems to have this contrast between Christian and non-Christian thought in view in Colossians. In 2:20-23 the anthropocentric theory, the view of the covenant-breaker who reasons in rebellion against his Creator, is exposed. Then in 3:1-4 the Christocentric faith, the view of the covenant-keeper who seeks to reason in obedience to his Creator, is presented.

The apostle's remarks here – as concise as they are – help us to understand that if we follow anthropocentric theories about reality and methods of reasoning, we will inevitably commit ourselves to an anthropocentric system of moral principles. But if we follow Christian theory and method, we will inevitably commit ourselves to the Christian system of moral principles. It seems axiomatic that the theist will at least acknowledge the possibility of moral principles rooted in deity, to which he may be obliged to give obedience. The atheist necessarily denies this possibility and accepts no such obligation. This being so, it is certain that the two systems will tend to devise mutually exclusive ethical systems. It should not surprise us, then, that the increasingly secular thinking of modern Western society is methodically eliminating Christian values from its culture.

Moreover, these three things – theory of reality, method of reasoning, and system of moral principles – are necessarily interactive; one of them can only be adjusted by making changes to the other two. So, I suggest, it is impossible to adapt our beliefs and practices to non-Christian theory or method, and at the same time maintain our commitment to Christian morality. Any shift in basic theological principles inevitably results in the change of ethical standards. Then, there is the disingenuous converse: when it accepts contemporary ethical standards, the modern church is driven to rewrite its beliefs.[137]

It is no surprise, then, that having carefully and quite comprehensively expressed basic doctrines of the Christian faith, the essential pre-eminence of Jesus Christ, and the necessity of a sound biblical philosophy, Paul now turns to the question of the moral implications of these things. He has mentioned that he prayed for the Colossian believers that they might "walk worthily of the Lord unto all pleasing" (1:10). We have briefly considered the general characteristics of such "worthy" behaviour (#1.2.2.), *and* the means by which the grace of God enables us to comply (#1.2.3.). But now, in 3:5-17, the apostle returns more specifically to both these things, writing about particular acts and attitudes that are at variance with the

---

[137] If today's churches are unable to speak with one voice about moral issues – as, for example, about abortion, the sanctity of marriage, divorce, homosexuality, social justice etc. – it is because they share no common, structured philosophy of life. There are perhaps two contributing factors to this dilemma: *first*, by drifting from biblical authority they have borrowed from various philosophies of this world, and this has resulted in conflicting moral systems; *second*, by compromising with the moral values of contemporary society to conciliate the non-Christian, they have adjusted their philosophy of life to accommodate the change.

principles of godliness, over against those that are consonant with them, *and further explaining how we might conform to divine standards.*

By commanding specific responses – "put to death", "put away", and "put on" (3:5, 8, 12) – Paul confronts the reader with *the practical requirements, the demands, of Christian ethics.*

When we read Colossians 3:5-17 as Christians, we are confronted by definite, unambiguous statements concerning activities that we should and should not be doing. But this is far from being a reintroduction of some form of Pharisaical legalism! Rather, the apostle is explaining what is the inevitable response of all people who are committed to "the word of the truth of the gospel", which by its own intrinsic worth and divine purpose bears fruit and increases wherever it is preached (1:5-6). He is describing the moral engagement in life that is to be expected from all who have put "off the body of the flesh in the circumcision of Christ, having been buried with Him in baptism", and have been "made alive together with Him" (2:11-13).

Paul, in other words, is opening up to us here the astonishing possibilities of Christian living!

Anyone who reads these apostolic words and finds them onerous, offensive, otiose, or simply obsolete in our modern generation, a section of scripture that is culturally dated, is dubiously Christian. Can any man, we might hear Paul saying, who believes that he is reconciled "by His blood" and anticipates being "holy and without blemish and unreprovable before Him" (1:20, 22), despise instruction that is designed to enable him to realize the fullness of the salvation we have in Christ? It is they that "hunger and thirst after righteousness" who "shall be filled" (Matthew 5:6). Here the reference is to those who truly love God and keep His commandments (John 14:15) in the pursuit of godliness. This is no sterile legalism, but the response to God's love in loving God.

However, the beneficial outcome of this Christian moral engagement in life is more than personal or individual, as it also strengthens the Christian community when believers are "knit together in love" (2:2). It seems to me that there is little value, but only insipid sentimentality, when we imagine that the response the love God requires of us can be divorced from ethical and social behaviour. We simply abuse the word when, for example, we excuse lustful, immoral conduct on the pretext that it was an act of 'love'.

Therefore, I would suggest, that we are only able to present and recommend the love of God to the world without crippling hypocrisy *when the church is seen to be a truly ethical community.* Jesus exhorted His disciples, saying, "Even so let your light shine before men, that they may see your good works, and glorify your Father which is in heaven" (ὑμῶν τὰ καλὰ ἔργα, Matthew 5:16). If we are to bear witness to our God, the non-Christian community which surrounds us must be able to see a distinguishing goodness in the things we do, and this involves moral quality.[138] And Paul ambitiously urges his readers to "be blameless and harmless, children of God, in the midst of a crooked and perverse generation ... holding forth the word of life" (Philippians 2:14-15). Our proclamation of "the word of life" will carry no conviction, but only the ring of insincerity, if we are not different, morally and otherwise, from the non-Christians of our own generation.[139]

Hypocrisy, as we all know, is exceedingly hard to avoid. In fact, a measure of hypocrisy is inevitable in Christian life and witness, because we proclaim in Christ the highest of moral principles and the perfection of human life. But we know all too well that we ourselves never attain unto the standards we uphold in Him, the standards we should never compromise. There is never a time when we can avoid the accusation that we do not 'practice what we preach', for we never do. Therefore, we should always be seen as repenting people, for "if we say that we have no sin, we deceive ourselves and the truth is not in us" (I John 1:8). This contrition should be evident in all we do, but particularly apparent when we are censured by others. The criticism of other people cannot wound a genuine and sincere Christian, for he has already acknowledged before the holy God that in himself there "dwells no good thing" (Romans 7:18).

But we would be doubly hypocritical if we made no serious attempt to grow in grace and in the knowledge of Christ Jesus. If we know that our sins wounded Christ and that we are only reconciled "through the blood of His cross" (1:20), we will surely endeavour to "walk worthily of the Lord" (1:10). We should be "obedient children, not fashioning (ourselves) according to (our) former lusts

---

[138] The word used in Matthew 5:16 for "good" (καλός) suggests a comprehensive axiology, involving both utility, beauty, righteousness, and ethical worth. It refers to the outward and open expression of life that is the product of inward purity. That is, Christians should be comprehensively good! True, this only comes with time and experience, and only reaches perfection in heaven, but it should be, even in this defective world, pursued diligently.

[139] The beautiful church building with its pillars and towering spire, its stained-glass windows, polished pews, works of art, carved high altar with woven reredos and resplendent, gold cross, are all in danger of being reduced to a duplicitous charade when the priest in his richly embroidered chasuble who presides over the silver chalice and elevates the Host, is an impenitent, practicing paedophile. The testimony is violated, the meaning is lost, and the glory has departed. The truth of the gospel and the beauty of Christ may well be more clearly seen among the humble, repentant few striving for true godliness, who meet in a remote, poor, mountain village in a bamboo shelter to break bread together in remembrance of Him.

in the time of (our) ignorance, but as He which called (us) is holy" it will be our ambition to be "holy in all manner of living" (I Peter 1:14-15).[140]

It is always possible to dissimulate, concealing our true thoughts and motivation. The pagan actor can mouth the words of Christian truth to play the part of a Christian saint in a theatrical production, even as many a man might recite the Apostolic Creed to impersonate the genuine believer in the church congregation (Matthew 15:8). The skilful and eloquent preacher will always attempt to appear sincere, even when proud, ambitiously 'professional', and secretly avaricious.

And, I suggest, the only hope we have of rising above any form of theatrical Christianity and concealed egoism is not to become better rhetoricians, to devise improved techniques, to acquire a greater sophistication, or to seek some empowering experience, but to seriously pursue, by the grace of God, a life of true, inner, godliness. Or, as Paul writes here in Colossians, to "mortify ... (our) members which are upon the earth" and "put on ... as God's elect ... a heart of compassion, kindness, humility, meekness" and "longsuffering" (3:5, 12).

Therefore, we must now follow Paul's words and seriously consider these moral implications of the gospel.

◆

A man's philosophy and/or religion must answer, or attempt to answer, the ethical questions of life. Some contemporary thinkers deny that there is any substance to the discussion of morality, suggesting that it is all irrelevant verbiage conjured out of nothing to devise a religious or political system that enables the powerful to control the gullible.[141] However, they could only espouse such a position – as some have brazenly dared to do – because they have already reasoned themselves into a nihilistic belief system. In other words, even they have in their own way answered the ethical questions according to their philosophy, as *all people must do.*

So, Paul now draws moral conclusions from his Christian philosophy, and in reference to the pre-eminence of Jesus Christ, as *all Christians ought to do.*

---

[140] It is difficult to decide who is the more obnoxious – the Christian who proudly preaches Christ as if he were good and noble enough to do so, or the Christian who smugly preaches the gospel as if his sinfulness, and a swaggering admission of his guilt, enhance his ministry.

[141] I recently heard an influential individual assert on radio: "... marriage and morality, neither of which are priorities in my life".

NOTE: It is the Christian's philosophy that provides him with a basis for his moral values and the motivation to adhere to them. There is no ethical superficiality or temporal moralizing in genuine Christian living. Our moral values are not pragmatically determined or 'situationally' devised, although they have intense practicality and immediate applicability. They are not superimposed by man on a supposedly neutral world, but are established in the mind of God and embedded in the very nature of created reality itself, and delineated in His revealed law.

It is evident here that as Christian conversion involves abandoning one way of thinking for another, previous moral practices and values must be repudiated, and "put to death" or "put away" (3:5, 8). But this is far from being a reduction or shrivelling of life through the arbitrary imposition of restrictive prohibitions. It is, rather, the excising of inhibiting evils that are destructive to man's joy and fulfilment. Then, as the new, biblical way of thinking has been embraced, there is much of ineffable worth to be "put on" (3:12). It is not the reduction, but the scintillating augmentation that is significant in Christian conversion! Indeed, it would be no exaggeration to say that not only has a new *worldview* been adopted, but *a new world* has been entered; we have been "delivered ... out of the power of darkness, and translated into the kingdom of His dear Son" (1:13).[142] Hence there is *a new life* to be lived (cf. Romans 6:20-23). There are both a new *context* and a new *content* for our morality.

However, our translation into the kingdom of Christ, as factual and as significant as it is, does not remove us from this "present evil world" (Galatians 1:4). We have already seen that although we are to set our "mind on things that are above, not on the things that are upon the earth", we have no other option than to live, as God intended, in the immediate environment in which we find ourselves (cf. #3.3.2. Third). We are citizens of heaven, who now live as strangers and sojourners on earth (I Peter 2:11); that is, we are in a familiar but nonetheless foreign situation. We must, then, work out the implications of our moral principles in the postlapsarian, corrupted world. And doing so is always conflictual. Not only does this place us at odds with the ethics of non-Christian society, but also, as we ourselves are not yet immune from the influences of evil, or without sin, each of us finds himself in conflict within himself. Therefore, it is still required of us that we "put off" as well as "put on" (3:8, 12). We are constantly confronted with the responsibility to make moral decisions.

---

[142] It is, I believe, a great tragedy that people generally – including many believers! – have been deluded into thinking that Christian morality is essentially negative, devoid of joy, and the diminution of wholehearted living and satisfaction in all that God has created. After all, Paul insists, "God ... gives us richly all things to enjoy" (I Timothy 6:17).

NOTE: I would suggest that we ought always to keep in mind that theoretically non-Christian philosophy and morality are diametrically opposed to Christian philosophy and morality, and they should not be confused or conflated. However, the distinction between non-Christian thinking and practice and Christian thinking and practice is often blurred. Non-Christians can and often do behave in a Christian manner, and Christians can and often do behave in a non-Christian manner. It should not surprise us that some non-Christians are decent, moral people because they are made in the image of God and "they show the works of the law written in their hearts" (Romans 2:15). And even the best of Christians cannot claim that they "have no sin" (I John 1:8).

However, just as the Christian has abandoned one philosophy for another, so he must also abandon one moral system for another. He must repudiate old ethical principles and behaviour and commit himself to new ethical principles and behaviour. There is both evil to be overcome and good to be achieved. And there is help in the gospel for us to do both (Philippians 4:13).

Therefore, our ethical system must have a *negative* as well as a *positive* aspect, the *prohibiting* and the *affirming*. Paul discusses both in terms of the required *practice* and of the *principles* that support the practice.[143]

3.4.1. PROHIBITIVE MORALITY (3:5-11)

We must not be dissuaded from the proclamation of a prohibitive morality. In fact, it would be morally reprehensible if we fail to do so, for love demands that we warn others of the disastrous consequences of violating divine law (3:6, cf. Ezekiel 33:1-9, Romans 2:1-11).

Hence, there remains a very strong "Thou shalt not" in the Christian gospel! Nevertheless, there is serious danger in proclaiming *only* a prohibitive morality, or to speak of it with an attitude or tone of superiority, for none is without fault (Romans 2:1). It should always be conjoined with affirmative morality. However, to follow the order in Paul's instructions here in Colossians, we will consider the two separately.

---

[143] I have often heard it said of late that 'Christianity is not a set of do's and don'ts.' Needless to say, I agree with these words – for Christianity is far more than the requirements of law. But I find I am often disturbed by the context in which such words are spoken and the emphasis they are given, leaving the impression that believers might happily ignore divine commandments and standards. Although Christianity *is not* a 'set of do's and don'ts', it does *contain* such a set of requirements.

3.4.1.1. THE PRACTICE OF PROHIBITIVE MORALITY (3:5-9A)

As Paul turns from his consideration of Christian philosophy to its moral implications, he imposes upon his readers an astonishing – even outrageous – injunction: "Put to death, therefore, your members which are upon the earth" (3:5, νεκρώσατε οὖν τὰ μέλη τὰ ἐπὶ τῆς γῆς). No doubt, these words are difficult to understand, considering the particular terminology the apostle is using.[144] His tone is so peremptory and his demand so draconian that our first response is puzzlement, if not resentment. What, we might ask, is he really asking his readers to do? In considering this, we should remember that Paul is encouraging them to think Christianly that they might walk worthily of their Lord (1:10), so the outcome he desires is clearly altruistic.

NOTE: A brief but important comment needs to be made about the word for "members" (3:5, μέλος) that Paul uses here. In the New Testament, it refers consistently to the physical parts of the body. But frequently the reference is metaphorical – as, for example, of Christians being members of "the body of Christ" (I Corinthians 12:12-27, cf. Romans 12:4-5, Ephesians 5:30).

But the reference is to our literal, physical member in those difficult verses in Matthew 5:29-30. Needless to say, our Lord is not advocating the violent dismembering of the body. He said, "If your right eye causes you to sin …" But it never does! If it did, we might be better without it, for sin is a deadly matter with eternal consequences. But the eye and the hand are only instrumental in sin, never the cause. Paul explains this when he writes that we should never present our "members … as instruments (or, weapons) of unrighteousness" (Romans 6:13). The problem was that "sinful passions … worked in our members" (Romans 7:5). And with this James agrees (James 4:1). *If there is to be a more felicitous use of our members, something must be done about the lusts and sinful passions that drive our actions.*

We suggested above that as we were created in the image of God, we should seek to be like Him in righteousness, holiness, and knowledge. But this is not to be abstracted from physical life, so we should also seek to live in such a fashion that "the life also of Jesus Christ may be manifested in our body" (II Corinthians 4:10,

---

144 Various attempts have been made to translate these words: ESV, "Put to death therefore, what is earthly in you: sexual immorality …" (this identifies the 'members' as 'sexual immorality …' etc.); NASB, "Therefore, consider the members of your earthly body as dead to immorality …" (this requires the reader to 'consider' done what Paul is asking them to do); NIV, "Put to death, therefore, whatever belongs to your earthly nature: sexual immorality …" (this begs some definition of 'earthly nature').

see #1.3.1.1.1.). If there is to be this physical reflection of the likeness of God in the way we behave, then the manner in which we use our "members" is of great significance. It is important, then, that we understand how we are to put "to death our members which are upon the earth", and that we do so.

To understand what the apostle requires of us here, we should note first of all, as the word "therefore" implies, that he is drawing a conclusion from the remarks he has just made in 3:1-4 (see #3.2.2.). And then, secondly, as we have seen before, we must interpret Paul's words here in reference to his writings elsewhere.

In the preceding paragraph (3:1-4), there are *two significant exhortations*:

- **First**, Paul wrote of *the new perspective for their thinking* that Christians adopt when they "seek the things which are above, where Christ is seated at the right hand of God" (3:1).

  Because of this, devout believers as they engage in life will – to the best of their ability – always think in reference to the sovereignty of Christ enthroned in heaven.

  Therefore, the *lordship* of Christ must become a determining factor in our thinking.

  This is important, because in this world there are those who would "make spoil of us", attempting to dominate us, by captivating us through their philosophy (2:8). These contentious individuals would illegitimately lord it over us, wanting to control both our minds and our lives (cf. I Peter 5:3). There are teachers and preachers who seek to be more than men who would humbly mediate truth to us, proudly presenting themselves as ultimately or unquestionably authoritative. Those who would engage in explaining or proclaiming the gospel should be advised of the solemnity of, and the moral dangers involved in the task (James 3:1). But let the listeners also beware!

- **Second**, the apostle would also have his readers follow *the new pattern for their thinking* which they have as they set their mind "on the things that are above, not on the things that are on the earth" (3:2).

  Because of this, and as they engage in life, believers will deliberately embrace the values that are commensurate with things above where Christ is enthroned.

  Therefore, the *character* of Christ must become a determining factor in our thinking.

  This is important because the things we now find on the earth are manifestly inferior, for "the creation was subjected to vanity" and is not yet "delivered from the bondage of corruption". There are both a diffused debility and a persistent malaise permeating the whole of our environment that leave us "groaning and travailing in pain". So, as Christians, "we hope for that which we see not", and will not see until "the redemption of our body" (Romans 8:20-25). We must look, then, beyond our present state for true and abiding values, and find in Christ the criteria we need to discern them.

It is impossible for us, once we have adopted the higher perspective, to rest content with any values that are commensurate with things that are on the earth (cf. 3.3.2. Third).

This does not mean that we despise the things of God's creation or fail to see their immediate significance and importance. The opposite is the case! Being aware that they are indeed *created* things, not the mindless results of happenstance, we highly respect them as *His* created things. Therefore, we are grieved by the despoliation this earth has suffered and are concerned and long for its restoration. We are now obliged to view all "the things that are upon the earth" through the eyes, as it were, of Christ the Creator *and* Christ the Redeemer. Things, that is, as they are now, and as they will be.

This *new perspective* contextualizes and this *new pattern* moderates the Christian's thinking. Then, and consequently, such thinking *contextualizes* and *moderates* the life he lives. And herein is the change, both in thought and in action, effected by Christian conversion.[145]

All this is consistent with Paul's teaching elsewhere. He writes of the change, or one aspect of the change, this renewed thinking effects in a man's life as a result of his conversion to Christ, in the following words from Romans 6:16-19:

> Know you not, that to whom you present yourselves as servants
> unto obedience, his servants you are whom you obey ... But
> thanks be to God, that, whereas you were servants of sin,
> you became obedient from the heart to that form of teaching
> whereunto you were delivered; and being made free from sin,
> you became servants of righteousness. ... for as you (previously)
> presented your members as servants to uncleanness and to

---

[145] I am deliberately using the words 'contextualize' and 'moderate' in the hope that they may help to clarify in the reader's mind the concepts I believe Paul is presenting to us. However, I am not referring to any attempt to contextualize the gospel to adapt it to varying social cultures, but only to the contextualizing influence the biblical worldview should constantly have upon all our thinking and practice.

iniquity unto iniquity, even so now present your members as
servants to righteousness unto sanctification.

The apostle is concerned here not with the destruction, but with the disposition of our "members". He explains that obeying the teaching they had received, Christians, as slaves of Christ, present their members "to righteousness unto sanctification" (τῇ δικαιοσύνῃ εἰς ἁγιασμόν) – and this affects their thinking and behaviour. The presentation to righteousness *moderates* their life in the acceptance of the moral principles of divine law, which is the result of the sanctification that *contextualizes* their life in the service of God.[146]

This is a conclusion inexorably drawn from Paul's theology. He has presented Christ in his letter to the Colossians as the one in whom "all things were created" and "consist" (1:16-17), so those who believe in Him think within *the context* of a universe designed and sustained by His power and for His glory. And He is also seen as the one "in whom we have our redemption" (1:14), through which the Christian gains an anticipation of a life "holy and without blemish ... before Him", so those who believe in Him think within *the moderation* of a life morally sustained and directed by His grace.

However, a serious problem confronts us!

If – and when – we give priority to, or are preoccupied with "the things that are upon the earth" (3:2), then we will not have our "minds set on the things that are above", as they ought to be. Consequently, we will not engage in life as Christians should, and our members will revert to the service of "uncleanness and ... iniquity" (Romans 6:19). This, I suggest, is a significant aspect of the battle in which all Christians find themselves as "the flesh lusts against the Spirit" (Galatians 5:17).

But if we are to present our members to righteousness and sanctification – as Paul requires – it is obvious that Paul does not want us to destroy them. What then does he require of us in 3:5?

We should note carefully that the apostle does not ask us to put to death our "members" as such, but our "members which are upon the earth". It is

---

[146] Both contextualization and moderation are required. We might moderate our lives according to good moral principles, but in the wrong context. For example, living righteously and honestly, but only in the service of our own reputation or financial gain. Alternatively, in the context of attempting to serve God, we might in our zeal be persuaded to employ devious practices. For example, we might fund church activities with misappropriated money.

the *relationship* of our members with "the things that are on the earth", our engagement in life as those who worship and serve "the creation (i.e. "things upon the earth") rather than the Creator" (Romans 1:25), that should be put to death. To use our members according to the materialistic values of men is to worship the creation, which is a pernicious manifestation of idolatry (cf. Romans 1:22-23). So, nothing substantial or corporeal is to be destroyed, but only the ill-advised relational aspects of our lives. (Similarly, Paul would have us "mortify the deeds of the body". Romans 8:13, τὰς πράξεις τοῦ σώματος θανατοῦτε. This is another difficult phrase, but we only need to note here that the "deeds", not the "body", are to be put to death.)

But lest his readers be confused by his acerbic exhortation, Paul gives some specific examples of what he has in mind. He is unhesitating in listing things that a person must not do! We should seek to eradicate, *inter alia*, these four things – sexual immorality, moral uncleanness, lustful passions, evil desires (3:5, πορνείαν ἀκαθαρσίαν πάθος ἐπιθυμίαν κακήν)[147]. But it is not, for example, our sexuality that we should mortify, for this is intrinsic to human life as God designed it, but the use of our sexuality that is driven by purely materialistic considerations, and is not subject to the lordship of Christ. Neither is it our desires that should be suppressed, for they also are vital aspects of our humanity, but the "evil desires" of the sinful heart.

We should, in other words, strive to eschew all that is wrongly contextualized and inappropriately moderated.

Now it is particularly interesting that Paul adds to this list of four aberrations, a fifth and perhaps a more destructive disorder – "the covetousness, which is idolatry" (3:5). This evil seems to be given particular significance here, being emphasized by the addition of the article – "*the* covetousness".[148] Then, by equating it with "idolatry", the apostle evidently sees it in some sense as the concentration of all evils. Idolatry is the anthropocentric reduction of the very idea of God, diminishing Him, in the minds of men, to that which is but the likeness of man himself – or even to that which is less than human (Romans 1:22-23). And by exchanging "the glory of the incorruptible God for the likeness of an image of corruptible man", we human beings have in effect made ourselves 'the

---

[147] These four disorders all imply moral aberrations and the sinful dispositions of the heart that drive them. Not only the practice of immoral acts, but the desire for them is condemned.

[148] The article is probably added also to isolate "covetousness" from the preceding evils itemized in this list, so that it alone is to be equated with "idolatry".

measure of all things'[149] and the axiological architects of all moral principles. And these fabricated principles are designed to justify all sexual immorality, moral uncleanness, lustful passions, and evil desires for our own sensual satisfaction, and to excuse our wicked behaviour.

Covetousness (πλεονεξία), as the Greek word here suggests, is a 'desire to have more'. But, we might suggest, in the biblical context, being the disposition of the sinful human heart, it is primarily the desire to have more than God has been pleased to give to us. It is, perhaps, the first of all evils! Adam and Eve desired the fruit that was forbidden them (Genesis 3:6). Hence rebellious man determined that if God forbids what he desires, he must find – or design for himself – another god that would accommodate his passions. And he continues to do so![150]

And this religious reductionism, this idolatry, is – as Paul explained – the immediate result of man's "refusal to glorify (God) as God" and his anthropocentric narcissism in "professing (himself) to be wise" (Romans 1:21-22). In other words, we might say, man de-contextualized his thinking when he failed to "set (his) mind on the things that are above" (3:2). Consequently, he "exchanged the truth of God for a lie, and worshipped and served the creation rather than the Creator" (Romans 1:25). This implies, in the language of Colossians, that he "set his mind ... on the things that are upon the earth" (3:2). In other words, we might say, he de-moderated his thinking. Now the things that he really desires, the things he most values are the material and sensual benefits of this world. And this inevitably gives rise to covetousness or greed – the acquisitive, grasping passion for the tangible and the carnal, the moderation of life in reference to wealth and indulgence.

Now man believes that the wealthier, the greater: and the more self-indulgent, the more liberated! Therefore, man's philosophy of religion is idolatry, and the practice of his religion is covetousness – because of his inescapable anthropocentricity.

Catastrophically, this de-moderation of fallen man's thinking, his grasping for material wealth and self-indulgence, has not proven to be to his advantage. The benefits he had anticipated – and still desires – from his purported enrichment and emancipation have proven to be a fantasy. His idolatry has not transported him into paradise! Rather, as Paul explains, "For this cause (i.e. man's rebellion)

---

[149] So Protagoras, Greek philosopher, c. 450 BC. Such an idea is very contemporary, but is certainly not new! Actually, it is regressive.

[150] Historically, man has shown himself to be very favourable towards religion – provided he is at liberty to design his own god. And in principle, this is true of the atheist as well as theists and polytheists. Designing a god that is nothing, the atheist reduces himself to the same.

God gave them up unto worthless passions" (Romans 1:26, εἰς πάθη ἀτιμίας).[151] Then he immediately – in the following verse in Romans – indicates the tragic loss of value in human sexuality, hence in all interpersonal relationships, and the consequent and devastating impoverishment of all life. *We cannot degrade our sexuality without depreciating everything else.*

But moral degradation is not the only – in fact, not the primary – impoverishment of life. Paul further explains that "as they refused to have God in their knowledge, God gave them up to a reprobate/ineffectual mind" (Romans 1:28, εἰς ἀδόκιμον νοῦν) – and this has left man "to do those things which are not appropriate". The moral malaise that disturbs humankind is coupled with intellectual mayhem! Or, we might say, the *de-moderation* – a matter very much about morality – is the concomitant of the *de-contextualization* – a matter very much about the use of the mind (see 3:10, #3.4.1.2.2.).

The *de-contextualization*, and the resulting "ineffectual mind" (εἰς ἀδόκιμον νοῦν), together with the *de-moderation*, and the resulting "worthless passions" (εἰς πάθη ἀτιμίας), combine to precipitate man into his fallen state. *And it all begins with idolatry – the misrepresentation of God.*

It is not at all surprising, then, that Paul adds "covetousness" to his list of sinful things in 3:5, or that he equates it with "idolatry". The implication is that if we are to escape human wickedness we must first abandon our idolatry – that is, we must rediscover God and His holiness, and "seek the things" that are commensurate with His values and intentions, and "be content with such things as (we) have" (Hebrews 13:5). And this requires a change so comprehensive that the apostle describes it as putting off "the old man with his doings" and putting on "the new man, which is being renewed unto knowledge after the image of Him that created him" (3:9-10, #3.4.1.2.). Old, evil-induced practices must give way as God-given knowledge is gained. *The passion to reduce God to a man-like idol must give way to a desire to regain the God-like image in man!*

Then, Paul adds an even more ominous comment! Not only are human life and interpersonal relationships impoverished, both intellectually and morally, because of man's idolatry, but also, and of far greater consequence, is the fact that this idolatry incurs the wrath of God. "For which things sake, the wrath of God" is coming (3:6, cf. Ephesians 5:5-6).

---

[151] This may well be translated 'dishonourable' or 'disreputable passions'. But I choose the word 'worthless' because, from a Christian point of view, whatever God judges to be undesirable, must indeed be considered worthless.

Alan D Catchpoole

The genuine believer, the man who has been "raised with (Christ) through faith in the working of God" and has had all his trespasses forgiven (2:12), whose "life is hid with Christ in God" (3:3), and who anticipates entering into His presence "holy and without blemish" (1:22), will reveal the authenticity of his Christianity by, *inter alia*, *his aversion to those things that incur the wrath of God*. Such things – "in which (he) also walked before, when (he) lived in them" (3:7) – are now an embarrassment to him. If he is honest with himself, he will acknowledge that he has not yet fully escaped their influence, for he is not yet perfect. Nevertheless, he will seek, by the grace of God, to "put to death (his) members which are upon the earth" (3:5), for he would not live in a manner offensive to his Lord. If he is genuinely converted, he need have no fear of the wrath of God, for he has been made "sufficient to be (a partaker) of the inheritance of the saints in light" (1:12). Nevertheless, as he is committed to live for the glory of Christ he would seek to do nothing to defame Him.

Therefore, Paul goes on to encourage his readers to "put ... away all these: anger, wrath, malice, slander, shameful speaking out of your mouth" (3:8). Again, the apostle is very specific. Evidently, he would accept no excuse! The genuine Christian must have done with these things.

Hopefully, all this might help us to understand what Paul requires of us when he instructs us to "put to death" our "members which are upon the earth" (3:5). This being an apostolic injunction, it demands our willing response. But it is not merely brute willpower that is required, nor is it only a matter of practising rigorous, austere self-discipline. It is not achieved solely by human effort without gracious, divine assistance. But as we have seen, it does involve proper contextualization and moderation, so what is required is *the answer of the will that is generated by engaging in pertinent thinking and in the commitment to appropriate values*.

To make the appropriate response, then, the will needs to be directed by clear understanding and true principles. We are not simply confronted by cold, relentless law with which we must struggle. Rather, we are invited to have the mind of Christ (Philippians 2:5) so that our thinking might conform to the will of God. Then, ideally, whatever we do will be done "from the innermost part of our being, as unto the Lord" (3:23, ἐκ ψυχῆς ἐργάζεσθε ὡς τῷ κυρίῳ, my paraphrase). We are encouraged to *re-contextualize* and to *re-moderate* our lives, to facilitate a joyful, meaningful, and volitional response to all that God desires for us. Then our behaviour should be evidently different. When we were converted, we put on "the new man" (3:10, #3.4.1.2.1.), and so we should now live in "newness of life" (Romans 6:4).

That we might further comprehend and participate significantly and meaningfully in this response, and mature in a life of true godliness, we will give some thought to the principles involved, as they appear in the following verses (3:9-11).

3.4.1.2. THE PRINCIPLES BEHIND THE PRACTICE (3:9B-11)

Now we must consider how we are, in the daily practice of Christian living, to deal with and to overcome the incessant temptation to engage inappropriately with "the things that are upon the earth", and how we are to cope with our own deficient moral capacity. We have already acknowledged that in proclaiming Christ and preaching the laws of God to the world, we expose ourselves to the charge of hypocrisy (#3.4.). We must humbly accept this criticism, and we dare not present ourselves as anything other than sinners saved by the grace of God. To be of lasting help to anyone we must not draw his attention to ourselves, but direct it to Jesus Christ. If we would be examples in any way, it must be above all else in this humility, but never in the arrogance of a pretentious piety or superiority. We must acknowledge that we will not be able to live perfectly as Christ requires, or even as we desire, until the day we see Him and will then be like Him. Nevertheless, having this hope, we now seek to "purify" ourselves (I John 3:2-3) – and admittedly, not with much success.

Therefore, preparing ourselves for "the hope which is laid up for (us) in the heavens" (1:5), and being troubled by our own feeble efforts to purify ourselves, we must take seriously Paul's instructions to "put to death" and "to put away" (νεκρώσατε, ἀπόθεσθε, 3:5, 8). These *two demanding imperatives* both suggest that with determination we must have done with the evils the apostle lists. The lists themselves are not intended to be exhaustive but are specific examples of the kinds of wickedness we should eschew.[152] Each of the items recorded is categorically prohibited. Wherever found, they are unacceptable and inexcusable – but thankfully, not unforgivable.

We should notice here an important distinction. In the two lists of things prohibited by Christian moral principles, in 3:5 and 3:8-9, there are *improper attitudes* – passion, evil desires, anger, wrath – and *improper actions* – fornication, uncleanness, slander, obscene speaking, lying. Wickedness is found, then, in both the disposition of our hearts and in the array of our deeds. And this obviously requires more than tolerance and forgiveness if the quality of human living is to

---

[152] Elsewhere in the New Testament, the apostles catalogue other evils that are not listed here in Colossians. See, for example, Romans 1:29ff, Galatians 5:19-21, Titus 1:5-9, I Peter 4:3, et al.

be significantly improved. There must be a solution to the problem of misconduct that arises from the possibility of transformation in character.

We might tentatively suggest, therefore, that there is *a difference between these two imperatives*. The first is far more drastic than the second: the first a matter mortification, the second a matter of modification: both destruction and discarding. The putting to death, as we have discussed above, seems to require that we deal with the *internality* of our sinfulness, seeking the grace of God that there might be a sanctifying of our *attitudes*. In contrast, the putting away – as removing clothing – seems to require that we deal with the *externality* of our sinfulness, seeking the grace of God that there might be a sanctifying of our *actions*. This explanation may demand too much of the words themselves, but there can be no doubt that we desperately need a refining of both attitude and action.

Any behavioural transformation that is not the result of attitudinal change is superficial, facile, fragile, pretentious, inconstant, and always specious.

Profound changes are needed. Perfunctory alterations to our practices are insufficient. Something of the depth of the transformation required has already been seen in our consideration of "circumcision made without hands" (2:11), in which all true believers participate. The outward sign, or token, of membership in the covenant God makes with His people – whether the circumcision or the baptism – as valuable as it is in itself, is of no worth without "a new heart" (see #3.1.3. Third, and #3.2.2.2. First, Second).

There seem to be *three underlying principles* that Paul has in mind here as he urges his readers to disengage their members from the "things that are upon the earth":

3.4.1.2.1. RECONCILIATION (3:9-10)

We ought not to "lie … one to another", or to engage in any of the other manifestations of wickedness in Paul's lists of human sins, because we – if we are Christians – "have put off the old man with its practices, and … put on the new man" (ἀπεκδυσάμενοι τὸν παλαιὸν ἄνθρωπον σὺν ταῖς πράξεσιν αὐτοῦ καὶ ἐνδυσάμενοι τὸν νέον).

It is important to notice here that Paul is not advising his readers to "put off … and put on", but he is taking it for granted that this they have already done. It is precisely because this change has been made that he commands them not to lie to one another. In other words, he bases his moral directive to speak honestly on the actuality of their transition from the "old" to the "new man". He is writing to those he believes are true Christians (1:2, 4, 8). Therefore, we must assume that the transition was effected when, at the beginning, they were converted, when they were "raised with Him from the dead" (2:12) and entered into "newness of life" (Romans 6:4).

The Christian is "the new man"; and to become a Christian is to "put on" the "new man". Or, in other words, someone is only a Christian when he had made this transition from the old to the new.

We ought not then, I suggest, to exhort Christians to put off the old and put on the new, for this they did when they put their "faith in the working of God" (2:12). Rather, we should explain to them that their conversion to Christ is no simplistic matter, no mere academic acceptance of a different philosophy of life, no desultory change in communal, religious associations. Something so significant has happened – if their conversion is truly a work of the grace of God – that they are to consider themselves as 'new men', and as now having refurbished and demanding moral obligations.[153]

And this change from the "old man" to the "new" is instant, categorical, comprehensive, and complete! It is irreversible, not to be repeated. We who were non-Christian men became Christian men. Whatever is involved in this transformation, it has been done. And Paul is encouraging us to proceed in our Christian living reckoning with the fact of its completion.

I have mentioned above that I have difficulty with the translation of "the body of the flesh" (2:11, τοῦ σώματος τῆς σαρκός) as "the sinful nature" (#3.2.2.3. Third, Fourth). Similarly, here I am not comfortable with interpreting the "old man" and the "new" (3:9-10, τὸν παλαιὸν ἄνθρωπον and τὸν νέον) as the 'old self' and the 'new self'. To do so leaves the reader, struggling to define or to discover just what the change is that is supposed to have taken place, anticipating a perceptible change in his created being, perhaps even in his personality.

However, there seems to be no biblical – or experiential – evidence that something we once identified as our 'self' no longer exists, or has been discarded, and that something distinctively different has taken its place. Indeed, many appear quite frustrated and even disillusioned by some forms of teaching that use such 'new

---

[153] Paul also writes about putting away "the old man" and putting on "the new man" in Ephesians 4:21-24. But again, he is not exhorting his readers to take this action, but reminding them of what they had been taught was necessary if they were to become Christians when they were first instructed in the truths of the Christian faith. Therefore, in a similar fashion to his words in Colossians, he then exhorts them to put away "falsehood" and to "speak truth each with his neighbour" (Ephesians 4:25).

self' language. The fact is that we all find ourselves to be very much the same person with the same 'self' after our conversion as we were before it. We find an affinity with Paul when, feeling his continuing deficiencies (Romans 7:14-18), he exclaimed, "O wretched man that I am! Who shall deliver me out of this body of death?" (Romans 7:24).

In vain will we search within ourselves to find a new self! We may in time, and God being willing, find an *improved* 'self', the created 'self' being morally restored, but it is the same 'self' we have always been. Paul has explained that having "heard the word of the truth of the gospel" we are to bear "fruit in every good work, increasing in the knowledge of God" (1:5, 10). Such development of character in the Christian is expected. Even so, we need to know in what aspects of our being the improvement is to be found. We are advised that "our outward man is decaying, yet the inward man is being renewed day by day" (II Corinthians 4:16). So, some change or renewing is to be anticipated. We shall give more thought to this below (#3.4.1.2.2.).[154]

But we should note here that this development of character is the ongoing process of a lifetime; but the putting off and the putting on that made each of us a new man in Christ is done conclusively, and in a moment.

In what sense, then, are we to consider ourselves to be "new" men? To understand, we need only return to our earlier consideration of our participation in Christ's baptism (#3.2.2.3. Fourth). Just as we saw then that we are to "reckon" ourselves "to be dead unto sin but alive unto God in Christ Jesus" (Romans 6:11), we are now to consider ourselves to be new men. But again, the newness is not to be found primarily in some inward change in our self, but in our relationship with God. We were, as we have seen, aliens and enemies (1:21), but now we are citizens and friends.

To illustrate, we might liken the change to the time a man enlists in the army. The moment he signs the appropriate document, he, in that instant, is transformed from a civilian to a soldier. He then puts on his uniform as an indication of his recruitment. But the significant change is certainly not in the externality of different clothing, which is, as it were, only a 'sacramental sign'. To use the terminology I introduced above, he, being enrolled, is at once *re-contextualized*,

---

[154] It is even more confusing when some suggest that the "new man" or the "new self" is the 'indwelling Christ'. What then are we to make of the "new man ... being renewed" (3:10)? In what possible sense is the 'indwelling Christ' to be renewed? Or if there is supposed to be some replacement of the "old" with the "new" and the "new" requires renewal, then the "new" is imperfect or inadequate. So, we suggest that the "new" is not a replacement, but a moral realignment.

moving from his home to the army barracks; and he is at once *re-moderated*, coming under military law. This is an immediate transition, resulting in a new relationship that is the beginning of a new life, with disciplined character, and modified behaviour.

And every believer has been chosen to be "a good soldier of Christ Jesus" (II Timothy 2:3). And this is a transforming relationship.

It is best, then, to understand the expression "old man" as referring simply to the unconverted man; independent, self-governing man; man in isolation from God; man in rebellion; the covenant-breaking man (cf. Romans 6:6, Ephesians 4:24). In contrast, the "new man" is the converted man; the man who recognizes his dependence upon God and his responsibility to obey Him; the man in submission to divine authority; the covenant-keeping man. That is, the *re-contextualized* and *re-moderated* man.

The deed has been done! The Christian is the person who has put off the "old man" and has put on the "new". But as this immediately involves him as a covenant-keeper in doing the work of God and serving in Christ's army, so it has immediate moral and behavioural consequences. What is contrary to the will and the standards of God must now be abandoned – "put to death" or "put away" (3:5, 8).

We might ask, how exactly did we put off the old and put on the new; or what action did we take to enter a new context and find a new moderating principle for our lives? We must surely acknowledge that our transition from the old to the new is the gracious, renewing activity of a sovereign God. Had He not intervened, we would have continued in our former condition, living in the lusts of the flesh, committed to our covetousness and idolatry, and probably remained devoid of any real interest in God. But in His mercy, He opened our eyes to see ourselves as we actually are, and He gave us the *repentance* we needed to acknowledge this disturbing truth (II Timothy 2:25) and the *faith* necessary for our salvation (Ephesians 2:8). The repentance corresponds to the 'putting off', even as the faith corresponds to the 'putting on'. And repentance and faith are the beginning of *re-moderation* and *re-contextualization* that set us on the path to a life of godliness that will continue until we are presented "holy and without blemish and unreproveable before Him" (1:22).

NOTE: The two imperatives, "put to death" (3:5, νεκρώσατε) and "put away" (3:8, ἀπόθεσθε), are beyond the moral ability of the unconverted no matter how dedicated and disciplined he may be. But they become feasible for the converted because he has "put off the old man" (3:9, ἀπεκδυσάμενοι τὸν παλαιὸν ἄνθρωπον) and has "put on the new" (3:10, ἐνδυσάμενοι τὸν νέον). Moreover, the unconverted has repudiated the obligation to obey the imperatives, but the converted has accepted the responsibility to do so.

3.4.1.2.2. RENEWAL UNTO KNOWLEDGE (3:10)

Compare, Holiness in character (#3.4.2.1.1.).

For the Christian, then, the putting off and the putting on are things he has done; they are past events. Indeed, they made him the Christian that he is, but they were only the beginning. He is now positioned to put to death his sinful attitudes and to put away his evil actions (#3.4.1.2.). He is now, Paul explains, caught up in *a process of renewal*. The "new man", the Christian man that the neophyte has become, "is being renewed unto knowledge" (3:10, τὸν νέον τὸν ἀνακαινούμενον εἰς ἐπίγνωσιν).

There are two things we should notice about the word used here for "being renewed":

- **First**, it is in the *present tense*, indicating that an ongoing process is in view.

  The *terminus ad quem* for this process is, we may assume, the moment when we are presented "holy and without blemish and unreprovable" (1:22) in the presence of God. Until that day no man can claim perfection, and he should not think that he can disregard the renewal process without serious consequences. Moreover, this renewal, as we noted above, is a progressive "day by day" process (II Corinthians 4:16), so it should be our daily concern as we recognize that we are not "already made perfect" and reach "forward to the things that are before" us (Philippians 3:12-14).

- **Second**, it is in the *passive mood*, and this implies that the Christian is not renewing himself, but is being renewed by God.

  We are, in every sense, saved only by divine grace. Paul as a mature believer lamented his own deficiencies and inability to improve his own life (Romans 7:14-18) and his only anticipation of deliverance from this pathetic condition was in Jesus Christ (Romans 7:24-25). Despite the many books written to the contrary, the Christian gospel is not, and does not supply a self-help manual, and does not offer any techniques for self-improvement. But it does invite us to "draw near ... unto the throne of grace, that we may receive mercy, and find grace to help in time of need"

(Hebrews 4:16). *What is advised is not self-help, but divine help; and the summons is not to effort, but to faith* (2:12).[155]

Now, *the ultimate objective of this process of renewal* is that those who are redeemed by grace might recover all God intended when, at the beginning, He created man in His own image (Genesis 1:27). It was His foreordained intention that His people should be "conformed to the image of His Son" (Romans 8:29). And we are assured that all believers are even now "being transformed into the same image from glory to glory" (II Corinthians 3:18). Paul has explained to the Colossians that Jesus is "the image of the invisible God" and the creator of all things (1:15-16), and now he boldly announces that the Lord's people are predestined to be restored to "the image of Him that created" them (3:10, this being an integral aspect of the apostolic hope, cf. I John 3:2). We are to be, and we should aspire to be in some way like Jesus Christ. He is our ultimate paragon.

But as we cannot be like Christ in His deity or share in His omnipotence and omniscience – for we ourselves are not and never will be God! – in what sense then are we to be like Him?

There is a tantalizing and intriguing indication in the New Testament that in the future consummation of our redemption there will be a physical component in our likeness to the incarnate Christ. When He returns, He will refashion our present "body", which in its fallen condition brings us considerable humiliation, so that it will conform to "the body of His glory" (Philippians 3:21). This will happen in the resurrection when "we shall all be changed in a moment", and then in a truly physical sense we will "bear the image of the heavenly" (I Corinthians 15:49, 51-52).[156]

I might suggest that this ultimate physical likeness with the body of Christ's glory – His tangible body, seen and touched subsequent to His resurrection – is something we should confidently *anticipate*. It is promised in the gospel! But it

---

[155] Here again we must be careful not to be confused. It is required of the Christian that he discipline himself and "labour and strive" (I Timothy 4:10) like an athlete in the contest (I Corinthians 9:25-27). This is because the work we have to do for the kingdom of God is difficult and demanding – in fact, dangerous. It requires our every effort! But this is that we might get done the job we have been given, not that we might conform ourselves to the image of God. Even so, Paul acknowledged that his labour and striving were only effective because God "works in (him) mightily" (1:29). It was, then, only as he was being "renewed ... after the image" of God (3:10) that he could begin and maintain any effort that would promote the kingdom and advance the work of the gospel.

[156] In I Corinthians 15:49 the "image of the heavenly" is contrasted with "the image of the earthly". In context, it seems most likely that Paul is comparing the resurrection body, fit for heaven and eternity, and the natural, dying body of people in this present world.

is not something to which we can *aspire*. That is, there is nothing we can do to prepare ourselves for it, and there are no physical prearrangements that we can make in readiness for this change. It will happen in "a moment, in the twinkling of an eye" (I Corinthians 15:52). And it matters not whether we are alive on earth when it happens, or long since dead and buried (I Thessalonians 4:16-17). But until that day, and as we have seen, "the outward man (our body) is decaying" (II Corinthians 4:16).[157]

Nevertheless, in other matters we should *aspire* to be like Christ, for he who hopes that he will be transformed into His likeness will even now be purifying "himself, even as He is pure" (I John 3:3). Here we return to the matter raised above concerning those aspects of our being in which improvement is to be found as we mature in our faith: the fruitfulness, knowledge, and walking worthily mentioned in 1:10 (#1.2.3., cf. #3.4.1.2.1.).

The renewing Paul writes about here is in reference to or "after the image of Him that created him" (3:10). In other words, the benchmark by which we ought to measure our development – as daunting as it seems – is, as it has always been, the image of God. This is wholly inclusive. Everything we are, think, feel, desire, and will, or do, construct, express, and articulate should reflect the likeness of God. Everything! Therefore, Paul writes that "whatsoever you do" should be done "as unto the Lord" (3:23). Whatsoever! To aspire to be like Christ is a breathtaking and exhilarating enterprise – but sadly, an enterprise few think worth much consideration, and most have given it no thought at all. *Contemporary Christians, possessed by an inflated notion of progress, seem to be more concerned to become something entirely new, rather than recover the original divine design!*

However, as I have suggested above, the Christian is advised to have the mind of Christ (Philippians 2:5, #3.1.3. Second) so that his thinking might conform to the will of God, which involves the re-contextualizing and the re-moderating made possible by our redemption. But then, if he thinks in the way Christ desires, he will respond "from the innermost part of (his) being" (3:23) to the will of God (#3.4.1.1.) This involved an "inward" – so subjective and subliminal – renewal (II Corinthians 4:16). Therefore, we might suggest, any significant change in our doing, constructing, expressing, and articulating requires a prerequisite change in our thinking, feeling, desiring, and willing. The productivity of our life is determined by the disposition of our soul.

---

[157] Even so, knowing that our creation in the image of God is all-inclusive, we acknowledge the importance of our body, even in its fallen condition. We are so to conduct ourselves that "the life of Jesus may be manifested in our mortal flesh" (II Corinthians 4:11).

Now there are, *inter alia, three specific aspects of the image of God* that must be seriously considered if we are to understand the renewal required to adjust, refine, and improve our inner disposition, to incline our hearts to keep God's law (I Kings 8:58, Psalm 119:36), and to gain wisdom and understanding (Proverbs 2:2). These three aspects are specifically associated in Paul's writings with putting on the "new man" – they are *righteousness* and *holiness* in Ephesians 4:20-24, and *knowledge* in Colossians 3:10.

So, if we aspire to be like Christ, we will have a primary and impelling interest is righteousness, holiness, and knowledge – we will, in fact, "hunger and thirst after righteousness" (Matthew 5:6), seek to "grow in ... knowledge" (II Peter 3:18), and be found "perfecting holiness in the fear of God" (II Corinthians 7:1). It is in the pursuit of these things, that we should aspire to be like Christ.[158]

We are to grow into the likeness of Christ, *not in part but in whole*. Therefore, we must, as it were, embrace the whole Christ! This, from Paul's perspective in Colossians, is Christ the Creator and Redeemer; the Christ in whom "all things consist" (1:17); the Christ in "whom all the treasures of wisdom and knowledge are hidden" (2:3); the Christ in whom we "are made full" (2:20); the Christ who died that His people might be "holy, without blemish and unreproveable" (1:22). This demands nothing less than that we set our hearts upon a life of righteousness, holiness, and knowledge – all three, and all three together.

NOTE: I suggest, then, that *the Christian scholar*, who pursues knowledge, will falter in his endeavours if he neglects the pursuit of righteousness and holiness. And *the Christian moralist*, who pursues righteousness, will falter in his endeavours if he neglects the pursuit of knowledge and holiness. And *the Christian devotee*, who pursues holiness, will falter in his endeavours if he neglects the pursuit of righteousness and knowledge.[159]

Paul was concerned to promote such an all-embracing pursuit of these *qualities of godliness* in the lives of those to whom he ministered. His stated objective was

---

[158] We might well hope and pray that Christians in our times will become more passionate about attaining righteousness, holiness, and knowledge – as they are to be found in Christ – that they might be godly, than they seem to be anxious to discover new techniques by which they might be successful.

[159] We might suggest that righteousness, holiness, and knowledge, being components of the image of Christ, should be the distinguishing characteristics of the true Christian. Certainly, the Christian is to be known by his love (John 13:35) – and this we should never forget. However, as that love is a disposition of a man's soul it is invisible, concealed within his heart. We only know that he is a man of love when it is displayed in the quality of the life he lives. *So, we might say that love has its fullness of expression in and through righteousness, holiness, and knowledge.* Indeed, without these three it is difficult to conceive what love might be! It is a strange love indeed – if it is love at all – that is concomitant with unrighteousness, wickedness, and ignorance! Sadly, such strange, vacuous 'love' has become commonplace.

that he might "present every man perfect in Christ". Therefore, he was at pains to admonish and to teach "every man in all wisdom" (1:28). And this, as we have seen, required guidance in moral living and instruction in knowledge (#2.1.4. Second). Maturation in both righteousness and knowledge is essential.

However, here in his letter to the Colossians Paul only mentions, and therefore *gives a certain emphasis to knowledge*, as he writes about the process of renewal (3:10). In context, this is perfectly reasonable. As concerned as he might be that his readers "walk worthily of the Lord ... bearing fruit in every good work", he is well aware that they will only be able to do this as they are "increasing in the knowledge of God" (1:10). They required, in other words, renewal unto knowledge that they might walk in the righteousness of good works.

Moreover, the apostle was obviously concerned that this process of "increasing in the knowledge of God" was being assailed by false teachers with their persuasive oratory and deceptive philosophy. These extraneous preachers were subverting, or attempting to subvert, the thinking of these young Colossian believers, and thereby to deflect them from a life of righteousness and holiness. *Therefore, it was important that Paul explain to them that putting off the old and putting on the new man – that is, being converted to Christ – initiated a new learning process, the gaining of knowledge in reference to the image of Christ.*

Paul's first concern here for the renewal process is that it leads the Christian continually into knowledge – to the very knowledge of God that is required for "every good work" (1:10). Therefore, the renewing is not primarily dynamic, but noetic (cf. Romans 12:2).

However, it is fatal to the whole principle of the gospel of grace to assume that what Paul is saying here implies a renewal *by* knowledge. That a man might be renewed by education is a notion more at home among secular humanists than Christians! Both Christian and non-Christian might agree that schooling for all people is most desirable. But the Christian is aware that learning does not renew a man, but only educates the man that he is. Send a criminal to university and he will not graduate as a good man but as an educated criminal.[160]

Rather, Paul is stating that the renewal *precedes* knowledge – the knowledge that is the companion of holiness and righteousness. In fact, this renewing must be

---

[160] Of course, I am aware that education may – or may not! – refine a man's character and thereby make him a better citizen. It may result in redirecting his thoughts and actions towards a more productive life, and this should be encouraged. But Christianity has something much more substantial to offer.

understood as a work of God's grace in the soul of a man that removes prejudice against God and sets him free from his restrictive, anthropocentric interpretation of the world. This work of grace opens up a man's mind to a Christocentric perspective, and hence to rightly contextualized knowledge. And this "renewing unto knowledge" is always in progress!

The practice of morality – negatively or positively, prohibitive or affirmative – is obedience to God's commandments or conformity to divine standards. But the commandments are addressed to man's mind and need to be known, appreciated, and their implications considered. Therefore, the work of God's grace in renewal unto knowledge, the redeeming of man's intellectual faculties, is an essential prerequisite to obedience.

3.4.1.2.3. UNIFICATION IN CHRIST (3:11)

Compare, Holiness in communion (#3.4.2.1.2.).

Here Paul writes of various classifications in which people in this world are distinguished from each other – Greek, Jew/circumcision, uncircumcision/barbarian, Scythian/bondman, freeman (3:11). Each couplet in order – as I have divided them – suggests distinctive *ethnic, religious, cultural,* and *social* backgrounds and characteristics.

Now the first and obvious thing to say about such classifications is that the gospel does not – and indeed, need not and cannot – eliminate them from human society. It is impossible for us to change our ethnicity, remaining for all our days as members of the race into which we were born. We may be able to change our religion, culture, and position in society, but we still remain religiously, culturally, and socially identifiable, for these in one form or another are the structures of the communities in which we live and of which we are an integral part. They are all ineradicable aspects of created human existence.

Therefore, being aspects of our created existence, they are not intrinsically evil or inevitably divisive. They were divinely designed, no doubt, for the enrichment and integration of the human community.[161] It would be a bland, colourless, insipid, and monotonous world without them! Nevertheless, they have all been corrupted, being contaminated by sin, and have become a source of divisiveness and conflict. We all too easily degenerate into racists, religious bigots, cultural snobs, and tyrants.

---

[161] We might compare Paul's words in I Corinthians 12:14ff.

So, rather than attempting the unnecessary and impossible task of diminishing or eliminating these categories from human society – as many of our contemporaries endeavour to do – we, as Christians, should work for their redemption. We should seek empathy with other races, and pursue the remediation of religion, culture, and society through the gospel of Christ. We desire to promote enrichment and congenial integration in the great plurality of the distinctive characteristics of humankind without compromising our beliefs.

It is no surprise to us, then, that although Paul writes here in Colossians 3:11 about various human classifications and, at first glance perhaps, appears to disparage them, elsewhere in his letters he encourages his readers to take them seriously, respect them, and engage with them. He was not, for example, averse to adapting himself to the cultural practices and social conditions of others when it was appropriate for him to do so, and advantageous for the higher principles of the gospel. Needless to say, how he did this without violating "the law of Christ" requires careful consideration (see I Corinthians 9:19-23). Christians must be discerning. We are not to follow thoughtlessly the customs of any community in which we find ourselves but must always remain true to the founding traditions of the apostles (see II Thessalonians 2:15, 3:6). In other words, we are not to destroy or disparage the created and necessary aspects of human society, but to seek their redemption by living according to and proclaiming the principles of the word of God in every aspect of our communal life.

However, if there is to be any enrichment in and integration of the diversities of the human communities, there must be *some unifying ground*, some universal principle, some shared essence, some undergirding commonality that makes consolidation possible. However, the bare, undefined, undifferentiated abstraction 'human nature' is far too nebulous to serve as the integrating fundamental. It could not be, as 'human nature' – however described – is intrinsically diverse, and the term itself far too diffuse.

From the historical perspective, a unifying principle seems to be excruciatingly elusive. But as far as Christians are concerned, it is found in the image of God, in which we are all created and according to which we are to be renewed. Therefore, the ethnic, religious, cultural, and social are to be redeemed by righteousness, holiness, and knowledge (see #3.4.1.2.2.). In other words, the various and diverse characteristics of human society are to be conditioned and consolidated by the invariable and universal qualities of godliness.

But it is also important to notice – and this is critical for understanding the apostle's thinking – that Paul writes that there is a place "where there cannot be" (ὅπου οὐκ ἔνι, 3:11) these classifications that distinguish various groups of people. That is, in at least one aspect of our thinking they are to be considered irrelevant and set aside – and this is in reference to the restoration of "the new man" (3:10). As important as the ethnic, religious, cultural, and social may be in *the created order* of things, they are unrelated to the "renewal" according to "the image" of God in *the redemptive order* of things. In other words, the renewal is neither hindered nor assisted by these distinctive categories in human community. We must not think anyone to be excluded from or included in Christian salvation and its benefits by race or by his present religion, custom, or status.

When Paul insists that there "cannot be" Greek and Jew, he does not imagine that Greek-ness and Jew-ness can be eliminated, any more than maleness or femaleness, or other basic socio-cultural distinctions. But he does indicate that the image can be manifested in all such categories. This image, then, is something far deeper and more fundamental in human life than personal characteristics, or any of the features that distinguish one person – or one people – from another. To be renewed unto the likeness of the God who created us does not expunge God-given personality. *So, we have here a unique understanding of humanity that both appreciates a fundamental unity and equality, and concurrently authenticates the validity of uniqueness and complementary individuality.*

The only important and consequential factor in the renewal is that "Christ is all, and in all" (3:11). This implies that in the restoring of the "image", Christ, in whom "all the fullness of the Godhead" dwells (2:9) is, in Himself and in all He supplies, "all" that is necessary. And then, He is also "in all" – that is, intimately associated with – those who have "put on the new man". As much as we might emulate good, Christian men (I Corinthians 11:1, Philippians 3:17), we should above all else seek to be "imitators of God, as beloved children" (Ephesians 5:1-2).

Paul makes a parallel statement in Galatians 3:28: "There can be neither Jew nor Greek, there can be neither bond nor free, there can be no male and female; for ye all are one in Christ Jesus".[162] This and Colossians 3:11, being much alike,

---

[162] Some suggest that the principle of Galatians 3:28 has been accomplished – or is being accomplished – in the historic development of the church. They propose, for example, that the distinction between Jew and Greek was overcome at the Jerusalem council (Acts 15), and that between bond and free many years later in the abolition of the slave trade in the early nineteenth century (thanks to men like William Wilberforce). But resolution of the male/female divide had to wait until the revolutionary thinking in the late twentieth century. But this was certainly not what was in Paul's mind. He did not write 'there will not be' or 'there should not be', but there 'is not' or 'there cannot be' (οὐκ ἔνι) these divisions in Christ. What he has in mind was and is a present reality. In fact, in neither Galatians 3:28 nor Colossians 3:11 does the apostle actually suggest that these human categories needed to be overcome, but only that they were irrelevant to the relationship between God and His people that he was considering.

immediately invite comparison. However, these two verses are not found in the same context, and this gives each its own significance. They also differ in that Galatians mentions that the Christian has "put on Christ" (Galatians 3:27), but in Colossians that he has "put on the new man which is being renewed" (3:10). And as we have mentioned above (fn. 154), the "new man" must not be equated with "Christ" because the former is progressively being renewed unto knowledge, and this could hardly be said of Him "in whom are all the treasures of wisdom and knowledge" (2:3). It is helpful to compare these two statements:

- **First**, at this point in Galatians, Paul is particularly concerned that we understand how we are to be justified and receive the advantages of the covenant God made with Abraham and his believing descendants; that we appreciate being "the sons of God" (Galatians 3:26) and the benefits this conveys. He likens the Law of Moses to a schoolteacher who, exposing our moral insufficiency, directs us to Christ who "gave Himself up" for our salvation. Under this tutelage, we were "brought unto Christ, that we might be justified by faith".

  It is in this context that it is said that we have "put on Christ", which the apostle associates with baptism (Galatians 3:18, 23-27). In this the Christian has gained all the benefits of Christ's death and the imputation of His righteousness (cf. #3.2.2.3. and #3.2.2.4.), and consequently is fully reconciled to God.

  The immediate result is that we have all become, as "sons of God", "heirs according to the promise" (Galatians 3:26, 29).

  The permanent, given *status* we have in the kingdom of God is in view.

  Paul is explaining what we are *in Him* because we have "put on Christ". This is the benefit of our justification, the result of what He did *for us*.

- **Second**, at this point in Colossians, Paul is particularly concerned that we understand how we are to "walk worthily of the Lord" (1:10); that we appreciate being the servants of God, and the importance of the moral transformation this requires of us. There are undesirable deeds and attitudes that the sincere Christian will be anxious to "put away" (3:8), and there are desirable deeds and attitudes that he will be concerned to "put on" (3:12).

  It is in this context that it is said that we have "put on the new man". In this, the Christian is progressively being renewed and restored to a life of godliness (3:9-10, #3.4.1.2.1.).

The continuing result is that we are being "renewed unto knowledge" and transformed into the "image of Him who created" us (3:10).

The progressing, moral *state* of our life in this world is in view.

Paul is explaining what we are *for Him* because we have "put on the new man". This is the benefit of our sanctification, the result of what He does *in us*.

We might suggest, then, that the two points at which matters of ethnic, religious, cultural, social and – now we might add from Galatians 3:28 – gender characteristics are irrelevant are in both the justifying and sanctifying relationship we have with Jesus Christ. No matter how a man might be classified in any one or in all of these communal categories, he may be redeemed and renewed by the grace of God. And, we might add, no matter how he might be so categorized, he should not be denied the opportunity of hearing the Christian gospel.

But here we must be careful not to confuse things that differ. In Colossians 3:11 and Galatians 3:28, Paul writes about justification and sanctification, *the redeemed relationship* Christians have with their God. In this relationship, all matters ethnic, religious, cultural, social and sexual are irrelevant. However, in *the human relationships* that we have with each other in this world they are of the greatest importance. Therefore, for example, the apostle does not contradict himself when he insists that *in union with Christ* "there can be no male and female" (Galatians 3:28) – where the distinction is of no consequence – and then instructs wives *in their marriage union* to be in subjection unto their husbands (3:18) – where the distinction is of considerable consequence. Neither does he contradict himself when, having explained that where His people have "put on the new man" there can be neither bond nor free (3:10-11), he instructs servants to obey their masters "in all things" (3:22). *And we must note that Paul makes corresponding demands of husbands and masters*, as we shall see below.

As Christians, we should be concerned not only to recognize these human categories but also to protect, promote and enhance them (cf. Titus 2:1-10). But it must be acknowledged that this is extremely challenging for the Christian community – at least for those who are committed to biblical standards – in the modern, secular world. But it would not have been easy, I assume, at any time in history.

What cannot be denied in all this is that there are biblical principles – divine laws, if you will – that are designed to structure the Christian community and to regulate interpersonal relationships among believing men and women. They are demanding – and so demanding that, especially in our contemporary and supposedly egalitarian age, we tend to question and even to resent them. Indeed, we might even fear them, knowing how we are prone to distort all things for our own advantage. In our day, it seems that whenever it is suggested that the definition of interpersonal relationships be qualified with words like 'subjection' or 'obey', there is vehement protest. Such qualifications are abhorrent to the avant-garde devotees of unlimited freedom.

However, we must remember that Paul is giving these instructions to those who have "put on Christ" and have "put on the new man". He is addressing the justified and sanctified. He is writing to a unique and significantly different society of people. Genuine Christians! And in this context, our response to biblical principles ought always to be confidently and unapologetically affirmative, and the notions of submission and obedience openly accepted as inoffensive.

The point is this: the justifying and sanctifying relationship we have with Jesus Christ, although not dependent upon, is nonetheless intensely relevant for all matters ethnic, religious, cultural, social, and sexual. It is through the benefits of justification and sanctification that the qualities of godliness – righteousness, knowledge, and holiness – can be restored to any and every aspect of human life and to all categories of human society. Or, in other words, the benefits of the grace of God in Christ are to penetrate into every corner of our lives and transform our individual and communal behaviour.

We must insist, then, that the biblical principles that are designed to structure the Christian community and to regulate interpersonal relationships are to be honoured and obeyed, and always pursued in righteousness, knowledge, and holiness. However, being aware of our own moral weaknesses and our irrepressible love for "the glory of men more than the glory of God" (cf. John12:43), it is most unlikely that we will effectively and faithfully embrace such a way of life unless we have a full appreciation of and constant joy in the total sufficiency of Christ, and fully trust in Him who "is all, and in all" (3:11). Without shame, we are to be like Him – and, inter alia, like Him in His humility, submission, and obedience.

NOTE: We insist that distinctive *ethnic, religious, cultural, social,* and *gender* characteristics do not advantage or disadvantage, privilege or exclude anyone from finding salvation and entering into the kingdom of Christ.

Therefore, we welcome every opportunity to share the gospel with *everyone, none excluded.*

Nevertheless, we must also affirm that the gospel we preach – or should be preaching – requires people to *re-contextualize* and to *re-moderate* their thinking (#3.4.1.1.) about the significance, nature, and implications of all these social relationships. The unalterable attributes of ethnicity and gender must be reconsidered within God's created order; and the variable religious, cultural, and social features of our lives must be restructured within God's redemptive order.

Therefore, we welcome every opportunity to relate the gospel to *everything, nothing excluded.*

There is a comprehensiveness about the gospel that makes it important for *everyone, everywhere,* and applicable to *everything,* and implies a Christian responsibility for both its proclamation and implementation. This is ineluctable if we conscientiously formulate our philosophy "after Christ" (2:8), in whom "are all the treasures of wisdom and knowledge hidden" (2:3).

3.4.2. AFFIRMATIVE MORALITY (3:12-17)

Paul has commanded his readers to take decisive action to rid themselves of attitudes and actions that are contrary to a life of godliness and that incur the wrath of God. They were to put to death their "members which are upon the earth" and to put away all aspects of an evil disposition (3:5-9, #3.4.1.1.). But although this demanded a meaningful, volitional response, it was by no means an exhortation to mere self-reformation. The task required of them was Herculean – in fact, Sisyphean! – and beyond the ability of even the most devout and most disciplined. There is a sombre note running through the scriptures exposing the pathetic incapacity of postlapsarian man to recover himself from his fallen condition and persistent contumacy (eg. see Genesis 6:5, Psalm 14:2-3, 51:1-5, Jeremiah 13:23, Romans 7:15-25). Despite whatever meagre moral improvement we might achieve in human society by our own efforts, we are not able to transform ourselves into intrinsically good people in the sight of God. Only "the Lord the Spirit" can do this (II Corinthians 3:18).

Therefore, the apostle reminded the Colossians of the advantages they enjoyed because of their "faith in Christ Jesus" (1:4) and their reconciliation "in the body of His death" (1:21). They are now markedly different men and women because of their restored, dynamic relationship with God, having "put off the old man" and "put on the new man" (3:9-10, #3.4.1.2.1.). And this, as we have seen, is the commencement of the process of renewal that God effects in His people, to conform them to the "image" of Christ, their creator.

The man of faith and understanding, then, does not rely on any ability of his own but recognizes that he is fully dependent upon the gracious intervention of God for the moral restoration of his life. Therefore, we may suppose, if he is seriously intent on living a life of godliness and walking "worthily of the Lord" (1:10), he will frequently "draw near with boldness unto the throne of grace" that he may "find grace to help in time of need" (Hebrews 4:16). He will not be a pretentious man who would be seen as more than he is, but a penitent man who would be known only as someone who has benefitted from the mercies of Christ.

Paul now brings this benefit to our attention here in Colossians by describing those he exhorts to "put on" the various graces of their redemption – those whom he anticipates will be transformed into the image of God – as "God's elect, holy and beloved" (3:12, ἐκλεκτοὶ τοῦ θεοῦ ἅγιοι καὶ ἠγαπημένοι). Anyone not in this category is without God and without hope (Ephesians 2:12). To make clear where the true Christian stands before God, the apostle uses in this description *three powerful ideas* to encapsulate the fundamental advantages of being "in Christ", that is, of being "reconciled in the body of His flesh through death" (1:21-22). These we must consider:

- **First**, the apostle refers to the believers as "God's elect" (ἐκλεκτοὶ τοῦ θεου).[163]
  They are, he is indicating, people whom God has selected for Himself. In this He exercised His sovereignty when He "chose us in (Christ) before the foundation of the world, that we should be holy and blameless before him" (Ephesians 1:4). Somehow Paul would have us conceive within our minds that which is inconceivable – that God had a saving interest in us before the earth was created!

  Therefore, we stand now, at this time in human history, as Christian believers because it was His eternal will that we should be so. Our conversion was not fortuitous or of our own design, but the direct result of His timeless intention. In pursuit of His own ultimate glory, His immediate purpose is that we should be "holy and blameless" (ἁγίους καὶ ἀμώμους) – and to be so is not only our *enrichment*, but also our *responsibility* (1:22, #1.3.2.3.3. Second).

  We must humbly acknowledge that had the Lord left us to ourselves, we would never have chosen Him, for "there is none that seeks after God" (Romans 3:11). We were, to quote the prophet, "as a firebrand plucked out of the burning" (Amos 4:11) – helpless until rescued.

  In the mercies of Christ, we find ourselves among the eternally elect of God.

- **Second**, Paul also refers to his readers as "holy" (ἅγιοι, as in Ephesians 1:4).
  This is the word translated "saints" in 1:2, 4, 12, and 26 (#1). And it is a cognate of the words elsewhere translated 'holy', 'sanctify', and 'sanctification'. So, the saints are those who are holy, or those sanctified.

---

[163] This word is variously translated 'chosen', 'chosen ones', or 'elect'.

But here it must be kept in mind that the basic significance of words in this group is that they imply being 'separated', 'dedicated', or 'set apart' for God's exclusive purposes.

Therefore, when the first Christians referred to themselves as "saints" they were reflecting their awareness that God had elected them to be His people that they might be at His disposal and serve Him in all things. They understood clearly, in other words, that they were "bought with a price" and should "therefore, glorify God" (I Corinthians 6:20). But as the service of God requires a measure of godliness, this word acquires the added idea of moral purification – being set apart *for* God requires a setting apart *from* sin and evil. Therefore, being sanctified, they should pursue after increasing holiness.

In the mercies of Christ, we find ourselves among the sanctified servants of God.

• **Third**, Paul further refers to his readers as "beloved" (ἠγαπημένοι).

The apostle would not leave us in any doubt about God's "great love wherewith He loved us" (Ephesians 2:4) that motivated Christ to give "himself up for us, an offering and a sacrifice" (Ephesians 5:2, cf. Romans 5:8, Galatians 2:20). It is, he wrote, "through Him that loved us" that we are "more than conquerors" in this troubled world, and he insisted that "nothing can separate us from the love of God which is in Christ" (Romans 8:37-39). His love for His elect is ineffable, irresistible, and eternal.

But we must not be so conceited – or so nonchalant – as to imagine either that we are intrinsically loveable, or that God is obliged to love everybody. We are not, and He is not! To have been 'brought into the company of those loved'[164] by God is an exquisite privilege, which not all will enjoy (Psalm 5:5, Romans 9:13).

In the mercies of Christ, we find ourselves among the undeservedly beloved of God.

In these three matters, God has the initiative. If we are elect, holy, and beloved it is entirely His doing and not ours. We are the beneficiaries because He chose, He sanctified, and He loved us. Being so positioned before God, we are *privileged* in His election, *purposeful* in His service, and *protected* in His love.

---

[164] I suggest this as a possible reading of "beloved" (ἠγαπημένοι, in contrast to ἀγαπητοί).

Here is reason enough for those who have "received Christ Jesus the Lord" to be forever "abounding in thanksgiving" (2:6-7). And motivation enough to pursue a moral life.

Moreover, being so advantaged, Christians may confidently seek God's assistance to "put on" the graces of a godly character – compassion, kindness, humility and the like (3:12-13). This divine assistance is not to be gained by our own merit, but thankfully accepted by faith as the gift of God's grace (cf. Romans 6:23). As we began with "faith in the working of God" (2:12), so we should continue – "from faith unto faith" (Romans 1:17).

NOTE: Now it is particularly relevant to note that Jesus Christ is also referred to in scripture as God's "chosen" or "elect" (Luke 9:35), as having been "sanctified" by the Father (John 10:36), and as the Father's "beloved" (Luke 3:22). Or, as God said of Him in similar words, "Behold my servant, whom I have chosen, my beloved ..." (Matthew 12:18, Isaiah 42:1).

Therefore, it may truly be said of Jesus that He also is "God's elect, holy and beloved"!

This implies that those who are "in Christ" stand before God even as Christ stands before His Father. So, we might say that in some sense God looks upon us as He looks upon His Son.

It is just because we have this position in Christ that we have the potential of being like Christ. We are only chosen, holy, and beloved because we are in Christ. And because we are chosen, holy, and beloved by God we are being renewed after the image of God in righteousness, holiness, and knowledge.

All this should give us the confidence to rely upon the assistance of divine grace when we give ourselves to the demanding practice of positive, Christian morality. With God's help, the pursuit of true godliness is not a futile exercise. Nevertheless, it should always be attempted in genuine humility, knowing that we will only be truly like Christ when we see Him (cf. John's anticipation, I John 3:2, and Paul's determination, Philippians 3:13).

Moreover, being privileged as God's elect, holy and beloved, we have an inescapable moral responsibility to pursue a life of godliness for the sake of His glory and praise.

3.4.2.1. THE PRACTICE OF AFFIRMATIVE MORALITY (3:12-14)

In the gospel, there is not only instruction concerning the negative things we should not do, but also concerning the positive things of true worth we should do.

258

Christians are not only saved 'from', but also saved 'for', and we must now give some thought to affirmative aspects of Christian morality.

We mentioned above (#3.4.1.2.) that in Paul's lists of things prohibited by Christian moral principles (3:5, 3:8-9), he mentions both *improper attitudes* – passion, evil desires, anger, wrath – and *improper actions* – fornication, uncleanness, slander, obscene speaking, lying. Wickedness is found, then, in both the disposition of our hearts and in the array of our deeds. Now, writing of things promoted by Christian moral principles which believers are obliged to "put on", he mentions *proper attitudes* – compassion, kindness, humility, meekness, longsuffering, love – and *proper actions* – forbearing, forgiving (3:12-13). Godliness is also found, then, in both the disposition of our hearts and in the array of our deeds.

The apostle is evidently not concerned here with the private pursuit of personal godliness in the isolation of some hermitic or monastic seclusion. Nor is he interested in individualistic piety in which a man might indulge only for the sake of his own benefit, religious gratification, or spiritual egocentricity. He is not writing about some form of mystical exercise that is of advantage only to the participant.

But he is writing about achieving, through divine assistance, the conscientious practice of Christian moral principles within the Christian community. He is advising his readers to "put away ... anger, wrath" and all associated malevolent attitudes (3:8), and to "put on ... a heart of compassion, kindness" and all associated benevolent attitudes, so that the community might enjoy unanimity in the "bond of perfectness" (3:12-14) – or, in other words, in "the unity of the Spirit in the bond of peace" (Ephesians 4:3).

NOTE: The genuineness of our godliness – the true quality of our character – is revealed in the communion of the saints. And if it cannot be seen there, then it is highly improbable that it will be displayed in the common concourse of secular society!

"God's elect", just because they are both "holy and beloved" (3:12), should behave in a manner that directly mirrors the attitude of God towards them in the gospel. Being "holy" they are taken up into God's *purpose*, and being "beloved" they are drawn to God's *person* – and, we might suggest, never the one without the other. If we care not to cultivate and enjoy a comprehensive worshipful relationship with God, it is most unlikely that we will ever be truly aligned with His purposes.

In this purposeful and personal reconciliation, the two most fundamental needs of inescapably dependent human beings are supplied – the need for *significance* and *security*. Although they are both provided to God's people *on earth* and are to be manifested in their lives *in this present world*, their ultimate source and final realization are *in God Himself* and *in His presence*. Therefore, the understanding Christian, although profoundly thankful for his temporal existence, will nonetheless seek to "lay up … treasures in heaven" (Matthew 6:20) because he knows that truly 'significant significance' and truly 'secure security' are only to be found in the Almighty. Hence, he "seeks the things that are above, where Christ is seated on the right hand of God" (3:1, #3.3.2.).

Such people will be seriously concerned with their involvement in the purposes of God and will be passionate in their love for the God who loves them. Therefore, it will be their genuine aspiration to be "holy in all manner of living" (I Peter 1:15). And this demands holiness in both *personal character* and *communal life*.

3.4.2.1.1. HOLINESS IN CHARACTER

Having this end in mind – the actualization of a life of genuine holiness – Paul exhorts the person who has "put on the new man" (3:10, ἐνδυσάμενοι) to "put on" attitudes that are consistent with the godliness expected of this new man (3:12, ἐνδύσασθε). His first concern, here in 3:12, is that his readers be clothed with the ways of thinking and responding that are appropriate for anyone professing faith in Christ and dependence upon His grace.

And this is a matter of genuine holiness of character.

The idea of God's people 'putting on' or 'being clothed' with specific characteristics has its roots in the Old Testament. That they might serve the Lord as He desired, the Israelites were to be clothed with salvation and righteousness (eg. II Chronicles 6:41, Job 29:14, Psalm 132:9, 16), the garments of intrinsic beauty (cf. Isaiah 52:1, 61:10, Zechariah 3:4). And God Himself is said to be clothed with honour, majesty, and strength as the almighty creator (Psalm 93:1, 104:1); and the prophet Isaiah implores Him to "put on strength" as the almighty redeemer to rescue His people (Isaiah 51:9).

Similarly, in the New Testament Christians are to "be clothed with power from on high" (ἐνδύσησθε, Luke 24:49), and they are to "put on the whole armour of God" (ἐνδύσασθε, Ephesians 6:11).

Here, in Luke and Ephesians, we are directed to the *enabling*, by the "power", and to the *equipping*, with the "armour", that our Lord makes available to us that we might stand against all the forces of evil and serve Him without fear. These two verses together help us to understand the apostle's words, "the weapons of our warfare ... are mighty before God" (II Corinthians 10:4, τὰ γὰρ ὅπλα τῆς στρατείας ἡμῶν ... δυνατὰ τῷ θεῷ)[165]. No matter how talented and well trained we might be, we will remain ineffective if we are not empowered by the Lord Himself (1:29). We act in concert with Him, or we fail. If we do not abide in Him, we can do nothing (John 15:5). God does not furnish us with the abilities and talents we need is deistic fashion that we might then act independently of Him. "Whatsoever is not of faith is sin" (Romans 14:23).

But more needs to be said in this matter. Being clothed with power and having put on the whole armour of God – as sublime as these may be – are not sufficient. We remain impotent in the service of God if we are concerned only with the instruments and the power of spiritual battle. *Accoutrements and strength – the weapons of our warfare – are not to be entrusted to those who lack the moral character that is required for a life of godliness.*

Therefore, we are not at all surprised that Paul exhorts the Colossians to "put on ... a heart of compassion, kindness, humility, meekness, longsuffering" and "love" (3:12, 14, σπλάγχνα οἰκτιρμοῦ χρηστότητα ταπεινοφροσύνην πραΰτητα μακροθυμίαν ... τὴν ἀγάπην). Although God is pleased to include us in His purpose and draw us to His person despite our moral frailty and imperfections, it is inconceivable that He would have us continue – let alone, encourage us to do so – in heartlessness, unkindness, pride, arrogance, intolerance, and lovelessness. Such attitudes are the very antithesis of Christ-likeness and in the Christian community can only be detrimental to the cause of His kingdom and the propagation of the gospel.

NOTE: In this modern age that is fascinated with technology and confident in its methodology, much of Christendom – falling under the spell of the technocratic theorists – now seems to think that it can effectively advance the work of the Church provided it masters the best contemporary techniques and secures for itself a position of influence in society. But this is a delusion!

Then, perhaps confusing their methodology and influence with divine equipping and spiritual empowering, they have little interest in holiness and disregard its demands. Then the application of their anthropocentric principles may well produce results of a secular kind, but we must seriously question whether

---

[165] This interesting expression "mighty before God" (δυνατὰ τῷ θεῷ) is variously translated. It could mean "powerful in the service of God", "made powerful by God", or "divinely powerful". But the significant point is that whatever "weapons" we have, they are not effective outside His will or without His presence.

they contribute much, if anything, to the kingdom of God. More often than not, they are a distraction and a hindrance.[166]

The urgent priority is for us to manifest compassion, kindness, humility, meekness, longsuffering, and love, before seeking to be clothed with power from on high or taking up the armour of God. This is because the Lord cares little for the "outward appearance" but "looks on the heart" (I Samuel 16:7); He "resists the proud, but gives grace to the humble" (I Peter 5:5); He considers the meek and the merciful to be blessed (Matthew 5:5, 7); and He strengthens His people "unto all patience and longsuffering" (Colossians 1:11). Moreover, we should commend ourselves as "ministers of God" in, among other virtues, "pureness, in knowledge, in longsuffering, in kindness" (II Corinthians 6:4, 6). The simple man in whom these things are found is more likely to serve the Lord well than someone who is influential and talented but lacks them. In a highly significant sense, our strength is perfected in our weakness, and we only achieve anything of worth "through the power of God" (II Corinthians 12:9, 13:4).

If, in seeking people to minister in our congregations, we have to choose – as we often do – between various nominees, we must be careful not to confuse personality and character. Better, I suggest, is the weak personality with strength of character than the strong personality with weakness of character. If our concern is for temporal success we might be tempted to choose the strong personality, but if our concern is for godliness and the glory of God we will do better to choose the strength of character.

The New Testament recognizes that God gives differing abilities to people that make each one of us unique. These "gifts" also constitute every individual as an integral element in human society, each having his own personality (see Romans 12:3ff, I Corinthians 12:4ff, Ephesians 4:8ff, I Peter 4:7-11). Such individuality in God's economy was intended to enrich, integrate, and harmonize the community.

But sadly, and at excruciating cost, fallen man has made matters of particularity and personality the source of endless conflict and division.

---

[166] If we are involved in preparing men and women for the work of the gospel we would do well to remember that, in truth, there is relatively very little we can do for them. If we would have them be good ministers of Christ we must do what we can to make sure that they are well nourished and trained in "the words of the faith, and of the good doctrine" (I Timothy 4:6) that in this they might be well equipped. But to empower them and to instill the attitudes of godliness into their hearts are the work of God alone, and in this we can but pray for them and with them.

The problem of 'personality conflicts' – or any other social malfunction – is certainly not a modern phenomenon. Paul wrote to the Corinthians about himself and Apollos, both of whom had ministered to that congregation. He was concerned that some were "puffed up for the one against the other" (I Corinthians 1:12, 3:6, 4:6). In effect, the apostle acknowledges that they were two distinct individuals, and variously gifted. But they differed only because of what they had "received" from God. Therefore, there should be no boasting in or about their giftedness as if they had achieved their distinctiveness by their own efforts (I Corinthians 4:7).

Whatever our abilities, we should not take pride in them, but be thankful that God so qualified us. "Every good gift ... is from above, coming down from the father ..." (James 1:17). Therefore, let no man "think of himself more highly than he ought to think; but to think to attain soundness of mind, according as God has dealt to each man a measure of faith" (Romans 12:3, my translation). We can be no wiser than our faith permits.

Those who are "puffed up" in their thinking, Paul notes, are deficient in love (I Corinthians 13:4), and this inevitably has a deleterious effect on their interpersonal relationships. He also suggests that this self-satisfaction results in "not holding fast the Head" (2:18-19), thus seriously affecting any possible relationship they might have with Christ. These are two catastrophic consequences of the "puffed up" mind! *Moreover, this implies that truly efficient thinking is vitiated not only by inadequate logic, but also by arrogance and prejudice.*

So, I suggest, that when we "think" about ourselves, considering our individuality, as we "ought to think" – and that we might become truly wise thinkers – we should not make our distinct personality a reason for pride, or the ground for claiming special rights, privileges, or honours. Rather we should understand that our unique individualities are predesigned that as "many members" we might cohere as the "one body in Christ" and realize the purpose for our life as "members one of another" (Romans 12:3-5). There ought to be, then, a depth of harmony and integration in the Christian community – such as, no doubt, God originally intended for the whole of humankind under His sovereign rule and desires to be manifested now in the church.

Now, from the Christian perspective, the reason why we live in a society that is fraught with interpersonal conflicts, marriage failure, family breakdowns, cultural wars, communal divisiveness, racial hatred, and tribal battles is that in our rebellion against God we assert the authority of our individuality *without any significant concern for – or even without any adequate understanding of – the divine requirements of moral virtue.* Chaos in community is the costly consequence of the loss of personal, ethical values.

We might say that as we are all created in the image of God, we share a common likeness (Genesis 1:26); and this common likeness is the basis upon which our multifarious personalities are to be integrated into a harmonious whole; and the integration is established and maintained only through the common values of moral virtue.[167]

We need both an appreciation of individual significance in *personality and talent*, and of common worth in *character and virtue*. Human society cannot be organizationally structured without the former, and it cannot be morally sustained without the latter. And perhaps one of the serious problems of contemporary, Western society is that it places greatly exaggerated importance on the former, considering the latter to be relatively insignificant. Today we tend to be more concerned to find, follow, and emulate people of talent, rather than those of virtue.[168]

Hopefully, all of this provides some background understanding that will help us to appreciate the great importance of Paul's exhortation to put on a heart of compassion, kindness, humility, meekness, longsuffering, and love (3:12, 14). These qualities should be pursued with urgency – indeed, with a sense of desperation!

NOTE: We must keep in mind that when God clothes Himself with majesty and strength, as we mentioned above, He necessarily draws upon His own glory, for such attributes are intrinsic to His being. But when the Christian puts on kindness, humility, meekness, and other such virtues, he necessarily draws upon God's grace. Such as he might have by nature of these attributes are only melancholy, marcescent elements of man's creation in the divine image; they are greatly impaired and in need of renewal.

Moreover, we must beware the subtle danger of putting on the mere appearance, an affected imitation of these values – and, even more dangerously, putting on a mere profession of them.

3.4.2.1.2. HOLINESS IN COMMUNION

Now Paul's concern, in 3:13-14, is that his readers be so clothed with the attitudes and principles that are appropriate for anyone professing faith in Christ, that this personal moral transformation should determine their relationships with

---

[167] Here we might see again the importance of a philosophy that is "after Christ" (2:8), and of thinking with a truly Christian mind. The world in which we live, especially in the contemporary era, has no sense of creation in the image of God, is more concerned that individuality be given greater significance than communality, and insists that there is no common set of moral principles that is applicable to all people.

[168] Not so long ago a job applicant needed above all else a good character reference, but now what is required is his impressive curriculum vitae. This, perhaps, reflects my concern.

and their actions towards each other. Godliness should characterize not only the individual but also the whole community; it should be effective in qualifying the social interactions of believing people. But the apostle mentions one attitude that he held to be "above all (the other) things" he had listed, and that should, therefore, be considered as of primary importance – "love, which is the bond of perfectness" (3:14). In this, he reflects the mind of Christ, who said, "By this shall all men know that ye are my disciples, if ye have love one to another" (John 13:35).

And this is a matter of genuine holiness in Christian communion.

We need, then, to give some thought to the following:

- **First**, we are to aspire after holiness in an imperfect community.

    Paul was aware that there may well be someone who has a "complaint against" another (3:13) in the Colossian congregation. Rarely would it be otherwise in any Christian community! The church is, after all, nothing more than the assembly of the repentant – that is, self-confessed failures, people who need help and know that they need help. Those who truly belong to it have acknowledged their sinfulness and are seeking the forgiveness of God and the assistance of His grace. Therefore, each of them ought in "lowliness of mind" (ταπεινοφροσύνη, or "humility", as in 3:12) to consider the "other better than himself" (Philippians 2:3), thus abating the possibility of any conflict.

    However, where believers are subject to the schismatic pressures of controversial, false teaching it is far more likely that such humility will be abandoned and complaints be made. In one sense this is understandable because most men and women are zealous to guard their own religious beliefs, as these are vital to their deepest concerns and expectations. Such personal beliefs are sensitive matters of the heart, and when they are challenged a person's sense of meaning and hope is undermined, and he is left insecure and distressed.

    And, as we have seen, the Colossian believers had been exposed to such theological controversy and suffered whatever bitterness and conflict it may have produced. Altercations may have arisen as a result. But Paul would not have them make this an excuse for avoiding their congregational responsibilities, but to see it as a situation in which it was more important than ever that they all pursue a life of godliness. Regardless of the difficulties, he would have expected them to be "blameless and harmless, children of God without blemish in the midst of a crooked and perverse generation, among whom" they should have been "seen as lights in the world" (Philippians 2:15).

Paul is obviously concerned with the practice of affirmative morality in the community of imperfect and distressed people. The pursuit of holiness in such a situation is a challenging task.

• **Second**, we are to pursue holiness in forbearance and forgiveness.

As we have seen, Paul would have his readers pursue holiness in reference to both their attitudes and their actions (#3.4.1.2.) Now, in the light of this, he requires of them that they respond Christianly to the attitudes and actions of any who have a complaint against them. They are to be "forbearing" (ἀνεχόμενοι) and "forgiving" (χαριζόμενοι, 3:13), as both are important responses in conflictual situations. And these we should consider.

This forbearance involves 'putting up with', 'suffering', or 'tolerating' others whose *attitudes* we find difficult or offensive, even as our Lord, distressed by the attitudes of the people of His day, rhetorically asked how long He must tolerate or "suffer" (πότε ἀνέξομαι ὑμῶν;) that "faithless and perverse generation" (Matthew 17:17). The very least this requires is that we neither ignore nor reject any members of the Christian congregation, no matter how weak their personality or obnoxious their character. A negative propensity should be meet with positive consideration. *We should seriously love others even as we are loved by God.*

But it is not enough that we tolerate difficult people in the congregation despite their irritating attitudes, for we must also forgive their offending *actions*. And we should be highly motivated to do so because in Christ God has "forgiven us all our trespasses" (2:13, cf. 3:13). *We should seriously forgive others even as we are forgiven by God.*

At the heart of the word "forgiving" (χαρίζομαι), a cognate of the word for "grace", that Paul uses here is the concept of being gracious or offering kindness and help to another.[169] It is used with this significance when it is translated "freely give" in, for example, "the things that are freely given to us by God" (I Corinthians 2:12, τὰ ὑπὸ τοῦ θεοῦ χαρισθέντα ἡμῖν), and "shall He not also with Him freely give us all things?" (Romans 8:32, πῶς οὐχὶ καὶ σὺν αὐτῷ τὰ πάντα ἡμῖν χαρίσεται;). I might suggest, then, that the apostle – by using this particular word – would have our forgiving to be graciously given, together with the sincere desire and intention to help and to enrich the offending persons. And this we are

---

[169] There is another more frequently used sword for 'forgive' that is used in the New Testament – ἀφίημι – which is equally important, but it does not have the same rich emphasis on the graciousness that supplies the forgiveness.

to offer to "each other" (3:13), none excepted, and it ought to be much, much more than the perfunctory dismissal of the offence.

It is perhaps too obvious a comment to make, but it is difficult to see how such forbearing and forgiving, as these are required of us in the New Testament, could possibly be found in any who have not "put on ... compassion, kindness, humility, meekness, longsuffering" and "love" (3:12).

These priceless attitudes that enable believing men and women to be "forbearing" and "forgiving" must ultimately arise out of this consideration: *We have nothing we can give and there is nothing that we can do to merit or to earn anything from God. Every benefit we have is the gift of His grace (I Corinthians 4:7, James 1:17).*

Therefore, as Paul has indicated, we must approach our Lord pleading for His grace as those who were once aliens and enemies (1:21) – and to do so with a measure of "fear and trembling" (Philippians 2:12). God is so intensely holy that we are warned, "It is a fearful thing to fall into (His) hands", because He is "a consuming fire" (Hebrews 10:31, 12:29).

We are all sinners! Each one of us should join with the apostle and confess: "I know that in me, that is, in my flesh, dwells no good thing" (Romans 7:18). We always need to be forgiven (I John 1:8-9), and we should never deceive ourselves into thinking otherwise. As difficult as it may be, we must acknowledge that there is nothing within ourselves that enables us, or entitles us to draw near to God.

Therefore, our first step towards a life of holiness is to realize that it is a step that we cannot take. Such is the drastic demand of true repentance! It is the cry of the helpless. In fact, we would not repent, or even think repentance necessary, if it were not given to us to do so (II Timothy 2:25). We are utterly dependent upon God's prevenient grace.

So long as we think otherwise and cling to a belief in our own competence to formulate the truth or to attain some measure of personal righteousness – thus following man's "philosophy and vain deceit" (2:8) – there will be a fatal flaw in our theology, and in our understanding of the Christian gospel. Then we will think more highly of ourselves than we ought to think (Romans 12:3), and in our folly, abandon the humility of genuine godliness. And then we will inevitably be more demanding and intolerant of others than forbearing and forgiving. Anyone who thinks he can stand tall in the presence of God because of his own intrinsic worth is a stranger to genuine humility and incompetent in the practice of holiness.

But to avoid any misunderstanding, the following distinction should be considered.

We may – indeed we must – continue to rely upon our natural, God-given abilities and developed skills in the interests of civil society, and to maintain some legitimate self-respect and sanity, and we should encourage all people, whether Christian or not, to do the same. These things are required of us as we are creatures in God's creation, being regulated by the commandment to love our neighbour as ourselves (Matthew 22:39), that we might be good and useful citizens (cf. Ephesians 4:28, I Thessalonians 4:11).

But this same love for our neighbour also requires that we make it known that none of these natural abilities and skills is sufficient to gain access into the presence of God, no matter how sophisticated they might be, or how diligently they might be applied. We can only "enter into the holy place by the blood of Jesus" (Hebrews 10:20), because through His death we ourselves receive the benefits of God's forbearance and forgiveness.

And only those who genuinely appreciate receiving the forbearance and the forgiveness of God will be disposed to be genuinely forbearing and forgiving themselves.

So then, as we are to aspire after holiness in an imperfect community, in which we will inevitably find disagreement between various parties and individuals, it plainly becomes necessary that we be forbearing and forgiving. And this we can only be when we "put on ... a heart of compassion, kindness, humility, meekness, longsuffering" and "love".

In fact, forbearing and forgiving are the overt evidence that a man has actually clothed himself in such graces. The attitudinal must find genuine expression in activity if it is to avoid hypocrisy.

Paul sees a time when someone may have "a complaint against another" (3:13). Being a common occurrence in the church, it is important that we discover how we might respond to such a situation lest it distress the community of believers and obfuscate the beauty of Christian reconciliation. However, the apostle does not recommend some process of 'conflict resolution' – at least, not in the contemporary meaning of this term – but advocates godliness of character, or true holiness. He would not have his readers merely make use of some artful technique to resolve the confrontation, but that they resort to the saving, forbearing, character-changing grace of God. In this Christ is to be emulated, and His people are to forgive "even as the Lord forgave" them (3:13).

But for this pursuit of communal holiness to be effective, those involved need above all else to put on love, which is the perfect bond (3:14).

- **Third**, we are to find holiness in the perfect bond.

Paul evidently considers love – genuine, Christian love – to be the one essential "bond" that will perfectly, or effectively unite Christians (3:14). Whatever integrating programs might be instituted to synthesize the congregation into a functioning and cooperating whole, whether to obtain internal harmony or solidarity in action, the result will be little more than a fragile, superimposed organizational structure if it is not deeply rooted in and motivated by love.[170]

It is evidently not *individual* perfection (τελειότης, or 'completeness', 'maturity') that Paul has in mind here, but the effective bonding together of the Christian community; or the maturation of *holiness in communion*. The perfection, I suggest, is in the bonding principle, and not in those who are so bound.

Forbearance for the obnoxious and forgiveness for the offending, with all complaints resolved, are required that "the peace of Christ" might be exemplified in the "one body" (3:15). It was our Lord's prayer that His people be "perfected in one" (ἵνα ὦσιν τετελειωμένοι εἰς ἕν), and this will be confirmation for the world to see that the Father sent Him for our redemption (John 17:23).

We can only lament the inefficiency and, perhaps, the indolence of the churches, in pursuing and attaining this "perfection" of love and in repenting of our own failures in this matter. This reflects our inability to "put on love" (3:14), or at least our ineptitude in doing so – and, in effect, it reveals our disdain for things holy. The modern church does indeed speak often about love and sometimes makes heroic efforts to be loving. And for this, we are thankful. But as it so frequently preaches love without any mention of holiness, it is promoting an ill-defined attitude, perhaps only an insipid sentimentality, that can only result in ill-conceived practices.

Nevertheless, as believing men and women we should long for, and seek the grace of God that we might have hearts of compassion, kindness, humility, meekness, longsuffering, and love, for the sake of the church and the glory of God. *And this should be a greater concern for us than any*

---

[170] Obviously, some organizational structure is necessary if God's people are to congregate and to cooperate in the ministry of the gospel. And arranging such administrative structuring ought to be done well, for we are the servants of Christ. But to imagine that the efficiency of the organization guarantees – or even that it is essential for – the proper functioning of the Body of Christ and the quality of its witness to the world, is to misunderstand the true nature and viability of the church.

organizational or programmatic schemes we might devise. The fumbling administration of the loving is to be preferred to, and will probably be longer lasting and more effective in things that really matter, than the proficient governance of the loveless.

Then it might be worth considering that *the organizational* can only be effective in *the congregation,* or specific gatherings and joint activities, of God's people. These functions have their importance, but in the life of the average believer, they, being occasional, take relatively little of his time. In contrast, Christian *communion*, the joint participation in all that the saving grace of God provides for His people, consumes the whole of his life.[171] He is *always* in communion, but *infrequently* in congregation. Therefore, it cannot be the organizational, but only his communion, that regulates his holiness.

And I might add to this that *the communion* of God's people, always there and diffused through the common society of all people, is by far the greater platform for Christian witness to the world than *the congregation* of God's people, occasionally gathered and distant from the common people. Therefore, if we are truly concerned for evangelism, we should give more time and effort to the promotion of holiness than to the multiplication and perfection of organizations and activities.

The importance Paul gives to Christian love in this respect cannot be underestimated. His summary of its effects in a person's life in I Corinthians 13:4-7, leaves us in no doubt about its necessity for maturing holiness and perfecting communion.

However, it must not be thought that at this point morality has been put aside for sentiment – although it often is by the sentimentally thoughtless. The moral law is not to be disregarded for the sake of some supposed but nebulous 'love'.[172] In Galatians 5:14 Paul writes, "For the whole law is fulfilled in one word, even in this; you shall love your neighbour as yourself". Love, directed by law, makes the greatest moral demand as it seeks the good of the 'other person' whoever that may be, the good that is defined by the commandments of God. Therefore,

---

[171] This, I believe, is the implication of biblical 'communion'.

[172] There is no word that is more frequently used by Christians than 'love' – and probably there is no word in their vocabulary that is more frequently taken for granted, with its meaning neither considered nor defined. Therefore, in much of our writing and speech it has little weight beyond its emotive effect. Sadly, through common and thoughtless usage, it has become a rather limp and lifeless word.

> love, needing the ability to discern between good and evil, is necessarily guided by God's statute laws (cf. John 14:15).
>
> Love is not an alternative to the law; rather, love is expressed in obedience to the law.

Within any imperfect community in this fallen world, forbearing, forgiving, and loving are all essential aspects of a harmonious and integrated society. And these can only be obtained with any degree of efficiency and sustainability, we believe, through Christian redemption. The removal of the alienation and enmity among men requires the removal of the alienation and enmity between man and God: only a man who is confidently at peace with God can anticipate being unreservedly at peace with his neighbour.

NOTE: We should not imagine that the pursuit of genuine holiness in Christian communion is a facile exercise. It is most demanding! But it may well be the one activity above all others that is necessary for the survival, the purity, and the true advancement of the Christian faith. If this is so, then it is important that we think about how it might be initiated and sustained, at least as far as it is required of those who would live for the glory of God.

3.4.2.2. THE PRINCIPLES BEHIND THE PRACTICE (3:15-17)

Now we must consider how we are, in the daily practice of Christian living, to effectively pursue holiness in community. How are we, despite our moral frailty, so to love one another that "all men" shall know that we are His "disciples" (John 13:35)? Or how are we to be, both visibly and convincingly, the followers of our Lord? How are we to be holy together?

These are not questions we can ignore if we are seriously concerned for the gospel and the glory of God. We must not sublimate holiness into some mystical experience and thus disregard its realistic, functional, and communal demands. And here we are faced with the immense practicality of another *three imperatives*: "Let the peace of God rule in your hearts", "Let the word of Christ dwell in you richly", and "do all in the name of the Lord Jesus" (3:15-17). These require our intelligent and volitional response.

But before we proceed to a consideration of these three requirements, we should yet again recall the circumstances in which this letter was written. As we have seen, Paul was deeply concerned for the congregation in Colossae because it was being influenced by subtle rhetorical arguments and dangerously deceptive philosophy that were contrary to the gospel. False teachers, with their heterodox ideas, were disturbing this young Christian community. This, as we might well imagine, would have tended to provoke disagreements and give rise to someone having "a complaint against" another (3:13). Theological disputes inevitably do this!

Consequently, the harmony and the unity of the church were – even as they continue to be in congregations in our day – seriously at risk, for we all suffer from a chronic inability to be of one mind (cf. I Corinthians 1:10).

The apostle sees that such a situation must be approached in holiness, seeking unity and peace through love, "the bond of perfectness" (3:14). Without a genuine concern for godliness in character and in communion, little peacemaking could be achieved. Only godly temperament will generate the kindness, humility, and meekness that are necessary to maintain "the unity of the Spirit in the bond of peace" (Ephesians 4:3).

However, the required unity is not and cannot be without meaningful structure – it must be a unity in substance and purpose (cf. I Corinthians 1:10). It is not a mutually agreed symbiotic relationship, moderated only by indiscriminate tolerance, between people of substantially different beliefs, moral principles, and ambitions.[173]

Paul, here in 3:15-17, is still concerned that his readers be "filled with the knowledge of His will in all spiritual wisdom and understanding, to walk worthily of the Lord" (1:9-10). This, after all, was his constant prayer for them. He obviously, then, had no desire that the church condone ignorance, folly, and misunderstanding, or that it disregard behaviour unworthy of Christ. To adopt such a latitudinarian, permissive attitude – as, sadly, is done far too often! – is only to eviscerate the church, destroying its validity, and extinguishing its witness.

Therefore, writing here about holiness in communion and the peaceful integration of the Lord's people "in one body" (3:15), Paul again stresses the absolute necessity of "the word of Christ", "wisdom", "teaching and admonition" (3:16). Truth and moral principles are not to be neglected, neither are they to be compromised. Only through the instruction of divine revelation in Christ and in the scriptures,

---

[173] But do not misunderstand! I am not suggesting that Christians should be intolerant of other people. As we are to love both our neighbour and our enemy (Matthew 5:44, 22:39), this must never be. However, there is a difference between the unity and the basis of unity we seek with all people, and the unity and the basis of unity we seek with fellow Christians. What we might tolerate in the secular society in which we live may be intolerable in the church. Moreover, we might well be tolerant with some people and at the same time be intolerant of their beliefs and behaviour. To disagree is not – or, ought not to be – to despise.

can the congregation be meaningfully structured, and genuinely united in belief and purpose. The organization that is structured and united upon any other basis cannot be considered to be a Christian church. It is only from this "word of Christ" that we can deduce appropriate contextualization and moderation for authentic Christian living.

We must now examine *the three principles* – the *three imperatives* – mentioned here (3:15-17) that are fundamental for holiness in communion. But it might be helpful to begin with a brief consideration and comparison of the three of them together because they are so integrated with each other that they either operate conjointly in congruity or they do not operate at all. That is, if one fails, all fail.

1. The Sociological. We are to "let the peace of Christ rule" in our hearts, and live as "one body" (3:15).

    From our Christian perspective, this is the most fundamental principle in our *sociology of redemption*, which should regulate the whole structure of the community of believers.

    This is the integrating or *moderating principle* that reconciles each individual believer with God *through Christ*, and subsequently each with other believers *in Christ*. It is this rather than any 'articles of association', as useful as they may be, that maintains "the unity of the Spirit in the bond of peace" (Ephesians 4:3).

    This peace, which we will consider further below, is obtained for us "through the blood of His cross" and overcomes all alienation and enmity (1:20-21). It is essential for the constitution of the church, and fundamental for the kingdom of God. It makes virtuous communion between God and man and between man and man possible.

    Where "the peace of Christ" does not "rule", the integrity of the "body" is subverted.

2. The Theological. We are to "let the word of Christ dwell in" us, that we all might participate, actively and passively, in the teaching and the admonishing of the community of believers (3:16).

    From our Christian perspective, this is the most fundamental principle in our *theology of redemption*, which should establish our faith and our philosophy.

    The word of Christ that provides teaching and admonition for the members of the body of Christ, enabling them to "be of the same mind" (Philippians 2:2), is the God-given revelation that facilitates access to "all the treasures of wisdom and knowledge" (2:3) that are to be found in our Lord. Having in this the means, then, we are to take seriously Paul's injunction that we "all speak the same thing ... perfected together in the same mind" (I Corinthians 1:10). In this, much is required of us.

As our praxis is ultimately determined by our theory, so our sociology must always be determined by our theology. It is evident in all that Paul has written here to the Colossians that our sociology – the functioning and the purpose of the community, the "one body" – and our theology – the beliefs and moral principles of the community – must both be Christ-centered, necessarily based upon *His* "peace" and *His* "word". And in this, of course, is the beginning of a Christocentric philosophy (2:8).

Not to accept the authority of His "word" is tantamount to rejecting the "rule" of His "peace", which results in eroding the integrity of His "body".

To avoid any such subversion arising from false philosophy, it is important that the Christian community, using the scriptures, be conscientiously engaged in "teaching and admonishing" (3:16), which I briefly discuss below. But we should note here in the interest of coordinating the three imperatives in this passage, that the "teaching" is required for true *contextualization*, and "admonishing" is required for true *moderation*.

However, as perhaps the Colossian believers were beginning to realize, the captivating philosophy of men (2:8) may be imposed upon or infiltrate into the thinking of Christian people so that it corrupts both their sociology and their theology, restructuring them according to, or amalgamating them with anthropocentric principles. And thereby, as I have suggested (#3.4.1.1., Second), the heretics would de-contextualize and de-moderate Christian thought and practice. The obliteration of our faith!

3.   The Moral. Therefore, to maintain a Christ-centered sociology and theology, it is critically important that we give serious thought to the third imperative and insure we do everything "in the name of the Lord Jesus" (3:17).

From our Christian perspective, this is the most fundamental principle in our *morality of redemption*, which should condition all behaviour in the community of believers.

So, if our sociology is to be determined by our theology, then both must be established in our community by our obedience to and emulation of our Lord Jesus, which, as we shall see, are the implications of doing "all in the name of the Lord Jesus". When our moral principles are eroded, subverted, or neglected, the integrity of both our Christian society and our Christian faith is degraded.

Doing everything "in the name of the Lord Jesus" (3:17) is the concomitant of seeking "the things that are above, where Christ is seated on the right hand of God" (3:1). And this, as we have seen, is the essential *contextualizing principle* of all Christian thinking and living (#3.3.1., Second, 1 & 2).

Not to accept the sovereignty of God in all things is to reject the authority of His "word", which is tantamount to subverting the "rule" of His "peace" and the integrity of His "body".

NOTE: I suggest, then, that to have a comprehensive appreciation and to maintain an effective implementation of our *redemption,* we must integrate our *sociology, theology,* and *morality.* They cannot be effectively implemented in isolation from each other.

Moreover, we cannot realize the fullness of our redemption – and, therefore, maintain a comprehensive witness to our faith – if we neglect any one of these three aspects of Christian praxis.

And as each one of the three involves holiness in communion, it is impossible for any one of us to realize the fullness of our individual redemption in isolation. So, we cannot privatize our religion – or entertain the idea that we can be effectively 'Christian' without 'church'.

Now, recognizing the interaction between them, we must consider the three imperatives individually.

3.4.2.2.1. The arbitration of peace (3:15)

Exhorting his readers, the apostle wrote, "Let the peace of Christ rule in your hearts".

To understand this imperative, we should keep in mind that in the scriptures "peace" is primarily an *interpersonal* and not an *intrapersonal* matter. It refers, in other words, to an amicable and harmonious relationship between two or more people or parties, rather than to a subjective, inward, individual, personal sense of calm or well-being.[174] This is an important distinction to make, because although there are times when a Christian might be deeply troubled and filled with anxiety, lacking what we might call 'peace of mind' – and this would not necessarily indicate any weakness or failure but, indeed, it might well be a most admirable, altruistic concern – he continues irrevocably, despite his feelings, to be at peace with God. And an understanding of and faith in this immutable peace, which was purchased for him by Christ through His death, provide him with the knowledge and confidence he needs to face his fears. Being "justified by faith, we have peace with God" (Romans 5:1), and this is peace that nothing can erode or impair.

So, I would suggest that it is not a personal tranquillity of heart, a sense of contentment, or subjective satisfaction, but *peace in the community* – to which they were called "in the one body" – that Paul has in mind here. This should be accepted as a ruling, societal concept. It is a fundamental aspect of the *moderating principle* in Christian living.

The apostle has already mentioned this "peace" earlier in the letter. In his theological presentation of the pre-eminence of Christ as our Redeemer, Paul wrote that He "reconciled all things unto Himself, having made peace through the blood of His cross" (1:20). *This, surely, is the "peace of Christ" that he now reintroduces as a moderating principle in the church's pursuit of holiness in communion.* If it required the death of our Lord to secure the peaceful integration of "all things", then this must be seen as a matter of paramount importance for obtaining harmony in the Christian community. The immediate problem may be as trifling as one individual having a complaint against another (3:13), but the solution is as momentous as the crucifixion of the Son of God!

And from this we might deduce that where there is no concern for reconciliation between Christians who have complaints against each other, there can be little genuine interest in the Cross of Christ. The devout believer cannot rest in the peace he enjoys with God who forgave his sins through the death of his Lord, and then refuse to forgive and find conciliation with anyone who sins against him (cf. Matthew 6:12, Romans 15:7).

---

[174] It may, for example, refer to the absence of war (Matthew 10:33, Luke 14:32, Acts 12:20), to cordial associations between different people (Acts 7:26, 9:31, Romans 14:19, II Timothy 2:22, Hebrews 2:14), and to the justified relationship between a man and God (Romans 5:1). It also appears to imply being reconciled to one's circumstances (Luke 24:36, John 14:27, II Thessalonians 3:16). The frequent greeting, "Peace be with you" (Romans 1:7, I Corinthians 1:3, Galatians 1:3, Colossians 1:2, et al), or something similar, is no doubt, as it were, a prayer that all these aspects of peace be enjoyed. There is peace to be found in Christ – being at peace with God – even when there is war, conflict, and tribulation, and this makes it possible to maintain "good cheer" even in such difficulties (John 16:33).

Paul refers to this "peace" in Philippians 4:7 as the "peace of God, which passes all understanding" that guards, or protects, our "hearts and … thoughts in Christ Jesus". But why, we might ask, is it beyond "all understanding"? It is "peace" that is greater than we can fully comprehend because it is rooted in the inscrutable mystery of the crucifixion of Christ. "Making peace" required that He abolish "in His flesh the enmity" (Ephesians 2:15). Evidently, then, His incarnation, His taking human flesh, His suffering, and His death were essential elements in God's solution to the disastrous consequences of the great cataclysm (#1.3.2.3.1.). We can only stand in awe and thanksgiving before the cross of Christ, knowing that here we are facing the incomprehensible, but nevertheless the indispensable prerequisite for ultimate peace on earth and the integration of "all things in Christ" (Ephesians 1:10). And therefore, we believe, the prerequisite also for the sincere resolution of any interpersonal conflict between individuals in the community of believers.

The inscrutable mystery – that "the Word became flesh and dwelt among us" (John 1:14) – becomes the reason for and the means of loving our neighbour and our enemy.

But if 'beneath the cross of Jesus, (we) fain would take our stand'[175] we have at least begun to appreciate that "God commends His own love towards us, in that, while we were yet sinners, Christ died for us" (Romans 5:8). Therefore, as Paul indicates elsewhere, the greater our appreciation of and faith in our Lord's redeeming death the more likely our "hearts" will remain calm and our "thoughts" steady (Philippians 4:7), and we be able to avoid being deflected by bitterness or doubt from our pursuit of holiness. And consequently, the more likely we will be to "rejoice in tribulation", with patience and hope (Romans 5:3-4). The "peace of Christ", then, does not consist in a calm heart and steady thoughts, but it is the prerequisite for obtaining and sustaining them.

Paul also explains elsewhere that the crucifixion of Christ is effective in bringing peace to His people, both in their relationship with each other and in their relationship with Him. Not only does it unite both Jew and Gentile, "creating in Himself of the two one new man, so making peace", but it also reconciles "them both unto God through the cross, having slain the enmity thereby". Therefore, our Lord came deliberately to preach "peace to (those) that were far off, and to them that were near" (Ephesians 2:14-17). This "peace of Christ", then, is comprehensive, intended to moderate the communion among God's people, and their communion with God Himself. And as the two are achieved by the one act of reconciliation, we must realize that genuine peace among the brethren is and always must be

---

[175] Hymn, Elizabeth C. Clephane.

concomitant with genuine peace between men and their God. A man is unlikely to love his neighbour as he ought – selflessly and sacrificially (John 15:13) – if he does not so love his God.

NOTE: If we genuinely believe that Christ is able to mediate between a sinful man and the holy God, reconciling them to each other, then surely we ought to trust Him to mediate between one sinful man and another sinful man and to reconcile them to each other. But for such peace to be found in the body of Christ, the church, each sinful man involved must approach the problem, the interpersonal conflict, as someone who would do "all things in the name of the Lord Jesus" (3:17, #3.4.2.2.3.)[176] And this, as I will suggest below, requires us to emulate Christ through the most wholehearted and all-embracing response in love for His person and obedience to His authority.

I hope I am wrong, but it appears to me that today's church members, knowing far too little of the significance of the Cross, are more likely to turn to the counselling of the psychologist or to the advocacy of a lawyer to restore the damage done by bitter and broken relationships, than they are to seek the intervention of Christ. Rather than "forbearing … and forgiving one another" (3:13), their first reaction in all probability is to resort to the "philosophy … of men". Manipulation and litigation are then preferred to letting "the peace of Christ rule in (their) hearts". Then, in effect, the person and work of Christ, and the gospel are trivialized.

Therefore, we can hardly claim to have any genuine interest in the "peace of Christ" if we desire only our own, individual, subjective satisfaction or tranquillity. Nor is our interest in this peace such as it should be if all we desire is the personal assurance of knowing that we have a good relationship with God, as immensely valuable as this may be. Our concern should be that the "peace of Christ" moderates our association with Him *and* with all the members of the Christian community – and, derivatively, with all the people with whom we have to do.

We cannot, then, know this exceptional and profound peace of Christ in hermitic isolation.

We may indeed desire harmony and unity among ourselves, and especially in the Christian community, but it is unlikely to be obtained or sustained unless

---

[176] This "peace of Christ", I believe, provides the Christian with something far more profound and effective than modern, psychological techniques for 'conflict resolution'.

the "peace of Christ" does effectively rule[177] "in (our) hearts" (3:15). And if it is to rule, then its *moral authority* must be acknowledged. If must be translated from the theory in our confession into the praxis in our church. The pure dynamic of this peace should energize our communion. For this reason, no doubt, Paul insists that it must have its influence not at the edges or, indeed, at the centre of our society, but at the core of our beings, in the "hearts" (3:15) of the believers. And if it is a ruling principle within and among us, then we will judge, decide, and act – individually and corporately – under its influence, and meet its demands in a manner that is most conducive to harmony in the community.

But here we must be careful not to trivialize the apostle's instructions as if he were only seeking an emotional response, assuming that all he asks for is a change of mood. As the word 'heart' in scripture refers to the whole, complex, human psyche, then what the apostle requires is that all we have considered above concerning the peace secured by the death of Christ should not only affect our emotions, but also direct our thoughts and motivate our will. And this can only happen when we so approach the cross of Christ that we are deeply moved in our affections, intelligently embrace new values and principles in our minds, and deliberately make those decisions that promote the peace for which our Lord died. And these are necessary aspects of putting on "the new man" (3:10).

The truly sanctified person will always react and respond, not for the sake of his own glory, to advance his own cause, or to secure personal contentment, but for the glory of Christ and to advance the cause of the Crucified.

Paul adds this explanation to the imperative: it is to the peace of Christ that we "were called in the one body" (3:15, εἰς ἣν καὶ ἐκλήθητε ἐν ἑνὶ σώματι). This no doubt implies that the Christian community should be a well-integrated and harmonious unity, for "in one Spirit were we all baptized into one body" (I Corinthians 12:13). And it is the presence of Christ with us through the ministry of the Spirit, uniting us as one, that makes Christian communion the most precious association we can enjoy as human beings. The apostle also explains that this association in the Spirit constitutes the church as "the temple of God", and we endanger ourselves if we do anything that might destroy it (I Corinthians 3:16-17). We should, then, "give diligence to keep the unity of the Spirit in the bond of peace" (Ephesians 4:3). This peace requires Christ's death and the Spirit's influence.

---

[177] The word used for "rule" (βραβεύω) – only found here in the scriptures – originally referred to umpiring in the games, deciding the winners, and awarding the prizes. But later, and about the time of the New Testament, it was used more generally of controlling or governing. However, as Paul has just mentioned the possibility of one person having a complaint against another, perhaps it retains here something of its earlier meaning – to judge, or decide.

Alan D Catchpoole

From this we might conclude that holiness in communion is of exceeding value, because it is profound in its resonance with God Himself, beautiful in its design, unlimited in its personal and interpersonal potential, enriching for the whole of human life – and as fragile as it is easy to grieve the Holy Spirit (Ephesians 4:30).

But more must be said. The apostle has already stated that Christ is "the head of the body, the church" (1:18). And he has warned his readers of some who were "not holding fast the Head, from whom all the body ... increases with the increase of God" (2:19), and thus they were creating divisions and discord. Having separated from the Head, they became a danger to the "body"! So, it is not simply a well-integrated human society that Paul has in mind, an alliance united only by sound organizational structures and corporate goodwill. Much, much more is required! None can be an integrated member of the society of the redeemed who is not first a member of Christ, a member of His body (I Corinthians 12:12-14, 27, Ephesians 4:15-16).[178] Nor will anyone effectively live as a member of His body without "holding fast the Head", and never resiling from his trust in and obedience to Him.

We are, then, only in the "body" when we are "in Christ", and only effective members of the body as we "walk in Him" (2:6). And we explained above, the dynamic for change in individual character and behaviour is to be found in this relationship with our Lord (#3.1.3.). Now I suggest that the communal "peace of Christ" only has its powerful dynamic in this same, vital association with Him.

Therefore, although we are morally obligated to order our own lives before God, we must not imagine – for it would be to miss the essential point of the gospel – that by conditioning our emotions, educating our minds, and disciplining our wills we can by ourselves and through our own techniques improve our character and cultivate peace among the saints. Such an idea was possibly an element in the false teaching that was disturbing the Colossians – as it certainly is in many churches today.[179] The divine dynamic is otherwise. We are to walk in Christ through repentance and faith, thus depending on Him and His presence to condition our emotions, educate our minds, and discipline our wills that we might grow in individual and communal holiness.

The truth is that we must maintain our walk in the Lord so that the "peace of Christ" will rule in our hearts and have its God-designed effect in the church.

[178] But this is not to say that he cannot be welcomed into the congregation of believers.

[179] There are numerous psychological, pedagogical, and disciplinary techniques – many promulgated in self-help manuals popular in the churches – now being recommended, that seek to achieve this end without any real need for faith in Christ. They are indeed *self-help* manuals!

Perhaps Paul has already indicated what influence this should have upon us when he wrote of himself that he rejoiced in "sufferings ... and ... afflictions ... for His body's sake, which is the church" (1:24). It should produce genuine love and concern for all the people of God, and the willingness to suffer for them. *And all that is required is a simple but sincere life of repentance and faith, that is inevitably expressed in love and obedience.*

There is here the gospel principle of forbearance and forgiveness in love, which surpasses – but does not supersede! – the principle of law and the standards of righteousness.

NOTE: It is significant that the apostle Peter writes in a similar manner, advising Christians to be "likeminded, compassionate, loving as brethren, kindhearted, humble minded, not rendering evil for evil ... for to this you were called" (I Peter 3:9, ὅτι εἰς τοῦτο ἐκλήθητε). He is also concerned for holiness in communion. With this in mind and quoting from Psalm 34:12-16, he addresses the person who "would love life, and see good days", exhorting him saying, "Let him seek peace and pursue it" (I Peter 3:10-11, ζητησάτω εἰρήνην καὶ διωξάτω αὐτήν). It is significant that both Peter and Paul mention that we have been "called" to aspire after such holiness of character and to prosecute this "peace" in communion. It lies at the heart of living Christianly; it is our vocation – and a significant aspect of our witness to the world.

Moreover, to "follow after peace with all men" cannot be separated from the pursuit of "the holiness without which no man can see the Lord" (Hebrews 12:14). Both are awesome responsibilities!

If we are to "let the peace of Christ rule in (our) hearts" (3:15) we must understand that as we seek God's forgiveness through the death of our Lord, we place ourselves under the solemn obligation to forgive those who sin against us (Matthew 6:12). To think otherwise is hypocritically incongruous.

3.4.2.2.2. THE INFLUENCE OF THE WORD (3:16)

Paul also exhorts his readers to "let the word of Christ dwell in (them) richly in all wisdom, teaching and admonishing one another".

It must not be thought that the "peace" which we have been considering is an unstructured concord or nebulous tranquillity, a peace without form or content, the peace of unrelenting, amoral tolerance, or 'peace at any price'. Such an indeterminate peace as this is no expression of genuine love. Thoughtless indulgence is nothing more than careless indifference.

As we mentioned above (#3.4.2.1.), the peaceful integration required in the Christian community is not and cannot be amorphous, without meaningful formation – it must be a unity in substance and purpose. Therefore, Paul now supplements his injunction concerning the rule of the "peace of Christ" with this following exhortation concerning wisdom and the "word of Christ". The implication is that the community cannot effectively maintain the former – being at peace – without the latter – being judiciously and authoritatively informed. Peace must be established, instructed, and directed by the Word of God. In fact, this Christian peace cannot even be rightly defined without divine counsel, let alone have any practical significance or purpose.

If we are to be ruled by the "peace of Christ" we must be taught and admonished by the "word of Christ".

NOTE: Through the *teaching,* we are instructed in the "philosophy ... after Christ" (2:8), and in doing so it *contextualizes* our thinking. In contrast, yet in concert, through the *admonishing,* we are instructed in the way we should "walk" (2:6), and in doing so it *moderates* our behaviour (cf. these two words in 1:28, #2.1.4., Second). I think it salutary to consider our communion – and reconsider our hymnology! – within these parameters.

It is not surprising or incongruous that the apostle makes the comment he does here about congregational singing.[180] This, no doubt, is an important matter in itself, or, at least, its importance has been emphasized – and often exaggerated – in contemporary dissertations and popular articles about worship.[181] However, we might ask why Paul mentions it at this point in his letter. One thing predominates in 3:12-15 – in forbearance, forgiveness, love, and peace the church should be united, and each individual concerned to promote the "bond of perfectness" among all the members. Therefore, when we congregate we all ought to minister to or serve one another. And there is only one, integrated, formal congregational activity in which this is done corporately, comprehensively, and involving everybody – the singing. Therefore, it should be carefully, wisely, and theologically crafted.

---

[180] Paul expresses a similar concern that Christians be "wise" and not "foolish", "understanding what the will of the Lord is", that, being "filled with the Spirit", they might speak "one to another in psalms and hymns and spiritual songs", in Ephesians 5:15-19. Evidently, much more than the enthusiasm of human emotion is involved.

[181] It is of great concern that in many churches today singing is virtually equated with worship – which is to seriously misunderstand worship – and then utilized primarily for its emotivity with little or no thought for its didactic function.

Here, in 3:16, the dominant concern is that Christians allow the word of Christ to dwell in them that they might teach and admonish one another wisely. *The intelligent maturation of the congregation through increasing understanding is in view.* And this cognitive, corporate benefit, at least as far as Paul's words here are concerned, is the important *objective*, and the singing is a *means* to this end. The singing is secondary, as there are situations where it may be impossible,[182] but the teaching of the word is always indispensable. Of course, the singing – as with everything else we do – should be worshipful, bringing glory to God, but these two aspects, the instruction and the praise, should never be dissociated, and the emphasis here is strongly on the former.

In the singing we all ought to be "teaching and admonishing one another" (3:16, διδάσκοντες καὶ νουθετοῦντες ἑαυτούς). While acknowledging that everything we do should be done for the glory of God, and that this is the *ultimate purpose* in all our activities as Christians, we must not forget that the *immediate purpose* for our congregational singing involves the intelligent education and the moral encouragement of the people. Both are concomitant, but it is most unlikely we will accomplish the first and glorify God if we are deprived of the latter, not being appropriately instructed and motivated as the Lord's people. Therefore, we should be concerned that *what* we sing is both biblically didactic and biblically principled, and that the *way* we sing is reverential.

Again, it is worth recalling that in his prayer at the beginning of this letter Paul asks that his readers be "filled with the knowledge of His will in all spiritual wisdom and understanding" (1:9). When considering this request (#1.2.1.2.), we suggested that this wisdom is '*the ability to use knowledge well*, but well in *the dual sense* of both efficiently and ethically' – that is, in a didactic and principled manner. Moreover, we also saw that the primary knowledge with which we ought to be concerned is derived from "the word of the truth of the gospel" (1:5). The wise Christian, then, is the person who not only knows the Bible but who also intelligently uses such understanding of it that he has with godly sagacity.

Now, it seems, the apostle is applying these principles to what I am referring to as holiness in communion, and this includes his reference here to the relevance of communal singing. This corporate activity should arise from and be given its content through the "word of Christ dwelling in you richly" ('Ο λόγος τοῦ Χριστοῦ ἐνοικείτω ἐν ὑμῖν πλουσίως). Whether this implies the abiding effect of the "word of Christ" among the people as a group, or in the individual lives of the members of the group, might be disputed, but I would suggest that the one necessarily includes

---

[182] As, for example, in a congregation of the deaf.

the other. The group can only be influenced by the scriptures as the members of it are affected by them. *And this requires that the word of Christ be truly, consistently, and fully – that is "richly" (3:16) – ministered in the congregation.* Only a wealth of biblical knowledge and understanding can ensure that any church activity will bring benefits to the people and glory to God. *Good hymnology is the product of sound theology and strong morality – not of religious sentiment.*

But as we have suggested earlier, knowledge alone is insufficient, as it is only used well by those who are also wise (#1.2.1.2.). Once the congregation has been enriched in biblical knowledge, they must then "in all wisdom" (ἐν πάσῃ σοφίᾳ, 3:16) teach and admonish one another.[183] And blessed is that congregation where there is a deep and pure well of biblical understanding from which all the people can draw the waters of divine wisdom! Indeed, it behoves us all to be students of the Bible, not only for our own individual maturation but also for the enrichment of the community.

Therefore, we need to be sensitive to the fact that we might truly have an extensive knowledge of God's Word, being sedulous Bible students, and yet fail to teach and admonish others "in all wisdom".[184] A little biblical knowledge well applied is far to be preferred than much biblical knowledge that is misapplied. Therefore, we should note again, that Paul prays that his readers might be "filled with knowledge" *and* with "all spiritual wisdom and understanding" (1:9). And for this, we would do well to pray for one another, even as the apostle interceded for the Colossians.

The apostle is indicating that the knowledge obtained from the teaching of the scriptures should be wisely promulgated, and that it is able to be so disseminated – in part – through congregational singing. Without this meaningful content, the singing may well be inappropriate, and in danger of doing nothing more than promoting passion without understanding. *Good hymnology is also the product of wisdom and understanding.*

NOTE: This demands, in effect, that all the "psalms, hymns, and spiritual songs" that we use in our congregational singing ought not only to be selected, or composed, with adequate knowledge of the word of God but also used appropriately and wisely. It should, in a sense, be as erudite an exercise as the preaching of the

---

[183] This verse is somewhat ambiguous. It might be translated "Let the word of Christ dwell in you richly in all wisdom; teaching and admonishing one another ..." or "Let the word of Christ dwell in you richly; teaching and admonishing one another in all wisdom ..." Either way, the importance of combining knowledge with wisdom is unavoidable.

[184] And this, I suggest, again indicates – as we have considered above – the importance of developing a Christian mind.

word and the practice of prayer. This is not to ignore the emotional effects of music, which in themselves may be most enriching. However, to be moved only by music's aesthetic influence without the contextualization and inspiration of Christian truth, or without the moderation and guidance of Christian ethic, will only stimulate misguided and possibly irresponsible passion. Music can be as perilous as it can be passionate.

As we also considered above (#1.2.1.2.), we can all too easily misuse even biblical knowledge in our folly. The truths of divine revelation must be understood, valued, honoured, and explicit in the words we sing. And this cannot be achieved by simply threading together a concatenation of phrases taken from the Bible, arranged in a rhythmic fashion and with pleasing assonance. This may have the semblance of worshipful music, with the sounds of biblical terminology, but not be a wise use of the scriptures. Indeed, it can be positively deceptive, when, having the emotional resonance of religion, it is obfuscating and distorting the true meaning of God's revelation.

Because we ought to be singing "unto God" (3:16), the whole exercise, even when appropriately joyful, is surely one of great gravity! We cannot assume that everything we sing and whatever music we choose are necessarily pleasing to God (see Amos 5:23). Neither can we suppose, remembering our fallen condition, that what we find aesthetically satisfying necessarily reflects His glory.

It is not too much to anticipate that the philosophy "after Christ" (2:8) will contextualize and moderate our understanding of the truth, our concept of the ethical, and our appreciation of the aesthetic; and that *Christian* – not secular – truth, ethic, and aesthetic will contextualize and moderate our living. These things together are the province of knowledge, righteousness, and beauty – which three things together are of the essence of holiness.

Paul's comments in 3:16 are important, but not primarily for whatever parameters they may – and do – set for acceptable church music. More immediately, they are significant for their emphasis on the importance of the community, the significance of congregation, the mutual reinforcing of one another's faith, the necessity of sagacious teaching and admonishing, and the centrality of biblical knowledge and wisdom. All these things are the outworking of 3:12-14 and critically important for holiness in communion. This is not instruction only for the choir leader or music director, but for all the people.[185]

---

[185] With this in mind, I find it sadly disturbing that in recent years, music, rather than being an integrating influence, has often become a divisive and disrupting factor in congregational life. Something has been seriously amiss.

Alan D Catchpoole

The Christian community should be noted for its wisdom (4:5).[186] But this can only be achieved when the "word of Christ", that is, biblical truth, "dwells in (us) richly". And this necessarily precedes and supplies the godly teaching and admonition that establish a true structure for a loving and peaceable community. The teaching and admonition are also the immediate justification of and purpose for congregational singing, which is as legitimate as a method for inculcating truth and for instruction in righteousness as it is for praising God – and all these elements should determine our hymnology.

The praise of God expressed in our singing amounts to little more than emotional self-indulgence if it fails to assist in promoting and sustaining the true contextualization and moderation of the thoughts and practices of those who sing, with results that are subsequently and increasingly manifested in their lives. We cannot claim that God is glorified if holiness in communion is not enhanced by knowledge, righteousness, and beauty.

However, although a proper and useful corporate method of mutual education and encouragement, Paul obviously did not intend singing to take the place of, or be given priority over the biblical teaching of wise and capable elders (Ephesians 4:11, I Timothy 5:17, Titus 1:9); or that the performance of the choir take precedence over the sermon.

Only the sermon can give significance to the song!

The practice of affirmative morality requires this wisdom of Christ's word and the teaching and the admonition of the Christian community. Therefore, the communion of God's people in both congregation and in daily life should resonate with compassion, kindness, humility, meekness, longsuffering, and love, being moderated by forbearance and forgiveness, while nourished, informed, and directed by the scriptures. And as we should coordinate and cooperate with one another in the practice of these things, being "called in one body" (3:15), we all share in the responsibilities involved.

---

[186] Christian wisdom may not be appreciated in the non-Christian world, but we ought nonetheless to give evidence of it in our own thoughts and behaviour (I Corinthians 3:18-19). *Inter alia*, it should distinguish the Christian community from the secular world. The unconverted should be able to see our wisdom, even when it appears to him to be arrant folly; and see our Christian aesthetic, even if unappreciated.

3.4.2.2.3. The lordship of Christ (3:17)

Affirmative morality, the apostle explains, also requires the Christian to "do all in the name of the Lord Jesus". And here it is most important that we do not take the words "in the name of the Lord Jesus" lightly. They are highly charged with formidable ramifications. It is worth taking time to consider the serious implications involved in this imperative.

Evidently, Paul did not think he had said all that was necessary about the peaceful and informed integration of the Christian community, so he now enjoins another significant requirement. As we have seen, to allow the "peace of Christ" to dwell in our hearts we need a profound appreciation of the redemptive death of our Lord; and for this peace to be rightly informed and to have true structure and content, it is critical that the "word of Christ" dwells in us "richly". But neither of these will be genuinely effective, or contribute meaningfully to holiness in communion, unless we do everything, in word and deed, in the "name of Christ".

The importance of this cannot be overemphasized!

There is always the possibility that people professing Christian faith, and thereby claiming to act "in the name of the Lord", may have "the form of godliness" – the outward appearance – but at the same time "deny the power of it" (II Timothy 3:5), knowing nothing of its true influence. Moreover, they may have "in the law" – or in their confessional standards – "the form of knowledge and of the truth" and yet dishonour God in their lives by failing to take His commandments seriously (Romans 2:20-23). There is the persistent danger – to which we are all exposed – of confessional superficiality, as we are all predisposed to hypocrisy. So, we must beware lest our profession of peace be merely ostensible and void of any substance, and lest our confession of faith be merely a formal statement of orthodoxy to which we do not conscientiously adhere, so that neither has any appreciable impact upon the way we actually think and behave. This is the dissimulation of those who honour God "with their lips" when their "heart is far from" Him (Matthew 15:8).

We would do well to ask, then, what is the prophylactic – or the therapeutic – for this hypocrisy? How are we to avoid pretence and superficiality in both communion and confession within the association of God's people?

The answer is to be found in this third, comprehensive imperative. Everything that we do, "all" our self-expression whether "in word or in deed", is to be done "in the name of the Lord Jesus" (3:17). By God's grace, this will be a much-needed corrective in our lives, because we all dissimulate to some extent to hide our true thoughts, desires, and motives. There is a passion within us to present ourselves as something other than we are, and so to gain adulation or acceptance that we do not deserve – and we do so primarily that we might *make a name for ourselves, even when pretending to glorify His name.* This is a relentless and divisive problem in every society and, for our consideration here, it is seriously detrimental to holiness in communion and peace in the church – and, moreover, it is a flagrant misrepresentation of Christian values to the world.

Therefore, how we present ourselves in what we do and what we say (cf. in "walk" and "word" in 4:5-6) is important in the Christian communion for the sake of its internal peace, and in society in general for the sake of our witness to the truth. We ought, then, to seek the grace of God that we might pursue holiness in "whatsoever" we do, in "all" things (3:17). There is nothing adiaphorous in Christian living. There should be no duplicity, no double standards, no attempt to present one persona in church and another in the secular world.

Paul explained elsewhere that Christians must be "of the same mind, having the same love, being of one accord", having "the mind of Christ", that they "do all things without murmurings and disputings" and "may be blameless and harmless, children of God without blemish". They should live in this fashion despite the negative and corrupting influences that impinge upon them in whatever "crooked and perverse generation" they find themselves. And this is required if they are to be "seen as lights in the world" (Philippians 2:2, 14-15).[187] Here again, we should notice that this placidity and harmlessness, the benign disposition of God's unblemished children, should be evident in *all things*.[188] The comprehensive influence of God's grace should be evident.

When we think of our waywardness of heart and our persistent arrogance, when we are conscious of our ignorance and moral frailty, the possibility that we might live as "children of God without blemish" (Philippians 2:15) seems to be very, very remote. Indeed, the task of living in such a manner, we must admit, is quite beyond our ability. However, to make this admission – which is the essence of repentance – is to take the first necessary, although hesitant step towards the impeccable behaviour required, which, as we have seen, will only reach its consummation when we are presented "perfect in Christ" (1:22, 28). Nevertheless,

---

[187] Here in Philippians 2, as in Colossians 3, Paul is as much concerned about holiness in community as he is about individual holiness of character.

[188] Our Lord Himself asks this of us, so that we "glorify (our) Father who is in heaven" that we might be the "light of the world" (Matthew 5:14-16).

this will always be the godly ambition of all those who resolutely pursue holiness (cf. I John 3:3).

Those who take this first step in the pursuit of holiness and in anticipation of ultimate perfection must realize that what is immediately required of them is that now they "do all in the name of the Lord Jesus" (3:17). Prior to their Christian conversion, they had in effect been doing everything for their own name in their egocentricity, or for the name of some luminary who had taken them captive "through (his) philosophy and vain deceit" (2:8). But now they are to live in a Christ-centred fashion that glorifies His Name.

But what exactly is required of us if we are – albeit imperfectly – "to do all in the name of the Lord Jesus"?

We must first appreciate that the words 'in the name of the Lord' – or some equivalent – are not to be used as a kind of divine imprimatur that somehow authenticates what we say or authorizes the things we do. The formal use of the words does not sanctify the deed. Neither does merely vocalizing or writing them guarantee that our motives are what they should be. Much evil has been and continues to be perpetrated in this world 'in the name of God' and much blasphemy and heresy has been promulgated 'in the name of Christ'.

Perhaps it is helpful for our purpose here, or at least as an illustration of my concern, to recall that the Old Testament warns us about priests who "despise (God's) name" by corrupting worship, presumably for their own advantage (Malachi 1:6); and that prophets were prone to "speak ... presumptuously in (God's) name" (Deuteronomy 18:20). Failing to respect the name of God is tantamount to dishonouring His person. Priests were appointed to represent the people before God and speak to Him on their behalf, and the prophets were appointed to represent God before the people and speak to them on His behalf. Therefore, when priest and prophet are themselves corrupted by failing to respect the name of the Lord – which is to disrespect His holy character – they inevitably misrepresent both God and the people in their respective offices, their mediation is ineffectual, and communion between people and their Lord is impaired. *Even so, possibly, with the Christian minister.*

So serious is this matter that Israel was solemnly commanded, "You shall not take the name of the Lord your God in vain, for the Lord will not hold him guiltless who takes His name in vain" (Exodus 20:7). Priest, prophet, and people were bound by this injunction. All Israel, as the Lord's covenant people, was responsible

Alan D Catchpoole

to embody the righteousness and the grace of God in a godless world – being, as a nation, prophet and priest to all people. *Even so with the Christian community.*

However, in contrast to and in fulfilment of the Old Testament order, the Lord Jesus is for us both our priest and our prophet. He came from heaven to earth to represent God among His people; and having made sacrifice of Himself, been raised from the dead, and returned to heaven, He is now interceding for us as our representative at God's right hand (Hebrews 1:1-3, 7:25). And in the process of doing so, He "glorified" God as He "manifested" His Father's "name unto the men" whom the Father had given Him (John 17:4-6). *He is, therefore, the only and the immaculate mediator between God and man (I Timothy 2:5), and in His godliness, obedience, and self-sacrifice He epitomizes a life lived for the glory of the divine name.*

Jesus both came into this world and did all His "works" in His "Father's name" (John 5:43, 10:25). This implies that the life He lived was always a manifestation of the divine character. Now the apostle advises us to do "all in the name of the Lord Jesus" (3:17). And this implies that we, as God's new covenant people, have the responsibility to embody the way Christ lived for the glory of God. Although our attempts to do so are obviously feeble, we are not to forget that the standards demanded remain extraordinarily high. To repent of our failures in this matter is not, and must not be, to resile from the obligation involved.

Moreover, we might conclude from this that to do all in His name requires *at the very least* that we live in constant dependence upon and with the most profound respect for Him, and for the inviolable redemption He provides for us. *We will not be doing anything in His name if we diminish or disregard all that He has done in the Father's name to make it possible for us to do something in His name.* If we fail to reflect as best we can the significance of His teaching, the quality of His life, and the redemptive power of His cross, then we have little respect for Him and not much concern for the glory of God. Any church that functions without serious consideration for the salvific death and triumphant resurrection of our Lord and the necessity of His mediation for us in heaven, has no right to call itself 'Christian'. It has betrayed the Name!

All this is reflected in Colossians. Because of our redemption, we are no longer "alienated and enemies" in mind and works, and we have been "translated into the kingdom" of our Lord (1:21, 13). We ought then, because of our Christian conversion, to both *think* and *act* differently, acknowledging our subordination to the sovereignty of Christ. We have, as we discovered, both a new *disposition* and a new *perspective* (#3.3.1. Second), so we are not surprised that Paul exhorts us to "seek the things which are above, where Christ is seated on the right hand of God" (3:1, #3.3.2. First).

And this subordination to God's sovereignty and submission to His providence is, as we have seen, the contextualization of all Christian thought and action. We should live deliberately and conscientiously in the environment of divine creation and redemption.

All this, surely, delineates the context within which we should find what it means to do "all in the name of the Lord Jesus". And it clearly implies much more than simply doing something 'for Him' or 'for His sake', because these lesser expressions indicate only a person's intentions, which may or may not be well directed or in accord with the will of God. Acting 'in His name' is a far more demanding matter, involving both inspiring privilege and intense responsibility – both exhilarating and terrifying!

So, I suggest the following:

- **First**, this exhortation requires initially that we recognize and appreciate the *character of the person who is designated* as "the Lord Jesus". It is a simple observation, but one that it frequently overlooked, forgotten, or deliberately ignored, that as Christians we are called primarily to serve a *Person* – not an ideology, a cause, or an organization. However, we cannot escape the fact that we can only serve Him appropriately when we are committed to the ideology of His Gospel, the cause of His kingdom, and the organization of His church. The faithful servant must act in harmony with his master's thinking, objectives, and methods.

   But serious problems arise when we become so involved in ideological discussion that theology becomes an end in itself, and our own academic prestige becomes our master; or when some cause becomes an end in itself, and our methodology becomes our master; or when some organization becomes an end in itself, and our status within it becomes our master. We quickly succumb to the allure of these things! We then face the danger of the impersonal mechanization of our religion.

   We must never forget that we serve Jesus, the Virgin's Child who is God's Son, the village carpenter who is the eternal King, the Man who had nowhere to lay His head who promised His followers residence in His Father's house, the Lamb of God who is the King of heaven, the itinerant Teacher who graduated from no university but instructs the world in wisdom, the gentle Practitioner who healed the sick but was crucified as a criminal, the One buried in a borrowed tomb who rose from the dead and is seated at the right hand of God for evermore.

This Lord Jesus – and no other! – must appear throughout and comprehensively, and be honoured in our ideology, in every cause we espouse, and in His great Church of which we are unworthy members.

I would suggest, then, that to do all things in the name of Jesus requires, among other things, that we live in a manner that is compatible with the character and the quality of life manifested by the Lord *Jesus* we find in the Gospels.

We are obliged to emulate Him.

• **Second**, this exhortation also requires initially that we recognize and appreciate the *authority of the person who is designated* as "the Lord Jesus". It is a simple observation, but one that it frequently overlooked, forgotten, or deliberately ignored, that as Christians we are called primarily to obey "the blessed and only Potentate, the King of kings and Lord of lords" (I Timothy 6:15) – not some head of state, church dignitary, or person in authority. However, we cannot escape the fact that we only obey Him appropriately when we are humbly living "in subjection to the higher authorities" He appoints in human societies (Romans 13:1), and in obedience to those in authority in His church (Hebrews 13:17).

But serious problems arise when we become so involved with heads of state, church dignitaries, and people in authority that, when we fail to "put to death (our) members that are upon the earth" (3:5, #3.4.1.1.), we forget that "we ought to obey God rather than men" (Acts 5:29). Then we are tempted to assert our own will, to seek our own advantage, and to obey our own desire for advancement in this world, and having been taken "captive" by the beguiling influences of others, we love "the glory of men more than the glory of God" (John 13:43).

We must never forget that we are to obey Him whom God "highly exalted", giving Him "the name which is above every name", that "in the name of Jesus every knee should bow", and that "every tongue should confess that Jesus Christ is Lord to the glory of God the Father" (Philippians 2:9-11).[189] Therefore, no matter how thankful we are that Christ took the "form of a servant", was "found in fashion as a man", and "humbled Himself, becoming obedient unto death" (Philippians 2:7-8) – and this must never be allowed to evanesce from our minds – it

---

[189] It seems to me that we must understand that when Paul mentioned the "name which is above every other name" he was referring to the name "Jehovah" of the Old Testament, the name that was considered by the Jews to be most sacred. This being so, the apostle is identifying Jesus as God, and hence worthy of the adulation and obedience due to the Almighty.

is to Him in His exalted, sovereign, and eternal position at the Father's right hand that we must bow our knee if we are of a mind to obey Him.

When Jesus had risen from the dead He said, "All authority has been given unto me in heaven and on earth", and with this prerogative He commanded His people to represent Him in this world (Matthew 28:18-20). Therefore, "let us have grace, whereby we may offer service well-pleasing to God with reverence and awe" (Hebrews 12:28).

This Jesus – and no other! – must appear in all that we do as the one above all others to whom we owe allegiance, and in obedience to Him we should humbly take our place, whether lowly or prestigious, in the societies of men on earth.

I would suggest, then, that to do all things in the name of Jesus implies, among other things, that we ought to live in a manner that is consistent with the teaching, the purposes, and the work of the *Lord* Jesus we find in the Gospels.

We are obliged to submit to Him.

- **Third**, we must say that to do what we do "in the name of ... *Jesus*" is a most profound and *joyful privilege* that ought to be a source of great delight and satisfaction for all who truly love Him. But, in contrast, we should add that to do what we do "in the name of the *Lord* ..." is a most profound and *awful responsibility* that ought to be a source of great gravity and circumspection.

The privilege and the responsibility are isometric in the service of God, and they are always concomitant so we cannot have one without the other.

It might be helpful if we consider this duality of privilege and responsibility in reference to one particular activity – but an activity that is singularly important as it influences all our other activities. Jesus invited His disciples to ask of the Father "in (Christ's) name" when they approach Him in prayer (John 16:23-24). Keeping in mind that prayer, our most intimate and profound communion with God, should be integral to "everything" in our lives (Philippians 4:6), then we must assume that it is also an essential element in doing "all in the name of the Lord Jesus" (3:17).

The privilege of praying "in the name" of Jesus must be coordinated with the responsibility of doing "all in the name of Jesus". Therefore, when we "pray without ceasing" (I Thessalonians 5:17) we are – or we ought to be – deliberately bringing all we do under His authority.

So then, if we are to act in the name of Jesus, it is imperative that we pray in the name of Jesus.

Now, that we can pray in the name of Jesus is, without doubt, the greatest privilege any person could ever have. It gives us, who are without righteousness of our own and deserving only His wrath, access into the presence of our most holy God without fear. Therefore, as Christians, we may have "boldness to enter into the holy place by the blood of Jesus" (Hebrews 10:19), with the confidence that He will always graciously respond to our requests "that (our) joy might be fulfilled" (John 16:24).

But this privilege must never be abused by intruding into the presence of God with requests that would be an offence to His character and detrimental to His purposes, interceding presumptuously and without sensitivity to His purity or understanding of His word. He is always gracious and forgiving, but this does not relieve us of the responsibility to honour Him and to ask only with respect for the name in which we pray. Therefore, it is important that we appreciate – and that we appreciate increasingly – both *the character of the person* and the *authority of the person* whose name we invoke.

As we trust in His name, we must be careful to request nothing that He would find impertinent. It is our obligation, then, to ask "according to His will" (I John 5:14), as best we are intelligently able, and with measured caution. Therefore, we are advised, "Be not rash with your mouth, and let not your heart be hasty to utter anything before God; for God is in heaven, and you upon earth: therefore, let your words be few" (Ecclesiastes 5:2).

Then, as prayer in communion with God is pivotal for the man of faith, this sense of privilege and responsibility before the Almighty should suffuse all that we do in every aspect of our lives.

And, I might add, if we are *to pray* with this joy and awe when we speak to God in Christ's name, we should be just as concerned *to preach* with this joy and awe when we speak to people about God in Christ's name. Both are most solemn exercises, not to be taken lightly, for in them each Christian functions in his simplicity as priest and prophet, and must avoid the condemnation implied in Malachi 1:6 and Deuteronomy 18:20 as mentioned above.

So then, we are to act in the name of Jesus even as we are to pray in His name; and praying in His name is fundamentally preparing our hearts and minds that we might act appropriately in His name.

Rightly understood and taken seriously, 3:17 is a most exacting verse, an exhortation from God that requires us to emulate Christ through the most wholehearted and all-embracing response in love – for His person – and in obedience – to His authority. Paul reinforced this command when he wrote, "Whatsoever you do, work heartily, as unto the Lord and not unto men" (3:23).

However, as demanding as this might be, the apostle would certainly not have us intimidated by it. He encouragingly states that as we do everything in the name of our Lord we should at the same time be "giving thanks to God the Father through Him" (3:17). And well we might be thankful, for herein we both discover the fullness and joy of being human, and also locate the significance and purpose of life.

In the modern world, it seems that many have been convinced that the 'good life' is only available to those who are fully in control of their own affairs, free to do as they please, and subject to no authority than their own will. It has, then, become increasingly difficult to convince anyone that the fullness of joy could possibly be found in servitude – even, or especially, in servitude to God. It is obvious that to be the slave of a wicked tyrant is a desperate and evil state, and for one person to be owned as legal property by another is abhorrent. And all Christians who know that they are to love their neighbour as themselves will work for the emancipation of all who are in such appalling, human bondage (cf. #3.5.3. Third).

Nevertheless, to be in the service of a good and just man (cf. 4:1) may well be the provision of security, fulfilment, peace, and kindness for many. But above all, to serve the Lord Jesus – He being who and what He is – can only result in great emancipation and enrichment now on earth and then in eternity. As He determines the "good works" that we should do (Ephesians 2:10), our lives are filled with activities of indisputable and eternal worth; as He strengthens us (Philippians 4:13), there is nothing relevant or important that we cannot do; as He will never "tempt/test (us) beyond our ability" (I Corinthians 10:13), we will not be left frustrated or defeated; and as He has promised that He will never "fail" or "forsake" us (Hebrews 13:5), we will never be abandoned.

Moreover, "knowing that from the Lord (we) shall receive the recompense of the inheritance: (we) serve the Lord Christ" (3:24). Not only were we "delivered out of the power of darkness, and ... into the kingdom of the Son" – whereby we were drawn into the service of the King – we were also "made fit/qualified to be partakers of the inheritance" (1:12-13) – whereby we are guaranteed ultimate gratification. We know that if we "seek first the kingdom of God, and His righteousness" (Matthew 6:33) nothing of worth shall be withheld from us.

The "good and faithful servant" of the good and gracious God will indeed "enter ... into the joy of (his) lord" (Matthew 25:21) – regardless of the fact that he is "unprofitable", having at best only done "that which was (his) duty to do" (Luke 17:10). And for this, we ought to be most thankful indeed!

Such is our servitude in the Lord Jesus Christ!

NOTE: I suggest that this "doing all in the name of the Lord Jesus" is in effect the outworking of all the principles I have written about in #3.4.1.1. And this requires that whatever one does *as a Christian* – and for the Christian, that should be *everything he does* – whether in "word or in deed", should be in love for and in obedience to the Christ we worship.

The following chart is a brief summary of all the above concerning the practical principles of Christian morality:

THE PRINCIPLES OF MORAL PRACTICE IN THE GOSPEL

PROHIBITIVE MORALITY "putting off" In practice: 3:5-9a In principle: 3:9b-11	AFFIRMATIVE MORALITY "putting on" In practice: 3:12-14 In principle: 3:15-17
RECONCILIATION Peace between God and man. ETERNAL CONTEXT of MORALITY	ARBITRATION of PEACE Peace between man and man. TEMPORAL CONTEXT of MORALITY
RENEWAL unto KNOWLEDGE Subjective and gracious principle of knowledge. THE "IMAGE" and MORALITY	THE INFLUENCE of the WORD Objective and ministering principle of knowledge. THE BIBLE and MORALITY
UNIFICATION in CHRIST The **efficient** cause of moral behaviour.	THE LORDSHIP of CHRIST The **final** cause of moral behaviour.

◆

3.5. THE SOCIAL IMPLICATIONS (3:18-4:1)

In these verses, 3:18-4:1, Paul makes some very pertinent comments about the social implications of the gospel. The apostle is still developing his primary exhortation that as we have "received Christ Jesus the Lord" we should continue to "walk in Him" (2:6, #3.1.). But his sociological concern, as suggested above, is – at least as he develops his thoughts in this letter – only *one of five important and interrelated aspects of Christian faith and living* (Introduction, B.). Therefore, I suggest, we will not truly value or fully appreciate his instructions here concerning marriage, family, and social status if we separate them from the implications of his religion, philosophy, and morality (2:8-3:17).

In other words, although 3:18-4:1 form a self-contained pericope, we must not consider it outside the context in which it is found in this letter to the Colossians. The apostle's social concerns are not derived from the "philosophy" or the "traditions of men" (2:8) but from his Christian theology and worldview.

Some suppose that Paul added these words to this letter because there were difficulties with or disputes about social relationships in the Colossian church that were perhaps reported to him by Epaphras. This may have been so, although the apostle makes no mention of it, but he does record that he had heard of their "love in the Spirit" (1:7), which might suggest that the opposite was the case. As previously mentioned, he makes no particular reference to the *false teaching* that had affected the congregation but chose rather to expound positive aspects of Christian belief. Similarly, he now makes no reference to any specific *antisocial behviour* but states the positive Christian principles that should regulate the community of believers in all circumstances and at any time.

We will, then, better understand and appreciate the instructions Paul has written here if we see them as flowing directly from the Christian gospel, as the intelligent application of biblical philosophy and morality, and not as a pragmatic attempt to resolve a temporary, historical case of communal discord. And if they have their origin in the law of God and the gospel, and not in contemporary circumstances, then these instructions have a timeless and universal application. We cannot dispense with them as if they are archaic, only relevant in the remote past, and therefore irrelevant in modern cultures.

If these instructions, as I believe, do have their origin in the gospel and the law of God, we need not assume that Paul cobbled them together by borrowing ideas from non-Christian writers, as some suppose. There are, I understand, numerous examples of similar ancient lists of regulations penned by men of other philosophical persuasions. The apostle may or may not have been aware of them, or of any influence they may have had. However, it need hardly surprise us that many intelligent people had given thought to these matters before and during the time of the apostles. The inescapable fact is that we all – Christians and non-Christians alike – live in the same world and we must all find some way of dealing with our sexuality, our family associations, and the social structure of our community (cf. #3.2.1. Fourth).[190] Everybody thinks about them and many people write about them – almost *ad nauseam!* So, it is no coincidence, and no proof of plagiarism, that their ideas sometimes have common characteristics.

Inevitably, Paul had to employ language similar to that used by others in discussing social matters. Obviously, he had no alternative but to use the same words for wife, husband, parent, child, master, and servant that were found in the works of pagan and secular writers. And in one sense, he had to use them within more or less the *same proximate context* as others, for he was dealing with the same human associations.

However, in another sense, he was writing in an entirely *different plenary context*. He was indeed dealing with relationships between people on this earth, but supremely in reference to their relationship with God. Hence, he introduces qualifying expressions that no one but a Christian would use – "as is fitting in the Lord" (3:18), "this is well-pleasing in the Lord" (3:20), "fearing the Lord" (3:22), "heartily, as unto the Lord" (3:23), and "you also have a Master in heaven" (4:1). (For further consideration of these expressions, see #3.5.2. Third.) No non-Christian could, or would want to discuss human associations from this perspective, as his anthropocentric philosophy and pagan presuppositions would prohibit him from doing so. These instructions are uniquely and powerfully Christian.

NOTE: Paul has advised his readers to anticipate a life that is "holy and without blemish and unreprovable" in God's sight (1:22), and to "seek the things which are above" and to "set (their) mind on the things which are above, not on the things that are upon the earth" (3:1-2). Moreover, he would have them "do all things in the name of the Lord Jesus" (3:17). It is, then, inconceivable in the light of these instructions that he would now in 3:18-4:1 be doing no more than advising them how to live in a manner compatible with – and acceptable in – the contemporary culture and practices of the non-Christian community in which they lived.

---

[190] We would do well, I think, to keep in mind that in our day there are potent forces that are deliberately and quite unashamedly attempting to change the traditional social structures of our community according to principles and values that are inimical to the Christian faith.

Our main concern, then, should be to discover the distinctively Christian features in Paul's advice, and, by the grace of God, to integrate them into our own social theory and relationships, and not have our lives shaped by the non-Christian culture of our day. As uncomfortable as it might prove to be at times, we should evidently be different – we are to be "seen as lights in the world" (Philippians 2:15, cf. Matthew 5:13-16, I Peter 2:12, John 12:36). *It is a fatal mistake for Christians to adopt the moral values and social principles of the pagan or secular community in which they live, or to imagine that they will be better able to befriend and communicate with the unconverted if they do so.*

We might say that Paul had no interest in a coldly pragmatic, humanistic, materialistic society, but only in a genuine and significant realization of the kingdom of God among men and women on earth – and to some extent, at least in the Christian community, its realization now! We must live in anticipation of perfection in this matter (1:5, 22), but should immediately adopt the principles involved (1:10, 13).

◆

I insert the following comments about moral principle and the modern age, hoping that they might make Paul's remarks here more immediately relevant.

MORAL PRINCIPLE AND THE MODERN AGE

When we consider the implications of our Christian morality in contemporary culture we are confronted by what is perhaps one of the greatest challenges we must face in the modern age. In one way or another, we are all caught up in the throes of communal restructuring which is the inevitable result of the turmoil of the many conflicting and aggressive ideologies to which we are exposed. Radical changes are being introduced that are transforming the ethical and social landscape.

But this is not altogether a new phenomenon. During the past two or three centuries, at least in the Western world, there has been increasing ridicule, together with widespread rejection of the principles of religion and philosophy that the apostle Paul has presented in this letter. Consequently, Christianity itself seems to have fallen into disrepute, its morality repudiated by many, and weapons of every kind are being used to eradicate its influence in the world.

For example, the apostle is assuming that his readers believe in "the word of the truth of the gospel" (1:5). But we live at a time when philologists question the possibility that any 'word' might have enduring meaning, philosophers impugn the very notion of 'truth', and theologians deny that some ancient 'gospel' or primitive religious theory can have any current relevance. So, we are now being told that to think we might have "knowledge of (God's) will" (1:9) is nothing more than superstitious self-delusion, and to imagine that we might "walk worthily of the Lord" (1:10) is to fantasize in a meaningless world. And to entertain any hope of "bearing fruit in every good work" (1:10), some say, is arrogant folly because 'goodness' is only a convenient, temporal, and artificial convention having no permanent substance.

But our belief in truth, knowledge, and goodness is rooted deeply in our conviction that all things have been created and are sustained by Jesus Christ, the Son of God (1:16-17), and that although much that is evil and corrupt has devastated our present circumstances, He will eventually "reconcile all things unto Himself" (1:20). Therefore, we look back to the divine initiative in creation, we reckon with divine providence in history, and we anticipate divine consummation in the future. In doing so, our beliefs are not haphazard or without foundation, but are comprehensive, integrated, and intelligible.

Consequently, those who would undermine our trust in "the word of the truth of the gospel" are determined to demolish our belief in creation, in the divine government of all things, and in the certainty of an eternal purpose. By any and every means they attempt to tear people away from biblical teaching and the idea that the Christian God might in fact stand at the back of all things, working out His own resolve in this world. They reinterpret history according to their chosen perspective, deny that Christianity has made any worthwhile contribution to humankind, and attempt to lay the blame for modern man's confusion and distress at the door of the church. They prefer to believe that man is alone in the universe.

I suggest that the passion many of our contemporaries display in their antagonism towards Christianity is energized and directed by one predominant force – *their determination to be free from any constraint other than their own desires.* But this attitude, this craving for unrestricted autonomy, is far from being a modern phenomenon, but is as old as the human race! When Adam revolted against the idea that he should live in God's world, according to God's law, and fulfil God's purposes, he deemed the circumstances of human life in the Garden of Eden to be oppressive. And modern man is Adam's child.

Throughout the generations, Adam's descendants have refined their philosophy, progressively redefining their concept of freedom. The first man decided – with more than a little satanic prompting – that he could gain freedom for himself by claiming to be like God and, therefore, able to decide for himself what might be good and what might be evil (Genesis 3:5). He would live according to his own moral values and on his own terms.

But evidently, this proved to be unsustainable, so man adjusted his 'theology' and, perhaps realizing that he could not really be like God, decided that God was basically just like man – in fact, just like fallen man (Romans 1:23). This lesser god was more malleable and could be shaped into whatever form gave the devotees the greater freedom to do as they pleased. So many and various gods were formed in the minds of men, so each individual could choose the one he might prefer. He would be free to worship in the manner he desired.

However, this approach to life in this world also proved to be inadequate for those who were still driven by an inordinate passion for freedom. The religions that proposed various gods also imposed religious regulations, and so they became a far greater source of bondage than of liberty. When men began to realize that even their idolatry (Romans 1:23) demanded servitude and gave them no real freedom, they made the momentous decision that religion itself – or, at least, religion in any of it numerous forms that proposed some kind of god that existed beyond or above man – had to be rejected. Therefore, they dispensed with belief in any ruling deity and chose to worship and serve "the creation" (Romans 1:25). They became what we now call *secular materialists*.

This remarkable change in human thought seemed at first to provide the freedom men desired. No longer did they have to bow before demanding gods or subject themselves to the requirements of religious authorities, for the gods did not exist and authoritarian priests and clerics were seriously deluded and needed to be silenced. With optimism – and an abounding self-confidence that had the characteristics of the old religious faith – they turned to search the world and their own psyche to discover the resources and the means to build their own utopia where they and all people would enjoy unlimited freedom. In modern times, such optimistic thinkers had faith enough in themselves to believe that science and its prodigious child, psychology, would at last deliver what Adam had craved.

It is obvious that this approach to life will aggressively oppose all Christian beliefs, and must reject the philosophy that is "after Christ" (2:8). What it finds particularly offensive are the imperatives of biblical morality, which it considers to be inimical to their concept of human freedom. That Paul wrote as he did in 3:18-4:1 – and elsewhere – is despised as the authoritarianism of a deluded, religious mentality, that can only result in continuing and increasing human bondage. And any society that follows these apostolic instructions is considered to be outmoded – if not dangerously recidivistic. Therefore, they demand that we live in their 'brave new world'.

And thus, incidentally, they would deny us the freedom to live as we desire, insisting that their notion of human liberty has, as it is the product of historic progress, a god-like authority that cannot be repudiated.

However, not all modern secular materialists have been able to sustain the original optimism that seemed to galvanize some earlier Enlightenment thinkers. The cold, brutal realities of recent world history, the persistent recalcitrance in man's behaviour, and the continuing disparity – and conflict – between the hopes and aspirations of various peoples have brought despair to many of even the most cheerfully ambitious among them.

It now appears that man's ancient, historic decision to worship and serve "the creation rather than the Creator" (Romans 1:25, ἐσεβάσθησαν καὶ ἐλάτρευσαν τῇ κτίσει παρὰ τὸν κτίσαντα), even as this materialistic vision is pursued with all the genius of today's science and sophisticated technology, has not delivered the freedom the would-be autonomous man desires. Whether he will admit it or not, *he still worships and serves*, he is still the devotee of the idol of his choice. The creator-less, impersonal, physical world that he adores has proven to be a relentlessly demanding master, and the modern, anthropocentric social system he has devised is threatening to become – indeed, it has already become in some places – a totalitarian tyrant.

There seems to be a tragic sadness about modern secular materialism. Its devotees have searched for some principle in this world or some natural characteristic in humankind that provides a basis upon which the 'free' society they desire can effectively be established. It presupposed that the present troubles in human society are the result of the imposition of restrictive regulations that crush man's purported natural and intrinsically noble tendencies. If these basic instincts are released and people enabled to express themselves without inhibitions, as they propose, then, they hope, the pure worth of the human race would soon be discovered.

But, sadly, no such benign, natural, innate feature has been found in man that is sufficient as a foundation for a just, perfect, merciful, and gracious world. The utopian dream remains agonizingly elusive!

The last few decades of human history have surely provided enough evidence to suggest that a materialistic, secular society has given no more – and probably considerably less – freedom to its people than many religious communities. I know many would dispute this. But subsequent to the great Enlightenment, the advance of rationalism, and the spectacular developments of science, devastating world wars that still live in our memories, and endless regional armed conflicts, Hiroshima, the Siberian Gulag, the Cambodian killing fields, death camps, rapidly spreading terrorism, the worldwide trade in lethal weapons, innumerable refugees, together with the rising drug culture in our communities, unstoppable human trafficking, the increasing instability in marriage and family, and similar circumstances give us serious cause for concern. We cannot, of course, blame Enlightenment thinking for all these evils, but we might ask what significant freedom the modern world and its love child, secular materialism, have provided for us to alleviate them. And how frail is it? Many years of Enlightenment thinking has done little or nothing to dispel the ravaging darkness of this troubled world.

Indeed, we acknowledge that religious man has done much evil in the name of his gods, but we also observe that secular man has done much evil in the name of his godlessness. The problem is man himself!

Then, from another perspective, we might say that secular materialism, being what is actually an irrational belief about the unknown, is nothing more than a modern superstition. It is, in effect, a religion that is making desperate efforts to disguise itself as scientific fact. We might well be thankful for the benefits we have gained from modern science – which, we should remember, has its roots as much in Christianity as it has in any other belief system, or more so – but it is difficult to see what possible advantages we may have gained from secular materialism. It is only an imaginative belief-system cunningly devised and skilfully propagated to justify a supposedly 'free' morality – but ultimately it is no more effective in improving life than any other "philosophy and vain deceit, after the tradition of men" (2:8). And, I might add, it is obvious for all to see that a person does not have to be an atheist to be a good scientist!

But in our day, maintaining its anti-religious rage and the Adamic spirit of rebellion, secular materialism is promoting yet another audacious venture in the search for the ill-conceived freedom it desires. And it seems to be that the more desperate it becomes to promote human autonomy and unlimited liberty, its schemes are becoming more frenetic, dangerous, and possibly suicidal.

Until now men have sought to be free from God or the gods and from the authoritative imposition of religious or civil laws, and have proposed the removal of any social regulations that deny them uninhibited self-expression. Their hopes have been based upon finding something good and adequate in the material world and in humanity itself that would provide the foundation needed for their utopian dream of unbounded liberty. But nothing of any significance has been found or achieved.

So, a new and breathtaking scheme is being entertained which requires yet another definition of freedom itself – *we need, it is now being proposed, to be liberated from the human beings we are, and from the material world as it is. We need to create a new reality!* For millennia, men have desired to be free *to be all that they are,* but now they want to be free *from what they are.* The desire is for an unfettered power to choose, with the will unrestricted by God, nature, reason, or morality – brute autonomy! This is a revolution that has, perhaps, no precedent in human history and one can only wonder where it might lead us, other than into the abyss.

No longer is it sufficient to defy God, deny His existence, and subscribe to the religion that worships and serves "the creation rather than the Creator" (Romans 1:25). Now we are being exhorted to rebel even against the creation! Not only must God be evicted from Eden, but the Garden itself must also be re-landscaped! The earth is no longer there to be enjoyed or to be exploited, but it is there to be conquered and brought under man's control. The sciences, and genetic engineering in particular, are to be employed to construct a new kind of man and a new kind of world. Already steroids are used to produce a new type of athlete, babies are 'made to order' and trashed if unwanted, and we are able – more or less – to change our gender if we are not comfortable with the configuration with which we were born.

And at the back of this is the relentless, continuing, compelling, and irrational desire to be autonomous – to be free!

Perhaps the modern children of Adam have returned to the original ambition of the fallen, founding father of the revolt against heaven – if it had ever been abandoned – and once again desire to be "like God", and create their own world and devise their own values. *Deity is no longer to be despised, but impersonated!*

I sense a fatal weakness in this ambition. If the secular materialist can find no fundamental goodness in man as he now is that will provide the freedom he desires, can he find in himself or in others the goodness necessary to design and create a genuinely good and free man – or only the corruption to redesign another monster like or worse than himself? And we should be aware that whatever science discovers it can do, someone somewhere will eventually do it! He, too, would be free! This modern man's only hope is some Nietzschean superman.

◆

In contrast to all this, the Christian begins with the belief that man is created in the image of God, so he does not need to be changed into another 'likeness', but to be restored to the Creator's original design (1:21-22). The solution to the problem requires, *inter alia*, that we rightly define the freedom that God would have us enjoy, and for which Christ died that His people might delight in it. And then *we must learn how we are to be what we are intended to be and move comfortably within the system that God has designed for our fulfilment and satisfaction, and for His own glory.* Perfect freedom, we would suggest, is only to be found in the service of the perfect God and Father of our Lord Jesus Christ, who is infinitely loving and righteous.

We must affirm that the Christian faith provides the most exquisite freedom, and that it can be obtained nowhere else. Here I will but mention some aspects of this liberty:

1. There is *freedom from ignorance*: true intellectual liberty. Jesus said, "If you abide in my word, then are you truly my disciples; and you shall know the truth and the truth shall make you free" (John 8:31-32).
2. There is *freedom from sin*: true moral liberty. Paul wrote, "But thanks be to God. That whereas you were servants of sin ... you became servants of righteousness" (Romans 6:17-18).
3. There is *freedom from the fear of death*: true liberty to enjoy the fullness of life. Christ took our humanity that "through death He might destroy him that had the power of death ... and deliver them who through fear of death were all their lifetime subject to bondage" (Hebrews 2:14-15).
4. There is *freedom from condemnation*: true liberty to enjoy communion with God. "There is, therefore, now no condemnation to them that are in Christ Jesus, for the law of the Spirit of life made me free from the law of sin and death" (Romans 8:1-2, and see Romans 5:1, Hebrews 4:16).

Much more could be said, but this must suffice for now to present some of the facets of the freedom that is enjoyed, or should be enjoyed, and, indeed, will be enjoyed by every Christian – even if it remains something of an enigma to the unconverted. But the four aspects that we have noted above refer specifically to the liberty of thought, morality, life, and worship *within the individual and in his relationship with God.* But the individual, Christian or not, does not necessarily enjoy freedom *in human society.* The present corruption in the world cruelly and viciously denies social liberty to many and restricts it for all.

However, when Jesus spoke of His ministry in the synagogue in Nazareth, He read from Isaiah 61:1-2, explaining that those ancient words have their fulfilment in Him. "The Spirit of the Lord" was upon Him, He said, and He would, among other things, "proclaim release to the captives" and "set at liberty them that are oppressed" (Luke 4:16ff.). Surely, human freedom *in society* is in view here.

This leaves us in no doubt that our Lord is concerned for the liberty of men and women in human society, and that as and when He establishes His kingdom on earth there will be none held in captivity and none oppressed. The freedom of all His people will be guaranteed by "the law of liberty" (James 1:25, 2:8-13). Indeed, it is only divine law that can structure and protect any free community. Now we have here in Colossians 3:18-4:1 direct and very specific applications of God's law to specific social relationships. And from this, we conclude that these apostolic imperatives are intended not to limit but to greatly enhance human freedom and promote joy, peace, and satisfaction in the community.

But it is only those who are free in the knowledge of the truth, free from bondage to sin, free to enjoy life without fear, and free in their hearts to worship in the assurance of the presence of God – those who are genuinely Christian and abiding "in (Christ's) word" (John 8:31) – who are likely to appreciate the relevance of Paul's comments about the social implications of the gospel (3:18-4:1) in this modern age.

◆

But we must return to Paul's sociological concerns, expressed in 3:18-4:1.

3.5.1. CONTEXTUAL CONSIDERATIONS

Paul's primary exhortation in 2:6 – that we walk in Christ Jesus the Lord, abounding in thanksgiving – is, more or less, repeated in the exhortation in 3:17 – that we do all things in the name of the Lord Jesus, giving thanks to God. However, these two imperatives are not identical, each having its own nuance:

The imperative of the former is grounded in the redemptive *privilege* of being rooted and built up in Christ.

The imperative of the latter is grounded in our subsequent *responsibility* as God's "holy and beloved" people (3:12).

And I would suggest that all the other imperatives in this letter – which are numerous – are dependent upon and are secondary to these two. The aggregate of all these instructions indicates the apostle's concern that his readers both enjoy the *privileges* and accept the *responsibilities* of belonging to Christ, and that they discover how they are to do so.[191] And this requires, as I suggest the context demands, at least the following *three things*:

- **First**, that we do in fact have a genuine sense of privilege and responsibility, which is only generated in our hearts by a true and adequate appreciation of Jesus Christ and of our association with Him. We will only value the prerogatives and the accountability of being Christian to the extent that we revere our Lord Himself who defines and distributes them, and as we recognizing His might and majesty. If our knowledge of Him has only a secondary place in our thoughts, if we know Him but vaguely, or if we lack any desire to know Him better, then we admire Him little.

  Then any sense of privilege and responsibility in His service will be diminished – or evanesce!

  Therefore, it is most important that we keep in mind Paul's Christology in 1:15-23 and delight in His majesty and mercy, so that everything we do "in word or deed" is an acknowledgement of the propriety that "in all things He might have the pre-eminence" (1:18). There is no substitute for this. *It is, in effect, our true worship.*

  We must live for the glory of God.

---

[191] As an aside, it seems to me that the concepts of 'privilege' and 'responsibility' are being increasingly denigrated in modern society as men and women are more and more beguiled by exaggerated notions of 'rights' and 'freedom'. And this probably contributes to the general abhorrence many express for biblical morality, and particularly for Paul's instructions here about the proper relationship between husband and wife.

> *This is a matter of correctly contextualized volition and motivation.*

- **Second**, that we understand our identification with Christ in His death and resurrection (2:11-14) and develop our philosophy "after Christ" (2:8), setting our minds "on the things that are above, not on the things that are upon the earth" (3:2). Our adoration of Christ must lead to the reorientation of our mind, enabling us to distinguish between eternal and temporal values, to appreciate the worth of both, and to comprehend the association and interaction between them (#3.3.2. Third). We will only exercise our privileges and discharge our responsibilities intelligently – as we are obliged to do – when our understanding of life is the result of and consistent with our religious beliefs.

    We must live purposefully in the anticipation that we be "with Him ... manifested in glory" (3:4).

    This is a matter of correctly contextualized knowledge and wisdom.

- **Third**, that, having "put on the new man", we put away evil attitudes and actions, adopt a proper disposition, and strive for improved behaviour, according to the morality required by the instruction and the commands of God's word (3:12-17). It is critical that we embrace the exemplary principles of scripture, and rise above the degenerate standards of fallen man – that, in other words, by the grace of God we rise above ourselves! Therefore, our lives in the community, and especially in the fellowship of believers, must be governed by our Lord's standards and requirements.

    We are, above all, to live in love, "which is the bond of perfectness" (3:14, cf. John 14:15).

    This is a matter of correctly contextualized ethics and values.

This is only to summarize from another perspective all that has been suggested above about the importance and the context of a life of godliness, and to emphasize the comprehensiveness of the gospel. *But it is my immediate concern here that we begin to discover how we are to incorporate our Christian volition and motivation, knowledge and wisdom, and ethics and values into our working sociology.* This is required if we are not only to theoretically develop, but also to effectively implement our philosophy "after Christ" (2:8).

The challenging exercise is to translate our theological theory into practical, everyday living.

Many contemporary Christians are passionately concerned for human society and the general well-being of men and women in this world. And for this we should be most thankful. Nevertheless, as commendable as their passion might be, we are sometimes troubled by the lack of a corresponding enthusiasm for biblical philosophy and morality. Hence, I fear, their sociology is frequently determined by the secular ideology and the prevailing ethics that are now entrenched in popular culture, following the "philosophy and vain deceit after the traditions of men" (2:8), and not governed by scriptural principles.

The trend among contemporary thinkers in general is, it seems, to consider Paul's instructions to husbands, wives, parents, children, masters, and slaves (2:18-4:1) to be pre-Enlightenment, obsolete, and intolerable. Which indeed they are in the context of anthropocentric modern thought! As men and women, especially in the Western world, have abandoned Christian beliefs and philosophy, they have necessarily sought to define a new system of moral values. This has produced a very different culture that re-evaluates interpersonal relationships, redefines marriage, family, and authority, and demands its own, innovative social standards and practices.

To challenge these 'progressive' innovations, it is necessary to uncover the philosophical – the pseudo-religious – foundations upon which they are built, and contrast them with our own.

So, as we have seen, the apostle believed that Christians "died with Christ" that they might not live "in the world" (2:20), or be conformed to its values and conventions. We have considered that belief in and a true appreciation of the death of Christ radically transforms our way of thinking and our whole approach to life (#3.3.1.). We acknowledged that it requires insight into our Lord's crucifixion to deliver us from the philosophies of fallen man, whether ancient or modern. Therefore, unlike the unconverted, we approach Paul's instructions and the principles of biblical morality from a different perspective and with a transformed – a redeemed – understanding of their significance.

However, if we, as Christians, can find a moment of honest introspection, we will all discover that our minds entertain many erroneous ideas, that we are very much the product of our times, and that we have absorbed a great deal of the cultural practices and ethics of the contemporary world. And through time our consciences have been inured to the ways of modern, secular materialism, and then calibrated accordingly, and rarely do they serve us well.

Having, then, been habituated to contemporary values, we are not always consistent with our own fundamental principles. Too often we claim to have "received Christ Jesus the Lord", but only inconsistently at best do we "walk in

309

Him" (2:6). We desperately need the mind of Christ! Holiness, in character and in community, must be diligently cultivated; it does not come easily. We constantly need to "grow in the grace and knowledge of our Lord and Saviour Jesus Christ" (II Peter 3:18). As reformers, we must, as it were, first be reformed ourselves.

3.5.2. MODERATING CONSIDERATIONS

My contextual considerations above are more or less designed to focus attention upon the manner in which the Christian should think about and examine himself as an individual who has inescapable social responsibilities. But in these obligations, his success or failure will be determined by his personal *motivation*, *wisdom*, and *values* (#3.5.1.). If these three factors are Christianly and biblically oriented, they will equip him to be a source of enrichment to any community; but when wrongly construed or neglected, the result is social impoverishment.

However, we are not at liberty – in fact, it would be impossible – to think about and evaluate ourselves simply as individuals in isolation, although much contemporary thinking seems to advocate such depleted self-assessment. For better or worse, we are individuals-in-community. "Neither is the woman without the man, nor the man without the woman, in the Lord" (I Corinthians 11:11). I cannot be a husband without a wife, or a son without a father, or a father without a child. So, what I am as man – husband, father, or son, and I cannot avoid being at least one of these, and potentially all three – is not to be considered only in reference to what I am in myself, but what I am in reference to others. And this not only defines what I am but it also, whether I like it or not, imposes certain ineluctable restrictions and responsibilities.[192] Moreover, God has integrated all Christians into the one body in Christ so we are "members one of another" (Romans 12:3-5), and we must consider ourselves in this redeemed communal context also.

Therefore, I suggest that if we are to appreciate Paul's instructions concerning social behaviour, we must carefully consider the moderating influences that make them distinctively Christian.

- **First**, it is *important*, as we have seen, to appreciate the *personal requirements* of holiness in character (#3.4.2.1.1.).

---

[192] Perhaps most people, at least in theory, would consider this to be painfully obvious. But is it? We live in a time – remembering that there is nothing new under the sun! – when a man or a woman might with impunity, and even with social approval, walk away from marriage and family to pursue a personal passion, desire, or ambition. Individual rights and freedom are now often valued above communal responsibility – and this reflects a radical departure from what might be considered more conservative social values. Now 'self' is all-determinative.

Paul does not expect his readers to embrace his instructions about marriage, family, and society unless they have "put on ... a heart of compassion, kindness, humility, meekness" and "longsuffering" (3:10, 12). Only when these characteristics of true godliness are appropriated will the commandments of God – and every application of biblical morality – be found to be eminently sensible and deeply fulfilling. We can hardly expect the unconverted – those not born again of the Holy Spirit – to fully appreciate Paul's imperatives here concerning marriage, family, and communal associations.

I cannot be a loving husband, an encouraging father, or an obedient servant in the manner that God would have me be in this fallen world, without a measure of Christ-like compassion, kindness, humility, meekness, and longsuffering.[193]

We must learn to live appropriately within the context of Christian redemption.

* **Second**, it is *equally important* that we have an appreciation of the *practical requirements* of holiness in communion (#3.4.2.1.2.).

If we are to recognize the value of, and follow Paul's instructions in 3:18-4:1 we must see that in these verses he is applying the imperative that we "do all in the name of the Lord Jesus" to social behaviour. The "whatsoever" and the "all" (3:17) that we are to practice are not simply pious exercises or personal 'spiritual' disciplines, but involve the full and wholehearted involvement in communal life – in marriage, in family, in society. Holiness is not a matter for the hermit in the seclusion of his desert retreat, or the troglodyte in his mountain cave, but for every believer as he engages in the common concourse of human society. Our Christian faith must never be reduced to the exclusivity of the pagan mystic or the monastic contemplative. So, for example, to suggest that celibacy is a state more conducive than marriage for a life of godliness and the service of God, from a biblical perspective, is ludicrous.[194]

If I cannot be holy as a husband, father, employee, or employer – that is, if I cannot be holy within the fundamental interpersonal relationships of the divine economy – then I cannot be holy at all.

We must learn to live appropriately within the context of God's creation.

---

[193] We suspect that because these characteristics of godliness are frequently despised, the commandments of God are found by many to be intolerable. In a brash, individualistic, self-assertive, ambitious modern life there seems to be too little time for compassion and kindness, and no time at all for humility and meekness.

[194] This is not to deny that some may wisely choose celibacy for meaningful reasons.

- **Third**, even *more important* than what we are in our own individuality or in society, is what we are and what we ought to be in the communion we have with Jesus Christ.

Ultimately our holiness, whether as an individual or in community, is determined by the quality of the relationship we have with our holy God. "As He who called (us) is holy", we ourselves are also to be "holy in all manner of living" (I Peter 1:15). As Christians, we must not assess the quality of anything we do in this life by the standards of this fallen world or in reference only to pragmatic ends.[195] They are to be appraised in the light of the pure holiness of God Himself, in whose image man was created.

However, it is difficult for any of us to effectively appraise our lives in comparison with the holiness of God, because in our present condition we are unable to comprehend just how holy the holiness of God is! He "only has immortality, dwelling in light unapproachable, whom no man has seen, nor can see" (I Timothy 6:16). He said of Himself, "You cannot see my face … and live" (Exodus 33:20).

Nevertheless, in this respect God has not left us to struggle helplessly in our ignorance and futile speculations, but has been pleased to reveal Himself to His people in a manner they can endure. "Seeing it is God, that said, 'Light shall shine out of darkness,' who shined in our hearts, to give the light of the knowledge of the glory of God in the face of Jesus Christ" (II Corinthians 4:6). His face – the face of the incarnate God – we can see, and live!

Moreover, our Lord said to His disciples, "He that has seen me has seen the Father" (John 14:9). It is this Jesus whom "the Father sanctified, and sent into the world" (John 10:36) as the embodiment of the divine character. So, John could say, "The word became flesh and dwelt among us … and we beheld His glory" (John 1:14).

Therefore, we can say that He is the incarnation of the holiness of God, the epitome of holiness in human life. He is no less holy because of His participation in our humanity, but we can see holiness in Him, muted as it were – but not distorted – by the incarnation, in a way we can comprehend and without fear for our lives.

Nevertheless, if we are to see the holiness of God in the incarnate Christ, we must begin with a meaningful and true, albeit limited, concept in our minds of the essence of holiness itself, and some measure by which we can discern and appreciate it. How are we to recognize it even when

---

[195] These are the two common criteria used by most people to evaluate things we do in this life.

we see it embodied in the person and life of Jesus?[196] What are we to anticipate we will find in His life that manifests holiness? How is holiness to be recognized for what it is? How can we avoid the danger of defining holiness only in reference to the "philosophy ... of men" and our own predilections?

When God instructed the Israelites to live in a manner visibly different from other people (Leviticus 18:2-3), He commanded them to "be holy, for I the Lord your God am holy" (Leviticus 19:2). But He left them in no doubt concerning what this required of them. In the following verses in Leviticus 19 He spoke of avoiding idolatry, caring for the poor, paying just wages, being kind to the disabled, avoiding gossip, viable farming methods, sexual morality, respect for the elderly, welcoming the stranger, and more – all intensely practical matters relating to life in this fallen world.

There are, then, laws that calibrate the measure of holiness, specifying social values, and defining the manner in which holy people live – the precepts that should moderate our behaviour.[197]

Paul could confidently write, "The law is holy, and the commandment holy, and righteous, and good" (Romans 7:12). It must not be neglected – especially by those who would be holy.

Therefore, if we are to rightly understand holiness we should listen to and appreciate the laws of God. But if we wish to see holiness truly manifested in this world, and in a manner we might emulate, we should look to the incarnation of holiness in the life of Jesus Christ.[198]

If we keep these things in mind, we can then make true and wholesome assessments of our lives in reference to the manifestation of divine holiness in the life of Christ. And this is evidently what Paul would have us do. When making application of Christian philosophy and ethics

---

[196] We should remember that many of our Lord's contemporaries did not see Him as the incarnation of holiness, but as a troublesome malfeasant that deserved to be put to death. Evidently, they had no concept of true godliness by which to judge Him. And neither do many of our contemporaries.

[197] And much more is said about holiness in Leviticus 18-20 – and elsewhere. The Bible leaves us in no doubt about the demands it makes upon us.

[198] Because Jesus is of renown in history and in religious thought, many people, whether Christian or not, seek to find in Him something with which they can associate or identify to enhance their own status or to find support for their own philosophy. But many are selective, only finding in Him aspects of their choice; others are destructive, imputing to Him attributes of their own imagination. Either way, such people redesign the biblical Christ for their own purposes. Perhaps our Lord warns us about this in Matthew 24:5, or Paul in II Corinthians 11:13. It is most important, then, that we allow the written word of God, the Bible, to fully and exclusively interpret the incarnate Word of God in Christ, and not the "vain deceit" (2:8) of human traditions.

in the daily life of the common society in which we live, we must only contemplate doing what is "fitting in the Lord" (3:18) and "well-pleasing in the Lord" (3:20). Moreover, we must be sure that we do all that we do "fearing the Lord" (3:22), "heartily, as unto the Lord" (3:23), and in obedience to Him as our "Master in heaven" (4:1). Note the repeated emphasis upon the significance of Christ and our relationship with him in these verses. These are moderating principles, qualifying expressions, and are discussed below.

Our holy Lord should determine both the *deeds* done and our *disposition* in doing them.

The centrality and the sovereignty of Christ are clearly seen here in Paul's sociology. The operative principles are not egocentric and psychological, or anthropocentric and pragmatic, but Christocentric and sanctifying. And it is – or it should be – this Christ-centered life and practical holiness that distinguishes Christian social behaviour from all others.

But it may be helpful to distinguish *two things* here:

1. Objective standards.

    When Paul refers to things "fitting in the Lord" (3:18, ἀνῆ κεν ἐν κυρίῳ) and "well-pleasing in the Lord" (3:20, εὐάρεστόν ἐστιν ἐν κυρίῳ), he is presupposing that there are objective standards that are intrinsic and original in God's being, and that are not fabricated by man or conjured by human imagination. Moreover, he assumes that we live in a created universe and a divine economy designed with inbuilt, irrefrangible values; and a man lives either in harmony or in conflict with them. It depends whether we are among the "alienated and enemies" or among those whom God "has now reconciled" (1:21); whether we "walk worthily of the Lord unto all pleasing" or not (1:10).

    Generally speaking, what are "fitting" (or "proper") and "well-pleasing" responses may vary in changing situations, as diverse circumstances make different demands.[199] However, Paul has a very specific, but plenary context in view here. He is not concerned for what might be 'fitting in the first century', or 'fitting for some pragmatic purpose', or 'fitting in contemporary culture', but fitting "in the Lord". It seems most likely that he

---

[199] As a controversial example, behaviour that is fitting at a rock concert may not be fitting in the gathering of the Christian congregation.

has in mind behaviour that is appropriate as Christians "walk in Him" (2:6, see #3.1.3.). And what is fitting "in Christ" is so always and universally. The plenary context is God's creation itself.

And what is "fitting" in our Christian "walk" is also "well-pleasing" in the Lord. These two stipulations are complementary. Insofar as a man's response is "fitting" it corresponds to the requirements of the *divine law, or principle*; and insofar as it is "well-pleasing" it is compatible with the *divine character, or person*.

We must not, then, consider the standards that should moderate our behaviour merely as abstract principles, as the requirements of an impersonal 'natural law', as moral values that somehow just evolved out of the mysteries of molecular biology, or as temporary, contrived, pragmatic necessities for achieving an immediate goal. Rather, they are the expressions of a personal, infinite, and holy God, originating in His heart, and quintessential for the governance of His creation and for the eternal benefit of people created in His image. They require a personal response from man to the personal expression of the Creator. Therefore, His laws are not, and could never be an alien intrusion into this world or an artificial, restrictive imposition upon human life. They are fundamental to all that is virtuous and beautiful.

Consciously *living in respect for the character of God* is in view here.

2. Subjective disposition.

Now, as our moderating standards relate to both the law and the character of God, our response should be primarily to the Person who is the Author of all true ethical and aesthetic values. And this implies that we will behave in a "fitting" *and* "well-pleasing" manner only when we act out of genuine, altruistic love for God (John 14:15).

We should be solicitous in all we do neither to offend or grieve Him.

Our behaviour may in a sense be "fitting" even when motivated by some egocentric desire for self-aggrandizement, or to gain or maintain social status and respectability, or to satisfy our spurious moral pride. That is, the act in itself *might conform to divine law*. But it will not be "well-pleasing" to God unless it is driven principally by the loving ambition to live for His glory and to enjoy Him forever. The intention and disposition behind the act *might not conform to the divine character*. And, we should remember, "the Lord looks on the heart" (I Samuel 16:7, cf. I Corinthians 4:5). It is obvious that good things can be done from base motives and with immoral intentions.

Paul, then, has serious interest not only in the activity of the Christian in his social relationships, but in his disposition in his actions. It is not only what we do, but also our attitude in doing what we do that is of concern.

Consciously *living in sensitivity to the presence of God* is in view here.

But when Paul encourages his readers to do all that they do "fearing the Lord" (3:22, φοβούμενοι τὸν κύριον), "heartily, as unto the Lord" (3:23, ἐκ ψυχῆς ... ὡς τῷ κυρίῳ), and as having "a Master in heaven" (4:1, ἔχετε κύριον ἐν οὐρανῷ) – *three daunting qualifications* which we will consider below – he is obviously concerned with the inner, personal attitude that is indispensable for appropriate Christian *living in human society*, and that is concomitant with and derived from living with respect for the character and in sensitivity to the presence of God.

In other words, our attitude towards God should be mirrored in our attitude towards our neighbour.

Therefore, if in love we would avoid offending or grieving God, then in love we should avoid offending or grieving our neighbour (Matthew 22:37-40). "If a man says, I love God, and hates his brother, he is a liar" (I John 4:20).

The first two of these three qualifications cited here are found in Paul's particular advice to those in the service of their masters. But as the apostle would have Christians everywhere "through love" to "be servants one to another" (Galatians 5:13, διὰ τῆς ἀγάπης δουλεύετε ἀλλήλοις), what he requires here should be universally found among all true believers.

And the third qualification is also universally applicable, because all Christians are answerable to their "Master in heaven".

So, I suggest that we are looking here at the subjective attitude of heart and mind that is essential for all believers if they are "to walk worthily of the Lord" (1:10), and that in one way or another should qualify all our social relationships.

We need to consider these qualifications that, by grace, we might 'Christianize' our attitude to God and to man.

- **Fourth**, it is also *vitally important* that we understand and appreciate these qualifications of the attitude that is essential if we are "to walk worthily of the Lord". I will consider each of these separately.

  1. "Fearing the Lord".

     "Fearing the Lord" (3:22) seems to be a concept that is almost lost to church-going people of this modern age. The reason for this is, perhaps, that we are no longer able – or are unwilling – to reconcile in our minds the two biblical requirements that we both love God and fear God concurrently. Mistakenly, and considering them to be mutually exclusive, many among us have chosen to entice people to believe in a God of love, and not to warn them of the necessity to repent before a God of wrath. This is the mood of our generation, which has no real appetite for the requirements of Christian morality, preferring a therapeutic religion; and the pulpits of our churches have adapted to such contemporary sentiments.

     The fear of God has been eliminated from the 'gospel' we preach to today's man. And this is tantamount to a form of idolatry: or a refashioning of God.

     Nevertheless, as difficult as it may be to grasp, we are instructed to "love the Lord (our) God with all (our) hearts" (Matthew 22:37), *and* to perfect "holiness in the fear of God" (II Corinthians 7:1). So, we need to understand the essential characteristics of both this love and this fear, and to appreciate that they complement and do not contradict each other.

     Paul, we might note, would have us "be in subjection to" the governing, civic authority and that we "fear" its power. The ruler is, he explains, "a minister of God ... for good" and "an avenger for wrath to him that does evil" (Romans 13:1-4). Evidently, in the divine order of things on earth, the Lord would have the leadership in every community monitor the moral condition of the people, promote all that is good, and restrain all that is evil. They are responsible for maintaining ethical standards and for disciplining the malefactors. And as they are – perhaps unwittingly – ministers of God, it is through them that God Himself would effect His own governance. So, if we are to fear secular jurisdiction, how much more should we fear the Lord who stands behind it?

We must remember that "God is not mocked: for whatsoever a man sows, that shall he also reap" (Galatians 6:7). This admonishment was written to the Galatian Christians, which implies that all of us who believe in Christ should understand that we violate divine standards at our peril. It is still possible that we who are the beneficiaries of God's redemption might even now in some sense "sow unto (our) own flesh" and "of the flesh reap corruption" (Galatians 6:8).[200]

Our heavenly Father – just because He is our heavenly Father – chastens us "that we may be partakers of His holiness" (Hebrews 12:10). He said, "As many as I love, I reprove and chasten: be zealous, therefore, and repent" (Revelation 3:19). Indeed, it is just because we "call on Him as Father, who judges according to a man's work" that we should "pass the time of our sojourning here in fear" although we know that we were "redeemed ... with the blood of Jesus" (I Peter 1:17-19).

We should, therefore, fear His judgement even as we trust confidently in His love that redeemed us.

There is a sense, then, in which the Father's love for us is an essential aspect of the context in which we should fear Him. His love demands that He maintain the ethical principles of His law for the well-being of His people. A god who abandons righteousness in ruling men is certainly not the God of love whom we worship! Such a god is only a god of chaos. Therefore, we should fear not only incurring His wrath, but we should also fear grieving His love (cf. Psalm 78:40, Ephesians 4:30). And this requires, as suggested above, that we aspire to meet the requirements of the *divine law* in a manner that is compatible with the *divine character*.

We must insist, then, that the Christian life never be reduced to a cold, impersonal legalism, without love, or to a sentimental, individualized emotionalism, without law.

---

[200] This is not to suggest that the genuine Christian, the true beneficiary of God's redemption, can ever lose his salvation. He cannot! But it is obvious to all that Christians can still do much damage to themselves, to the church, and to the world – and to the good name of Christ. Paul would have us beware the consequences of such misbehaviour.

The fact is that we, as sinners, must first face the wrath of God before we can truly appreciate His love; that is, we must repent that we might believe (Mark 1:15). If we know nothing of our condemnation and its consequences, we will never truly value our justification and its benefits; or if we have not felt something of the pain of our alienation from God, we will never fully treasure our reconciliation with Him. In other words, if we have not learned that "while we were yet sinners, Christ died for us" we will never really comprehend that in doing so "God commends His own love towards us" (Romans 5:8).

All this is to suggest that if we have not clearly seen in the Cross of Christ the expression of the intense holiness of divine righteousness, neither have we seen in it the expression of the intense holiness of divine love.

The relevant point is that whether a man is yet to find salvation in Christ or now rejoices in the salvation he has found in Him, it is exactly the same intensely holy God he is obliged to worship. So, every man in his finitude, as well as in his present imperfections, must always fear such infinite holiness. In fact, we might suggest that the person who has "no fear of God" has suppressed all awareness of His might and authority, is in rebellion against Him, without faith, and knows nothing of "the way of peace"; he is more a source of "destruction and misery" than of love and kindness (Romans 3:16-18).

The church that knows nothing of the fear of the Lord is, then, only a vague and vapid example of what it ought to be, and has failed to appreciate, let alone to achieve the calibre and resilience of the love that God desires from His people.

But to avoid confusion, it is important to note that there are various categories of fear referred to in the scriptures. Of these, we might briefly consider the following.

For example, when Paul mentions the fear that reduced him to trembling, he is probably referring to his disquiet about his own ability to meet the ministering standards God demanded from him (I Corinthians 2:3, cf. II Corinthians 2:16, 3:5, 12:9-10). He also feared that some people to whom he had ministered might have their thoughts "corrupted from the simplicity and the purity that is towards Christ" (II Corinthians 11:3), or that he might have "bestowed labour upon (them) in vain" (Galatians 4:11). This concern was in part, no doubt, altruistic, born of an anxiety lest others, being beguiled, turn aside to false teaching (cf. II Corinthians 11:28); but it also suggests his apprehension that he may not have served them, or God, as well as he should. He feared, it seems, that he might fail to fulfil the commission his Lord had given him (1:25).

The apostle, then, evidently feared because of both his own *frailties* and *failures* as he sought to discharge his responsibilities in serving his "Master in heaven" (4:1). And this is most commendable because both these fears are the prelude to the *faith* that stimulates a man to trust in the grace of God for the outcome of his ministry and not to depend upon his own abilities or techniques. Only such a man will appreciate that nothing of worth can be accomplished without "His working, which works in (him) mightily" (1:29). Those we really do not want in the ministry of the gospel are the brash and self-sufficient – or, we might suggest, the fearless!

Then, one other fear – dark, looming, and inevitable – must be mentioned in this context. It was God's specific intention in the incarnation of Christ and through His death to "destroy him that had the power of death ... the devil ... and ... deliver all them who through fear of death were all their lifetime subject to bondage" (Hebrews 2:14-15). Death may be feared because of the trauma and pain that might cause it, because it prematurely terminates all our hopes and ambitions, or because of the unknown that lies beyond it. But the Bible's main concern is that "the sting of death is sin; and the power of sin is the law" (I Corinthians 15:56). Here is the most terrifying thing about death – it is divine judgement against human rebellion and immorality.

But the Christian answer to this incapacitating fear is both exquisitely profound and profoundly simple! It is an essential element in our belief that if we "confess that Jesus is the Son of God, God abides in (us), and (we) in God". And because of this reconciliation, God's "love is made perfect among us" that we might have "boldness in the day of judgement" because "perfect love casts out fear" (I John 4:16-18), this dread of condemnation.[201]

Christian fear of and trust in the righteousness of God gives birth to Christian trust in and fear of the love of God, and confidence in the righteousness and in the love of God dispels the fear of death. But the justifying love of God that dispels all fear of death must be distinguished from the sanctifying love of God that chastens His people and calls for our fear.

Therefore, we are to worship and serve God with the appropriate love and fear. If we trivialize the fear, we attenuate the love; and if we sentimentalize the love, we depreciate the fear. Either way, the gospel is eviscerated, and Christianity itself is replaced with ersatz alternatives.

• *If we do not fear God, then our relationship with Him will be frivolous.*

2. "Heartily, as unto the Lord".

"Heartily, as unto the Lord" (3:23) implies a subjective quality of Christian living we seem to find more agreeable and sometimes think it to be, mistakenly, the antithesis of "fearing the Lord" (3:22). It is not, I suggest, mere enthusiasm, although exuberance is not to be despised. Paul, for example, expressed his eagerness to preach the gospel (Romans 1:15, τὸ κατ' ἐμὲ πρόθυμον καὶ ὑμῖν ... εὐαγγελίσασθαι). Nevertheless, enthusiasm can be impetuous and ignorant in a foolish and unconverted, or even in an unsanctified and yet converted life. This can be, and often is a problem for Christians – unsanctified enthusiasm! Therefore, this qualification needs to be more carefully considered.

---

[201] There seems to be a growing tendency both in the pulpit and in the translating of scripture to replace the word 'fear' (φόβος) with euphemisms such as 'reverence' or 'respect'. This is troubling. These latter words imply that we are looking here at *the projection of our response in admiration or veneration to God's holiness as we acknowledge His perfections* and worship Him. This is commendable, but we flatter ourselves if we imagine that any reverence or respect we may have for God is unaffected by our sinfulness. Our worship itself, as with all our activities, needs forgiveness. Rather, fear is reflected in our anticipation of *the projection of God's response to us as He acknowledges our sin* and imperfections. Reverence anticipates no judgement or chastisement, but fear does. Or reverence has no accompanying sense of answerability, but fear does. Perhaps this modern tendency is the result of the resurgence of Pelagian and semi-Pelagian thinking and a renewed misguided belief in intrinsic human goodness. Or it may be because in our lust for freedom we have no appetite to serve a Master.

The words "work heartily" in this verse are more literally translated "work from the soul" (ἐκ ψυχῆς ἐργάζεσθε).[202] *The implication here is that whatever we do should be done in a manner that is not dictated solely by external demands, but is motivated primarily by a positive inner disposition.* The apostle is here applying the principle that we should not be "fashioned according to this world" – or external demands – but "transformed by the renewing of (our) mind" – or inner disposition (Romans 12:2).

Similarly, our Lord's greatest desire is that we love Him "from all (our) heart, and ... soul" (Mark 12:30). Therefore, John exhorts his readers saying, "Little children, let us not love in word, neither with the tongue; but in deed and in truth" (I John 3:18). What is required, whether of our work or our love, is a genuine correspondence between our attitude and our activities and speech – that is, without hypocrisy (James 3:17 et al.).

As Mark 12:30 (ἐξ ὅλης τῆς καρδίας σου καὶ ἐξ ὅλης τῆς ψυχῆς σου) suggests, there is a strong similarity – if not near identity – between the two phrases 'from the heart' and 'from the soul', both taking us into the very centre of our being, into our thoughts, emotions, and volition. At this point in Colossians we should remember that Paul only makes social demands after he has explained the moral implications of the gospel, as noted above. Therefore, he would not anticipate that anyone could truly serve their masters or their fellow Christians "from the soul" without putting on "a heart of compassion, kindness, humility, meekness" and "longsuffering" (3:12) – *both soul and heart*. But the reality of these gracious characteristics will completely elude us if we do not take seriously the biblical instructions to "love the Lord (our) God with all (our) hearts" (Matthew 22:37), and to perfect "holiness in the fear of God" (II Corinthians 7:1). They will simply be reduced to vacuous words in our religious vocabulary.

We should serve, then, not with resentment or begrudgingly, and always without superficiality and dissimulation, being

---

[202] The word "soul" is polysemic, having different nuances in the New Testament. It may, for example, refer to life itself that is lost at death (Romans 11:3, I John 3:16, "life"); or metonomically to people (Acts 3:23, as in English, 'few souls were saved'); or to that component of our humanity that survives death and awaits the resurrection of the body (I Peter 4:19, Revelation 6:9). Then it may also refer to that point of origin in us of our desires (Luke 12:19) and our emotions (Matthew 26:38, Acts 14:2, "embittered their minds") – and more.

driven primarily by godliness of character, and despite the distractions of a worldly environment. Or, as the apostle writes elsewhere, we should "do all things without murmurings and disputings, that (we) may be blameless and harmless, children of God, without blemish in the midst of a crooked and perverse generation, among whom (we) are to be seen as lights in the world" (Philippians 2:14-15).

- *If we do not live "heartily, as unto the Lord", then our relationship with Him will be perfunctory.*

3. Having "a Master in heaven".

Living in the knowledge that we have "a Master in heaven" (4:1) ought to be an entrenched attitude in the soul of every believer. We became Christians when *we called* "upon the name of the Lord" (Romans 10:13) – that is, called upon Him whom we recognized and acknowledged as our Lord – and when *we were called* by Him "to be saints" (I Corinthians 1:2) – that is, called into the service of God. There are serious and abiding implications in this relationship. We cannot call upon Him as our Lord to become a Christian and then continue in neglect of His lordship, for this would be to repudiate the responsibility to live as "saints", God's holy people.

Lest we miss the force of Paul's meaning we must note that the word 'master' or 'masters' in 4:1 – so translated here because it is used in the master/slave context the apostle has in mind – is the word "lord" (κύριος), the same word that is used frequently in the scriptures of God and of Christ, and in reference to their divine sovereignty. And as we have just considered, we are required to do everything "heartily as unto" *this* "Lord" (3:23).

I have suggested above that modern man desires unfettered freedom, and that this libertine passion is probably the reason for his hostility against Christianity, which, he perceives, denies him the autonomy he craves.[203] He deceives himself in his reveries about the possibility of fulfilling his ambition in this regard, but he is correct in his understanding that Christianity will not provide the kind of unconditional freedom he demands. Paul explains in some detail that conversion to Christ is – rightly understood – not an escape from bondage

---

[203] See #3.5, MORAL PRINCIPLE AND THE MODERN AGE.

into absolute freedom, but the escape from the tyrant sin into the service of benevolent righteousness; the only alternative we have to the bondage of evil is to "become slaves of God" (Romans 6:17-22).[204]

The incomparable blessing in being a Christian is that we now have an incomparable Master of infinite wisdom, justice, mercy, and love. To serve Him is perfect freedom.

We must remember that we were "bought with a price" – that is, like a slave, we are owned by our Master – therefore, we are to "glorify God in (our) body" (I Corinthians 6:20) and not become "the slaves of men" (I Corinthians 7:23). In this sense, we cannot serve two masters (Matthew 6:24, but cf. #3.5.3.3.1.). So, the apostles unashamedly introduced themselves as the "slaves of Christ" (Romans 1:1, Philippians 1:1, Titus 1:1, James 1:1, II Peter 1:1).

Of course, we love God as our Father, because He has adopted us into his family (Galatians 4:5); but we also serve Him as Lord, because He has "translated us into the Kingdom" of His Son (1:13). And we love to serve Him!

- *If we do not live as having "a Master in heaven", then our relationship with Him will be sycophantic.*

NOTE: The development of Paul's thinking is integrated, sequential, and profound:

If we have been "buried with Him in baptism" and "raised with Him through faith in the working of God" (2:12), *we are redeemed* to "walk in Him" (2:6), following the philosophy that is "after Christ" (2:8).

Then, if we "seek the things that are above, where Christ is seated on the right hand of God" (3:1), and "set our minds on the things that are above" (3:2), *we are intelligently positioned* to live as Christians.

Further, if we put off "anger, wrath, malice, blasphemy, shameful speaking" (3:8) and the like, and put on "a heart of compassion, kindness, humility, meekness, longsuffering" (3:12) and such things, then *we are morally prepared* to live as Christians.

Then, when we are so redeemed, so positioned, and so prepared, and only then, will we begin to "do all in the name of the Lord Jesus" (3:17), and our present life in human society will be converted to the holy ways of Christ. But there is a continuum here that requires progressive and comprehensive maturation.

---

[204] The word translated "servant" in Romans 6:17-22 is the same word "slave" (δοῦλος), which is also used in Colossians 3:22-4:1.

And all this necessitates serious application, and to this end, Paul provides the following instructions for Christian life in community.

3.5.3. Specific Considerations

All that we have considered above concerning objective standards and subjective disposition makes it abundantly clear that God desires our approach to social behaviour to be always altruistic, never egocentric – always motivated by a genuine concern for the well-being of the other person, and with the preparedness to be self-effacing and self-sacrificing. This is, I suggest, the outworking of "the love … to all the saints" (1:4) the apostle mentioned in his initial thanksgiving for the good report he had received about the Colossian believers. The intelligent willingness to do what is best for the other person – without any demand for or expectation of a recompense or reciprocation – is the strong distinctive of Christian love. It is the inevitable, distinguishing characteristic of those who "put on … above all … love, which is the bond of perfectness" (3:12, 14).

But this is not, as some suppose, a love that overrides moral considerations, much less a driving emotion that legitimizes whatever behaviour it demands. It needs to be understood within the entire biblical context, and, in particular, to be seen epitomized in the life of Jesus Christ, in whom God "commends His love towards us" (Romans 5:8). In this "we know love", John explained, "because He lay down His life for us: and we ought to lay down our lives for the brethren" (I John 3:16). To gain an adequate appreciation of the love God requires of us, we should consider Jesus Christ – and seek to emulate His love. And only when we love God with all our heart, and soul, and mind, will we be able to love our neighbour as ourselves virtuously (Matthew 22:37-39). Our love for Him is paramount, and prerequisite if we are to love others as is appropriate for His followers. In fact, the evidence that we are Christ's disciples is our "love one to another" (John 13:35).

Now, because we should live and love in reference to both God's law and God's character,[205] we must never prescind this primary, eternal, 'personal' factor – the holiness of God and our communion with Him – from our daily moral and social considerations. *It is with God we must reckon when we reckon with our neighbour!*

We cannot escape this reckoning with God, because all people, whether they realize it or not, have a personal relationship with God that is the central dynamic that determines the way they live. They may consider or ignore Him, love or loathe Him, obey or disobey Him, receive or resist His presence, seek His face or

---

[205] See above, 1. Objective standards.

turn their backs, relate to His sovereignty or rebel against His lordship, live for His glory or for their own. But none can escape the fact that "in Him we live, and move, and have our being" (Acts 17:28, cf. Colossians 1:17). A man's relationship with God may be that of an alien and enemy (1:21), but it is a personal relationship nonetheless. But if he is a Christian, he will enjoy the relationship as a son and servant, to love and to fear.[206] And whether he recognizes it or not, whatever the relationship might be it has an immediate influence upon him and eternal consequences for him. Living in alienation from God is as negatively efficient, as living in reconciliation with Him is positively so.

We believe that anyone who thinks that he is living in what is ultimately a totally impersonal universe of nothing but force and matter is self-deluded. He has, as Paul wrote, "suppressed the truth in unrighteousness" (Romans 1:18). In contrast, believing in divine creation, we understand that at the back of all things and the origin of them is the intensely personal presence of God.

Moreover, behind all things and giving meaning to all human life is that God in whose image we are created, and who eternally exists in three persons, Father, Son, and Holy Spirit. In Him, then, interpersonal relationships are eternal, and the most foundational and important aspect of all reality. Believing this, as Christians do, is to understand that personal existence, with interaction between persons, is the ultimate significance of all being and the source of the greatest of all values and satisfaction. Therefore, all interpersonal relationships, even the temporal associations between people on earth who were designed to reflect the likeness of God, are meaningful, and important, and ought to be guarded, preserved, refined, enriched, and, when necessary, redeemed and reconciled.

To engage in interpersonal relationships in genuine love and holiness is perhaps the most eloquent manner in which we might manifest our creation in the image of God.

In a sense, then, Christian sociology is unique because it is ultimately rooted in the biblical doctrine of the Trinity.[207] Moreover, reckoning with the fact that man is created in the image of God, and acknowledging that in Him "we live, and move,

---

[206] It is wrong to tell the non-Christian that what he needs is a 'relationship with God', as seems to be an increasingly common approach to evangelism. The fact is that he is in the inadequate situation in which he finds himself because he already has a relationship with God – a seriously defective and dangerous relationship! What he needs is reconciliation in his relationship with God.

[207] Those who deny the orthodox, biblical doctrine of the Trinity undermine all Christian beliefs, inevitably subvert the value of human being, necessarily embrace an anthropocentric sociology, adopt a different value system, and are committed to an entirely different philosophy of God and reality.

and have our being" (Acts 17:28), the Christian sociologist can conceive of no truly functional and viable society that is not consciously theocentric. Therefore, there is always a redemptive element is Christian sociological theory and practice.[208]

Therefore, Paul does not hesitate to introduce this eternal 'personal' factor into his consideration of all our social relationships, whether as wives and husbands, children and parents, or servants and masters – or any other. If we are to follow his instructions, we must reckon with the importance of the presence of a personal God in all our communal associations. If we do not, then we will be greatly impoverished and our interpersonal bonds will be seriously eroded. In the final analysis, people are estranged from each other because of their alienation from God (see Romans 1:28ff.). For this reason, Christian social order finds its foundations in both divine creation *and* divine redemption, and asks what kind of people were we designed to be and how we can achieve the "good works which God has prepared that we should walk in them" (Ephesians 2:10).[209]

Our individual, personal relationship with God will determine, one way or another, the quality of the relationships we have with other people in the human community. Therefore, for example, the apostle can write: "As the church is subject to Christ, so let the wives also be to their husbands"; and "Husbands, love your wives, even as Christ also loved the church, and gave himself up for it" (Ephesians 5:24-25). If husband and wife would know what is required of them in their union, then each must understand the redeemed union they have with God in His church. The less they value the latter, the less they will treasure the former. And, *inter alia*, they should value their marriage as a manifestation, or an embodiment in time of the eternal communion the Lord has determined for His people among themselves and with Him, which is to be perfected when they are presented "holy and without blemish and unreproveable in His sight" (1:22, cf. Revelation 19:6-9). *If the church fails, marriage is imperilled.*

The true paradigm, then, for Christian marriage – in fact, according to biblical principles, for every marriage – is the relationship between Christ and His people. There is, in other words, a sublime interpersonal relationship *beyond marriage* that defines the virtuous relationship that should exist *within marriage*. In

---

[208] And it is this redemptive element that makes the practice of Christian sociology unacceptable in modern, secular societies.

[209] Such a definition of sociology is abhorrent to most modern thinkers who deny that man is anything other than what he wants to make of himself, and that society must be manipulated to achieve humanistic, ideological aspirations. They may break free from the divine order, but in doing so they take the appalling risk of falling into bondage in their own!

Christian wedlock, we should aspire to this divine criterion, and not to variant, contemporary, cultural patterns and values.

And the same basic principles apply to Christian parent/child and master/servant associations also, because in both there is a pertinent divine order, as the apostle explains.

◆

With all these things in mind, we must now consider Paul's advice to his Christian readers concerning their involvement in the demanding associations of human society. They are to implement their faith in all the affairs of everyday life that they might maintain the relevant moral values in marriage, family, and work, and do "all in the name of the Lord Jesus" (3:17).

And in doing so they will be eloquently expressing their beliefs – with and without verbal explanation – in the general community, and this, as I suggest below (#3.6.), is the most fundamental context of the church's responsibility to evangelize and make Christ known to the world.

The most expressive proclamation of the gospel must emanate from and be seen to be significant within the ordinary concourse of daily life, within the structures of God's creation – not in some mystical or ritualistic deracination.

3.5.3.1. WIVES AND HUSBANDS (3:18-19)

Paul wrote at some length in Ephesians 5:22-33 concerning Christian marriage, explaining the nature of this relationship in reference to the union between Christ and the church. His account of the matter there is most profound, and this suggests that we should not take his brief comments here in Colossians too lightly.

I shall not compare the two passages except to point out that they both require wives to *submit* to their husbands, and husbands to *love* their wives; and to remark that Paul in Ephesians make these requirements formidable – wives are to be subject to their "husbands, as unto the Lord ... in everything", and husbands are to "love their wives as Christ loved the church and gave Himself up for it" (Ephesians 5:22-25). In fact, these stipulations are so daunting that we will either ignore them, or we must make a serious attempt to understand what the apostle means and the implications of his instructions. In effect, he is explaining that in marriage – the most intimate and sensitive of all interpersonal human relationships – Christ should "have the pre-eminence" (1:18). Christians should commit themselves to marriage according to His covenant constraints and subject to His lordship.

However, with Ephesians in the background, I shall limit my comments here to Paul's succinct remarks in Colossian 3:18-19, where there are *two unequivocal imperatives, or responsibilities*:[210]

> The imperative addressed to wives that they "be in subjection to (their) husbands", and this is qualified by the following words, "as is fitting/proper in the Lord" (3:18).
> The imperative addressed to husbands that they "love (their) wives", and this is qualified by the following words, "and be not bitter against them" (3:19).

> These are *respective responsibilities* that should be intelligently and gladly undertaken by men and women when they enter into the covenant of marriage, especially if they are professing Christians who should do so thoughtfully and willingly.
> They are *distinctive responsibilities* as nowhere in the New Testament are husbands asked to submit to their wives, or are women required to love their husbands.[211]
> They are *defining responsibilities* that establish a marriage, grounding it upon God-given principles, to ensure that it has strength and stability to survive as a safe and lifelong context for consortium, intimacy, passion, and mutual support. *And this is a privileged relationship.*

Needless to say, this is a very traditional view of marriage – at least in Western cultures – but it is being increasingly impugned and rejected in modern times. The most plausible – although specious – argument against it arises, perhaps,

---

[210] They are unequivocal, despite the pussyfooting around of many who would deconstruct Paul's words, equivocate about cultural relativity, mussitate over exegetical minutiae, and finally yield to modern – or postmodern – vacuities. Anything to assert their human independence of divine sovereignty!

[211] Strictly speaking, Titus 2:4 is no exception. Whenever men are commanded to love their wives the Greek word *agapao* (ἀγαπάω) is used, but here in Titus Paul uses the compound word *philandros* (φίλανδρος). The latter has the somewhat weaker meaning of 'being companionable' or 'showing affection', lacking the notion of self-sacrifice that the former gained in its Christian usage (cf. John 3:16, I John 3:16). This does not mean that women should not love (*agapao*) their husbands, because all Christians are so to love their fellow Christians – and their neighbours, and even their enemies (John 13:34, Matthew 5:44). However, what Paul is doing in Colossians 3:18-19 is to specify the particular elements that constitute the distinctive relationship that should be sustained between husband and wife, and what is required of each in a godly, Christian marriage.

from the misunderstanding that subordination implies inferiority, and to suggest that for someone to take a subordinate position is demeaning. Understandably, women who have been influenced by modern thinking in this regard may well be indignant.

Here is an example of the problems that arise when we allow ourselves to be influenced by the "philosophy and vain deceit, after the traditions of men ... and not after Christ" (2:8). Paul explains that the wife's subjection to her husband is "proper in the Lord", or the fitting manner for any married woman to behave if she has "received Christ Jesus as Lord" and, as all believers should, seeks to "walk in Him" (2:6). The context of her union with Christ should moderate her union with her husband.

Her subordination is not, and ought not to be imposed upon her by either society or her husband, for it is required by a divine, not a human ordinance. *It is something that in obedience to Christ she offers to her husband – not something that her husband is entitled to demand from her!*

Then, no one who rightly understands the biblical doctrine of the Trinity could ever think that subordination necessarily implies inferiority. In that God "sent ... His Son into the world" (John 3:17) and that He came to "accomplish the works" the Father gave Him "to do" (John 17:4), we must understand that within the Godhead the Son is subordinate to the Father in the sense that He obeys the Father's authority. Nevertheless, as the Father and the Son are both coequally God, we must not entertain any thoughts about the Son being in any way inferior.[212]

Similarly, because both men and women are coequally created in the image of God (Genesis 1:27) we must insist that neither is inferior to the other. But this evidently does not imply that God cannot require one to be subordinate to the other – which He does (I Timothy 2:11-12) – without derogation or deprivation. *The equality is in the image, or the creation of God; the relationship is in the economy, or the governance of God.*

In Ephesians 5:25 Paul requires that the husband's love for his wife be sacrificial – as "Christ ... gave Himself up for" the church. Here in the Colossian letter, his concern is that the husband's love should be unalloyed, or, in other words, that he be "not bitter against" her. These two correlate – the man who will sacrifice himself

---

[212] This – the doctrine of the Trinity – is a complicated and technical subject of theological debate, and much disputed. Nevertheless, it is relevant for the biblical doctrine of marriage and needs the most careful consideration in this matter. If our philosophy is to be genuinely "after Christ", then it must be "after" the biblical Christ of the biblical Trinity.

for his wife will never feel or act in bitterness towards her. We cannot countenance the idea that there was bitterness in our Lord's heart when He sacrificed Himself for His people (Romans 5:8).[213]

However, this requirement in Christian marriage, it seems, is also considered to be obsolete traditionalism by many contemporary thinkers, following the "philosophy and vain deceit ... of men" (2:8). As a result, if there is cause for bitterness or resentment in the relationship this is too frequently considered grounds for divorce or justification for adultery. Surely, it is claimed, the man marries primarily for his own fulfilment, not to sacrifice himself!

But his self-sacrificing love is not, and ought not to be imposed upon a man by either society or his wife, for it is required by a divine, not a human ordinance. *It is something that in obedience to Christ he offers to his wife – not something that his wife is entitled to demand from him!*

And all this apostolic advice to both wives and husbands should, in theory, be no problem for the serious and devout Christian, if he or she has "put away ... anger, wrath, (and) malice" and has "put on the new man, which is being renewed ... after the image" of God (3:10) and is concerned to "put on ... a heart of compassion, kindness, humility, meekness" and "longsuffering" (3:12). And elsewhere Paul requires that "all bitterness ... be put away" and that we be "kind to one another, tenderhearted, forgiving ... even as God also in Christ forgave" us (Ephesians 4:31-32).

I am tempted to add to these brief comments and write more about Christian marriage, it being a matter that is ferociously disputed in our times, both inside and outside the church. It is now at the centre of an unprecedented social and sexual revolution. However, these remarks must suffice, as my primary purpose is only to indicate what I believe are the implications of the words in 3:18-19, and to point to the demands these may make upon us.

However, I might add that as contemporary forms of the "philosophy and vain deceit, after the tradition of men" (2:8) are so radically changing the structures and mores of modern society, then it is important for us – if we would live for the glory of God – that we allow the "philosophy ... after Christ" to determine the structures and mores of Christian society, including marriage. If we do not,

---

[213] I am not comfortable with the translation "be not harsh with them", instead of "be not bitter against them" in 3:19. The advice given to wives and husbands here mainly concerns their *attitudes* towards each other, and not their *behaviour* towards each other. And "be not harsh" implies a behavioural, not an attitudinal response.

then we will cease to be "the light of the world" – and our witness on earth will be muted.

The church must be courageous enough to remain faithful to the Lord and to His law. And individual Christians need to be courageous enough, *inter alia*, to honour Him and His principles in their marriages, that their union might generate and radiate true light in the growing darkness.

Nevertheless, being the morally inadequate and egocentric people that we are, neither subordination nor self-sacrifice is easy for us. But, as suggested above, we have the grace of God in Christ to enable us to pursue personal and communal holiness that we might increasingly live for His glory.

The challenge is that we ascertain from scripture the required quality and demands of godly marriage, and that we find in Christ the assistance we need to order our lives accordingly. And at best we will but approximate to the ideal, so we should proceed in marriage with humility, grace, repentance, and forgiveness.

3.5.3.2. PARENT AND CHILD (3:20-21)

Paul, in Ephesians 6:1-4, also penned advice concerning the parent/child relationship in the family. His account of the matter there, as with his remarks about marriage, is somewhat more extensive than we find here in Colossians. But it is particularly interesting that in the former he grounds his instructions upon the law found in the Ten Commandments (Exodus 20:12). Evidently, then, he was not intending merely to give his personal opinion, or to request that his readers be sensitive to contemporary values, but that he was stating what he believed to be an unchangeable, divine requirement, proclaimed from the fire of Mount Sinai. Apostolic teaching was always based upon and compatible with the Old Testament scriptures.

Again, I shall not compare the two passages except to point out that they both require children *to obey* their fathers, and fathers *not to disturb*[214] their children. Nevertheless, I think it helpful to give some consideration below to the apostle's remarks in Ephesians advising fathers to "nurture" their children "in the discipline and instruction of the Lord", whereas here in Colossians he only requires that the young be not "discouraged".[215]

---

[214] I tentatively suggest 'disturb' as a word that captures Paul's concern in both Ephesians and Colossians, where two different words are used (παροργίζω and ἐρεθίζω).
[215] And from this we might anticipate that the young are far less likely to be "discouraged" if they are nurtured "in the discipline and instruction of the Lord".

However, with Ephesians in the background, I shall limit my comments here mainly to Paul's succinct remarks in Colossian 3:20-21, where there are *two unequivocal imperatives, or responsibilities*:

> The imperative addressed to children that they "obey (their) parents in all things", and this is qualified by the following words, "for this is well-pleasing in the Lord" (3:20).
>
> The imperative addressed to fathers that they "provoke/disturb not (their) children", and this is qualified by the following words, "that they be not discouraged" (3:21).

> These are *respective responsibilities* that should be intelligently and gladly undertaken by parent and child within the family, especially if they are professing Christians who should do so thoughtfully and willingly.
>
> They are *distinctive responsibilities* as nowhere in the New Testament – no doubt unexpectedly! – are parents asked to obey their children.
>
> They are *defining responsibilities* that establish the family, grounding it upon God-given principles, to ensure that it has strength and stability to survive as a safe and lifelong context for nurturing, encouraging, companionship, trust, and mutual support. *And this is a privileged relationship.*

Again, it seems to me that although this is a very traditional view of family – or perhaps because it is! – it is being challenged, the relationship increasingly attenuated, and familial bonds seriously eroded.

As marriage is depreciated, and sometimes even disdained, it is no longer generally considered prerequisite for sexual intercourse or binding for life, and is with growing frequency terminated in divorce. Therefore, the home has become increasingly problematic, and children traumatized by the separation of their parents. This is generating an environment that inevitably reduces the respect that children have for their parents, and diminishes the commitment parents have to their children. It is a dismal occurrence in a miserable community when individuals can abandon spouse and child in pursuit of a paramour or a profession without their reputation being impugned or anyone being particularly concerned. We have become inured to such deplorable behaviour.

Thankfully, because of the common grace of God there are still many good and well-integrated families in our community and the natural love between parent and child is commonly found among us. For this we should be most thankful, for what kind of society would we have if it were to disappear completely? But because many are being led astray by today's "philosophy and vain deceit, after the traditions of men" (2:8), the principles and moral values that are necessary to sustain the traditional Christian home are being subverted, and children dissuaded from honouring their parents.

So as with Christian marriage, a Christian family, wherein parents and children relate to each other in a godly manner, will stand as a source of and witness to the light, love, and truth of God in this darkening world.

And surely it is the responsibility of believing parents to encourage – indeed, to invite – their children to join with them to establish their home for the glory of God and in obedience to Christ.

Paul requires children to obey their parents in everything. There is, as far as I can discern, no time limit set to the child's obligation to do this. It is not restricted to the infant or the youth, but should be a lifelong commitment (see I Timothy 5:4). However, the character of the relationship and the expressions of obedience will change with maturation, while the responsibility remains. Thankfully, most people seem to sense and accept this requirement instinctively, which does not surprise any who believe we were created in the image of God. Nevertheless, the human heart is soon hardened, we become preoccupied with our own interests, and we easily grow neglectful and begrudging.

To respond willingly to this familial requirement, the child must obviously be of sufficient maturity to understand its implications. Hopefully, as he develops he will appreciate that the primary motivation for him to obey his parents is that it is "well-pleasing in the Lord" (3:20, εὐάρεστόν ἐστιν ἐν κυρίῳ).[216] It is important, then, for the parents to pray for their children even as Paul prayed for the Colossian Christians, "that (they) might be filled with the knowledge of (God's) will in all spiritual wisdom and understanding, to walk worthily of the Lord, unto all pleasing" (1:10, εἰς πᾶσαν ἀρεσκείαν).

But it is important that parents do more than pray for their children that they might mature in a godly fashion. If they are to be "filled with the knowledge of (God's) will in all spiritual wisdom and understanding" it is necessary that their fathers "nurture them in the discipline and instruction of the Lord" (Ephesians 6:4, ἐκτρέφετε αὐτὰ ἐν παιδείᾳ καὶ νουθεσίᾳ κυρίου). It is an ancient requirement of the Judeo-Christian religion that those who "love the Lord" both keep the

---

[216] That is, in other words, because "this is right" (Ephesians 6:1).

commandments of God, and that they also "teach them diligently to (their) children, and shall talk of them when (they) sit in (their) house, and when (they) walk in the way" (Deuteronomy 6:4-9). Parents, in other words, are required to generate a godly atmosphere in and around the home in which they raise their children, living by and articulating the Word of God.

It may help us to understand Paul's exhortation here if we consider the following:

- **First**, although children are to obey their "parents" – both father and mother – Paul makes the father primarily responsible for the "nurture" of the children "in the discipline and instruction of the Lord".

  It is evident – at least from a Christian perspective[217] – that both father and mother are required for the upbringing of the child and both are to be involved in creating and sustaining a godly atmosphere for their family. However, it is a corollary of Paul's ruling that wives be in subjection to their husbands (3:18) that the father has authority in the household. Therefore, if the child is to discover the Christian principles of love, trust, and obedience, which believing parents hope their children will eventually direct to the Lord Himself, these responses must first – and best – be seen in the appropriate relationship between father and mother, and be learned in a loving relationship with the father in a godly home.

  I suggest that we first learn instinctively to love and trust in our infancy within the family, but if we are not then given the opportunity to do so it becomes a much harder lesson to learn later in life – or perhaps never truly learned at all. Moreover, if the father gives his child no substantial reason to love and trust him, being no example of the lovable and the trustworthy, where then will the child discover what it means to love and trust our heavenly Father?

  The father should accept this authority in fear and trembling, for it is a great responsibility given to him by God. If he would have his children learn to address God in prayer as "Our Father" (Matthew 6:9) with understanding and devotion, then he must seek by grace to present a noble and sanctified image of fatherhood to his family.

- **Second**, in exercising this authority, the fathers must take the greatest care not to "disturb" their children (3:21, μὴ ἐρεθίζετε τὰ τέκνα).

---

[217] The modern proponents of 'gender fluidity' and 'marriage equality' – following "the wisdom and vain deceit" of the contemporary world – necessarily deny this. In debating this matter, we need to be aware of the conflicting presuppositions upon which opinions are being founded. And, as Christians, we should approach this and all present social disagreements with understanding and compassion.

In this matter, Paul expresses his concern by using two different words – *parorgizo* (παροργίζω) in Ephesians 6:4, and *erethizo* (ἐρεθίζω) in Colossians 3:21. The difference is perhaps that the first implies 'to anger' and the second 'to frustrate'. The latter may be used in a good sense, 'to stimulate', as in II Corinthians 9:2, so possibly it suggests here the danger of asking or expecting too much of the child, leaving him unfulfilled or embittered.

The objective is to "nurture them in the discipline and instruction of the Lord" (Ephesians 6:4) in such a manner that the children are not "discouraged" or "disheartened" (Colossians 3:21, ἵνα μὴ ἀθυμῶσιν). The father must be sensitive enough to recognize when his children are being discouraged, and may God forbid that they should ever be driven to lose heart. Permanent, personal damage might be done to the child.

This is not to deny that God can – and does – graciously repair the damage done by clumsy parenting. Neither would I imply that we can be immaculate role models for our children, for we are all diminished by the fall. Nevertheless, we must remember that it is only within the human community – the community of those who were originally created in the image of God – that we find the structures and experiences that give us the values and the vocabulary, the intellectual architecture, that enable us to think and to talk about the life we live – and here in particular, about a life of love and trust. We ought, then, to provide our children with the most transparent display and the most articulate explanation of these things – with the least possible hypocrisy, and with genuine repentance and apology when we fail.

- **Third**, Paul obviously believed that "the discipline and instruction of the Lord" (Ephesians 6:4, "chastening and admonition" in KJV), administered by the father, need not provoke anger and frustration, or be discouraging. It ought to impart principles and values that engender joy, security, and satisfaction.

In this, he is assuming that the father will approach this God-given task with the appropriate disposition. This father is the husband who will love his wife without bitterness, and sacrifice himself for her, as we have seen above. Such a man will have heeded Paul's advice to put on "a heart of compassion, kindness, humility, meekness" and "longsuffering" (3:12), and these attitudes will condition his relationships with all people, and especially with his children. Love, compassion, and the like do not discriminate. They are instilled by the grace of God into the very character of His people, moderating their every thought and action. Therefore, the father, who would instruct his children without frustrating them, must concern himself with the pursuit of his own true, personal godliness. It is critically important that he be such a man in reference to his own children, for whom he has particular responsibility.

But it is also important that this caring father understands what "the discipline and instruction of the Lord" are (Ephesians 6:4, ἐν παιδείᾳ καὶ νουθεσίᾳ κυρίου), making no assumptions or merely following the cultural norms or the sophisticated techniques of secular society. The added words "of the Lord" – one word in the original language – are, I suggest, most significant. They require that we practise only the discipline and instruction that are required by God and are consistent with His character.[218] Here again, we must see the importance of not following the philosophy of this world, but the philosophy that is "after Christ" (2:8) – and that we learn to distinguish between the two, for our children's sake.

The word "discipline" (παιδεία, and the corresponding verb παιδεύω) has the basic meaning of 'raising a child', training in *the practice of life* – and for us, the practice that is compatible with Christian beliefs and congenial in the Christian community.[219]

We might note three verses in particular where this word, "discipline" or "training", is used. We read that Pharaoh's daughter trained the child Moses "in all the wisdom of the Egyptians" (Acts 7:21-22). Then, the young apostle Paul, before his conversion, was "trained according to the strict manner of the law of the (Old Testament) fathers" (Acts 22:3). In both these situations, the child was being prepared to behave in a fashion acceptable in the respective social situations in which they were nurtured. In contrast, the grace of God in the gospel came "training us, to the intent that denying ungodliness and worldly lusts, we should live soberly, and righteously, and godly in this present world" (Titus 2:12). Here we have three different situations, and three very different objectives in view – to train a child for life in a pagan world, a life under the law, or a life in the redeeming grace of God.

The last of these three verses provides the paradigm for the Christian father who would rightly discipline his children. He must warn them of the moral weaknesses – the ungodliness and lusts – that inhabit their own souls, and train them in sobriety, righteousness, and godliness

---

[218] See #3.5.2., Third, 2. Subjective disposition.

[219] The strength of this word varies with its use. Hence, in Luke 23:16 – 'chastise' or 'punish' – it no doubt refers to punitive flogging. In contrast, it is used in Hebrews 12:10 of our heavenly Father's gracious 'chastening' of His children to promote their holiness.

that they might be prepared to live for the glory of God in the evil environment of this fallen world.[220]

The word "instruction" (νουθεσία, and the corresponding verb νουθετέω) has the basic meaning of 'putting in mind', directing in *sound thinking* – and for us, the thinking that is compatible with Christian beliefs and congenial in the Christian community. As it is used in the New Testament it also has the significance of admonishing or warning (see I Corinthians 4:14, I Thessalonians 4:14).

And this note of warning is not surprising, as the Bible recognizes that life presents us with many intellectual and moral pitfalls. Here in Colossians this instruction or admonition is associated with "teaching" (1:28, 3:16). It seems inevitable that if we are to teach truth we must concurrently warn about error, and when we instruct in what is morally good we must concurrently alert to the dangers of evil. But we cannot sincerely or convincingly instruct our children in godliness if we ourselves deny fealty to the Christ of all knowledge and holiness.

As intimidating as this task may be for the caring and devoted father, he is not without support – or at least he ought not be! – within the Christian community. As we have already seen, the apostle considered it his responsibility to admonish and teach "every man in all wisdom" (1:28, #2.1.4., Second), and congregational members are to teach and admonish "one another" (3:16, #3.4.2.2.2.). We might conclude from this that whether in leadership or simply in membership, every believer in the church is to contribute to the didactic, admonitory environment that encourages intelligent and ethical maturation. In this atmosphere, fathers also should be encouraged and enabled to encourage and enable the child.

By coupling these two words, "discipline and instruction" (Ephesians 6:4), Paul seems to be suggesting that the father's responsibility is not simply to train his children in the *way* they should live, but also to explain to them *why* they should so live. In the appropriate manner and measured to their ability, he should give them good reason for pursuing a life that is "well-pleasing in the Lord" (3:20). In other words, he should impart to them sufficient Christian comprehension that they might continue in the faith after he is no longer by their side to guide them. This is simply an extension of the apostle's concern that all the members of the Christian community be "filled with the

---

[220] The 'handbook' best suited to guide the father in this task, enabling him to effectively give training to his children, is the Bible (II Timothy 3:16-17).

knowledge of His will in all spiritual wisdom and understanding" (1:9), and that they teach and admonish one another (3:16).

This responsibility for the Christian nurture of their children – the discipline and instruction that is necessary for the young to be guided, according to the philosophy after Christ, to think and act Christianly – presents the parents with a most challenging task. In this perhaps more than in anything else, we must acknowledge, as Paul did, that we can only admonish and teach as we ought "according to (God's) working, which works in" us (1:28-29). We are never sufficient in ourselves (II Corinthians 3:5).

We should constantly seek the grace of God in this matter for at least two reasons: first, we ourselves also need constant "teaching and admonishing" (3:16), so we should invite our children to learn with us; and second, we live in a world that is determined to conform our children to the thinking and acting that is congenial to its ideology and secular values, so we should stand with and guide them in all their learning. We have, then, a problem with our environment and with ourselves – so the proper contextualizing and the true moderation of our own lives are essential. The home we establish as believing parents, the cognitive content of our conversation with our children, and the moral principles by which we conduct our own lives provide – for better or worse – the primary context in which our children are exposed to Christ and the gospel.

The task is the more fraught with danger in that all parents desire their children to 'do well' in the community in which they live, and we applaud when they have good success in education, in sport, and in other social activities. And rightly contextualized, this is admirable – our sons and daughters need encouragement. But the obvious problem is that in doing so we must be careful to make clear to them the difference between human adulation and divine approval. It is vital, then, that we encourage our children to join us in setting their "mind on the things that are above, and not on the things that are upon the earth" (3:2).

Surely, we do not want our children to be taken captive by the "philosophy and vain deceit ... of men" (2:8)!

3.5.3.3. MASTER AND SERVANT (3:22-4:1)

Paul now addresses "slaves" (οἱ δοῦλοι) or, as this word is softened in different translations, "servants" or "bondservants". Some in the Colossian congregation may well have been slaves, as would have been common in most communities in those ancient days of the Roman Empire. Society was then composed of free men and those in bondage, and the apostle is concerned that every Christian should behave Christianly no matter what his social status may be.

This does not imply that Paul is condoning or sanctioning slavery as it was then practised, or that he is compromising with contemporary culture – far from it! – but only that he is giving advice within the realities of the flawed social order of his times and advising his readers accordingly. Christians often find themselves in difficult, corrupt, and unjust situations in which they – and others – suffer. They may well work and pray for improvement and the establishment of justice – indeed, they should – but in doing so they must maintain a witness to the supreme Lord whom they serve, always acting in a godly fashion, even when unjustly treated by their "masters according to the flesh" (3:22). This may require them to endure disadvantage graciously and without complaining, even as our Lord Himself suffered (I Peter 2:18-23).

The enslaved Christian may well seek freedom from his bondage, and if he has the opportunity he should take it if he can use it advantageously. But he should always remember that the "slave is the Lord's freeman" and the freeman "is the Lord's slave". He has been bought with a price – the death of Christ (I Peter 1:18-19) – so he should not, in this respect, consider himself to be the slave of any man (I Corinthians 7:21-23). And this implies that if a Christian is bound to an earthly master, he ought to serve him in the knowledge that his ultimate obligation is to serve his God. He should acknowledge the sovereignty of God who has placed him in the position in which he finds himself and he should act appropriately – behaving Christianly (see below).

◆

SLAVERY AND SERVITUDE

Here, perhaps it is pertinent for us to ask what our attitude, as Christians, should be towards slavery, which continues to be rampant in this world in various configurations. This is a question we do well to consider not only because of the problem itself but also because many non-Christians reject our faith – or more precisely, they reject the Bible, which is the authoritative basis for our faith – because of the references to and laws concerning slavery contained in the Old Testament. So, to avoid misunderstanding, we should be able to explain where we stand in this matter. Moreover, we need some basic knowledge of the relevant biblical teaching if we are to appreciate Paul's instructions here in Colossians and if we are to find in them any advice relevant to our own position in modern society.

The issue is particularly complicated, because slavery is generated in different circumstances, and appears in various forms. So, a few very brief, general comments about these may be helpful.

There is the slavery generated by the appalling barbarity of rapacious criminals who, for their own financial gain, forcibly kidnap others with the intent of selling them in the markets of human trafficking, depriving them of all freedom and protection. This chattel slavery is abhorrent to God and forbidden by the scriptures (Exodus 21:16, Deuteronomy 24:7, cf. Amos 1:6, 9). It was against this practice that William Wilberforce and members of the Clapham Sect fought persistently for decades until it was banned from the British Empire in 1833. And this they did because they were people of profound Christian conviction.

Then there is the slavery generated by war when people are taken captive in battle. This can result, and often has resulted, in appalling abuse and cruelty. As difficult as they are, we find laws in the Old Testament that regulated this situation (Deuteronomy 20:10-18). With this in mind, we might infer that there is a form of war slavery that in some circumstances, as ugly as they are, is almost inevitable in this present evil world, and we might well endorse it on occasions as a necessary practicality. But if we do, we should do so Christianly, insisting that protection, adequate care, and a measure of liberty are provided. For example, I once had a delightful German friend who was taken captive by allied forces early in the Second World War. He was shipped to North America where he was interned until the cessation of hostilities. He and others were then taken to England where for some time they were required to assist with the rebuilding of that war-torn country, working as labourers on the farms. He was, in effect, enslaved! Interestingly, although he was aching to be reunited with his wife and family in Germany, he told me that those days in England, thanks to the Christians in the community who befriended him, were among the happiest in his life. In other words, the rule of law and Christian conscience regulated his bondage in the most humane way possible. But here, of course, the whole question is complicated and very problematic.

The Mosaic Law also regulated the situation in which a man becomes poor and finds it necessary to sell himself into bondage to repay his debts (Leviticus 25:39ff, Exodus 21:2ff.). Such a person and his family were to be treated humanely, and his service was never to be enforced for longer than seven years. Such servitude is not, in principle, uncommon or necessarily unacceptable. Anyone who contracts himself to serve another in order to pay his debts is, in effect, bound by restrictive conditions. Or when a malefactor is required by a court of law to 'repay his debt to society' by a period of 'community service' he is in a sense – perhaps to overextend the use of the word – 'enslaved'. In such circumstances, some authority has – or assumes – the right to command the use of another's time, and to that extent to deny him liberty. Somewhat in this sense, then, the manager and the office boy working in a business together are both bonded.

Maybe this is at least enough to suggest that the Bible is not as naïve or barbaric in its references to slavery as some might think, and to indicate that there is no single, simple description of a master/servant relationship. However, not nearly enough has been said here to make a reasonable evaluation of the matter, nor is it my intention to do so as I restrict my comments to Paul's advice to the Colossians.

◆

Little of the above consideration of slavery and servitude, however, is directly relevant to the apostle's advice to the Colossians in this letter, wherein these matters are not discussed. Paul has something different in mind.

Although we must acknowledge the horror attending various forms of slavery, be it in sheer brutality or as the result of, say, unjust industrial laws (sweatshops and the like) – and as Christians we are morally obligated to do whatever we can to ameliorate these evil situations – we should perhaps recognize the legitimacy of some benign forms of indebted service. Such is the case, for example, when a man is conscripted to serve his country in the armed forces; or when an apprentice is indentured. Moreover, it is inevitable in this fallen world that Christians in various cultures and circumstances will find themselves in different kinds of servitude.

In fact, what the apostle does say here is relevant to us all, because the inescapable fact is that we will find ourselves at some point in our life bound to some authority that has a proprietary right to our time and service. There are situations in which we must respond in obedience to others. Indeed, when appropriate, it is our moral obligation to do so. Then, even in the most congenial and egalitarian situations, we are, as mentioned above, to "be servants one to another" (Galatians 5:13).

So, Paul's concern is that we, as Christians, know how to behave Christianly in such situations, whether we are either master or servant. We may work for change, but how should we deport ourselves in the interim?

We should note, as with his remarks concerning marriage and family, that Paul also wrote at some length about the relationship between servants and masters in Ephesians 6:5-9. And again, I shall not compare his instructions there with those we find in Colossians, except to point out that they are remarkably similar, both emphasizing that whether slave or master the Christian must above all else act at all times in obedience to Christ, the common Lord of all men.

However, with Ephesians in the background, I shall limit my comments here mainly to Paul's remarks in Colossian 3:20-21, where there are *two unequivocal imperatives, or responsibilities:*

> The imperative addressed to servants that they "obey in all things them that are (their) masters", and this is qualified by the following words, "knowing that from the Lord (they) shall receive the recompense" because they "serve the Lord Christ" (3:22, 24).
> The imperative addressed to masters that they "render unto (their) servants that which is just and equal", and this is qualified by the following words, "knowing that you also have a Master in heaven" (4:1).

> These are *respective responsibilities* that should be intelligently and gladly undertaken by master and servant, especially if they are professing Christians who should do so thoughtfully and willingly.
> They are *distinctive responsibilities* as the nature of the relationship itself imposes differing obligations.
> They are *defining responsibilities* that establish in society an order that regulates working relations for the effective functioning and security of the community. *And this is a privileged relationship.*

When we do find ourselves in a subordinate situation, by our own choice or by compulsion, it is vital that we remember and adhere to Paul's advice given to servants here in 3:20-25.

The correlative is that when we find ourselves in authority over another person, by our own choice or by compulsion, that we remember and adhere to Paul's advice given to masters in 4:1.

And it is worth considering that an individual Christian may be master in one situation and servant in another, and even concurrently, so he needs to be adept in both. In fact, I am tempted to suggest that only those who have learned how to be efficient and obedient servants have the prerequisite requirements to become godly masters – this principle being implicit in Colossians 4:1.

3.5.3.3.1. What, then is required of godly servants?

The servant should, together with all Christians, be cognizant of and responsive to all that we have considered above concerning objective standards and subjective disposition (See #3.5.2. Third, 1. & 2.). He is, in other words, to act according to the requirements of divine law as he intelligently pursues a life of godliness, and to do so within the context of the servant/master relationship in which he finds himself, no matter how adverse this might be. Only as he does so will he "adorn the doctrine of God, our Saviour, in all things" (Titus 2:10).[221] The reputation of the gospel of Christ is paramount.

In this, his behaviour should be rightly moderated.

But to do this confidently and effectively, the Christian must have adequate knowledge of and sufficient trust in God as He is revealed to us in the Bible – the God who has created all things and reconciles all things to Himself (1:16, 20). This is the God of whom we heard in "the word of the truth of the gospel", which assures us of "the hope which is laid up in heaven" for us (1:5). Or, as Paul writes elsewhere, this is the God who "works all things after the counsel of His own will" (Ephesians 1:11), thus guaranteeing that "all things work together for good" (Romans 8:28) for His own people.

In this, his thinking should be rightly contextualized.

If God were anything less than this almighty, providential Lord of the Bible – or if there were no God at all – we would be living in a world in which things happen that neither God nor man intended or controls, a world of chance and chaos. Then all events are merely accidental and can have no immediate significance or ultimate purpose. They can only be the product of meaningless confusion or of blind, impersonal fate. But such is the kind of world, in one form or another, which the pagan and atheist seem to prefer.

But things are very different from a Christian perspective. As perplexing as some situation or incident may be in human experience, in the world of an almighty and sovereign God it cannot be without meaning or utility. Therefore, there is no 'unredeemable' event, because God is able to reconcile *everything* unto Himself (1:20), and so bring it to its intended purpose. Moreover, we are assured that He

---

[221] Paul was similarly concerned for himself. Although being "in bonds" or "in prison" – perhaps more severely confined and restricted than a slave – he desired to make the truth about God and Christ clearly known, even in such inauspicious circumstances (4:2-4).

will direct the whole of His creation to its predetermined objective (Romans 8:20-21).

It is our confident belief in this almighty and sovereign God that makes it possible for us to accept whatever situation we are in, to trust that it is for our ultimate good and God's glory, to maintain our "hope in the gospel" (1:23), and to lay up "treasure in heaven" (Matthew 6:20).[222] In other words, we ought to recognize that our present circumstances are not accidental but providential, that they provide us with opportunity to do good and glorify God, and that they are not an end in themselves but the means to a far greater, eternal, and heavenly purpose (see II Corinthians 4:17).

Within this context, Christian servants should moderate their behaviour by obeying "in all things them that are (their) masters" (ὑπακούετε κατὰ πάντα τοῖς κατὰ σάρκα κυρίοις), always acting "in singleness of heart, fearing the Lord" (ἐν ἁπλότητι καρδίας φοβούμενοι τὸν κύριον, 3:22, #3.5.2., Fourth, 1.).

We have already considered the importance of godly fear in a believer's subjective disposition (#3.5.2., Third, 2.). But now Paul specifically links this godly fear with the Christian servant's obedience to his earthly master "in all things". *The fear of God facilitates and moderates our appropriate obedience to men.*

And this, it seems to me, imposes a complicated, twofold demand upon the servant, which reflects the apostle's prohibitive and affirmative moral principles (#3.4.). He sharply contrasts the attitude that is inappropriate – "not with eyeservice, as men-pleasers" – with the attitude that is appropriate in the Christian servant – "with singleness of heart, fearing the Lord" (3:22). The former, in the spirit of those who would follow the "philosophy and vain deceit" of men, is evidently anthropocentric; whereas the latter is clearly theocentric. The eyeservice is characteristic of men-pleasers, but the singleness of heart is characteristic of those who fear the Lord.[223]

So, I suggest two things:

---

[222] But it is obvious that this does not mean that we tolerate or condone evil, accept the decrepit conditions of sinful society, capitulate to the demands of the world, are passive in the midst of human suffering, or in any way compromise our moral standards. The purpose Paul has in mind here is that, knowing that we are where the Lord would have us be, we therein maintain the appropriate testimony to our beliefs.

[223] The "eyeservice", I suggest, is directed to men, hence anthropocentric; but the "singleness of heart" to the Lord, hence theocentric.

- **First**, concerning insincerity.

    If the Christian servant lacks true godliness he will *not* be well motivated to do the things that his earthly master requires of him when, and in the manner, that his heavenly Lord would desire.

    Therefore, he will be inclined to obey only "with eyeservice, as men-pleasers" (3:22, ἐν ὀφθαλμοδουλίᾳ ὡς ἀνθρωπάρεσκοι).

    The first of these two words, "eyeservice", seems to suggest action taken in a manner that attracts attention, to present a good appearance; or even, perhaps, dissimulation to conceal one's true motives; and all to avoid *the master's displeasure*.

    The second of these two words, "men-pleasers", seems to suggest action taken, perhaps in a sycophantic manner, granting the one served the satisfaction he desires; and, perhaps, all to gratify his own lusts, while pandering to *the master's pleasures*.

    Both words imply that the service given is disingenuous, devoid of sincere moral principle, and given primarily to gain advantage for oneself.

    Herein is duplicity or insincerity, which is to be forsworn.

- **Second**, concerning integrity.

    If the Christian servant has a measure of true godliness he will be well motivated to do the things his earthly master requires of him when, and in the manner his heavenly Lord would desire.

    Therefore, he will obey his Lord "in singleness of heart" (3:22, ἐν ἁπλότητι καρδίας). And this, I suggest, is the very opposite of "eyeservice, as men-pleasers", being the absence of duplicity.

    If he does so serve the Lord "in singleness of heart", then all the values of his godliness will become evident in the manner in which he works for his earthly master; there will be no compromise of moral principle or denial of faith. He who serves his Lord "in singleness of heart" will be neither dissimulative nor sycophantic.

    Herein is true integrity, which is to be embraced.

But here we are faced with a persistent problem that has always confronted Christians as they seek to live for God in a godless world, or as they serve God when under the dominion of a godless master. What are we to do when a choice must be made between obeying God or obeying man? We may readily agree with the apostles that "we must obey God rather than man" (Acts 5:29), but what does this require of us? And with this high – and perhaps perilous – ambition, how are we to make the best decision in any such moral dilemma?

We have already seen that Paul would have his Colossian readers set their "mind on the things that are above, not on the things that are upon the earth" (3:2). I suggested that this involves the reorientation of the mind and the embracing of a new set of values (#3.3.2., Third), and these provide us, as Christians, with a new pattern for our thinking (#3.4.1.1., Second.). There is potential in this to effectively re-moderate our lives.

Our Lord similarly advised His disciples not to lay up "treasures upon the earth", but to lay up "treasures in heaven" (Matthew 6:19-20). This involves precisely the same reassessment of our values as Paul requires in Colossians, and demands a courageous decision to live for the "things that are above", eschewing the merely materialistic benefits that this world offers and men covet. This is not to despise the created things of earth, but to realize that they are only of immediate, instrumental, and penultimate worth, and are not the source or the substance of eternal satisfaction. There are far greater things to be considered.

Then our Lord indicated that to make and to consistently adhere to such a decision is not at all easy. The problem is, He explained, that we should "lay up treasure in heaven" because "where your treasure is, there will be your heart also" (Matthew 6:21). If we make a wrong assessment of where the things of greatest value are to be found – as we often do – our hearts will be seriously led astray. We will then invest in the immediate, the frivolous, the evanescent, the vacuous, the vicious, and the vile – things that are ultimately worthless.

We must, therefore, *focus our minds*. Christ said it is important that our "eye be single" (ἐὰν οὖν ᾖ ὁ ὀφθαλμός σου ἁπλοῦς) not "evil" (ἐὰν δὲ ὁ ὀφθαλμός σου πονηρὸς ᾖ, Matthew 6:22-23); and Paul requires that we avoid "eyeservice" (ὀφθαλμοδουλία) by our "singleness of heart" (ἐν ἁπλότητι καρδίας, 3:22).[224] Our 'eye' should be fixed on the only ultimate goal of any enduring worth – the glory of God.

Then, in effect, our Lord raised the problem to which we refer, saying, "No man can serve two masters. ... You cannot serve God and material wealth" (Matthew 6:24).[225] He appears to be personifying 'material wealth' as the 'second master', where we might have expected Him to refer to 'man' or even 'Satan' as the alternative. *I suggest that He speaks this way to distinguish the two very diverse value systems that differentiate the one master from the other.* There are those for whom *God Himself* is the ultimate value and those for whom *the creation* is the

---

[224] Both Christ and the apostle use forms/compounds of the words "eye" and "single".
[225] Our Lord used the word 'mammon' here (μαμωνᾶς).

ultimate value. In other words, there are those who "worship and serve" God and those who "worship and serve" the creation (Romans 1:25).

In one significant way, then, it is the values we choose that determine the master we ultimately serve.

Christians value God above all, so they gladly serve Him before all.

The antagonism of which we speak, then, is not primarily or necessarily in having two personal masters, as it is theoretically possible that the two could be compatible. In fact, it is recognized here in Colossians that the Christian servant, whether he likes it or not, does have two masters – both a heavenly Lord and an earthly lord. But the problem is that each might subscribe to differing moral and religious principles.

The conflict is fundamentally between different value systems.[226]

In principle, this conflict of value systems should not arise when a devout Christian servant is in the employ of a devout Christian master.

However, our Christian value system requires us to love our enemies and pray for them (Matthew 5:44), and to do good even to them that hate us (Luke 6:27) – love is to be extended to all people. Therefore, the Christian servant, if he has a measure of true godliness, will always be concerned for the well-being of his master, whether Christian or non-Christian, no matter how onerous this may be or unrewarded the task. But he will not be of any lasting or genuine benefit to his master if he behaves duplicitously in a dissimulative or sycophantic manner, being primarily concerned for his own advantage, and forsaking those eternal values and moral principles that should moderate his own life.

For the Christian to abandon his own integrity is to violate his service to God and obfuscate – if not, nullify – his testimony to the truth. He will no longer be walking "in wisdom toward them that are without" (4:5) – or, in particular, towards his master.

However, as our Lord explained, life will not always be comfortable for the Christian in this world in its present condition (John 15:20-21, 16:33). We should not be surprised when we are faced with "fiery trials" and "reproached for the name of Christ" (I Peter 4:12-14). There is every possibility, then, that we will both suffer

---

[226] This, hopefully, would not be the case if servant and earthly master were both true Christians.

and witness considerable injustice. Then we may well be troubled by the inequalities of our times and wonder why this is so, knowing that God is righteous. We may ask with the prophet, "You are righteous, O Lord … why then does the way of the wicked prosper?" (Jeremiah 12:1, cf. Psalm 37:7 and Job's perplexity).

In whatever way we seek an answer to this question, or in whatever situation, we must be careful not to impugn God's holiness or righteousness, or disparage His sovereignty and governance.

One of the most disquieting features of biblical theism is its constant insistence upon the immutability of divine justice. God always has and always will act according to His own principles of righteousness. To ignore or violate them would be to contradict Himself and to assault His own intrinsic holiness, which He cannot do (II Timothy 2:13). Such an unswerving commitment to His own immaculate values is, to say the least, intimidating! We cannot relegate Him to some world of relativity, volatility, and compromise. It is in the presence of such an immutable God that we all live now, and before Him we must all at some time stand in judgement.

Nevertheless, this feature of biblical theism is also, when rightly understood, a source of great comfort and assurance. In such a world as ours that is fraught with injustice, all people to some extent – and for many, intolerably – suffer from inequality, corruption, and exploitation. Justice is frequently denied them, and ultimately, as often no resolution is found, most die unrecompensed. And the perpetrators of evil so often die unpunished. But we are assured that the God we find in scripture, the "judge of all the earth", will always and necessarily do what is "right" (Genesis 18:25).

Paul makes reference to this inexorable, divine justice here in Colossians, writing, "He that does wrong shall receive again the wrong that he has done; and there is no respect of persons" (ὁ γὰρ ἀδικῶν κομίσεται ὃ ἠδίκησεν,καὶ οὐκ ἔστιν προσωπολημψία, 3:25).[227] Interestingly, the apostle, writing concerning the same servant/master relationship, makes a parallel but positive comment about God's

---

[227] I have translated this "receive again the wrong that he has done" (κομίσεται ὃ ἠδίκησεν) rather than the usual "receive again *for* the wrong". I have done so because the expression seems to emphasise that a measured, just, and equal repayment will be made. God is neither vindictive nor indulgent. Perhaps this reflects the unsettling words, the *lex talionis*, of Exodus 21:23-24, Deuteronomy 19:21. The harshness of this Old Testament regulation was presumably to be a deterrent. Nevertheless, it was also a limitation, prohibiting excessive retaliation. It was, I suggest, the measure of righteous judgement, not a prescription for retribution or vengeance. The Bible does require of us that we be forgiving and merciful, always remembering our own moral frailty. And as Christians, we always hope that the miscreant will repent.

judgement in Ephesians 6:8: "Knowing that whatsoever good thing each one doeth, the same shall he receive again from the Lord, whether he be bond or free" (εἰδότες ὅτι ἕκαστος ἐάν τι ποιήσῃ ἀγαθόν,τοῦτο κομίσεται παρὰ Κυρίου εἴτε δοῦλος εἴτε ἐλεύθερος).

These verses together indicate two things:

Divine judgement.
It is God Himself who performs the evaluation and makes the condign response for each act, whether unjust (ὃ ἠδίκησεν) or good (ἀγαθόν). It is – in the divine economy – heaven's court that decides these matters, not some earthly magistracy. What is received is "from the Lord".

Divine justice.
The principles apply equally to both "bond and free", to both servant and master. Therefore, we can safely assume that 3:25, coming as it does after advice given to servants and before advice given to masters, applies equally to the two parties. Servants and masters alike are answerable to God for their behaviour. With God, there is "no respect of persons" (3:25). His judgement is not made in reference to social status or privilege, but according to His own impeccable standards.

We may have confidence, then, that in the divine economy no injustice will prevail forever and no good left forever unrewarded. There will be the "restoration of all things" (Acts 3:21). This is an integral element in "the hope which is laid up for (us) in the heavens", about which the Colossians had evidently been informed by "the word of the truth of the gospel" (1:5-7) that was preached to them by Epaphras. The whole convoluted and corrupted story of human life on earth will conclude with the grand denouement of a righteous resolution.

No matter how unjust and iniquitous their earthly masters might have been, God will not leave His faithful servants without recompense for their faithfulness. And no matter how denigrated or degraded His servants may be in their servitude in this world, they will be manifested "in glory" with Christ (3:4). Ultimate reward for their obedience is guaranteed by God, even when no immediate or temporal remuneration or benefit is received.

However, the immutable rule of sovereign, divine law, which is the assurance we have that *ultimately righteousness will prevail*, is not in our case, as Christians, simply a matter of our works being weighed in the balance and our good being found to exceed our failures. We know that we are not saved by our works, but by the grace and the righteousness of Jesus Christ. Although the commandments of God and our love for Him moderate – or ought to moderate – our lives, educating us in the ways of holiness and guiding us into a life that brings glory to our Lord, we dare not claim that this alone qualifies us for any heavenly reward. The fact is that even the best of our good works condemns us, falling far short of God's standards both in motivation and in execution (cf. I Corinthians 4:4-5).

The assurance we have that *ultimately we will prevail over all injustice* is that the "Father ... made us meet to be partakers of the inheritance of the saints in light" (1:12). Therefore, Paul explains that we should serve "in singleness of heart ... as unto the Lord ... knowing that from the Lord (we) shall receive the recompense of the inheritance" (3:22-24, see #1.2.3.4. First).

Because our "recompense" is our "inheritance" – bequeathed to us by our Father – we must conclude that it is considerably more than we could possibly deserve. This is because all that we do in our "labour" and "striving" in His service only accomplishes anything of worth because of "His working, which works in (us) mightily" (1:29, cf. Philippians 2:13, 4:13). The glory, then, is always God's! He is able and willing to make use of our less than useful works to prosecute His own purposes (Philippians 2:13). He redeems our blunders!

But there is no divine inequity in this! The law remains irrefrangible. Yet, without contradicting Himself or violating His righteousness, God is able to give 'good' even to him "that does wrong" (3:25). This is because He justifies His people "freely by His grace through the redemption that is in Christ", and doing so in a manner that enables Him to "be just, and the justifier of him who has faith in Jesus", but only through "propitiation ... by His blood" (Romans 3:23-26). As a direct result of this divine intervention through our Lord's incarnation and crucifixion, sins can be forgiven and the "righteousness ... which is through faith in Christ" (Philippians 3:9) can be obtained. Every benefit we gain through our salvation, even the "reward" we receive for such "good" works as we may do, is the pure gift of the grace of God. Apart from Him, we can do nothing (John15:5).

So, it might be worth repeating: *we have been freely forgiven, but there is not and could not have been free forgiveness* (#3.2.2.4., First). We might also say: *we will be freely rewarded, but there is not nor could there be any free reward.* Both the forgiveness and the reward have been obtained for us by the merits and the works of Christ. We only inherit as coinheritors with Christ (Romans 8:17), and we are only rewarded as fellow workers with God (I Corinthians 3:9). If then we are to boast, it should never be in our own accomplishments – regardless of the accolades and awards we might receive from men! – but only "in the cross of our Lord Jesus Christ" (Galatians 6:14), which unites us with our God.

It is "the cross" that guarantees our salvation, and our indissoluble union with Christ, and our access to His grace while here on earth, and our eternal life, and our place in God's kingdom, and our entrance into heaven, and our eternal reward and inheritance. Therefore, through "the cross of our Lord" we find all that is required to contextualize and moderate our present life, to discover true significance and purpose, to redeem every moment, and to glorify our Redeemer – *regardless of our social position and notwithstanding our moral inefficiency.*

3.5.3.3.2. WHAT, THEN, IS REQUIRED OF A GODLY MASTER?

The master also, together with all Christians, should be cognizant of and responsive to all that we have considered above concerning objective standards and subjective disposition (See #3.5.2. Third, 1. & 2.). He is, in other words, to act according to the requirements of divine law as he intelligently pursues a life of godliness, and to do so specifically within the context of the master/servant relationship in which he finds himself.

And again, as mentioned above in reference to those in servitude, our Christian value system requires us to love our enemies and pray for them (Matthew 5:44), and to do good even to them that hate us (Luke 6:27) – love is to be extended to all people. Therefore, the Christian master, if he has a measure of true godliness, will always be concerned for the well-being of his servant, no matter how onerous this may be or unrewarding the task.

So, it is perhaps sufficient to say that what is required of Christian masters is, in one sense, precisely the same as that which is required of Christian servants, for both are the servants of Christ. The relationship the believing master has with his heavenly Lord should determine the relationship he has with his own servants.

But we should note in particular, that Paul requires masters to "render unto (their) servants that which is just and equal" (τὸ δίκαιον καὶ τὴν ἰσότητα τοῖς δούλοις παρέχεσθε, 4:1). When he wrote this, it would have been unprecedented, perhaps even outrageous, for the contemporaneously traditional and socially sensitive. I can only speculate, but considering the slave economy of the ancient world and the legal system – such as it may have been – that permitted it, this apostolic requirement must have sounded revolutionary at that time.[228]

The average citizen in the days of the apostle would have found the idea that slaves should share equally with other people and be governed in accordance with the same principles of justice to be quite incomprehensible. They would have had neither the religious nor the social categories in their minds – having adopted the "philosophy ... after the traditions of men" (2:8) – to be able to process such transforming ideas and make any sense of them. Nor would they have been able to do so until they turned to the "philosophy ... after Christ" (2:8). The gospel has always required and facilitated radical rethinking!

The apostolic message – "the word of the truth of the gospel" (1:5) – has profound implications that, *inter alia*, challenge the principles and convert the practices of non-Christian cultures. And this gospel, "bearing fruit and increasing" (1:6), re-contextualized and re-moderated the entire praxis of those who responded to it. Throughout history, this Christian influence has invigorated decaying communities and has civilized nations. It has introduced to many societies the high values of biblical equality and justice that are according to the "philosophy ... after Christ" (2:8).[229] These concepts, and the very idea of a sovereign God of pure righteousness and love that gives them substance, would have been foreign and bewildering in a pagan world. The ancient pantheon was utterly devoid of such a God, and their philosophers – as brilliant as some of them were – lacked the imagination to envisage, and the motivation to worship such an intensely holy deity.

Today, especially in the modern, so-called 'post-Christian world',[230] these ideas – or at least the vocabulary – of 'equality' and 'justice' are assumed to be desirable by most people without much thought and little definition. But now they are usually attributed to some unspecified 'natural' system of values. However, they are, in the main, only the tattered remnants of a Christian heritage. Irrational

---

[228] In fact, the arrival of the Christian gospel had far reaching effects, revolutionizing the thinking of men, generating a kinder disposition and a more benevolent community, bringing hope and purpose that most had never known.

[229] It is evident that the apostles – following the example of their Lord – openly challenged the non-Christian philosophies and cultures of their day, recognizing their incompatibility with Christian philosophy and culture. Subsequently – and as in our day – a compromising tendency in the churches has been attempting an impossible marriage between the two, producing only confusing amalgamations.

[230] The term 'post-Christian world' seems to have found some currency in recent literature. But I question its value, sensing that it is used as a diversionary tactic. Seeing there has never been a 'Christian world', it has yet to be 'posted'!

'rationalism' has rejected religion but has attempted to appropriate the religious, moral principles it has plundered from its cultural legacy.

Having been prescinded from Christian faith and philosophy, both equality and justice are now being reinterpreted from various ideological perspectives. The vocabulary has been recharged with new cognitive significance, acquiring its own strong emotive force, especially when it is built into political slogans. What is now considered to be 'equality' or 'justice' depends entirely upon the viewpoint of those who use these words. These terms are in danger of being reduced to small, diminishing packages of emotional jargon, and will continue to be so if they are not bonded to a belief in absolute values.

People of diverse political and sociological persuasions, and the parties they form, strive for equality and justice on *their terms* and according to *their axiological systems*.[231]

And as Christians in these days of moral, religious, sexual, sociological, political, and intellectual revolution – troublesome times, but not altogether different from the tumultuous circumstances that our Christian forebears had to navigate – we are obliged to strive for genuine equality and justice for all people, for we are the servants of Christ. Having been "translated ... into the kingdom of the Son of His love" (1:13), we must be true to both the sovereign rule and the love of God, and this precludes unscrupulous injustice and loveless inequality.

But as we strive for equality and justice, the conception of these things we entertain in our minds and promulgate in the world must be determined by the "philosophy ... after Christ" (2:8). And as we have seen, this requires that we "seek the things that are above, where Christ is seated on the right hand of God" – His sovereignty – and that we "set our minds on the things that are above" – His principles (3:1-2, #3.3.2.).

Therefore, as Christian people, we must work for the equality and the justice that are established by *the terms set by our sovereign Lord,* and according to *the axiological system of heaven.*

We should keep in mind, then, that when we and our non-Christian friends and neighbours discuss equality and justice, we are not necessarily talking about the

---

[231] The danger of de-contextualizing the concepts of 'equality' and 'justice' and separating them from Christian belief, is massively demonstrated by the appalling redefinition and distorted application of these words in modern states that were established on the principles of atheistic Marxism.

same things, using the words with the same cognitive content, or working within the same system of values. Contextualization is critical!

We, like all who are obligated to promote and administer equality and justice, should act according to the requirements of divine law as we intelligently pursue a life of godliness, as suggested above. And we have little doubt that if we do so, then in some situations and to some degree we will be considered social misfits – even dinosaurian! – by the devotees of atheistic materialism, radical humanism, and popular secularism.

Nevertheless, this unwelcome derogation from our critics establishes Christian masters here on earth – be they potentate, politician, or proprietor – in a strategic position in which to bring glory to God and exemplify divine standards in the human community (cf. 3:17) by giving unto their "servants that which is just and equal" (4:1). In this, their resolve to exalt the name of our Lord is paramount.

And herein is my justification – or my apology! – for making much of Paul's advice to masters. If a 'master' or 'lord' (κύριος) is essentially one who has authority over another, then he might be found as the butler over the scullery maid, the manager over the office boy, or the prime minister over the country. But be he butler, manager, or prime minister *and* a Christian, then he is obliged to heed the apostle's imperative in this verse.

As surely as a Christian in service to an earthly master, whatever his situation, is able to manifest the grace of God and a measure of Christ-likeness in his attitudes and behaviour, so the master also, whatever his situation, is able to do the same. No condition in life in this fallen world is beyond the redemptive intervention of God, and the amelioration of His mercies.

◆

CHRISTIANITY, EQUALITY, AND JUSTICE.

A fair case can be made, I believe, for the suggestion that the true ideals of social *equality* and *justice* were bequeathed to the modern Western world by its Christian forebears. It is certainly difficult to see how materialistic atheism could have convincingly developed any such values on the basis of its own presuppositions. So, we suspect that contemporary, naturalistic ideologies have simply commandeered their ethical principles that are of any worth from church traditions to utilize for their own purposes. Unfortunately, in doing so they have de-contextualized them and made them instrumental in de-moderating human life.

Hence the words 'equality' and 'justice' have been plasticized by our contemporaries, made into vehicles for the 'politically correct', and voided of their original, Christian content. They define them in reference to anthropocentric ambition and fabricated social structures, and not in reference to the holiness of God and the economy of heaven. And their efforts in all this are presented to our generation as sophisticated modern thinking and progressive ideas, although, it seems to me, they are astonishingly regressive, returning to paganism.

Our concern in this regard, as Christians, is at least twofold: *first*, we should seek to re-contextualize these concepts according to "the things that are above, where Christ is seated on the right hand of God" (3:1), and redefine the words 'equality' and 'justice' in reference to the character and righteousness of our Lord: and *second*, through the preaching of the gospel, we should seek to explain that an equal and just society is ultimately dependent upon the redemption that enables us to put off the old man and to put on the new, being renewed unto knowledge and conformed to the original image for which we were made (3:10).

We should work for the rehabilitation of *Christian equality* and *Christian justice* in our community – and this requires precise understanding of their objectivity, significance, and substance, together with the ability to clearly articulate them to our generation. But first, we must consider, define, proclaim, embody, and manifest them within the visible life of the church. How else are we to escape being only an insipid reflection of this world's melancholy culture, darkness, and confusion, and be seen as a distinct "city set on a hill" that "cannot be hid" (Matthew 5:14)?

The Christian faith has much to say about marriage, family, and 'industrial relationships' within the context of true equality and justice. We cannot, then, isolate our beliefs about these standards and associations in some hermetically sealed, encapsulated private existence, as if our religion is irrelevant in social and communal affairs. We cannot separate our beliefs from our participation in the whole of life, any more than the devotees of other religions and philosophies can – or will – sequester theirs. We are to let our "light shine before men" (Matthew 5:16).

Then, unlike other ideologies – in fact, in sharp distinction from them – we admit that the kind of social behaviour we envisage cannot be achieved simply through imposed regulations or sociological engineering. Ultimately it requires, we believe, divine intervention and the grace of redemption. So, our sociology, as suggested above, must be rooted in our understanding of the pre-eminence of Christ and the philosophy that is consistent with "the treasures of wisdom and knowledge" we find in Him (2:3).

We would, then, advance the well-being of our society primarily through the preaching of the gospel of Christ and the proclamation of the values of heaven, that individuals might be redeemed, the kingdom of God advanced, and our community permeated with the qualities of godliness. This has happened before in the history of the church, and, by the grace of God, it can happen again despite increasing social – and perhaps, legal – inhibitions that would prohibit the open proclamation of our beliefs.

Working towards this end, we have confidence in Christ that divine equality and justice will eventually prevail over all oppression and discrimination. We look forward to "a new earth, wherein dwells righteousness" (II Peter 3:13). This prospect is *strong justification* to work for the kingdom of God in the service of Christ. And as we accept that our social responsibilities arise from our moral principles, this is *strong motivation* that greatly exceeds that of any configuration of pragmatism.

And all this makes the Christian gospel far, far more progressive than any contemporary alternative.

◆

3.6. THE EVANGELISTIC IMPLICATIONS (4:2-6)

We might say that up to this point in this letter, Paul has been concerned with *the Church in Christ*, what it is in itself; how it is contextualized by its belief in the pre-eminence of our Lord as sovereign creator and redeemer, and how it is moderated by its obedience to His moral and sociological principles. But now he is concerned for *the Church in the world*; that is, he would have the believing community to be seen by the unconverted for *what it actually is in Christ*.

Although this is a matter of importance, Paul's concern for it is only briefly expressed in these five verses (4:2-6), but the weight of what he is saying here is considerable and not to be underestimated. He is clearly drawing conclusions from all that he had written before in this letter. In this regard, we should note the following:

- **First**, Paul's reference to his own ministry: the proclamation of the gospel of Christ.

    Paul requests *prayer for himself* that he might have the opportunity "to speak the mystery of Christ" (4:3). In doing so, he is referring back to comments he had already made about his God-given responsibility in the ministry of the gospel (1:24-29). Therefore, those who were to intercede for him intelligently would do well to remember the extensive responsibilities and the complexities of the work in which he was engaged (#2.1.).

    They needed, in other words, a genuine – and hopefully, increasing – understanding of what is required in the proclamation and the extension of the kingdom of God.

- **Second**, Paul's reference to his readers' behaviour: the renewal of the people of Christ.

    Paul exhorts his readers to "walk in wisdom ... redeeming the time" (4:5). In doing so, he is surely reminding them of *his prayer for them* that they "walk worthily of the Lord unto all pleasing" (1:10, #1.2.), and of his instruction that as they had "received Christ Jesus the Lord" they should "walk in Him" (2:6, #3.1.). If, then, they were to behave in a manner that would truly and effectively influence the unbelievers – "them that are without" (4:5) – they should ponder, embrace, and effect in their lives all the apostle has been explaining to them about their relationship with Christ.

    They needed, in other words, to realize all the implications and practicalities of having "put off the old man" and having "put on the new man", and of being "renewed unto knowledge after the image of Him that created" them (3:9-10, #3.4.).

NOTE: It is only as we keep in mind these two things – the proclamation and the renewal – that we will comprehend what *the Church in the world* ought to accomplish; and that we will appreciate the resources *the Church in Christ* has at its disposal to accomplish what it ought. In this context – and only in this context – will evangelism become the powerful, faithful, humble, and meaningful expression of the gospel that it ought to be.

It is worth recalling once more that Paul develops his thoughts in logical sequence throughout this book. So, we see that, in expanding his exhortation in 2:6-7, he writes first about the redemptive aspects of salvation and the believers' association with Christ (2:18-19), and on this he then builds his philosophical view of reality (2:20-3:4). This order should never be reversed, as the natural man would attempt to do. The unconverted, being fundamentally creature-worshippers (Romans 1:25), insist upon establishing their philosophy of reality first, and then they attempt to build upon it a religion of some kind. At least, this is their theory! In actual practice, they surreptitiously begin with their own, often undisclosed, religious presuppositions.

Then, continuing to develop his thoughts, Paul makes his Christian philosophy the basis for his moral principles (3:5-17). These in turn provide a Christian foundation for appropriate and exemplary social practices (3:18-4:1). Finally, Paul introduces his evangelistic concerns (4:2-6). In doing all this, he provides us with a very significant and logical order which should inform and direct our service on earth as ministers of the gospel of Christ. We outline this order thus:

Religion/redemption → philosophy of life → moral principles → social order → evangelism.

Concerning our proclamation to the world, the first two – our religion/redemption and philosophy of life – must *contextualize* our evangelism, giving it true substance; and the second two – moral principles and social order – should *moderate* our evangelism, giving it true expression.

First, then, what we believe and the way we think – as those who have "heard … the word of the truth of the gospel" (1:5), and are committed to "the philosophy" that is "after Christ" (2:8) – establish the only appropriate *content* for our proclamation to the world. And, second, the extent to which we have absorbed the moral principles of heaven and have translated these into the fabric of our social life on earth – having put on a "heart of compassion" and the associated characteristics of "the new man" (3:12ff.), and "in singleness of heart, fearing the Lord" (3:22) – provides the appropriate *behaviour* for our evangelism.

Without these two factors, I suggest, we will neither "walk in wisdom towards them that are without", nor will our "speech be always with grace" (4:4-5), as Paul requires.

Neglecting this order, or failing to incorporate our contextualizing and moderating principles in our presentation of the gospel, is to trivialize evangelism, reducing it to a facile, often vacuous, recruitment technique, and rendering it virtually irrelevant to the non-Christian.

But this is not to imply that the Christian should *first* engage in social action *before* he begins to evangelize. Neither is it to suggest that he might use philanthropic activities as a form of pre-evangelism to establish a favourable relationship with the unconverted of this world to gain a hearing with them. Rather, it is to state that genuinely altruistic and transparent evangelism cannot take place outside the structures of true religion, sound understanding of life, holiness in character and in communion, appropriate private and interpersonal moral behaviour, and social integrity. Prescinded from this comprehensive context, the *motive in both our philanthropy and our preaching* is in danger of inadequate moderation, and even of duplicity; and our *manner in evangelism* may well be incongruous with the Christian message itself and its pure values.

In other words, our social action and personal morality are not a prelude to, but indispensable, intrinsic elements in evangelism.

Or as Paul explained elsewhere, it is only as we "do all things without murmuring or disputing", being "blameless and harmless" as "children of God without blemish", that we will be "seen as lights in the world" (Philippians 2:14-15). Without this humble involvement in "all things" as sanctified children of God, our light will be obfuscated, and our evangelism will become little more than proclamation in a vacuum, reverberating with all the hollow sounds of cheap, ersatz religion.

- **Third**, the search for the essential content.

    Contemporary churches – in a manner similar to those in preceding generations – are considering how best to accommodate themselves to the changing culture of the times, and measuring how much of modern society's values and practices they might assimilate; and today many seem to be involved in a convoluted attempt to proclaim the gospel in some non-confrontational or culturally neutral manner. In some ways, much of this is inevitable as we cannot escape our environment, and there is certainly biblical precedent for a wise and careful appraisal of and adaptation to our circumstances (eg. I Corinthians 9:18-23, #3.6.1.2. First 1.).

However, I suggest that it is critical at this present time that the churches balance their thoughts about adaptation and assimilation with a far greater sense of responsibility for the manifestation of Christian culture in contradistinction to prevailing trends, and – even more importantly – to ask themselves how much they are actually being influenced and guided by the Bible's philosophy, and how much by "the philosophy ... of men". Christians are to be seen as lights in the darkness – they are to be conspicuously different!

The question here is, to what extent is our supposed evangelistic practice determined by external, cultural considerations, and how much is determined by internal, theological considerations? And, we must ask, how are we to correlate cultural and theological considerations without resorting to pragmatic compromise? Moreover, we should consider the cost we might have to pay to maintain a truly Christian expression of our faith, as and when it is opposed by popular opinion and current standards.

Permit me to be provocative, to exemplify the problem. The witness of dynamic, talent-led congregations in hi-tech auditoriums, and in their spectacular 'worship' extravaganzas is, I suggest, a somewhat problematic approach to the presentation of the truths and the moral demands of the gospel. There is, among other impediments, always the imminent and insidious danger that, to accomplish their immediate goals, such congregations are forced to attract, and to continue attracting numerous people and considerable finance – if only to pay their bills – and to be attractive they must be popular – at least in that segment of the community that appreciates their particular music and style – and to be popular, they must compromise. And as they compromise, the tendency is always to diminish or distort the Christian message, vitiating their testimony. Being what it is, the gospel makes no claim upon or appeal to popularity, although – sadly – those who would promulgate it often do.

This is not to suggest that there is anything intrinsically wrong with modern auditoriums, electronic equipment, or large congregations, but to think that these things provide the only, or even the best environment or atmosphere in which to present the gospel is not only false, but also meretriciously deceptive. Compare the small country church in a sparsely populated rural area, which struggles even to find someone who can play the piano: or the poor and remote tribal village church in the distant mountains of some undeveloped country, which has neither electronic equipment nor electricity. These, of necessity, will function according to different architectural, instrumental, organizational, and cultural formations. So, we must ask, what is *the essential, central, common element that constitutes any of what are very disparate congregations as genuine, Christian expression?* There must be something in each of them that is clearly and decisively Christian, which can be seen as distinct from and uncluttered by whatever might be the local influences, transient values, contemporary preferences, and contrived emotional atmospherics.

We need to be clear in our understanding of just what this essential, universal, and biblical common element is, and to be sure that it provides the contextualizing and the moderating factors in all our evangelism. It must become the genius of our Christian expression, and never obscured by the irrelevant and the incongruous. Therefore, we must gain an appreciation of true gospel theology before we can rightly formulate an appropriate evangelistic methodology – or, to restate my concern, we must seriously contextualize before we attempt to moderate.

The essential, common element, to state the matter in the simplest, yet the most profound way, is nothing less than the preaching, the presentation, and the presence of the living Christ in and through the lives of believing individuals in the church, made evident in their "walk" and "speech" (4:5-6). But this must be expressly the biblical Christ, not the Christ of popular imagination or commercial fabrication! The mere mention of the name of Jesus does not Christianize the evangelism (cf. #3.4.2.2.3.).

To be more explicit, it is the presence and the presentation of the pre-eminent Christ who is proposed in all that precedes in this letter to the Colossians. Christ preached by and manifested in His people!

- **Fourth**, the search for the appropriate locus.

    It is obvious, surely, that the greater part of evangelism must be outside the 'church in congregation'. It is in the secular or pagan communities of this world that the vast majority of the unconverted is to be found.

    So, we must ask whether *the church in congregation* is the most effective locus for evangelism. There is good reason to anticipate that unconverted men and women, having been presented with the truth, will be converted when meeting with Christian believers (cf. I Corinthians 14:23-25). In fact, a statistical investigation would probably reveal that many are.

However, the proclamation of the gospel that Paul writes about here in Colossians 4:2-6 is not that of *the church in congregation*, but of *the church in the world* – Paul himself being "in bonds" (in prison, 4:3) and the Colossians Christians mingling among "them that are outside" (in the world of the non-Christians, 4:5).

The Christian witness that really matters – the light that we should all bring to this world – is not in the hi-tech auditorium, but in the home, in the marketplace, in the workplace, and in the common concourse of life. It is not best communicated by the skilled, charismatic pulpit orator to the congregation, but by the godly father and mother to their children, believing people to their friends, or the converted businessman to his colleagues. It is not best seen in the brilliant performance of the extravaganza – which the secular world does much better than the church anyway! – but in the love, honesty, and trustworthiness of humble believers going about their daily affairs in a Christian manner. Perhaps it is such considerations as these that Paul had in mind when he wrote Philippians 2:14-16 (see above).

We really must make a serious evaluation here, according to the moderating principles of the gospel. What is of greater evangelistic worth? One hour a week in the artificiality of a theatrical auditorium, or twenty-four hours a day in the realities of everyday life? The presentation of scintillating dramatics, or the manifestation of sanctified living? The skills of the charismatic performers, or the godly quality of the whole community of genuine believers? And all this I ask, not at all to deny the value of the preaching of the pastor or the evangelist, or the congregating of God's people, but to provoke a more considered and expansive comprehension of what is required of us all in the church's witness to the world. The task, being as broad as the whole inhabited earth, cannot be compacted into the auditorium!

And, I might add, we should indeed be most thankful for charitable organizations that are constantly bringing help and hope to suffering people in this world. Most of this kind of activity in contemporary society, even in secular welfare institutions, has its historic origin in Christian philosophy and sociology, and in the preaching of the love of God in Christ, even when this provenance is not acknowledged. To love your neighbour, even to love your enemy, is a very Christian thing to do! Nevertheless, there are problems here that we should beware. These organizations have become so structured and so regulated that they are now more a demonstration of anthropocentric philanthropy – sometimes a state-funded distribution of public wealth – than the distinctive practice of Christian compassion; and many have lost both the ability

363

and the freedom to "do all in the name of the Lord Jesus" (3:17). If truly Christian and the silent witness of their good work is left unexplained – that is, if it is decontextualized – it tends to become indistinguishable from the secular.

But more concerning, perhaps, is that these charitable organizations become a substitute for our own love for our neighbour. Rather than being active to assist the needy, we leave it to these institutions and convince ourselves that we have done what is required of us if we make a cash donation to the cause. Or we might even shrug off all responsibility, insisting that it is the government's problem! Of course, many, many people in such organizations are generous and well-meaning, and truly helpful, for which we are thankful. But it is our own personal motivation and involvement that should be our first concern.

We do well to remember that Jesus would be pleased to be able say to each of us individually in the day of judgement: "I was hungry, and you gave me food: I was thirsty, and you gave me drink: I was a stranger, and you took me in: naked, and you clothed me: I was sick, and you visited me: I was in prison, and you came unto me" (Matthew 25:35-36). If we have no concern for these things we are in danger of decontextualizing our evangelism.

The locus for our evangelism is out there in the broken world.

Now, all this is relevant to the things Paul writes about in 4:2-6. Here the apostle is obviously concerned for the proclamation of the gospel – the Christian testimony to the world – both through his own words and in those of his readers. We are all to speak of Christ! However, he has explained that whatever they do in "word and in deed" was to be done in the name of the Lord (3:17). Both word and deed! What is proclaimed and what is practised are to be compatible, corresponding with each other; the two should always be in agreement. Therefore, if we do not manifest something of the characteristics of holiness (3:12ff.) or care little about living in society as we ought (3:18-4:1), then, when we preach the gospel, or speak about Christ, we will sound decidedly unconvincing and our evangelism will ring with sounds of insincerity. We are to be "the light of the world" in and through our "good works" that others might "glorify" God (Matthew 5:16-18).

NOTE: I would suggest that persistent and irresistible evangelism flows *not from specific organizations, dedicated programs, or technical specialists* – as helpful as these may or may not be – *but from a vibrant community of genuine Christians*; that is, from the homogeneity, integration, and moral quality of those who are "elect, holy and beloved" (3:12), from men and women who pursue holiness in character and in communion, from those who do "all in the name of the Lord

Jesus" (3:17), those, in other words, who having "received Christ Jesus as Lord" are determined to "walk in Him" (2:6).

This is demanding in the extreme, touching every believer in every way!

Therefore, I suggest that we must broaden our understanding of evangelism, thinking of it as the interpretation of the whole of life in reference to Christian faith and practice, coupled with our complete involvement in the whole of life in a genuinely Christian manner.

Certainly, in our modern, multicultural Western world, as unfettered individual freedom has become the aspiration of many, and where there is little common moral or aesthetic axiology, we must rethink the manner in which the church can effectively and most faithfully represent Jesus Christ in our community. And although written to an ancient church in a culture different from our own, and that knew nothing of the remarkable social and technical developments of our sophisticated age, *Paul's brief remarks in Colossians 4:2-6 are as relevant now as they ever were.*

We discover here, in reference to evangelism and the interaction of the Christian community with the secular world in which it is found, that the apostle discloses his immediate concern for the believers' sense of *dependence* upon God, which is – or should be – evidenced in their *prayer*, and for the believers' *obedience* to God, which is – or should be – evidenced in their *behaviour* or *walk*.

Therefore, before concluding this letter with some personal references (4:7-18), Paul penned these final words of general exhortation (4:2-6) to the church in Colossae, which contain *two imperatives – first*, that they "continue steadfastly in prayer" (4:2); and *second*, that they "walk in wisdom towards them that are without" (4:5). Therefore, we might suggest, having written so powerfully about the pre-eminence of the Christ and the privileges and responsibilities of the Christians, his final instructions are that through prayer his readers maintain an effective and meaningful *life before God*, and that through wise behaviour they maintain an effective and meaningful *life before the people* of this world. Not the one without the other, but both concurrently and in concert. This should result in the open expression of their privileges and responsibilities as redeemed men and women, and this expression is the essence of their evangelism.

Therefore, we should note the following:

3.6.1. Prayer: and Contextualizing Evangelism (4:2-4)

By requesting as he does in these verses that his readers "continue steadfastly in prayer" (4:2), the apostle is indicating that evangelism, as with all aspects of

Christian living, comes under the sovereign and providential government of God, upon whom we are totally dependent. The Lord, as is acknowledged here, commissions His people to preach the gospel, provides them with opportunities to do so, and enables them in the task (4:3-4). *So, whatever we might think about prayer, we can with some confidence say that at least, but essentially, it is the conscientious and deliberate acceptance of the contextualizing of life within His will and purposes.*

3.6.1.1. ATTITUDE IN PRAYER (4:2)

There are *three things* mentioned here that we should consider:

- **First,** persistence.

  Paul advises his readers to "continue steadfastly in prayer" (4:2, τῇ προσευχῇ προσκαρτερεῖτε). It is recorded elsewhere that the first Christians "continued steadfastly in the apostles' teaching and fellowship, in the breaking of bread and the prayers" (Acts 2:42). Such tenacity in praying is significant, and from the beginning was evidently accepted without question as an essential aspect of practical faith, being highly valued as a necessary adjunct to, *inter alia*, "serving the Lord, rejoicing in hope", and patience "in tribulation" (Romans 12:11-12). It relates directly, then, to our work, our joy, and our perseverance – and, no doubt, to every other aspect of Christian living (I Thessalonians 5:17).

  Even if we have only a limited understanding of the issues Paul has presented to us in this letter, this emphasis on persistent praying should not seem surprising or incongruous. We have been confronted with our own human frailty and dependence. We are creatures of the Son of God (1:16), in whom "all things consist" (1:17), and "in whom we have our redemption" (1:14). But we have yet to obtain the fullness of our salvation, as we are waiting for the day when we will be "presented ... holy and without blemish ... before Him" (1:22). In the meanwhile, we are caught up in the process of "being renewed unto knowledge" (3:10). Therefore, what we were created to be, and what eventually we will become by His grace, is all determined by our God. In all this, we are totally dependent upon Him.

  Without Him, we are nothing and can do nothing (John 15:5). It is only "in Him" that we are "rooted and being built up" (2:7) and are "made full" (2:10). Therefore, maintaining and enjoying the interpersonal relationship we have with Him as a result of our reconciliation is a matter of the greatest importance if we are to realize all our intended human potential. The disciplines and techniques we may practice to regulate our Christian lives are totally impotent outside of this personal association with the omnipresent God.

And genuine prayer is rooted in this total dependency, acknowledges it, and accepts it with gratitude; prayer expresses the believer's confidence in the Lord's goodness and mercy; prayer is the Christian's personal response to an intensely personal God; it is affinity of the most exquisite kind.

Prayer, then, and steadfastness in it, is far more than a cultic duty or the perfunctory performance of a religious requirement. It is more than the means of acquisition, or merely a technique for achieving a self-determined end. It is not instrumental in gaining meritorious approval, or simply a meditative procedure for finding personal solace. And it is never a mechanism for manipulating the divine will. Genuine prayer cannot arise from such egocentricity that lies at the heart of these things.

The Christian who knows and loves God, and is aware that to a far greater extent God knows and loves him, is impelled into prayer by the spontaneous response of his faith in and worship of a Lord so magnificent and merciful as Jesus Christ. He may well pray as a considered duty, and do so diligently and systematically through the prayers of the church liturgy – and both duty and diligence are commendable – but these may soon decay into lifeless formalities unless driven intelligently by an informed, passionate, and willing heart (cf. Matthew 15:8).

And, we might suggest, when such is our dependent disposition in and thankful enjoyment of steadfast praying, it will inevitably embolden us to intercede and to petition for ourselves and for others. Because it is the most intimate communion with the Lord we love, it embodies the altruistic desire to see the purposes of God fulfilled and to participate constructively in them. Hence, Paul does not hesitate to ask the Colossians to pray for him and his colleagues (4:3-4).

Genuine prayer arises from the personal Christo-centricity that lies at its heart, which also establishes it as a persistent Christian proclivity.

- **Second,** perspective.

Then, Paul would also have his readers be actively "watching" in their prayer (4:2, γρηγοροῦντες ἐν αὐτῇ). This requires vigilance, with perhaps an element of urgency. It at least advises us against carelessness or complacency in our praying.

But why, and of what should we be watchful?

Elsewhere in the New Testament, we are advised to "watch and pray, that (we) enter not into temptation", for "the spirit is willing but the flesh is weak" (Matthew 26:41). Moreover, we should "be watchful" because our "adversary the devil, as a roaring lion, walks about, seeking whom he might devour" (I Peter 5:8). In our praying, then, we ought to be realistic about our own moral weaknesses, and alert to the almost irresistible evil enticements and wicked forces that would corrupt our behaviour. We should proceed with a sense of our dependence upon the grace of God in Christ Jesus that we might grow in holiness.

Therefore, I suggest, our moral inadequacies demand that we be watchful in prayer.

Paul warned the elders of the church in Ephesus that "grievous wolves shall enter in among you ... and from your own selves shall men arise, speaking perverse things, to draw away the disciples". Therefore, he advised them to "watch", keeping in mind the truths he had taught to them for three years (Acts 20:29-31). Presumably, when watching in prayer they should also manifest a concern for the theological well-being of the Christian community; that its members "be not carried away with every wind of doctrine" (Ephesians 4:14). We also should be alert to these dangers that continue to threaten the church's well-being. But as we are all in the process of "being renewed unto knowledge" (3:10) – and, as we have seen, this is a work in progress (#3.4.1.2.2.) – none of us is yet as wise in the things of God as he might be; we are all exposed to the dangers of being "deluded ... with persuasiveness of speech" (2:4, #2.2.2.).

Therefore, I suggest, our theological vulnerabilities demand that we be watchful in prayer.

Then, there is a third and eschatological dimension to this "watching". Jesus spoke to His disciples about His "coming, and the end of the world", when "heaven and earth shall pass away", and believers separated from unbelievers in the "day and hour" known by no man. In this context, He advised His disciples, "Watch therefore, for you know not on what day your Lord comes" (Matthew 24:3, 35-36, 38ff., 42). We are to live in anticipation of the day when Christ returns – in fact, we are to live *for* that day – being careful to "lay up treasures in heaven" (Matthew 6:20). In the light of this Christian hope, the understanding Christian would, when his Lord returns, be found "watching", being careful to be about his Master's affairs, ready and prepared for His arrival (Luke 12:37), knowing how easily we are distracted.

Therefore, I suggest, our God-given, vocational responsibilities demand that we be watchful in prayer.

There should be, then, an ethical, a theological, and a vocational component in our watchfulness: we ought to pray out of an awareness of our susceptibility to evil, of our intellectual gullibility, and of our vacillation in purpose. We need to be constantly vigilant! Prayer maintains our true focus.

• **Third,** persuasion.

However, although we must be watchful because of our own inadequacies and, perhaps, our lack of self-confidence, our prayer must never be the whimpering of the querulous or the badgering of the hubristic. It is, rather, the grateful expression of the humble, because it is – if truly prayer – always offered "with thanksgiving" (4:2, cf. Philippians 4:6).

The Christian, having confidence in the ministry of Christ in His office as our great High Priest, boldly approaches the "throne of grace" knowing that he will receive from God "help in time of need" (Hebrews 4:16). In fact, our Lord invites us to "ask" in His "name" that our "joy may be fulfilled" (John 16:24). He evidently desires that we find such confidence and satisfaction in Him and in His grace, that we pray with unpretentious assurance.

Those who truly believe in Him and appreciate His person and redemptive work, and who know something of divine love, would be most foolish to think that their prayers remain unheard in heaven or are dismissed by God as foolish or inconsequential; or, alternatively, to be so crass as to think that they might receive more attention if they pleaded in some name other than Christ's.

And perhaps we would be just as foolish were we to think that our prayers, by virtue of our intensity or some technique, will determine what God's response will be. Those who imagine that this might be so may well be disappointed. We are advised not to be "rash with (our) mouth" or "hasty to utter anything before God", for He "is in heaven" and we "upon earth"; "therefore let your words be few" (Ecclesiastes 5:2). We pray from a very circumscribed – and introverted – standpoint, and with more ignorance than understanding. We are not able to match wits with God!

Therefore, our faith may well encourage us to approach God boldly in our prayers, but such knowledge as we have of His infinite majesty should make us aware of how little we know of His purposes and, therefore, diffident respecting what we say to, and what we ask of Him. The sobering fact is, "we know not how to pray as we ought" (Romans 8:26).

Why, then, should we be thankful whenever we pray?

Above all, I suggest, because when we pray as we ought, we cast "all our anxiety upon Him", knowing that "He cares for" us (I Peter 5:7). We should reach out to Him as a child to its father, being aware that the "Father knows what things (we) have need of, before (we) ask Him" (Matthew 6:8-9). And although we "do not know how to pray as we ought", we have confidence that "to them that love God, all things work together for good". Moreover, it is guaranteed that despite the inadequacy of our own praying, "the Spirit Himself makes intercession for us" (Romans 8:26-28).

Therefore, that for which we should be most thankful – above and despite all other things – is simply and overwhelmingly God Himself and our inalienable fellowship with Him.

Knowing Him is to be persuaded that we are privileged to commune with Him and that our prayers are not in vain; and so, we should always be "abounding in thanksgiving" (2:7, cf. Ephesians 5:20, I Thessalonians 5:18).

3.6.1.2. Particular Requests (4:3-4)

Having noted the appropriate – indeed, the essential – attitude, as indicated by Paul's words, that Christians should have in prayer, we now consider his request that, in particular, the Colossians pray for him and his ministering companions. As he prayed constantly for them (1:3), so he now requests that they do the same for him and those with him (4:3). This mutuality in intercession was clearly important in the apostle's mind.

Elsewhere Paul asks others to pray for him that, *first*, he might be protected from disobedient, unreasonable, and evil men (Romans 15:30-31, II Thessalonians 3:1-2); and that, *second*, he remain bold and forthright in preaching the gospel (Ephesians 6:19-20), and bring no shame upon himself in failing to do so even when intimidated by the possibility of death (Philippians 1:19-20). He was clearly a wise enough man to realize that the dangers he faced in preaching the gospel arose from two sources – the hostility of the world, *in which* he preached, and the condition of his own soul, *from which* he preached. Constantly facing both these perils, he was aware that he needed the sustaining and sanctifying of God's grace, and was unashamed to admit as much when asking his friends to petition the Lord of his behalf (cf. #3.5.2. Fourth 1.).

There are, then, two corresponding aspects of his request:

- **First**, for an opportunity: "may open unto us a door" (4:3).
  Being "in bonds" (4:3), Paul was in no position to make any plans for his own itinerant preaching. But we need not assume that he was only requesting here that the Colossians pray for the opening of the

prison door to release him from captivity – although this may well have been in his mind. He was aware that even incarceration could itself provide a fruitful occasion for evangelism (cf. Philippians 1:12-14). No doubt his first concern was that he might capitalize on the situation in which he found himself, whatever that might be. It was his passion, the apostolic aspiration, that "the word of the Lord may run and be glorified" (II Thessalonians 3:1), regardless of the circumstances, and should be preached "in season" and "out of season" (II Timothy 4:2). As he desired for his readers, he also would be found "redeeming the time" (4:5, #3.6.2.1. Second).

Whatever dangers or difficulties the hostile world may present to him, the apostle was always confident that God would make it possible for him in some way to speak about "Jesus Christ and Him crucified" (I Corinthians 2:2). Even when his own plans were frustrated – by whatever means – he evidently saw this as the intervention of the Holy Spirit, guiding him in his travels, for example, and bringing him and his companions to the place where God would have them be (Acts 16:6-10). When opportunity to preach the gospel came his way, he saw this as a "great door" for effective ministry that God had "opened" for him (I Corinthians 16:9, cf. II Corinthians 2:12, Revelation 3:8).

Therefore, when Paul asked the Colossians to pray that God would open a door for him, he was, no doubt, realistically acknowledging that this world, in which we are surrounded by disobedient, unreasonable, and evil people (II Thessalonians 3:1-2), presents many obstacles to the advance of the gospel and is an environment hostile to the preaching of Christ. But this was no reason for despair!

To ask that God would provide an evangelistic opportunity is to trust Him, and to reckon with His sovereign, providential management of all things.

- **Second**, for the ability to do the task well: "as I ought to speak" (4:4).

Paul's concern was not only that he might have an open door "for the word, to speak the mystery of Christ" (cf. #2.1.3.), but that he "make it manifest, as (he) ought to speak" (4:3-4, τοῦ λόγου λαλῆσαι τὸ μυστήριον τοῦ Χριστοῦ ... ἵνα φανερώσω αὐτὸ ὡς δεῖ με λαλῆσαι).

He writes similarly elsewhere of his desire that others pray for him that "utterance (or, "a word") may be given" him "in opening" his "mouth to make known with boldness the mystery of the gospel" as he "ought to speak", he being responsible to do so as Christ's ambassador (Ephesians 6:19-20, ἵνα μοι δοθῇ λόγος ἐν ἀνοίξει τοῦ στόματός μου, ἐν παρρησίᾳ γνωρίσαι τὸ μυστήριον τοῦ εὐαγγελίου ... ὡς δεῖ με λαλῆσαι).

In these verses, we see that both *his circumstances* and *his preparedness* were matters of prayerful concern; an open door and an open mouth were both in some way dependent upon divine intervention. He relied upon God's providence and His personal assistance that he might preach the gospel "boldly" – that is, openly and clearly – as he "ought to speak".[232] We have already considered his awareness of his God-given stewardship (#2.1.) and of his constant reliance upon the Lord's "working" in him (1:29). But now he is referring these two matters to the intercession of his Colossian friends, admitting his need of their "supplication" and "the supply of the Spirit" (cf. Philippians 1:19). Ambassador for Christ he may have been, but a self-sufficient representative or an independent agent he was not![233]

Such a combined sense of obligation and of dependency no doubt motivated Paul to preach the gospel and provoked him to preach it appropriately – being driven by the divine imperative. And to discharge this responsibility he would have been concerned – as he advised his Colossian readers – "in word and deed" to "do all in the name of Jesus" (3:17), and to "work heartily, as unto the Lord" (3:23).

Therefore, to serve His Lord in the manner best suited to the task, he may well have had in mind the following:

1. When writing to the Ephesian church, as we have seen, Paul requested prayer "that utterance may be given" him – or, as we might translate, "that a word be given" him – "in opening" his "mouth to make known with boldness the mystery of the gospel" (Ephesians 6:19, ἵνα μοι δοθῇ λόγος ἐν ἀνοίξει τοῦ στόματος).

    If a man is to speak with boldness, it surely requires not simply the courage to stand up and talk to people openly, but also the confidence of knowing that he has something worthwhile and appropriate to say. Paul explained elsewhere that he approached an opportunity to preach the gospel with sensitivity to the situation and an understanding of the mind of those he was addressing (I Corinthians 9:18-22). And from Luke's record of the apostle's ministry we see that he adapted

---

[232] The phrase "ought to speak" may refer to Paul's sense of obligation to preach the gospel, or to his sense of responsibility to preach the gospel carefully and faithfully. But considering the solemn importance of the task, and his divine commission to engage in it, the apostle would hardly have distinguished between the two – it is as if he said, 'I ought to preach the gospel, and I ought to preach it well!' Both his motivation and his manner in ministry, I suggest, are reflected here.

[233] Paul well explains his own attitude in and his understanding of his ministry in Romans 15:17-18.

his presentation of the message to his audience – for example, he preached the gospel to the religious people in Antioch in a significantly different manner from the way he addressed the philosophical academics in Athens (cf. Acts 13:16ff. with Acts 17:22ff.).

Perhaps, then, in this request in 4:3-4, the apostle is revealing his desire that God assist him in speaking as he "ought", both in the *manner* and with the *content* – or "word" – that was best suited for his audience. When writing the Colossian letter, as we have seen, he was in prison. Could it be, then, that he was thinking about how best to present the gospel to his fellow prisoners, to the jailors, or even to the judge when brought to trial – or to all three?

Each situation requires a distinct and apposite "word" – or presentation of the Christian message – to communicate the inviolable truth of the gospel to disparate ears.

2.   So, in reference to his responsibility to preach "the mystery of Christ", Paul writes that he desired to "make it manifest" as he "ought to speak" (4:3-4). By bringing together the two words "manifest" and "speak", he seems to add another dimension to his sense of accountability as a preacher, and to indicate something of the demanding, personal prerequisites such ministry requires.

It could be, as some translations convey, that this combination of words implies no more than 'speaking clearly' or 'openly' – suggesting, in other words, that if he was to manifest the mystery he must preach effectively. If so, then Paul is saying much the same here as is implied in his concern to "speak boldly" as mentioned in Ephesians 6:19-20. And such open and bold preaching is desirable, as it does little good to obfuscate the plain message of the gospel with an overly simplistic or an unnecessarily sophisticated presentation. Hence the need for an appropriate "word", as explained above.

But it seems to me, in the light of Paul's comments elsewhere, that there is something more implied here – and something of considerable importance. The manifestation of the truth requires, I suggest, more than intelligible speech.

We must keep in mind that manifesting the mystery, or revealing the truths about divine things, *is pre-eminently the work of God Himself.* Earlier in this letter, Paul wrote that "the mystery" which "had been hidden" in times gone by, has now "been manifested to His saints" (1:26-27, cf. #2.1.3.). This evidently is in reference to the revelation of the gospel in the life, death, and resurrection of Jesus Christ (cf. John 21:1, I Peter 1:20, I John 1:2, 3:5, 3:8).

Moreover, we must also remember, as the apostle explains elsewhere, that God has manifested himself in creation (Roman 1:19), and in the scriptures (Romans 3:21, 16:26).

Therefore, the divine "manifestation" of the "mystery" cannot be separated from the work of God in creation, and in the incarnate Christ through His works and words on earth, and in the revelation of God given through the prophets and in the scriptures. It is an immense – indeed, a spectacular – exercise in divine self-revelation![234]

From God's perspective, manifesting the mystery involves not only 'speaking clearly', which in a real sense He does, but much, much more.

We might suggest, then, that any subsequent and secondary manifestations of the mystery in and through the ministry of God's people, if they are to be of any real communicative value, must surely be rooted in and reflect something of all these facets of the primary, divine manifestation, and be more than the verbalization of our beliefs. Divine revelation in all its forms is the very *substance of the gospel* we should preach, and it conveys the very *significance of the life* we should live. And our involvement in both – preaching and living, and doing so concurrently and in concert – delivers us from hypocrisy and gives weight to our Christian witness.

Therefore, when Paul accepted the responsibility to "make ... manifest" the revealed mystery (4:3-4), he would have identified himself with, and aligned and committed himself to the entirety of this divine manifestation in the creation, in the incarnation, and in the Bible. So, if he was to minister as he ought, he must not only expound the scriptures openly and effectively, but also embrace all that is involved in being

---

[234] One of the serious problems, if not the most serious, that we face as Christians when we would preach the gospel to the people of this world, is that the self-revelation of God, which seems to be so open and self-evident before our eyes, cannot be seen by those "whom the god of this world has blinded" (II Corinthians 4:4).

"in Christ" and a beneficiary of His life and death, and live lawfully according to God's ordinances and intentions in this world. Everything he did was to reflect and to communicate the comprehensive revelation God had given of Himself.

The task, then, involved more than eloquence, which, in a sense, is the least requirement – so let those who would preach beware! He who would *speak* in the Name of Christ ought also to *live* by the Name of Christ. There is blasphemous hypocrisy in honouring Christ with our lips if our hearts are far from Him (Matthew 15:7-8). The manifestation of the mystery must be, as it were, in both the words and in the character of the evangelist, and every Christian.

Moreover, here in Colossians 4:4, Paul remarks that he – a mere man, with distinctly human limitations – was responsible to "manifest" the mystery. This may be a particular reference to his own unique task as an apostle; which personal responsibility seems to be implied in his words in 1:25-26. He was evidently taught the truths of the gospel directly by God (Galatians 1:11-12) and specifically given an "understanding in the mystery of Christ" (Ephesians 3:3-5). And this equipped him to be an authentic apostle, with particular concern for the evangelism of the Gentiles (Galatians 2:8) – and we must never forget the uniqueness of the pristine, founding authority that was given to all the apostles to establish the church in the first place, immediately after the death and resurrection of our Lord.

We understand, then, that Paul's unique, apostolic work in manifesting the mystery evidently made tremendous demands upon his whole life (cf. Philippians 1:18-21), which probably included trials and adversities greater than most men could bear (cf. Acts 9:15-16, I Corinthians 4:9-13, II Corinthians 6:4ff.).

Nevertheless, we do ourselves no favour if we think, because we are not apostles, that less is required of us in our own lives – in commitment and intention, if not in ability or accomplishment; or if we seek to serve God with less than apostolic dedication. Paul requires us to "be imitators of" him even as he was of "Christ" (I Corinthians 11:1). In Jesus Christ is the definitive example of manifesting the truth in human life (John 1:14, 18, 14:6-10). And Paul was concerned that his readers be "renewed unto knowledge after the image of Him that created" them (3:10), and grow more like Him.

Besides, as we have seen, "whatsoever we do, in word or in deed" is to be done comprehensively "in the name of the Lord Jesus" (3:17). This is an all-embracing stipulation. And when, through faith and obedience, we do effectively Christianize all we say and do, then, no doubt imperfectly but in a truly meaningful sense, the whole of our lives begin to manifest the truth.

However, if we are to imitate Paul in this ministry with the same commitment we will inevitably – if we take the responsibility seriously – be overwhelmed by the immensity of the task. We will then exclaim, even as the apostle himself did so many years ago, "Who is sufficient for these things?" (II Corinthians 2:16).

Indeed, who is? The person least sufficient for the task is he who – perhaps looking at the framed certificates on his wall – shamelessly thinks himself to be well equipped and adequate!

Paul asked this question because he was aware that "God … makes manifest through us the savour of His knowledge" everywhere, and he in no way underestimated the most solemn implications of this ministry. Those through whom God is pleased to "make manifest … His knowledge" are indeed a "sweet savour" to God, but among men they bring the scent of death to some and the scent of life to others. It was and is always a matter of life and death – in fact, of eternal life and eternal death (II Corinthians 2:14-16). Faithful preaching of the gospel will always, in one way or another, present this alternative. We must not, then, think lightly about our Christian witness to the world, or give it only perfunctory – or, I might add, merely professional – attention. It is best undertaken in "fear and trembling" (I Corinthians 2:3, #3.5.2., Fourth 1.).

However, in this work of manifesting the truth, God is the active principal and Christians but the responsive – and responsible! – agents in making known "His knowledge". Therefore, the apostle can say, "Not that we are sufficient of ourselves … but our sufficiency is from God" (II Corinthians 3:5).

This divinely given and sustained sufficiency provided for the "ministers of the new covenant" (II Corinthians 3:6) is critically important, for at least two reasons. *First*, in our witness to the world, we carry the burden of knowing that the end result of our involvement is a matter of the life or death of other people. We are, then, in some measure instrumental in the determination of their eternal loss or well-being. *Second*, in our witness to the world, we also carry the burden of representing God Himself in all that we do. We are, then, in some measure instrumental in bringing glory – or dishonour! – to our Creator.

But herein are responsibilities far, far too onerous for any mortal man! So, we must always look beyond ourselves, our abilities, our resources, and our methods – using, perhaps, but never relying on any of them.

Nevertheless, despite these grave responsibilities, Paul assures us that we have the assistance of the Holy Spirit, and "therefore seeing we have this ministry, even as we have obtained mercy" we are not discouraged (II Corinthians 3:17-4:1). This is the apostle's assessment of our position in God's service. When done in faith, we need not be dispirited.

The task is demanding, but there is no need to lose heart.

Here we should note that Paul associates the ministry he has received with the mercy he had been given (διὰ τοῦ το,ἔχοντες τὴν διακονίαν ταύτην καθὼς ἠλεήθημεν). This implies that he would have had no ministry at all but for God's mercy (cf. Romans 15:15-16, Ephesians 3:8). Neither, for that matter, could he have received mercy without ministry! That is, he was aware that the privilege of being a Christian carries the responsibility of representing Christ here on earth (cf. Romans 1:13-14). And in this, he was assured that the work to which he was commissioned was sponsored by the Lord and supported by His grace. And this, he explains, is why he and his companions were not discouraged. This divine patronage is the context in which the apostle – and we who might seek to emulate him – could find the strength to persevere even in the most difficult circumstances (See II Corinthians 4:7-12, and cf. I Timothy 1:12-17).

The apostle was also aware that within this context certain moderating principles are required if there is to be a genuine "manifestation of the truth". There has to be a renunciation of "the hidden things of shame", a refusal to walk "in craftiness", and the truthful "handling" of "the word of God" (II Corinthians 4:2). This requires, as Paul's words here imply, a people who are truly and transparently repentant, openly honest in their intentions, and constantly faithful to God's self-revelation, all as a result of God's merciful intervention in their lives. In other words, it is the witness of men and women who are being transformed into the image of God (3.10, II Corinthians 3:17-18).

Such a person, when he "speaks the mystery of Christ" (4:3), will be in a position to commend himself "to every man's conscience" (II Corinthians 4:2); but not because of some assumed moral superiority, but in the genuine humility of a repentant sinner, well aware of his own weaknesses. *Therefore, it will not be his primary concern to commend himself to the intellect of others, but to confront their sense of moral inadequacy by confessing his own.* So, he will present himself as a simple man of humility, sincerity, and faith, because what he desires from those who listen is, first of all, meaningful repentance, which requires the agitation of their conscience. Conversion begins only when the moral question is taken seriously, therefore it is critical that the evangelist be, and be seen to be a person of Christian integrity.[235]

Paul cautions his readers that although we possess great treasure in Christ and in the gospel, we ourselves remain but "earthen vessels", frangible instruments, and the power of our ministry is God Himself. Therefore, the traumas we might face in life, the threatening situations, our frequent perplexities, and the extent to which we might suffer in our body the "dying of Jesus", are in themselves no impediment to our witness, if we desire that in every moment "the life also of Jesus might be manifested in our mortal flesh" (II Corinthians 4:7-11). The fact that "the gospel ... is ... in all the world bearing fruit and increasing" (1:5-6) – as it has been doing relentlessly for thousands of years – through the ministry of frail and dying human beings, is in itself evidence that Jesus is alive and revealing Himself through His people! And in all this, all Christians should be involved.

We must not, then, separate our evangelism from all Paul wrote above about Christian morality and holiness in character

---

[235] I deliberately use the expression 'Christian integrity', as distinct from 'moral integrity'. Only Christ Himself has the latter. The former is a matter of humble repentance and honest dependence. We are aware of our hypocrisy (cf. #3.4. Third, #3.4.1.2.). And there is a sense in which Christian *integrity* must have priority over Christian *intellect* in true ministry, although both are indispensable. Paul, we might note, is about to instruct his readers also to "walk in wisdom".

that should be evident in our lives, as we seek to manifest the truth.

But now we must consider how we might intelligently and effectively take our place among the myriads of Christians who throughout the ages and across the world have been and are involved in manifesting the mystery of Christ to a dying people. Having given a little thought to prayer and the contextualizing of evangelism (#3.6.1.), we must now give further consideration to things Paul has to say in these verses in Colossians about the appropriate *behaviour* and the required *speech* that should moderate evangelism, and by which we might effectively present the gospel.

3.6.2. Behaviour and Speech: and Moderating Evangelism (4:5-6)

If, in the interests of the gospel, for the salvation of the lost, and to glorify our God, we are to manifest the mystery of Christ in every aspect of our lives – and we have suggested that this is our responsibility as His servants – then it is imperative that we "walk in wisdom toward them that are without" and that our "speech be always with grace" (4:5-6). This indicates that if we are to bridge the divide between us and the non-Christians with genuine concern for their eternal well-being, we must approach them in an appropriately moderated manner, in both our demeanour and our conversation.

But the readers of this letter have been prepared for this imperative. When we were considering the moral strength and fortitude Christians need to live as they ought in this present, evil world, we saw that Paul prayed for the Colossian believers that they might "be filled with the knowledge of His will in all spiritual wisdom and understanding, to walk worthily of the Lord unto all pleasing" (1:9-10, see #1.2.). If the Lord so ministers to them, then their demeanour will be moderated by both God-given wisdom and knowledge, and not by the philosophies of men. Now, as the apostle advises them to give serious thought to their behaviour and speech, these two factors reappear – they are to walk in "wisdom" and to "know" how to answer others (4:5). The Lord provides not only the specific *ethical* insight but also the definitive *noetic* comprehension that are required for faithful Christian living and significant conversation. Moreover, to "walk worthily of the Lord" is to "walk in wisdom" towards the outsider.

Therefore, having prayed that God might enable the Colossians "to walk worthily of the Lord", that they might be "pleasing" to Him (1:10), Paul now has no hesitation in requiring that they "walk in wisdom towards them that are without", that they might be Christianly presentable to them (4:5). Both – pleasing to God and presentable to men – must be their concern, for if they give attention to the former, they will be efficient in the latter. Then what was once impossible for them – godly behaviour – is progressively achievable with divine assistance. And as a result, they will be able to manifest the mystery of Christ, albeit at first – and often subsequently – with stumbling hesitation, but nonetheless effectively. *But this demands that our true 'presentability' be the result of grace and godliness, and not a superficial, sycophantic, adaptation to contemporary, fashionable modes and morals.*

We must not be so foolish, then, as to imagine that we might present ourselves in one way to our non-Christian neighbours, and in another before the throne of God. Duplicity is extraneous and inimical to godliness. This means that what we are in our private communion with the Almighty is directly relevant to what we will be in public engagement with the people of this world. Or, if we are not rightly and thoroughly contextualized by our prayers, we are unlikely to be rightly and thoroughly moderated in our evangelism.

3.6.2.1. Behaviour (4:5)

Paul is referring to the appropriate, Christian demeanour when he commands his readers to "walk in wisdom". Although we may be judged to be fools by others (I Corinthians 3:18) and our motivating ideas thought to be inane (I Corinthians 1:21), we ought nonetheless to be guided in all we do by the wisdom that is from God, even as we are being "renewed unto knowledge" (3:10) by His grace. We are well advised by the apostle elsewhere to walk carefully, "not as unwise, but as wise" (Ephesians 5:15).

Whatever else we – or others – might think about wise behaviour, we can with some confidence say that for the Christian it necessarily involves consciously accepting the moderation of life through increasing knowledge of God and by intentionally living within His will and purposes. In this, Christian wisdom is unique, markedly different from and should never be confused with the wisdom which is the product of the "philosophy … of men" (2:8). Therefore, it is critical that we learn how to distinguish between "the wisdom … from above" and that which is "earthly, sensual, devilish"; a distinction, as James makes clear, that is evident not only in abstract theory and logic but, more significantly, in attitude and conduct (James 3:13-18). To "walk in" God's wisdom makes a tangible and discernible difference in life. Wisdom that produces only verbal conundrums and seemingly irrefutable syllogisms, whatever their value, may contribute little or nothing to the wisdom that gives birth to a life of godliness.

We do the world around us no good at all if we allow its wisdom – its philosophy after the traditions of men – to moderate our ways and practices. If we yield to their persuasive speech (2:4) and follow their customs, we will do no more than give our assent to their confusion of thought and compound the darkness of their minds. And if we embrace the logic of their reasoning, we will soon find ourselves walking in their ways.

I shall say no more about the uniqueness of Christian wisdom here, having mentioned it briefly above (#1.2.).

However, I might add, to walk in wisdom – true, Christian wisdom – is not an attempt to complement or redirect the wisdom of the world, as if to make some contribution to the existing worldview of the non-Christian mind. Rather, it is to offer the world, and exemplify before it, a fundamentally different way of thinking and behaving altogether – even when we are judged to be simpleminded by our contemporaries (I Corinthians 3:18-21).

Therefore, if we are to be faithful ambassadors for Christ, we cannot overlook the importance of the way we present ourselves. This obligation to live in the godliness that is generated by true wisdom, and the importance of such conduct in evangelism, is often stressed in scripture (eg. Matthew 5:16, 10:16, II Corinthians 4:2, Philippians 2:14-16, I Thessalonians 1:5-7, Titus 2:5,7-8). Hence, the Colossians are advised to consider their "walk" for, among other things, the sake of "them that are without" (4:5), the unconverted.

The apostle mentions here two aspects of appropriate Christian behaviour, or "walk":

- **First,** walk and wisdom.

  Facing this imperative to "walk in wisdom", we must acknowledge both our *responsibility* and our *privilege* to do so as Christian believers if we are to live conscientiously in this world as ambassadors for Christ (see #3.5.1.).

  The apostle makes reference to the Christian's walk elsewhere, giving us a number of indications of the *character* or quality of such godly conduct. Those who behave accordingly will do so "honestly" (Romans 13:13, I Thessalonians 4:12), in "good works", "worthily of the calling", "in love", "as children of light", and with precision (Ephesians 2:10, 4:1, 5:2, 8, 15). This provides some explication of the "newness of life" which we should manifest as a result of our being "united" with Christ in His death and resurrection (Romans 6:4-5, cf. Colossians 2:10-15).

This should leave us in no doubt about the responsibility we have as Christian men and women.

Being the beneficiaries of Christ's death and resurrection places us under the obligation not to "let ... sin therefore reign in (our) mortal body, that (we) should obey (its) lusts" (Romans 6:12). If God has made it possible for us to live honestly, in love and good works, then we are required to do so. We cannot excuse ourselves simply by pleading our conspicuous moral and intellectual inadequacies; neither can we absolve ourselves by simply complaining that God has done too little to help us.

However, if we are honest with ourselves, we will admit that all our accomplishments in the service of God lack perfection, and are only accepted by Him because He is merciful. Nevertheless, we must not resile from our responsibility, or modify its requirements for our own convenience.

Paul has also given us at least two clear indications of the *means* by which we might maintain a godly walk. It should be "not after the flesh, but after the Spirit" (Romans 8:4, μὴ κατὰ σάρκα περιπατοῦσιν ἀλλὰ κατὰ πνεῦμα), and "by faith" (II Corinthians 5:7, διὰ πίστεως γὰρ περιπατοῦμεν) – the vital presence of God's Spirit and our trusting response. This indicates that in the exercise of godly living we are completely dependent upon the assistance of the Spirit, and that we will not find the necessary resources we need solely within our own being, our "flesh". Therefore, we must proceed in deliberate and sincere reliance upon His grace.

This should leave us in no doubt about the privilege we have as Christian men and women.

Being born again by the Spirit of God, and empowered by Him to live for the glory of God is an inestimable advantage that the non-Christian knows nothing about. Our Lord has not only made us "more than conquerors", but has guaranteed that nothing "shall be able to separate us from the love of God" (Romans 8:37, 39). But these things are to be enjoyed by us precisely because He has promised, "I will never leave you nor forsake you" (Hebrews 13:5).

We are invited, then, not only to live *for* the Lord, but also to live *with* Him!

All this, I suggest, requires more than casual interest; it demands some serious and intelligent thought and a positive and persistent response.

If we are to present ourselves to the world as Christ's ambassadors to beseech others to be reconciled to God (II Corinthians 5:20), we must be armed with an appreciation of all that is involved in this responsibility and privilege. If we are not, then to "walk in wisdom towards them that are without" will be beyond us – we will only stumble in our folly. Renewed understanding provides the knowledge we need to give substance to our wisdom (see #1.2.1.2.). Then we need to make clear to those we would advise to become Christians precisely what will be required of them if they do – and this we cannot do effectively if we ourselves are unsure of, or careless about the requirements.

To summarize, if we are *to walk wisely* we must be knowledgeable about our God-given responsibilities and privileges. Moreover, if we are to effectively communicate and implement the knowledge we have of God and His ways, we also need *to be wise*. Therefore, we would do well to acknowledge our frequent foolishness and ask God for the wisdom we truly need (James 1:5).

- **Second,** walk and time.

We are required to manifest the mystery of Christ in this very tangible and tiring world of space and time, the world of joy and pain, of beauty and ugliness, of good and evil, of plenty and famine, and of hope and despair. The gospel is relevant in any and every situation in which we find ourselves, and cannot be restricted to the occasional, the purely subjective, or the ethereal. It must be seen to be significant and sufficient in all circumstances, whether these are desirable or undesirable, and to be powerful in both life and death.

Those who look for a religion that is significant only in particulars that they designate as important for themselves, and that does not make plenary demands upon the whole of life, will not find it in Christianity – at least, not in the pristine faith of our Lord and His apostles. Numerous sub-Christian groups may, and often do, offer spurious, self-indulgent alternatives in the name of Christ. But such substitutes for the original are only manifestations of idolatry because they are built upon misunderstandings of God Himself – and this is a problem we should constantly beware (I John 5:21).

It is because of this very troubled world with its conflictive and contradictory circumstances that Paul advises his readers to "walk ... redeeming the time" (4:5, τὸν καιρὸν ἐξαγοραζόμενοι). He gave similar advice to the Ephesians concerning wisdom and their behaviour in evil days (Ephesians 5:15).

But these words, "redeeming the time", seem to be used here idiomatically, and the apostle's exact meaning is to some extent obscure and, hence, they are variously translated.[236]

However, it is interesting that the word Paul used here for "redeeming" (ἐξαγοράζω) is derived from the noun for 'marketplace' (ἀγορά) and implies 'buying', 'buying back', or 'buying up'. And it does seem to retain something of this original meaning in the way the apostle uses it. In Galatians 3:13 and 4:5 (in active voice) it refers to our redemption from "the curse of the law" that leads to the "adoption of sons". It is, as it were, the purchase of the slave that he might be adopted into the family of God. The underlying principle is the change of ownership or possession, and, hence, one's future.

Now, I see no reason why we should not find the same basic principle in Ephesians 5:16, and here in Colossians 4:5, where the same word is used (in middle voice). If the "days are evil" and the "time" corrupted, then they are possessed by evil forces, both human and satanic, and used for villainous purposes. It is our responsibility to 'buy them back' and possess them for the glory of God. We should no more abandon time to the violation of wickedness than we should stand by and do nothing about the defiling of the physical. Indeed, it would be impossible to care for the one and neglect the other.

Then, the other word Paul uses here is also significant – "time". He has chosen to use the word 'kairos' (καιρός), rather than 'chronos' (χρόνος). These two words for 'time', both being found and so translated in the New Testament, are not exact synonyms, although they interrelate with each other and overlap in meaning. Oversimplifying, but to indicate the difference, we might say that the latter refers to a specific time – a time 'at which' – or to a period of time – the time 'during which' – something happens or may happen. But the former refers to the nature or the quality of the period or the 'season' in view – such as a good time, a bad time, a troubled time, a chaotic time, "a time to weep, and a time to laugh; a time to mourn and a time to dance" (Ecclesiastes 3:1ff.).

As he chose this particular word, 'kairos', I suggest that Paul is not advising his readers to manage their diary well and to avoiding wasting the hours and the days they may have – as good as this advice might be (cf. Psalm 39:4, 90:12, James 4:14). It was not the chronology or length of the times, but the characteristic components of the times that concerned

---

[236] They are sometimes paraphrased with expressions such as "using the time most effectively", or "making the best use of the opportunity".

him. He is requiring, then, that they, walking in wisdom, should be cognizant of the actual quality and constitution of the times in which they live, being aware of the factors determining the intellectual, moral, and social conditions of their current situation, so that they might be able to redeem their days from evil – buying back time from satanic corruption. How are chaotic days to be converted to times of peace? How can wickedness be expunged from the daily life of the community except it be recognized, deliberately and intelligently confronted, and replaced by godliness?

And what source of godliness is there except in the Christian gospel? And how is it to be introduced and established in society except through Christian evangelism? Truly effective evangelism will not only bring redemption to the individuals who believe, but will also redeem the times, and generate wholesome and genuinely productive seasons in life – and, hopefully, in history.

When the mystery of Christ is truly manifested in the lives of God's people, culture is enriched, and the course of history may well be changed for the better. This has happened, and can happen again! And the more this change is effected in the Christian community, the greater its influence in the world.

But all this obviously requires the critical and practical thinking of true wisdom, which we have discussed above (#1.2.1.2.).

Perhaps we can better understand Paul's concern here if we consider his advice to Timothy: "Preach the word; be instant in season, out of season ... for the time will come when they will not endure the sound teaching" (II Timothy 4:2-3, κήρυξον τὸν λόγον,ἐπίστηθι εὐκαίρως ἀκαίρως ... ἔσται γὰρ καιρὸς ὅτε τῆς ὑγιαινούσης διδασκαλίας οὐκ ἀνέξονται).

The apostle is reminding Timothy, his young associate, that there will be a "time" (kairos, καιρός, a 'season') that will be configured by people who do not accept "sound teaching", who, we might assume, prefer the "philosophy and vain deceit ... of men" (2:8). To the extent that they are influential, their thinking will determine the intellectual, moral, and social conditions of their day. Then, whether we feel comfortable or not within that environment, it will be in those conditions that we must manifest the mystery of Christ – or, evangelize. We will have to contend with teachers – and preachers! – who fashion their theories to condone the corrupted passions acceptable in their community, and to provide the pleasurable words that the people desire to hear. Hence Paul refers to those who have "itching ears", and desire to be instructed according to "their own lusts" (II Timothy 4:3).

Paul's advice to Timothy – and hence, also to us – is that he "in the sight of God, and of Christ Jesus, who will judge ... preach the word" and "be instant in season and out of season" in doing so (II Timothy 4:1-2, ἐνώπιον τοῦ θεοῦ καὶ Χριστοῦ Ἰησοῦ τοῦ μέλλοντος κρίνειν ... κήρυξον τὸν λόγον, ἐπίστηθι εὐκαίρως ἀκαίρως). He was, in other words, to preach the message of the gospel, being constantly aware that he was ministering in the sight of God, realizing that the Lord was assessing the work he did and the things he proclaimed. It mattered little how his contemporaries might evaluate his message, for he knew that he was answerable to Christ Himself. The opposition might be intimidating, his social status imperilled, and his professional position endangered, but it was critical in this service that in word and deed, he did all "in the name of the Lord" (3:17).

Moreover, Timothy should be ready (ἐπίστηθι) to do this, whether the occasion presents itself 'seasonably' or 'unseasonably' (εὐκαίρως ἀκαίρως). The two adverbs used here are compounds of the word for "time" (kairos) – suggesting times both good and bad, convenient and inconvenient, when safe to do so, and when dangerous. We are not so much, then, to trust God for the resolution of the difficulties of the times that we might freely preach the gospel, but to trust Him in the difficult times as we preach the gospel even when there is no immediate solution for the problems, anticipating that the preaching of the gospel might well be instrumental by the grace of God in redeeming the time. We are not to wait for the 'right' or the propitious time before we preach, or manifest the mystery of Christ, but to make this enterprise a constant and a consistent feature of the manner in which we live and speak.

When war brings fear and loss to our community, we should preach the gospel; when peace brings complacency and affluence, we should preach the gospel – both times having their own difficulties for us. However, neither the one nor the other is 'off season'! Each has its own features and requires the appropriate Christian response. I have suggested above that evangelism involves the interpretation of the whole of life in reference to the gospel, and this involves making a 'gospel evaluation' – a Christian analysis – of every 'season' and every situation in which we find ourselves. If we do not, how will we be able to position ourselves intelligently and strategically that we might "walk in wisdom toward them that are without" in our "time" (4:5)? How else are we to be lights in the darkness?

We might well keep in mind that Paul rarely preached in times that were propitious!

Our behaviour – the manner in which we live as Christians in a non-Christian world – must then be moderated by a wise understanding of our 'privileges' and 'responsibilities' in the service of our Lord, and by an analytical appreciation of every 'season', making use of them all for the glory of our God. Only then will our evangelism be as comprehensive and as significant as it ought to be.

But now we must consider how Christian behaviour involves *the godly use of language*, a matter of great importance that is more often than not neglected, or simply taken for granted without much thought.

3.6.2.2. SPEECH (4:6)

Godliness in behaviour is indispensable for our witness to the world, but as evangelism is also very much a matter of articulating – as well as manifesting – "the mystery of Christ", effective Christian speech, an integral aspect of our conduct, is also essential. Our verbal expression should be of the highest quality, being moderated by our holiness. The Christian, acknowledging that God has chosen to reveal Himself to us in words[237], should have the highest regard for their use in human conversation. This is a vehicle for interpersonal communication we must not abuse or degrade. We should "always" (4:6), as Paul indicates, take care for the manner in which we talk and be meticulous about what we say.

- **First**, the problem with language.

    There is an abundance of evidence that biblical authors were acutely sensitive to the deleterious effect the fall and human sinfulness can – and constantly do – have upon language and its use. *Our speech, as with every other aspect of our lives, is in need of redemption.* The ancient wise man, for example, noted that "a fool's lips enter into contention", "a fool's mouth is his destruction", and that "death and life are in the power of the tongue" (Proverbs 18:6, 7, 21). Being aware of the extreme damage the misuse of speech can do, the Psalmist – that master of words! – prayed, "Set a watch, O Lord, before my mouth; keep the door of my lips" (Psalm 141:3). He also advised his readers, "Keep your tongue from evil, and your lips from speaking guile" (Psalm 34:13, cf. I Peter 3:10).

    To appreciate the complexity of this problem and to discover some solution to it, we must recognize that the damage the tongue generates is, I suggest, the result of at least two aberrations:

---

[237] He spoke, for example, to Adam in Eden (Genesis 1:28), to the "fathers in the prophets", and "in His Son" (Hebrews 1:1-2).

1. *Moral seduction,* in which language is used with the intention of corrupting or demeaning others and *enticing their passions,* often for the most sordid of reasons – in, for example, blasphemy, lying, gossip, calumny, slander, disparaging, tempting, and the like.

2. *Intellectual deception,* in which language is employed to academically manipulate others with the intention of propagating a spurious ideology and *enslaving their minds,* often for the most sophisticated of reasons – in, for example, cunning rhetoric, deliberate catachresis, newspeak, propaganda, deliberate ambiguities, sophisticated paralogisms, assertions resulting from assumed knowledge, distorting or concealing relevant data, and the like.

The Psalmist and Peter, as referred to immediately above, probably have in view the first of these aberrations when they write about keeping the "tongue from evil", the moral problem; and to the second in their comment about "speaking guile", the intellectual problem. However, we need not make too much of this distinction as every act of malevolent speech is inevitably a combination of both, attempting to entice the passions and to enslave the minds of others. And this should not surprise us because language always has both emotive and cognitive content, each being susceptible to misuse and abuse.

- **Second,** the origin and extent of the problem.

We might say that the abuse of language – whether morally or intellectually – lies at the heart of the whole human dilemma; it is an instrumental cause of the tragic circumstances in which we find ourselves. It is far more profound and pervasive than perhaps most people imagine, and it cannot be dismissed as trivial persiflage. Moreover, it is ancient in origin, runs deeply and influentially in every culture, it is a weapon 'mightier than the sword', and a persistent problem that has always confounded the Christian's testimony to the world.

Therefore, I suggest, it is of the utmost importance that we, to the best of our ability, discover how to deal with this problem, and to realize, implement, and promote the beauty, the worth, the effective nuances, and the power of godly human speech. We must take in hand "the sword of the Spirit, which is the Word of God" (Ephesians 6:17) – that commanding, authoritative, divine word which provides, I suggest, the ultimate directive, rationale, and moderating principle for all interpersonal communications – to the end that we might rightly defend and propagate our beliefs. That is, in other words, we would do well to learn the excellent use of language by emulating the Creator and Master of all language.

When Satan in the Garden of Eden asked the first critical question, "Hath God said …?" (Genesis 3:1ff.), he not only impugned the validity of God's word, but also subverted the reliability of all verbal expression – and in doing so he had the temerity, like many of our contemporaries, to use language to deconstruct language! He was implying that God could not effectively communicate His ideas through words, and if He, the Almighty, could not do so, then words cannot be sufficient for that purpose, and language ceases to be a suitable vehicle for the truth.

Moreover, as the enemy of our souls insinuated, if God deliberately used words to deceive Adam and Eve, then words cease to be a reliable and authoritative vehicle for moral instruction and cannot express axiological absolutes, being initially a contrivance, designed by the Almighty, for deception.

Satan, then, disputed the intellectual viability and the moral adequacy of language itself.

And, as some of our modern contemporaries contend, because language fails to relate us to truth or to values, we have no procedure for discerning, let alone communicating, any significant meaning at all. Then life becomes a 'tale told by an idiot, signifying nothing'.[238]

And when language fails, we turn to the intuitive, the subjective, the mystical, and the Gnostic, isolating ourselves within our own, lonely, depleted self-consciousness. Godly rationality, with true wisdom, beauty and goodness, are lost in the labyrinth of relentless, idiosyncratic relativity.

What the devil did in Eden was to decontextualize the words God had spoken, advising Eve not to understand them in reference to God and His purposes, but to evaluate them in reference to herself and her desires. She was enticed to view God's words from the perspective of her own milieu; she was to determine for herself the trustworthiness, the value, the applicability, and the significance of things her Creator had said. Or, I might suggest, she was asked to culturally re-interpret them. In her response, she professed herself to be independently wise and inevitably became a fool (cf. Romans 1:22).[239]

---

[238] Shakespeare, Macbeth, Act 5, Scene 5.

[239] In effect, we might say, Eve denied the significance – or the accessibility – of authorial intention in God's words, and was only concerned about the reader's response. And many modern linguistic critics and theologians follow her example!

Ever since the disaster in Eden, man in rebellion against God has continued to have serious difficulty with language, using it, as often as not, in a devastating manner. If God has not or cannot express truth in words to communicate knowledge and instruction to man made in His image – as those committed to the "philosophy ... of men" (2:8) usually insist – then words and verbal communication are cut adrift from meaning and become nothing more than mundane instruments that people use primarily for their own purpose, usually as weapons of conquest to gain influence over others, to "make spoil" of them (2:8). Our 'word games' become 'power play'![240]

It is evident that when language is deprived of its integrity and viability in human discourse, it eviscerates not only human-to-human but also divine-to-human communication. Therefore, I suggest, the redemption of the former is dependent upon the recovery of the latter. It is the Christian hope that if God can convey truth to man through words, then there is the redemptive possibility for man to convey truth to man through words, but only when man's words are moderated by divine words. But this recovery in interpersonal communication requires the restoration of the necessary integrity and viability in human discourse through the return to godliness of character which is only effected by the grace of God.

Therefore, as the beneficiaries of being "in Christ", those who believe in Him ought to be notably more articulate and communicative – at least in having better things to say, more gracious ways of saying them, and altruistic motives in doing so.

In other words, if we are to speak Christianly and effectively articulate the truths of the gospel, we need something far more important and basic than oratorical skills and good elocution – it requires the moral character that is only found "in Christ".

If God has spoken and does effectively communicate knowledge and instruction, then we might well anticipate finding in His words the means to redeem human language itself by anchoring it in the mind of our Creator. Moreover, as God has prescribed that He be made known through preaching, it follows that He intends to redeem human language for that purpose (cf. I Corinthians 1:21, 2:13). And this divine intention is at the back of Paul's advice to the Colossians here, where he exhorts his readers to speak as they ought.

---

[240] And today, with the vast possibilities of electronic media to communicate ideas, this 'power play' – often illogical and unprincipled – is a vast, ominous, and often anti-Christian force.

Moreover, if language is powerful and delicate, susceptible to use and abuse, and if it is both an essential instrument in the proclamation of the Christian gospel as well as a weapon for the propagation of evil, then, because of our evangelistic responsibility, we must employ it with care, sensitivity, and responsibility as men and women concerned for the holiness of the whole of life, including the sanctity of speech. And to this end, we should consider Paul's advice to the Colossians in this regard.

- **Third**, the apostle's advice.

Paul was obviously perturbed by the misuse of language and its deleterious effects. We have seen that he cautioned his readers not to be confused by the deceptive and misleading speech of the false teachers who were attempting to turn them away from the Christian faith (2:4, #2.2.2.). Here is a warning not only about the danger of a false philosophy but also about the misuse of language in its propagation – the dual problem of erroneous content and insufferable method. The apostle would certainly not have wanted the Colossians to use the same deceptive, misleading, and manipulative rhetoric to defend their own theological position, any more than he would have wanted them to compromise their own teaching. It would simply be immoral to do either – to propagate an erroneous message or to employ intolerable methodology! *Their use of language was to be sanctified.*

We should not be beguiled into thinking that we can defeat our opponents by using their oratorical methods, verbal arguments, deceptive reasoning, and emotional manipulation. This would not only obfuscate the very message we wish to convey to the world, but it would also abandon the responsibility we have for redeeming language through the moderation of holiness, leaving the whole human community further impoverished and confused.

The apostle, in his advice to the churches facing the constant, contra-Christian influences of secular and pagan thought and propaganda, makes *two astute comments* concerning this problem that we should consider and compare. *First*, he advised the Romans about the danger of "smooth and fair speech" that might "beguile the hearts of the innocent" (Romans 16:18, διὰ τῆς χρηστολογίας καὶ εὐλογίας ἐξαπατῶσιν τὰς καρδίας τῶν ἀκάκων). And, *second*, he would not have anyone "delude" the Colossians "with persuasiveness of speech" (2:4, ἵνα μηδεὶς ὑμᾶς παραλογίζηται ἐν πιθανολογίᾳ).

In these verses, there are a number of important matters we should consider:

1. Two threatening, motivational dangers.

There are *two active dangers* here: Christians – let alone the unconverted – might be 'beguiled' (ἐξαπατῶσιν), and they might be 'deluded' (παραλογίζηται). The *first* word here suggests deliberate trickery, or seduction, such as would corrupt the innocent, or inexperienced. It seems to convey the idea of the unethical being employed for an illicit, possibly carnal, purpose.[241] The *second* word suggests the subtle, but erroneous use of reasoning and logical argument, to deceive others into turning away from the "wisdom and knowledge" that are in Christ, and to commit themselves to some false ideology.

If this is the correct distinction, then we might see here reference to the *moral seductions* that debauch language, in Romans 16:18; and to the *intellectual deceptions* that pervert language, in Colossians 2:4; to which we referred above.

The Christian should beware these motivating dangers in those would influence him. He should also beware the possibility that he might himself be similarly motivated when attempting to influence others.

Again, to appreciate the integration of Paul's thinking, we should remember that he has written of the gracious advantages the Christian enjoys (2:8-19, #3.2.), the intellectual principles of the Christian's worldview (2:20-3:4, #3.3.), and the values of Christian morality (3:5-17, #3.4.). *There is, then, grace given in our faith that we might recognize and overcome intellectual perversion and that we might discern and rise above moral debauchery. Then, when we make use of these mercies, we will neither succumb to such influences nor be tempted to use them.*

Therefore, we would do well to pray for each other that we might "be filled with the knowledge of His will in all spiritual wisdom and understanding" – avoiding intellectual perversion – and that we might "walk worthily of the Lord … bearing fruit in every good work" – avoiding moral debauchery (1:9-10).

I suggest, then, that anyone who would converse Christianly and preach faithfully ought to give serious thought to these matters. Grace is our only defence against hypocritical motives.

---

[241] Hence the reference to the perpetrators serving not Christ, but their own "belly/appetites" in Romans 16.

2. Three devious, instrumental means.

There are indications in Romans 16:18 and Colossians 2:4 of *three instrumental means* – three ways of abusing language – that effectuate these *two motivational dangers*. These are seen in Paul's words "smooth", "fair", and "persuasiveness" of speech. These might be translated: "useful words" (χρηστολογία), "encouraging words" (εὐλογία), and "persuasive words" (πιθανολογία). All these terms might be used in a good sense, as I have attempted to indicate with the expressions I have used here.[242] Language can and does have a useful, encouraging, and persuasive applications that may well enrich human associations and facilitate communication. Indeed, at its best, this is what language should do.

Nevertheless, because language can also be used destructively, the best of expressions can be employed deceptively. So evidently these basically *good words* are used by Paul with an implied *bad connotation* in the verses we are considering. Therefore, they are variously translated, "smooth and fair speech", "smart talk and flattery", "fair and flattering words", or something similar, in Romans 16:18; and "plausible argument", "fine-sounding words", "beguiling speech", or something similar, in Colossians 4:2. The context imparts something ironic, or even sinister, to their use.

All these words and what they indicate, then, may have legitimate use and positive meaning, being just words. Language can and should be practical, reassuring, and convincing, but it can be all these for either a good or for an evil purpose, depending upon the motivation and intention of the speaker. We can consider every word as a small vessel that comes to us filled with meaning given to it by its history and by any nuance imparted to it by the user. Then the clever rhetorician, or author, can surreptitiously manipulate both the cognitive and the emotive content of the word, and use it to control the minds and hearts of the hearers, or readers, to divert them from the truth.

The very fact that Paul uses these three words as he does, shows that he recognized this subtlety in human language

---

[242] The second, for example, "encouraging words" (εὐλογία), is elsewhere in Paul's New Testament letters translated "blessing" and "generosity" (cf. Romans 15:29, II Corinthians 9:5, Galatians 3:14, Ephesians 1:3).

and was aware of the danger. Wholesome words were being used with evil intent by those who would corrupt the people, including Christian believers, to distort their thinking, and pervert their morality.[243] Thereby they cleverly appeal to selfish ambition, inveigle the proud ego, and flatter the sophisticated mind – using smooth, flattering, and plausible vocabulary. And often the greater the plausibility, the subtler the deceptiveness.

We must be careful, for example, when listening to some who eloquently promote the cause of 'freedom' – surely a righteous goal? – lest their concealed agenda is libertinism, licentiousness, and unprincipled passion. Or we should beware those who argue the cause of 'justice' – another virtuous objective? – as a means of imposing the restrictive and selective regulations of their own dubious ideology. And how often in our contemporary society is the word 'love' use for the promoting of sensuality and lust?

All this involves using noble words for the most ignoble purposes – the advancing of wicked causes in the guise of kindness and benevolence, or of 'progress'.

The Christian, in his pursuit of holiness and for the glory of God, must strenuously eschew any such deceptive and immoral misuse of language. Therefore, the apostle insists that our "speech should always be with grace, seasoned with salt" (4:6).

The words "speech (or, word) should always be with grace" (ὁ λόγος ὑμῶν πάντοτε ἐν χάριτι) may be mildly translated, 'always speak kindly', or something similar. However, in the powerful context of all that Paul has been writing in this letter, I cannot but sense that he had much more in mind.

There is a similar comment in 3:16,[244] where the apostle is writing about using language in song – as verbal exchange – to teach and admonish one another. This should be done, he explains, "with grace in your hearts" (ἐν χάριτι ... ἐν ταῖς καρδίαις ὑμῶν). Here it is required that grace affects a man from within, for the sake of genuine communication, not simply that it modify the words used. The genuineness and sincerity of speech must be generated in the soul, that is, in the

---

[243] Consider, for example, how frequently statements of false doctrines are 'Christianised' by the inclusion of biblical terms and phrases.

[244] The word "grace" is only found twice in the Colossians letter, in 3:16 and 4:6. Both in reference to the use of language.

gracious character of the speaker, for they cannot be produced by the mere formation of the words, which, as we have seen, can be most disingenuous. As we know, 'speaking kindly' can be deceptive, seductive, and even secretively vicious! It is only the godliness of the man that determines whether his "speech" will "always be with grace".[245] This, perhaps, is what Paul means by "seasoned with salt" (4:6), being people of true character.[246]

And this grace (as suggested immediately above, 1.), is defensive and enables the Christian to avoid intellectual deception and moral seduction in both behaviour and language. But it is also powerfully and positively effective when it drives both our way of speaking and the content of our speech; and when it does, elocution and illocution become rich vehicles for grace itself, being filled with mercy and blessing.

If it is correct, as I proposed above (#3.5.2. First), that Paul does not expect his readers to embrace his instructions about marriage, family, and society unless they have "put on ... a heart of compassion, kindness, humility, meekness" and "longsuffering" (3:10, 12), then we might assume that he would not anticipate that anyone would speak always in grace without these same benefits.

Speaking "always with grace" presupposes living "always with grace" – or the life lived is only a manifestation of reprehensible hypocrisy.

NOTE: If these two threatening dangers and the instrumental abuses of language are facing us in the world today – and we have no doubt that they are – then we need to learn not only how to maintain our moral probity in a pagan, secular society, but also how to sustain our intellectual integrity in the educated and sophisticated non-Christian environment in which we find ourselves. And as

---

[245] In the phrase "always be with grace" (πάντοτε ἐν χάριτι), the first word is highly significant – "always". A form of graciousness, especially in speech, can always be contrived, put on in pretense for some ulterior motive. It can be an oratorical performance, perhaps too often practiced in the pulpit. However, to illustrate the importance of grace in the whole of life, Paul was insistent that the church leader must be "one that rules well his own house" (I Timothy 3:4). We might say, then, that if he is not gracious in his own home, he will not genuinely be so in the congregation – "always ... with grace" demands a compelling consistency. A wise man said to me many, many years ago, 'The greatest danger to the Christian ministry is the closed manse door.' It took me some years before I really began to appreciate his words.

[246] The word 'salt' does refer, I suggest, to character in Matthew 5:13, Mark 9:49-50, and Luke 14:34-35.

morality and understanding are mutually interdependent, if we fail in one we will fail in the other.

Therefore, among other things, it is incumbent upon us as Christians as we seek maturity for ourselves, to equip our children in our homes and in our churches that they might be able to conserve and to emulate the ethical standards and the rational principles of Christ, in the face of all opposition. We fail in our duty if we leave them ill-equipped to resist the beguiling and devastating influences of this world and its deceptive rhetoric.

We ought, then, not only to teach our sons and daughters to beware being morally seduced by some erethistic paramour when we send them to college or university, and to maintain their Christian virtue; but also, to give them understanding that will enable them to avoid the intellectual seduction of their sophisticated, unbelieving teachers, and to maintain their Christian beliefs. *This also is our evangelistic responsibility.*

◆

COLOSSIANS 4:7-18.

4. PERSONAL REFERENCES

As the apostle concludes this letter to the Colossians, he makes reference by name to ten of his friends and fellow workers. Perhaps the most significant aspect of these few verses is the overall picture they give us of the ethos of the early church and of the fascinating diversity of the people who were at that time engaged in the ministry of the gospel. This is no ethereal scene depicting mythical characters or the heroes of the Elysian fields, as if in such company we should find examples of the kind of people we should be; neither is it a catalogue of perfect saints we should consider impeccable. Rather, we see only normal, everyday people, simple men and women just like ourselves, who gave themselves to live in an ordinary manner, and to do so in the common concourse of life in – despite the cultural, social, and lifestyle differences that have developed over the years – essentially the same world as that in which we now find ourselves. These were human beings living in the realities of a material world!

But I suggest that what is particularly noteworthy about these ancient men and women is that they were found living in this world for the glory of God, evidently inspired by the hope of the gospel and the love of Christ. They were, no doubt, anxious to contribute to the progress of "the gospel … in all the world", and that it continue to bear fruit and increase (1:5-6). And in this, *inter alia*, they are prototypical Christians.

There are a few things about these archetypal believers that I think are worth briefly considering, as I rapidly bring to an end these studies in Paul's letter to the Colossians. They appear as the kind of people the apostle would invite to be his co-workers in the service of the gospel.

Three of those Paul named were Jews – Aristarchus, Mark, and Jesus Justus (4:11, being "of the circumcision") – and the others, Gentiles. One was evidently a woman and house owner – Nympha. One seemed to have stumbled in the early days of his ministry (Acts 13:13, 15:37-38), but recovered to author one of the four gospels – Mark; another, in contrast, resiled from the ministry he had with the apostle, being distracted by his love for "this present world" (II Timothy 4:10) – Demas. One was a converted, sophisticated, and scholarly doctor – Luke; and another was a converted, runaway slave (Philemon 10) – Onesimus. Then, Aristarchus had proven to be a longstanding and courageous companion and fellow-prisoner of the apostle (Acts 19:29, 20:4, 27:2); Tychicus to be both beloved and faithful; and Epaphras both hardworking and prayerful as a "servant of Christ". Archippus was perhaps a younger man in the ministry, in need of some encouragement. And of Jesus Justus, we know nothing.

This was truly a motley of people from various races, societies, and cultures. They had evidently been united together in the common cause of proclaiming the gospel in the service of the Lord. There is enough evidence to suggest that they were equipped with different talents, for among them we find such as the theologian (Paul), the writer (Mark), the historian/physician (Luke), the evangelist (Epaphras), the pastor (Archippus, possibly), the messenger (Tychicus), and the hostess (Nympha).[247]

However, it is, I believe, particularly important to note that Paul does not recommend any of these people to the church in Colossae, or to his readers, because of their abilities or qualifications, but because they were beloved, faithful, and sedulous servants, slaves of Christ (4:7, 12). *It was undoubtedly their holiness of character and their devotion to their God that made them the people they were and, above all else, equipped them for their Christian service.* In this, they were men and women who, to a greater or lesser degree, had realized the benefits of being crucified and raised with Christ (2:12-13).

We might assume that, being friends and colleagues of the apostle, they were familiar with Paul's teaching, even as this is outlined in his letter to the Colossians. And if so, they knew how to walk in Christ (2:6), and were careful not to be ensnared by the "philosophy ... of men" (2:8). They would have "set (their) mind on the things that were above, not on the things on the earth" (3:2). They conscientiously sought to live a morally acceptable life as they "put away ... anger, wrath, malice" and the like (3:8), and "put on ... compassion, kindness, humility" and kindred attitudes (3:12). They would have recognized and honoured the social

---

[247] Not that I would limit the ministry of any of these individuals to only one of these disciplines – some, no doubt, exercised their service in several, if not all categories mentioned.

values of Christian community (3:18-4:1). And their "speech" would have been "with grace" (4:6).

This is not to suggest that they were *perfect people*, but only that they were highly *principled people*. They would have been driven by the desire to do everything "in the name of Christ" (3:17). And since their day, myriads of such people, being similarly motivated, have followed them in succeeding generations of believers – and so it must always be in the Christian Church. And today, if we are truly serious about being involved in our Lord's work in modern society, we need men and women of the same calibre – *people committed to the highest principles of the gospel and willingly obedient to the commandments of God*.

We should also remember that Paul and his associates were extremely few in number, but they courageously faced – and, in a gospel sense, sought to conquer in the name and the love of Christ – the whole world of their day, the world of multiple religions, philosophies, and worldviews, comprising numerous and intermingled cultures and value systems. They worked in societies that were morally corrupt and often pitiless; where life was cheap, infanticide was common, immorality was frequent, and the economy was slave-driven. It was a time of militaristic nations and frequent wars; travel was arduous and often dangerous. They faced constant and sometimes fierce opposition from enraged crowds and civic rulers, their lives were frequently at risk, and they were incarcerated and flogged (cf. II Corinthians 11:25-27).

Moreover, from our perspective in the prosperity and technological advantages of our day – at least in the West – they went about their business to preach the gospel to all the nations, using only the simplest of means. As far as I can see, the only equipment they had at their disposal was pen and parchment. And I assume, without any evidence, that they might have been able to purchase or hire a donkey or two to assist them in their frequent travels! Then, once churches were established – probably only in small congregations as they met in people's houses, owning no ecclesiastical property – and began to "teach and admonish one another with psalms, hymns, and spiritual songs" (3:16), they may well have had some musical instruments. But at times they lacked even the simple essentials of life (cf. II Corinthians 11:27, Philippians 4:11-12).

But it was this small and ill-equipped band of Paul and friends who, in effect, were at the forefront of the religious movement that turned the whole of Europe – and subsequently, much of the world – away from paganism and towards the Christian faith. Their influence in history is evidence of God's "working, which (worked) in (them) mightily" (2:29). And in a real sense, we are all the beneficiaries of their faithful – albeit imperfect – service, and so we should honour these men and women of the early church by finding ways and opportunities to emulate their simple obedience, continuing the work that they began.

And to this end it is imperative that all of us who have "received Christ Jesus the Lord" learn, responsibly and intelligently, how to "walk in Him, rooted and being built up in Him, and established in (our) faith" and that we be well taught in "all the treasures of wisdom and knowledge" that are to be found in Him (2:3, 6-7).

◆

Printed in the United States
by Bookmasters

Printed in the United States
By Bookmasters